PRINCIPLES OF EVALUATION
IN PHYSICAL EDUCATION

Evaluation as It Was. (From E. J. Marey,
Animal Mechanism, London, King, 1874)

HARPER'S SERIES IN

SCHOOL AND PUBLIC HEALTH EDUCATION,

PHYSICAL EDUCATION, AND RECREATION

under the editorship of

DELBERT OBERTEUFFER

Principles of Evaluation

in Physical Education

1962

Philip A. Smithells
Peter E. Cameron

Harper & Brothers, Publishers, New York

TO

the memory of

THE LATE REGINALD E. ROPER OF BRITAIN

AND CHARLES HAROLD McCLOY OF AMERICA

without whose inspiration

this book would never have happened

CONTENTS

PART IV.   APPLICATION TO VARIOUS ACTIVITIES

PREFACE

IN BOOKS written by more than one author the problem of style arises. The two authors of this book have markedly different styles, and we have not attempted to fuse them into a style which would be foreign to both of us. Nor do we agree absolutely in detail, and in the institution where we both work, we both hope there will always be a measure of friendly disagreement. If it disappears we will know that our minds have become sterile.

We feel, therefore, that we should say that Part I (Chapters 1–6), Part III (Chapters 12–16), and Part IV except for Chapter 21 were written almost entirely by Philip Smithells. Part II (Chapters 7–11), the statistical and testing section, was written by Peter Cameron, who lectures in this field and guides students in testing and measuring studies. Philip Smithells acted as editor for the book.

Books to some extent write themselves and this book, which was conceived in general as a guide to purposeful evaluation, has turned out to be much concerned with the principles of evaluation in our field. We feel that it would have been both impudent and impossible to try to trump the many excellent books full of practical tests, already published in the United States.

In writing we have had mainly American readers in mind, but one of us knows Canadian physical education well and also something of European physical education. We make no excuse for trying to write a book in the English language (even using English spelling) which we hope can be read on both sides of the Atlantic and north of the 49th parallel, as well as by the English-speaking world below the equator.

Many people have helped us with this task. It is impossible to acknowledge all the help we have received. We would particularly like to thank the editor of the series, Dr. Delbert Oberteuffer, for his patience and encouragement and for entrusting non-Americans with writing a book for the American market—living as we do in a very distant and isolated part of the world.

We would like to thank, too, various people who have allowed us to use pictures, diagrams, and quotations. Several ladies have helped in the various typings of the manuscript—Mrs. Clarice Leaver, Miss Mary Cox, and, for the finished script particularly, Mrs. Joan Salter, who took on a tremendous task at short notice. We would also like to thank our wives and children, who recently have seen much less of us than is reasonable.

Philip A. Smithells
Peter E. Cameron

The University of Otago
Dunedin, New Zealand
January, 1962

part i

BASIC CONCEPTS

INTRODUCTION

Books beget books, but the method of conception remains a
mystery.

JONATHAN SWIFT

No BOOK written on evaluation in physical education in the middle
of the twentieth century can hope to be, or indeed should try to be,
entirely original. A book on this field has to take its place in the proces-
sion of the famous writings that have appeared since about 1900—the
articles which appeared at first sporadically in professional journals,
then after World War I, a few isolated books, and finally new books on
evaluation which began appearing yearly. There is little doubt that the
interest of physical educators in testing and measurement is an off-
shoot—a reflected pattern—of the major attention which the field of
education as a whole has given to evaluation in this century; and there
was also a feeling among some that there was more dogma than science
in our profession. We freely and gratefully acknowledge the help and
inspiration of the many general and physical educators who have
fought hard and led the way in the battle for the ousting of dogma and
prejudice, and the introduction of scientifically and philosophically acceptable methods of assessment.

A new book in this field can only be justified if it has a new slant on
problems, shows them in a different light perhaps, and puts, where possible, difficult ideas more simply. We believe that there is probably no
greater need in our young profession at this stage than to develop its
quality of thinking and expression. We feel that our capacities in this
area have lagged behind our capacities for teaching, organisation, and
action in general. The quantity of published material on physical education has increased—but has the quality always kept pace? The true
strength and quality of a subject, if it is to rise above the merely technological, must be reflected in the philosophy, powers of self-criticism,

3

and intellectual curiosity of those who work with it. We feel that these essentials should be found more than anywhere else in the evaluation of our work.

It is noticeable that nearly every book in this field since the end of the 1930s has tended to aggregate more and more quotations from previous writers—their ideas, their tests and procedures—until some such books are in danger of becoming mere handbooks or encyclopaedias of testing and measurement. We feel that it is redundant to reproduce what others abler than ourselves have devised or collected, and in no way do we regard this as a comprehensive study of what has been suggested and tried in the field of evaluation in physical education. We regard this as a book to be read with other books on the field, and not one which gives all the answers.

Scope of the Book

We wish to make it quite clear that this book is intended as an undergraduate book for use in the senior year. It is not a book on how to write a master's or doctoral thesis, nor is it a book on how to do research. There are other guides for that. We hope that occasionally graduates may browse through this book, and that it may shake any complacency they have.

Nor is this a book written to bolster convictions at a time when our profession is threatened, but one which asks that we shall examine ourselves as people and our conventions and basic assumptions. We have not pulled any punches out of cultural considerations; yet no offence is meant if we are loath to accept things as they are. The book will undoubtedly irritate some people and provoke others. If it sets any healthy controversy going, we shall feel we have been successful.

Wrangling

At Cambridge University, the student who comes out first in the final undergraduate mathematics examinations is still known as the Senior Wrangler. In earlier days the finals students had to show their capacity for wrangling—a word now debased in meaning. The modern equivalent might be being put through one's paces by a doctoral committee (the "oral"), only in earlier days even as an undergraduate, one had to face the assembled faculty and senior students, and hold one's own in debate and cross-questioning.

We feel that this sort of thing should be happening in the senior undergraduate year in our field. We feel too the doubts expressed in the *Quarterly of the Carnegie Corporation of New York*,[1] in an article which suggests that graduate schools may be losing some of their function as disseminators of liberal education and the traditional culture of Western man. Part of that culture is the tradition of frank discussion and the willingness to hold an individual viewpoint, even an unpopular one.

PRELIMINARY THINKING AND SOUND RESEARCH

It is a truism to say that answers are inadequate if questions are not properly understood, it having been said more than once that the business of philosophy is the proper stating of questions. We feel that the time has come for a fresh examination of testing and measurement, an evaluation of evaluation maybe, so that there can be some winnowing of the more valuable wheat from the interesting, but often irrelevant chaff, such as that which indiscriminate enthusiasm on the part of some of those preparing theses for degree requirements may have added to our store of knowledge. A great pioneer in this field, C. H. McCloy wrote, in acknowledging the Clark Hetherington Award given to him at the annual meeting of the American Academy of Physical Education in Chicago in 1956: "I feel today we are not conducting too much research, but we do conduct too much research that is not based on sound preliminary thinking."

This is, we believe, a profoundly important statement, and one which should pull us up in our tracks and make us take a look at ourselves, coming as it does from so eminent a pioneer and leader in this field of evaluation.

THE SENIOR YEAR AS CRUCIAL TO PRACTICAL EVALUATION

Our avowed aim is to catch if we can the mind of the specialist-to-be as he comes into his final undergraduate year—the period when the critical faculties may have begun to mature, and the period im-

[1] VIII, no. 1 (January, 1960).

mediately before he faces the hard reality of his first job or the tougher discipline of postgraduate work. For many, the first job can be a disillusionment, particularly when it is found that much that has been painfully studied and learnt, even enjoyed, seems suddenly not to be pertinent in the rush of regular teaching, organisation, and the diurnal pressures of routine. It is at this period, we feel, that many reject much of their most important learning, because it seems not to matter, not immediately purposeful. This we feel is a crisis in teaching, and one which must be prepared for. Indeed, some will once more enter the field of evaluation, when they begin to accumulate a higher degree; however, only a portion of teachers will take such degrees or will choose evaluation as a thesis topic. In this we also see a danger.

We suggest that research done for examination awards does not always involve that compelling curiosity which true investigation needs. In fact, such research can become a mere formality. We consider that the attitude of mind—the sincere desire to try and find the truth, the drive to examine one's own efforts and appraise them—is as fundamental as the technology and technique of research. There are, we realise, two views about this. One often held by the ordinary teacher and also by distinguished leaders in the sphere of the university is that research is properly the province of a select group of special ability, and should only be carried out at a highly refined level. The other view, a minority one, is that although certain types of research can only be carried on at this high level, all workers, at all levels, in a given professional field should be trained so as to be able to think about examining and appraising all that they do. We tend to agree with this minority view. We have the utmost respect for high-level research— though we have some doubts about examination-requirement theses— and we feel that the majority of ordinary practitioners in our profession could learn to evaluate parts of their work. What is even more important, through the habit of evaluation, they might approach their work with an open mind.

Evaluation for the Schoolteacher

If we are to catch the enthusiasm of the ordinary practitioner, we must make sure that this final undergraduate-year course is not far above his head, that it is immediately meaningful and makes clear sense. We realise that for every group in their senior year only a few will have high potential in serious investigation; however, our own experience suggests, and our conviction is, that this period is a fertile one, a tide not to be missed. We know that there will always be cynics and skeptics regarding new ideas, but we feel that unless the main body of our profession catches the spirit of evaluation and realises how important it is and how much it can mean to each of us, there will be a fatal division among us. We suspect there is at present a division between the common man and the scientist—a grave danger in any part of society. Just as in society at large the ways of the scientist are barely understood, and to many, science is but magic; so we feel that in our profession a parallel division may exist.

Our hope is that this book, by its rather different approach, may catch and hold the imagination of the senior student or perhaps one pursuing a master's degree. It may give him something that, from the first, in his career in school and community, becomes part of his philosophy of work, which inevitably pervades his thinking and his activity, and this of course includes self-evaluation. Perhaps the idea is summed up best in the archaic term: a touchstone.

chapter 1

CHOOSING

Ickle ockle black bottle
Ickle ockle out.
O-U-T spells out
Out you must go,
If I say so.
CHILDREN'S CHOOSING
GAME

DISCRIMINATION ESSENTIAL TO LIFE

EVALUATION is not a subject; it is a way of doing things, a way which all of us use in everyday life from quite early in our development. Animals and quite simple organisms evaluate, and so do plants. In lower organisms the choice is often automatic. The growing root tip burrows and wriggles till it finds water, rejecting dryness; the stem tip seeks the light and rejects the dark. To survive, living things must discriminate. Some vines will send their roots a mile to find water.

At what level the power to choose becomes voluntary, as opposed to automatic, has long been a subject for scientific investigation and philosophic speculation. At the primitive level choosing is concerned with comfort (restoring biochemical equilibrium) or survival or reproduction. At the highly complex human level, we are faced continually with making choices—in fact, one of the trials of civilised living is the continuous pressure of choosing. The incapacity to choose, the failure to make up one's mind, to decide on the desired end-result, can lead to that disintegration of the personality which in popular terms we call a

8

nervous breakdown. This is perhaps why an increasing number of people seek the simpler life, with fewer choices, of camping in the wilds, as a rest and a change from the pressures of the city. The escape world of the cinema, television, radio, comic strips, and drugs, which provide vicarious living, also provide temporary release from problem-solving. A neurotic state similar to a nervous breakdown can be produced in rats or mice by fooling and double-crossing them over matters of choice, where rewards of food and punishment by electric shock are mixed up.

HEALTH INVOLVES CHOICE

So choosing and evaluating are intimately tied up with health, and choosing can be a pleasure or pain. How do we choose and evaluate? In the simpler situations, with only two alternatives, we are guided by experience on a pleasure-pain principle. Faced with drinking salt and water, or sugar and water, our taste buds and general physiological re-action are sufficient. In general sugar is satisfying, while salt is an emetic. Normally, we can tolerate one but not the other, although it is important to realise that, even in this apparently crudely simple ex-ample, the choice depends to some extent on our own state chemically. If we live in Kenya, where salt is such a rare commodity that, until relatively recently, wages were paid in it, our innate need for salt in terms of the actual chemical state of our blood—having lost so much salinity by sweating—is so great that we might wisely prefer the salt and water. So too, if we worked in a malting-house or at another over-hot occupation, we might desire salt. On the other hand, if we had diabetes and were in a hyperglycaemic state, we might simply reject the sugar. The moral of this is that choice is a relative thing, based not only on experience and sensory pleasure, but also sometimes by some-thing subjective in our very make-up—in this case our own chemical consistency. We shall come back to subjectivity later.

THE NEED TO IMPROVE DISCRIMINATION

In general, the process of learning to live in a given society consists of improving our capacity to choose wisely, where voluntary choice can be made. The degree of available choice depends on the society. We build a capacity to sort things out; we develop scales of values. Choices may be as simple and mundane as preferring one kind of ice cream, or a necktie, or they may be as difficult as deciding our exact interpretation of one of the Ten Commandments (if they are one of our value scales). We may resent or admire our neighbour's Cadillac, without realising that covetousness (or in modern terms the destructive emotion of envy) is one of the things our religion has taught us to beware of. Although we may think we have a reliable scale of values, we may at times ignore it or not be aware of all to which it applies. And although we may think we have a free will in making choices, this is only partly true, insofar as we are subject to pressures from without to sway our choice. These external pressures may be general social ones, such as to have a crew-cut because other guys have, or to make love in a certain way because the pattern in our society is like that, or something more general such as keeping-up-with-the-Joneses as part of our way of life (even if it does break the Tenth Commandment). So in a sense we and our environment are inseparable, and just as any modern biologist studies the interplay of organism and environment, not the isolated organism, or the first thing a psychiatrist wants to know about a problem child is what its parents and siblings are like, so the degree of effectiveness of our *free* will is difficult to ascertain. Inevitably we make choices partly in response to external pressure. How great such pressures sometimes are, and the way in which they affect the merit of our evaluation, will be brought out later. An example of a major external force in civilised living is the highly potent and subtle one of advertising, which is quite simply organised opinion-swaying.[1] This is a huge, expensive, and effective force that not only affects our choice of breakfast cereal, car, or toothpaste, etc., but which makes many problems of healthy living considerably more difficult. We shall examine this particular force more carefully later.

So a great deal of living involves choosing, or evaluation, whether we realise it or not. We may evaluate the neighbour's daughter's early morning piano practising by a few well-turned phrases, we may evaluate a missed putt on the last green in a monosyllable, or we may write a sonnet to our mistress's eyebrow, or a 1000-page novel about the evils of some political creed. It is all evaluation, and these examples make one point that is quite fundamental and not always understood about

---

[1] Vance Packard, *The Hidden Persuaders*, New York, McKay, 1957. (American publishers are given book references although in some cases books were first or subsequently published in Great Britain.)

ways in which evaluation can be expressed. Some perfectly sound and accurate evaluations can be made in words; others may be made in numbers; others, as we will show later, need not be expressed in either. Some people are apt to regard that which cannot be measured as inferior; they see some essential difference in kind between calculation and description. We shall have to go into this fairly deeply because it is one of the traps in this field of evaluation.

Special Forms of Choosing

But to turn from special experts in evaluation such as the scientist, poet, or painter to our less able selves, it can be seen that in a private or professional life, we are forced willy-nilly into the situation of making judgements. The choosing may be difficult, but it is often a pleasure; it is certainly a major aspect of our becoming an educated person or good at our job. To be a person of good taste and good judgement is never a defect—in fact, it is a major sign of being a good citizen. But it is never easy to be an impartial judge, and we must examine more closely the factors that influence us, internally and externally. Most of us would admit for instance that hasty judgements made in a temper are apt to be erroneous, that is, when strong emotions are aroused, errors of evaluation may increase. So when we are in love and have no awareness of how love affects our judgement, we make erratic evaluations. In anger we invent reasons why what has angered us is bad, and in being in love, we invent reasons why we and our loved one were made for each other. This tendency to make our reasoning fit our emotions is a major danger about which we have to be most vigilant. It can occur in work, in sport, in love—in almost all endeavours, including science. The general name given to it is *rationalisation*, the inventing of reasons to justify feelings.

Emotion Clouds Clarity of Judgement

Most of the time emotions are fairly near the surface and come into play with very little stimulus. Much of the time we are barely aware that they are operating. It is an interesting experience to turn on the radio or TV and, deliberately ignoring the seductive and catchy music, to dispassionately analyse the words of popular songs, in terms of whether they make sense, are logical, or contain advice which one believes is sound. We may say that it is only the music we care for, but is this a completely honest answer? Another pastime—an evaluation game, if you like—is to examine cold-bloodedly advertisements in magazines, or "plugs" on radio or TV, and write down for each one the emotional devices which are being used to sway your judgement and affect your evaluation of the product concerned. You will find pride, envy, fear, social ambition, vanity, sex (often), shame, and the magic appeal of scientific authority by dazzling the ignorant with pseudo science. The advertisement maker is a shrewd psychologist; he knows that most people are potential suckers, if only he can find the right bait, and he may even employ a psychiatrist to help him. Dr. Goebbels, the Nazi Propaganda Minister, first crystallised the idea by saying that if you tell a big lie often enough people will believe it; the advertising expert knows that. The number of times you mention a name and the number of ways you get at clients, directly or indirectly, all help to condition them to buying the product. The advertisement writer is not a manufacturer who has made something the public needs, and announces it boldly so that people may know. He is a very special type of social psychologist who discovered by experience, long before the social sciences developed, what will sway opinions.[2] He amounts to an employee of the manufacturers. He knows possibly that there is really no significant difference between one type of toothpaste and another. He probably knows that toothpaste is unnecessary anyway. But is he successful? You know the answer. Why do you use the toothpaste you do use, or the soap, or the cigarette, or the gasoline, or the make of car, radio, TV set, golf club, or baseball bat? Make a cool and careful judgement of how you have evaluated these everyday objects.

MINDS HAVE SOMETHING OVER MACHINES

Some of this may seem a far cry from evaluation in physical education, but all the tests and statistical techniques available will be relatively useless unless it is realised that the human mind is not just a calculating machine and entirely rational, like a modern computer.[3]

[2] Even when a TV comedian in an advertising interval says that the high-grade car which his sponsors sell has a thinking man's oil filter, his cynical wise-crack probably serves only to reinforce this piece of conditioning—flattery used by the original advertisers of a cigarette.

[3] Though these apparently develop "bugs," making them appear temperamental.

The electronic computer is well protected from extraneous and irrelevant influences. The living human mind is open to influences which confuse its capacity to evaluate. But get this right, the human mind is and always will be infinitely more complex and in most ways more capable than any machine can be. It has the capacity to create, whereas the computer can only deal with what has been fed into it. No calculating machine will ever produce a King Lear, a Robinson Crusoe or a Huckleberry Finn—or another calculating machine.

IT PAYS TO ADVERTISE

Big money, yours and mine, for we the consumers always pay for advertising, has gone into swaying our judgement in what we buy. Approximately 75 percent of the retail cost of all packaged goods in the United States comes from the cost of advertising, and no country has developed this form of opinion biassing to such a great extent. But there is also big money (and money is a form of power) in sport and all that goes with it. The fact that a head football coach in a university can be paid considerably more than a world-famous professor in the same university, or that a university graduate may be offered $20,000 to play football professionally, as opposed to the $6,000 which would be the starting salary commanded in his field—such are factors which cannot be ignored in studying evaluation in physical education. For we are all part of the society in which we live. We cannot escape its pressures on our judgement. Whether we live in a democracy or a totalitarian state, the pressures are there. The sworn creed of the democrat gives him the inalienable right to choose. But choosing is difficult, in a free country more so than in an avowedly authoritarian one. The ideal citizen might be one who has developed the capacity to choose without bias and prejudice, who has confidence in his detached and coolly made judgement, whether in his home, his work, or in his community. Evaluation takes many forms, but it is always a question of *quality* of judgement, as well as *quantity*. How to attain both of these in relation to one special and limited field is the business of this book, but our special problems must be seen in the context of the general problem of our society. The capacity of the group to sway the judgement of the individual is tremendous; it is a force which is only just coming to be really understood.

So this book deals with evaluation in a broad sense. It is not a book full of answers on how to measure and how to test. Certainly it includes sections in which well-established procedures of an elementary statistical kind are described, with suggestions as to how and when they may be used. However, it has two main aims: (1) to emphasise that evaluations is essential and inevitable; (2) to emphasise that one cannot find answers till one asks questions, and the framing of questions and the habit of questioning are essential to evaluation.

chapter 2

WE CHOOSE ANYWAY

Woo't weep? woo't fight? woo't fast? woo't tear thyself?
Woo't drink up eisel? eat a crocodile?

Hamlet, Act V, Scene 1

THE CULTURED MAN

IN THE first chapter we tried briefly to show that all civilised people
evaluate often, and that their capacity to evaluate well is one of the
measures of their efficiency, status, and degree of education and culture.
Many people want to acquire culture. It is not too much to say that
the most difficult part is not in gaining experience or knowledge, but in
learning to have taste, learning to evaluate—in a sense, gaining wisdom. Visiting Ann Hathaway's Cottage at Stratford-on-Avon may be
an interesting and even a romantic experience, but it is not a way of
acquiring literary or any other sort of culture. Having read, pondered,
and discussed and compared say twenty of Shakespeare's thirty-seven
plays is more likely to start the process of culture—and that can be
done in Hoboken or Pasadena.

ACQUIRING TASTE

All countries have a culture of their own, but older countries tend
to have accumulated more, not only due to the passage of more time,
but to the increasing level of informed criticism, the sharper standards
of evaluation. The United States has developed fine cultural values in

15

many fields; it has produced good writers, architects, painters, composers, scientists, engineers, philosophers, and scholars of all kinds, as well as some of the world's greatest literary critics. But as recently as thirty years ago the country was not confident about its cultural development, and so trips to Europe, to "do" Europe (just as one "does" chemistry), were a felt need. *Punch,* the English equivalent of the *New Yorker* (the *New Yorker* is incidentally a very fine evaluatory journal respected throughout the English-speaking world), had a picture of an American tourist emerging from the Louvre, the most famous art gallery in Paris. He is looking at his wrist watch and saying "I did the Louvre in twenty minutes flat and could have cut it down to twelve if I had had roller skates." This might be a nice example of misapplied evaluation. Today the sort of superficial and phoney approach to culture implied in this joke is probably disappearing, to be replaced by a more studious one, involving the development of taste, not by collecting labels and experiences, but by learning how to discriminate and describe and compare differences in things.

OUR PARTICULAR FIELD

There is probably a parallel though slower development in our field of physical education, and for that matter recreation and health education too. Although this book is specifically devoted to physical education, it is impossible to separate the topic entirely from recreation and health education, and we shall not try to do so. Many of the main objectives, and indeed basic arguments, for the existence of physical education are concerned with recreation and health, and we would be intellectually dishonest in introducing artificial borders to our field of study.

WE ALL EVALUATE TO SOME EXTENT

The development of awareness of the need for effective evaluation in our profession is by no means universal, in spite of attempts by pioneers to promote it, over the last thirty years at least. But although we may not realise it, all of us in this profession evaluate continually. Whether we do it well or badly, we rate people as to physical skills, capacity to play well with others, and capacity to stand up to competition, and we pick teams. We do all these things and many more, whether we have had a course in evaluation or not. Some would be content to say that this is a matter which is taken care of satisfactorily in the free enterprise of the athletic world. Well-picked teams win a reputation; coaches who pick well succeed, while coaches whose teams lose, fail. Bad picking eliminates the bad pickers. So too, of course, lack of capacity to tumble keeps a man out of the tumbling display; a fumbling pair of hands or inadequate height keeps a player out of the basketball team. "This is life," some people will say. "By a process of natural selection—the survival of the fittest—everyone finds his own level." And they may add another somewhat erroneous platitude, "You cannot change human nature." This view holds true if life in physical education is regarded as having, and desirably so, the same sort of nature as life in the jungle. But this is certainly not the pattern of civilisation, and particularly not the pattern of democracy. Nor is it the accepted pattern in education.

All Children Matter

Rightly or wrongly in education, if not in commercial society, we have abandoned the jungle pattern. We try to teach a child to spell whether he has a natural aptitude or not. We teach all children who can (however much trouble it may be) to do those simple calculations essential to our sort of living. We teach the blind to use other senses which substitute for the missing one. We give the deaf hearing aids and teach them sign language and lip-reading. We teach the paralysed to play basketball in wheel chairs and to swim. We teach crafts to the mentally retarded. One of the unwritten credos of education is that no one is unworthy of our teaching, and even if it costs more to educate a slower child than a more normal one, we feel society should do this.

The World Drive for Education

On a wider front it can be said that never in the history of mankind has there been such a drive to educate all peoples throughout the world as in the mid-twentieth century. One leader[1] with much international experience considers this demand terrifying. All countries are trying to educate their own backward peoples, and international agencies have

---

[1] C. E. Beeby, former Director of Education in New Zealand, and former Assistant Director General of UNESCO.

sprung up to help the less fortunate on a world-wide basis. UNESCO, WHO, and local plans such as the Colombo Plan are phenomena unheard of, and indeed unthinkable, in the past. It was considered a truth by intelligent and kindly people, as recently as fifty years ago, that the capacity to learn—educability—was strictly related to level of culture, to environment, and to racial stock. And even to this day there are men with university degrees who regard Kaffirs as little more than baboons. Now it has been shown without doubt that basic ability to learn and profit by learning is independent of race, and is thwarted or developed by environment. Be he Eskimo, red Indian, African pygmy, Hottentot, Tibetan shepherd, Chinese coolie, or one from that most primitive of all cultures, the stone-age Australian aborigine, he can, given the opportunity, learn as quickly and successfully as the child from the most fortunate family in New York or London or Paris.

One Cause for Hope

This realisation of the educability of mankind is one of the important developments of this curious century. It is in keeping with the teaching of the great religions, and is of course evidence that visionaries have been right, that Lincoln's famous speech at Gettysburg was revealing an unsuspected truth. Do not let us pretend that "malice towards none" prevails, but we know for certain that "all men are created equal" in a sense. Why the modifying clause, "in a sense," is necessary will be seen later when we come to look at statistics and the distribution of intelligence or other qualities in a given group. For the moment, let it suffice to say that there are some stone-age aborigines from Australia who, given the education, could hold their own at Harvard, Oxford, or the Sorbonne.

Evaluation Diminishes Prejudice

How do we know this? The main answer is simple—we have learned to evaluate effectively, and this capacity has swept away some of the cobwebs of prejudice accumulated over thousands of years. How have we come to evaluate effectively? By two main processes, the first of which is often forgotten. First, we have *wanted* to make sure. We have had doubts about our judgement, doubts cast by thinkers, philosophers, religious leaders, scientists—all of whom are phenomena of the last page in the history of man. If man has lived in the world for the equivalent of a thousand pages of history, it is only the last page of which we know anything at all for certain, and only the last line can we read quite clearly. In brief, we have evaluated man's capacities, be he primitive or civilised, because we had doubts about our previous judgements. Doubt is sometimes the beginning of wisdom.

The Spread of Scientific Techniques

The second reason for our development of evaluation has been concerned with know-how—the technique of evaluation—which in this century has improved to an amazing degree. This is really the impact of the scientific way of thinking on everyday problems. Although there are some who may think that scientists have not given the strength of their minds to moral and ethical values, there are relatively few today who would doubt the scientists' special ability of devising means of finding out the truth. Science, which in the nineteenth century was confined to certain recognized fields—chemistry, physics, medicine, mathematics, astronomy, zoology and botany, and geology—has in the twentieth century spilled over into psychology, education, sociology, anthropology, economics, geography, and even into more surprising spheres such as history, art, and language studies. It also seems possible that theology and science will become reconciled, as has been predicted by some leading theologians.

Misjudging Science

The dangers of this are also present, and as one writer has said, science may be becoming a sort of sacred cow.[2] The dangers which affect us, and probably others, most are phoney pseudoscience on the one hand, the sort so often used by the advertisers (see examples), and the still more grave danger, dealt with in the next chapter, of *undervaluing* judgements which are not expressed in scientific terms. The graven image which we should not worship in this century is not only Mammon, but the robot. There is not space here to discuss fully the relation between men and machines, but the dangers of the machine dominating men have been pointed out by many thinkers.

[2] A. Standen, *Science Is a Sacred Cow*, New York, Dutton, 1950.

SOME OF OUR PROBLEMS

How can evaluation help us in physical education particularly? There are many ways, some obvious, some more subtle. Let us examine some.

A Multiplicity of Claims

We claim that we give children physical education for some good reason, and we expect the children to benefit in some way. The reasons given so far have been legion. They range from completely material, organic ones, such as the idea of gaining strength, perhaps cardiovascular or musculoskeletal strength, to wider and more abstract social concepts, such as fuller development of the personality, better citizenship, democratic experience, and—in the view of some protagonists—development and improvement of a spiritual kind. A list of the supposed gains from physical education abstracted from its objectives as put forward in hundreds of books in the English language would be a formidable list indeed, and would probably be regarded as extravagant, and certainly optimistic, by someone unacquainted with our profession. Most of the claims put forward would be unsubstantiated or not admit of substantiation.

Do We Want to Evaluate?

Without going further at the moment into the Babel of our promoters' philosophies, let us simplify the issue by saying that each of us should have some aim in view, even if it is only as simple (and inadequate in our view) as providing fun or filling in time. Do we not want to see if, in fact, we succeed in doing what we set out to do? More than that, is it not useful to us to be able to say, "This, that, or the other thing happened apparently as a result of our teaching." Honesty compels one to stick in the word *apparently,* because certainty is difficult to achieve in all problems of cause and effect. It is a grim truth, apt to be forgotten, that changes occur that have nothing to do with us, and some of which we would like to think were due to us. A fallacy, epitomised in the Latin tag *post hoc, ergo propter hoc* ("after this, therefore because of it") is a constant man-trap of which the enthusiast must be aware. A crude example will explain this type of error.

You may claim that we shall have better growth, taller and heavier children, as a result of physical education. You weigh and measure children at the beginning of the fall semester and again at the end of the spring semester. The children are heavier and taller. It would be a bold or stupid person indeed who said this was due solely to the physical-education teaching. This very simple example shows the principle and the difficulty. Sometimes it is much harder to find the error in the reasoning. For instance in Fiji, a drink called *khava* is consumed in long ceremonial gatherings. Some Europeans felt wobbly at the knees after a *khava* ceremony and concluded that the drink, though nonalcoholic, contained a drug which affected their knees. This was accepted until someone discovered that *khava* is drunk in a cross-legged sitting position and that knees often become wobbly because Europeans rarely undergo the strain of this position. Of course there are ways round this kind of error in some cases, but it is still very common.

But surely there is no doubt that we should be able to produce some sort of evidence of the effect of our work.

WHAT IS OUR STATUS?

Or take the status of our profession. Is it all that we would like it to be? We may know in our own minds that we may do good, but do our teaching colleagues always think so? Does the general public think so, does the politician? It may be remembered that in 1955 there was a public scare about the poor fitness of American children, and the President was shocked by a report on the state of American youth. A White House conference was called. Was it to the physical educationists that the conveners of the conference turned? Rightly or wrongly, it was not.[3] Now, well-versed physical educationists will argue as to whether fitness is one of our main objectives; they will argue what fitness is; they may even argue that the evidence on which the scare was based was not acceptable, but one thing is clear—the physical education profession was not thought of immediately as the group of people who should have a major contribution to make to the discussion or as the people who, by using evaluation, had clear evidence on the subject. No, the conference consisted more of sports leaders—fine people, but with little training in scientifically understanding a difficult problem such as

[3] In 1961 another chance has come—from another President. Let us hope the profession is ready this time.

this. The answer sometimes given, that the people in the public eye were politically more acceptable for such a conference, is an unsatisfactory one. Governments are sensitive to what the public wants, what pressure groups are after. If the physical-education profession was generally thought of as the expert group in this field, then any government would have crowded the conference with physical educationists.

The Necessity for Liaison with Medicine

These recent public airings of the question of fitness have proved a challenge to the profession, and the profession is responding; however, it is also an example which shows that evaluation in this field is still not highly developed or widely accepted in the United States. It is no exaggeration to suggest that in some countries, Scandinavia, Germany, or Hungary (although tests and measurements are less highly developed there), physical educationists would have been in the forefront of the discussion, and the government would have regarded them as entitled to a major voice on the problem. Without analysing it further at the moment, it is suggested that the closer the relationship of the medical profession and physical education, the more the physical educationist is expected to be an authority in this field.

Whatever Our Goals, We Must Evaluate

The ways in which we have suggested evaluation may be used by our profession may be minor or major, but each one of us is faced with evaluation problems each hour of our professional life. We may differ as to goals, aims, and objectives, and it may be a good thing we do, but we cannot escape evaluation. We *have* to divide our children into groups, we *have* to pick children for teams, we *have* to comment on how they perform a certain skill, and we *have* to suggest improvements towards which they should strive. If we are doing any sort of a job, we are continually appraising and evaluating.

Most Teachers Evaluate

So are our colleagues in the other parts of the school. Testing and assessing devices are in continual use to diagnose and to assess achievement in relation to previous status and in relation to expected standards for a given grade or age. Although the amount of formal written essay examinations has decreased (perhaps too much) in schooling, continuous use is made of testing and measuring devices, and continuous refinement and improvement of them are attempted (witness the establishment of such a body as the United States Educational Testing Service). Basic factors such as general intelligence (or components of general intelligence, such as spatial awareness), maturation, or readiness to learn (as in reading readiness tests) are assessed. Conscientious teachers are always trying to equate what they teach with whom they teach, so that the best over-all result for each individual is possible. Group progress in the classroom is of secondary importance. The group may do a good project, act a play well, or sing a song in harmony, but the teacher is constantly alert to individual needs and individual progress, or so it is hoped. There are, of course, critics who say that evaluation has tended to replace actual instruction too much, and it may well be that, in some teacher's enthusiasm for a relatively new approach, the balance of teaching and evaluation is awry. This is a phase to be expected when a new approach supplants the old. The old grind of rote-learning without understanding, exposure to subjects whether there is any innate ability or not, emphasis on being head of the class, crude and inaccurate forms of assessment, lack of realisation of fundamental difference in abilities or of the limits on possible progress—all these are defects which we are well rid of, because they were unscientific and unfair. They amounted to an ignoring of and denial of the truth, though we may have lost some motivation in the process.

Self-evaluation Is Essential

The wise teacher is continually evaluating, not only his pupil's abilities and the results of his work, but himself as teacher. He is a major part of the child's environment and as such is affecting the child's achievement and emotional stability. It takes, for example, little imagination to see that if a teacher is lethargic, lazy, unprepared, and uninspiring, the children, whatever their basic abilities, are unlikely to be outgoing or enthusiastic. We probably realise too that a tense, on-edge teacher stimulates tension in pupils. There are also much more subtle factors operating in teacher-pupil relationships, many unmeasurable mathematically, but nonetheless quite real.

SENSITIVITY

The quality of sensitivity in a teacher is a fine one, and includes sensibility, or the capacity to feel what a child is feeling about you, its task, or its peers—the ability to put yourself in the child's place. Gone is the day of the martinet ignoring the nature of his pupils, but dragooning them into a supposedly desirable pattern,[4] and using physical force and mental cruelty to make the pupils conform. This was the mechanistic view of teaching. Instead, we expect teachers to be aware of themselves and, as far as possible, their impact on individual children. It used to be thought that a dominating personality—the capacity to overawe the child—were hallmarks of the good teacher. Indeed, the teaching situation, where some sort of order is generally necessary so that each child can get on with learning, does need a teacher who can, if necessary, exercise group control, and at times absolute control. But the balance between dominating and sensitive qualities is a difficult one to achieve, and with most teachers needs a great deal of self-awareness—an awareness that should make some teachers see that they must tone down the aggressive side of their personality, while others must learn to exert rather more control than would be their natural inclination. We shall deal with means of self-evaluation later; there are several, and the process is a wise and essential one in any teacher.

SELF-EVALUATION AND MOTIVE

What about self-evaluation in our profession? Are we as a whole people aware of ourselves in our impact on others? This is a question of major importance, and one which our profession does not appear to have spent undue time considering. It is a salutary experience to talk to people outside our profession about ourselves as people, as human beings. This in itself might be a profitable field for a carefully planned evaluatory survey. Of course, a variety of opinions will be met, but there will be some very unflattering ones, if frank answers can be obtained. Such phrases as "too hearty," "too dominating," "too concerned with getting your own way," "too blind about others' enthusiasms," "too attached to the goals of youth," "too insensitive," "too unaware that

---

[4] Although archaic methods of class organisation can still be recommended. See "Deploying a Group for Physical Exercise," *The Physical Educator,* XVI, no. 4, 147.

others do not share your athletic enthusiasms," may appear among the opinions given. These are not abusive terms to be ignored, but are remarks which should make us think and do some self-examination:

Why have we chosen this profession?

What were the characteristics and abilities in ourselves that motivated us towards majoring in this field?

Was it our own athletic prowess?

Was this the main source of ego-satisfaction?

Was it our success in adolescent leadership, as expressed in schooltime popularity and influence?

Was it the enthusiasm of some teacher or coach who saw in us someone who would improve his own reputation?

Was it an unperceived desire not to mature—to be a Peter Pan, with eternal youth?

Was it a feeling that the fame we had then was something to cling to?

Was it a feeling we were a pretty important guy, or pretty smart girl?

If no wise friend whom you respect could make any of the implied criticisms about you, and you could say no confidently to the questions suggested, then you need not think of this particular issue much more. To very few people would *all* of these criticisms apply, and to very few perhaps *none* would apply, but whether we like them or not, it behooves us to see past the criticisms and think deeply about what might have produced them.

Ourselves as People

Let us look first at ourselves as people, and then at the sort of work we do. What is there in any way special about us? Let us hazard some informed guesses. We will tend to be well built and reasonably strong. If we are men, we may even be very powerfully built, and proud of it. We may be built like a tank, or a race horse with a strong, lithe figure. If we are women, we may be fine games players, swimmers, divers, or dancers. We will probably have been exposed to adulation for physical prowess if male, less certainly so, in America, if female. We will probably excel in some form of motor skill or be an above-average all-rounder. One of our first attractions to this field of work is likely to be that we like the sort of physical activity involved and which we do well at. At the age at which we chose, it was a major part of life. There is the sheer pleasure of the exercise, the confidence that comes from success, the social approbation that comes from our contemporaries, from being a minor or major "star" in motor skill. Do we stop to think that, in the adult world, these things we enjoy so much, although they may be of considerable importance as entertainment, are not considered to be of intellectual, cultural (in the more high-brow sense of the word), and social importance? Although a middle-aged lawyer may get ulcers from seeing his favourite team lose the Rose Bowl game (although the public wants its gladiators), do we as individuals have as much status among adults as a physical educationist with good motor skill, as we did among our adolescent peers and juniors at school? Do our doctor, lawyer, engineer, artist, teacher, or clerk friends rate us by what once gave us so much status? Some may, particularly those who were skilled like ourselves, but who chose other professions or trades. But the general answer is surely no. Many of our contemporaries have set aside "childish things" and regard us perhaps as having failed to grow up.[5] This is unpleasant to admit, but let us face it. Do not many adults, particularly the well-educated ones, be they fellow-teachers or in some other field, express silent doubts about our profession? The silence is broken sometimes by candid friends who ask what an intelligent person can find in such a profession.

We Must Accept Criticism

These suggestions will undoubtedly evoke a hostile reaction from some readers, but they would not be made unless felt to be true, and based on experience in several countries over many years. Some adults, very successful when grown up, have not been particularly successful athletically at school. They have seen others with natural athletic aptitude receive social approbation, teacher praise, even stardom. They have seen that as adults their own former schooltime inadequacy is of little importance, provided they are good at their job, or a good citizen. It was the Greek dramatist Euripides who said on one occasion, "No one is a greater potential menace to the state than the great athlete." It was the Roman satirist Juvenal who wrote, *"Orandum est ut sit mens sana in corpore sano"* ("It is to be prayed that there is a healthy mind

---

[5] This attitude, that "physical" activity is childish, is a fallacious one, but does it not spring from the way it may have been presented to the child at school?

in a healthy body")—a very different thought from the truncated version of the full quotation which is trotted out so glibly in support of our profession. The plain truth is that not all healthy bodies contain healthy minds—and vice versa. So too in the adult world, athletic prowess and rude health, and the heartiness of manner that sometimes go with these, are not necessary adult virtues, and indeed are anathema to some perfectly good citizens.

Minds and Bodies

It has been suggested from the days of Hippocrates that the mind is to some extent affected by the sort of body in which it lives. Not only have scientists and doctors been interested in the idea, but poets too, and once more Shakespeare can exemplify when he puts into Caesar's mouth:

> Let me have men about me that are fat;
> Sleek-headed men and such as sleep o' nights.
> Yon Cassius has a lean and hungry look;
> He thinks too much: such men are dangerous.

Caesar, a soldier reasonably robust and rugged, could not appreciate the man of leaner build. There is some evidence in modern times that highly mesomorphic people downrate those who are high in ectomorphy or endomorphy. Modern work in this field has been considerable and will be referred to in some detail later. It has been established that there is a wide variety of bodybuilds. Successful adults have been of all manner of build, but those drawn to physical education as a career tend to have some common characteristics. Certain builds are almost never attracted to this profession. It has been suggested by W. H. Sheldon, and there is other evidence to support this,[6] that the qualities of muscularity and drive are apt to go together, and with these qualities, very desirable in some professions, there is sometimes found to be less sensitivity than in some other builds.

All Physiques Are Important

In a primitive civilisation, ours is probably the best sort of physique.

[6] For example, work in the United States Armed Forces showing a preference for sportsmen as leaders. See also the studies of R. W. Parnell in Britain.

Then only the fittest survive (up to a point). In modern warfare (World War II variety) the majority of, say, fighter pilots are shown to be of this sort of build (dominantly mesomorphic), and by their high death rate show how much we have modified the tendencies of natural selection. But in peacetime adult life, all kinds of build and all kinds of mind and temperament must work together, and maybe these innate qualities of ours—particularly in the men[7]—are a partial explanation of an incomplete acceptance by our adult peers. It is also important to realise that there are probably more mesomorphs among delinquents than among nondelinquents. If in our work we ignore or are insensitive to those of delicate build, or fat and heavy build, who have no athletic drive, and we teach blindly with an unstated philosophy of "You too can be like me," it is no wonder that some adults, when they emerge from the sport-idolatory phase, regard us as atypical. Some such adults become headmasters, inspectors, or superintendents of education, and when their turn comes to preside over curriculum construction, unconscious memories of what they may have suffered at the hands of an insensitive physical educationist in a society of athletophiles may affect them. These memories may result in less place in the sun being given to our profession. So self-awareness, self-assessment, self-evaluation are desirable tools in both our individual interest and that of our whole profession.

RECOMMENDED READING

Glueck, S. S., and E. Glueck, *Physique and Delinquency*, New York, Harper, 1956.

Kluckhohn, Clyde, *Mirror for Man,* New York, McGraw-Hill, 1949.

Parnell, R. W., *Behavior and Physique*, Baltimore, Williams & Wilkins, 1958.

Reeves, J. W., *Body and Mind in Western Thought*, Baltimore, Penguin.

Roper, R. E., *Movement and Thought*, London, Blackie, 1938.

---

[7] Although women physical-education majors can also be the target of abuse by both men and women students and teachers, on the grounds that they are just a lot of muscular hoydens, this is by no means such an informed judgement as that made of men. It is an interesting example of social prejudice that, in an academic atmosphere where there is restiveness about men physical-education majors being the muscular heroes of the stadium, this is transferred automatically to the females too, few of whom are heavily built and many of whom are critical of men's athletics. The women physical educators may be said to suffer because of a myth.

chapter 3

VERBAL EVALUATION

The ill and unfit choice of words wonderfully obstructs the understanding.

AUTHOR UNKNOWN

The dead hand of the past still produces effects in the present through the conservatism of language. We still struggle on with the same linguistic equipment long after the accumulation of facts has ceased to be accommodated by it.

J. H. WOOD, *Essays on Growth and Form*

THE TOOLS OF PERSUASION

THIS may seem to some an odd title to include in a book devoting much space to measurement, but it is our feeling that this is a basic topic so far almost neglected in our literature. It is one which merits perhaps more than one chapter, as we hope to show. All of us use words far more frequently than numbers, and possibly they are our most important tools of persuasion. This is an attempt to see how we use them, where we fail, and what we might do about it.

THE DEVELOPMENT OF LANGUAGE

It is necessary before examining types of verbal evaluation, to look into the human mechanisms involved in word use. There is still some doubt about how human speech emerged from the grunts and squeals of pre-man, but there is no doubt that the enormous potential vocabulary of modern man (some 10,000 to 15,000 words at maturity), with all his languages, and the constant birth of new terms, whether in science, slang, or elsewhere, represents an advanced stage in a long development. The increase of complexity from the very limited vocabulary of the first speaking man to modern speech almost beggars description, and certainly has brought with it far greater potential *discrimination in meaning*, i.e., evaluation. The key word here is *potential*, because there is no evidence yet that actual vocabulary increases proportionately with the potential, since much of the potential vocabulary is limited to use by specialists. In fact, there is a new danger that scientific and technological fields are coining words so fast that before long communication between specialists will become very difficult. In a sense this is not a new phenomenon in that those who handle words most skilfully—the poets—have always tended to be a gifted minority, appreciated only by a few.

> True Wit is Nature, to advantage dressed,
> What oft was thought, but ne'er so well expressed;

as Alexander Pope wrote, or, as another critic said, "The best words in the best order."

Vocabularies

Most people have remained limited in vocabulary, especially in speech and the evaluatory colloquialisms of ordinary talk. These, while kept continually fresh in the United States by vigorous new word and phrase coining,[1] have tended to keep in circulation terms of little exact meaning, such as *swell, nice, cute, dandy, lousy,* and so on—words which save the speaker from making an exact evaluation. The late H. L. Mencken's examination of living language in the United States, or the works of Stuart Chase, S. I. Hayakawa, and others, bring this out. Many studies have been made of vocabulary used in certain social groups, including the monumental one by Thorndike, at Columbia University. Of course, the anthropologists, lexicographers, linguists, etymologists, and philologists have been listing and sorting out vocabularies throughout the world. Some of these endeavors have been due to the pure curiosity of science, others have been for a practical purpose.

---

[1] Someone has called this the "presentness" of American speech.

GENTEELISM AND COLLOQUIALISM

One such has been in Australia, a country with many new immigrants from many different lands. In order to assist and speed up adaptation and assimilation, a careful study by psychologists with tape recorders and other devices has been listing the 2000 words most commonly used by Australian working people. Australia (like New Zealand, a quite separate country) is a daughter country of Britain, quite independently governed since 1901. The common language while still nominally English, like that in America, has developed usages of its own. In both polite and general use an Australian vocabulary is in its way different from English in England, which is the type of English, if any, studied before by immigrants. However, while in the United States, there is almost proud use of slang and a warm informality in speech, there are traces of genteelism in the Australian investigation, since some of the pithiest and most frequent epithets of the Australian are not included in the survey. This represents perhaps, an earlier stage of postcolonial independence than that so clearly celebrated in America each July Fourth, since Australia is not entirely weaned verbally and retreats to a genteel correctness at times—derived far more from nineteenth-century Britain than from that country in the mid-twentieth century.

PLAIN WORDS

Indeed, there has been a move in Britain since the early 1920s to simplify English usage and call a spade a spade. This move surged up in the 1930s and was given further impetus when Churchill emerged as a national leader. In those famous broadcast speeches which have now become part of the cultural heritage of Britain, he used everyday terms, chosen of course, with great wisdom and appropriateness. Even such a term as *guts* for courage, determination, and fortitude was used publicly by Sir Winston. A recent head of the British Civil Service, Sir Ernest Gowers, conducted a campaign to cut out the gobbledygook, or indirect and often meaningless language, used in civil service documents. His books, *Plain Words* and *The ABC of Plain Words,* printed by the government itself, ought to be compulsory reading for writers of educational and psychological textbooks, and are a fine guide to anyone who would tighten up the exactness of his language. Later in this chapter, examples are given on which readers may work if they wish.

Our Use of Language

This excursion into matters seemingly far from physical education, has been deliberate, in order to emphasize two points—one fairly obvious; the other perhaps more subtle and fundamental. It is the writers' belief that much of the published literature in physical education is full of jargon, loose verbiage, and gobbledygook, used perhaps in an unconcious attempt to gain intellectual respectability by means of polysyllabism. Poverty of thought may be draped in a cloak of words lacking clarity. We have reason to believe we are not alone in this viewpoint. Friends within the profession in several parts of the English-speaking world have put forward the same views, and, just as important, critics of standing, outside the profession, whose good will we need, have also emphasized our poor capacity with words and our tendency to follow the jargoneers. We feel that a move toward simplicity, accuracy, clarity, and honesty of verbal use is needed. As a philosopher once said, "What is clearly understood can be clearly expressed." Many of the ideas in physical education are simple ones, lending themselves to simple description.

All of this, of course, is a comment on our powers of evaluation. An escape into figures will not excuse or cover an incompetence with words or lack of philosophy.

Psychology and Word Use

The second idea is concerned with psychology and word use. The ordinary layman probably makes a distinction between *reasoning* or *thinking* and *feeling* or *emotion*. The academic psychologist used to make a similar distinction between *cognition* and *affect*. Such divisions imply that we feel without thinking and that we think without feeling—or at least that we can do so. The earlier psychologist went one stage further and identified our will, drive, and determination as another entity—conation. As Hamlet puts it:

> And thus the native hue of resolution
> Is sickled o'er with the pale cast of thought

or in out-dated psychological jargon, "cognition inhibits conation." Is not the point that feeling, emotion, thinking, reasoning, and drive are all functions of one indivisible nervous system and a closely associated and actually connected endocrine system. We react as a *whole* to our environment, not one part at a time. All the evidence from neurophysiology, neurosurgery, psychotherapy, and psychosomatic medicine points to this unity. A stimulus here, impinging on one group of neurones, radiates some stimuli throughout much of the vastly complex nerve network, which permeates every intimate region of our being. We cannot generally isolate voluntarily the effect of a stimulus, so that it merely triggers off neurone circuits in a strictly limited part of the total system, any more than a bomb dropped on Hiroshima (whether justifiably or not is beside the point), cannot help having repercussions on the minds and emotions of people throughout the world, then and now—through space and time.

SPEECH INVOLVES THE WHOLE BODY

As John Donne, poet and Dean of St. Paul's in the mid-seventeenth century, wrote, "No man is an island . . . send not to know for whom the bell tolls. It tolls for thee." So no nervous impulse in the conscious living being (human or lower) acts in isolation. Words are the result of actions—by our brain, lips, tongue, teeth, etc., or our handmuscles and our pen. Words are like actions,[2] as we can see if we examine such an everyday concept as posture, a term sometimes used in our own field.

POSTURE—A COMPLEX

Posture is not a simple mechanical problem. At all times when we are conscious, several areas of our nervous system are involved, involuntarily and without our awareness, in fighting the continuous battle against the pull of gravity. We may voluntarily modify these patterns of activity by deciding to try and stand in a special way—maybe as we

---

[2] As Edmund Jacobson has put it, "It is even conceivable that mental activities are not uniquely determined by brain circuits alone, but only by the neuromuscular patterns, at least to some extent" ("Relaxation Methods in Labour," *American Journal of Obstetrics and Gynaecology*, LXVII (1954), 1035). There is also the story of the two young Frenchmen brought before a judge handcuffed. When they gave no answer to the judge's questions, counsel for the defence interjected, "But sir, they cannot speak unless their hands are free."

think a physical educator should stand, or a mannequin, or a soldier on parade, or as a quarterback waiting for the snap. That is, we choose to assume a certain posture. Suppose however, we are strolling across the campus, when suddenly the smell of burning rubber impinges on the smell-sensitive nerve endings in our noses. Automatically we alter our posture, the better to smell (our nose behaves somewhat like an insect's antennae), perhaps sniffing slowly to increase the number of particles reaching our yellow epithelium (i.e., better sampling) so as to verify that the smell is indeed burning rubber. We may turn our head to locate it, checking with our eyes, which scan the rough zone suggested by our nose (a rather crude direction and rangefinder). Our ears too, perhaps hear crackling, shouts, sirens. Eye and ear trigger stored neurone circuits of memory—"the tyre-factory, northwest of the campus." Perhaps fear operates at this point and we pale (superficial vascular constriction controlled through autonomic nerve centres). We may sweat (sudoriferous secretion from mepicrine glands, not the normal heat-losing sweat). Our hairs may stand on end—"like quills upon the fretful porpentine [porcupine]" (erector pilae muscles come into play for reasons lost in the mists of our ancestors' experiences). We may remember a person, perhaps a friend, or the friend of our uncle, or our sister's boy-friend, who works at the factory, or nearby, and this triggers other anxieties and memories. We break unconsciously into a run, and so on, and so on.

The Integrative Action of the Nervous System

All these developments are inseparable from the original reaction to an infinitely small particle of a vapour which drifted into our nostrils. Thus a small stimulus can set off a complex multiple reaction. It is the same with words. If we come on the word *serendipity*[3] it may merely annoy us, and cause us to curse the user thereof; we may feel it is a reflection on our ignorance. We may slam the book down and read no further. It triggers no stored memory. Of course, on the other hand, we may be word-curious and go and look it up in a dictionary, and later increase our self-esteem by trying it out on someone else (like a new car, joke, or gimmick). Words are not just convenient symbols, so many

[3] I am grateful to the 8-year-old-son of a well-known American leader in physical education for giving me this word.

bricks of thought for building structures called sentences. Man just does not communicate with man by means of words dragged from his memory in an entirely simple, cognitive, nonfeeling way. Words involve visual memory, the speech mechanism, ear memory, hand-co-ordination, memory at least, and very often associated feeling too. For instance, two words rather alike, MacArthur and McCarthy may both prompt strong emotionally toned reactions in Americans.

WORD MEMORY

Memory of a word may include the first occasion on which it was heard. It may have been used by someone whom you admire, or in a situation involving fear. Maybe it revives some special context of the word when first met. The word *enchanted,* ever since *South Pacific* was staged, has an inevitable connotation, and an Anglo-Saxon monosyllable has helped a musical to run for a long time on Broadway. Sometimes in college life a word from a professor is only half-understood at first hearing. When we produce it again we are not sure of our accurate use of it, and we may wonder if we shall make fools of ourselves in using it.

Of course not all words have emotional significance, but many that we use in making value judgements (evaluation, indeed) do have. Extremely familiar words—articles, conjunctions, pronouns, and prepositions—have little emotional impact unless spoken in a special way or in a special context, but nouns, adjectives, adverbs, and verbs often do. It is significant that some of these are the key terms used by adolescent groups. The word *square,* which since before Pythagoras has been dominantly geometrical, has suddenly in the middle of the twentieth century become pregnant with meaning, at least temporarily. So too, *dig* is no longer associated only with spadework. It is with the clever manipulation of words that the orator, the mountebank, the politician, the preacher, the advertisement copywriter, and the Elmer Gantrys sway our judgement, through emotion rather than logic.

FORGETTING AND PUNNING

As in so many other aspects of the workings of our mind, Sigmund Freud added to our understanding of how words affect us. For instance, how the seemingly senseless forgetting of names or words was explicable, when the emotional experience related to the word or a similar word in our past was understood. So too, the punning effect, or the tendency for one word to fire off another similar in sound but with different meaning, can be explained from the knowledge of the way memory operates, having come to us through Freud, and also modern study of the brain.

THE FLEXIBILITY OF LANGUAGE

There are, of course, many ways of saying the same thing. Sometimes accuracy is the point; sometimes it is good to reinforce fact by using imagination. Look at these examples, for instance:

1. a. On the gong stroke it will be exactly three minutes and twenty seconds after four o'clock A.M.
   b. Now is the very witching time of night
      When hell itself breathes forth contagion to churchyards.
   c. The glow-worm shows the matin to be near
      And 'gins to pale his ineffectual fire.
2. a. The temperature is 15 below zero. Humidity nil.
   b. The air bites shrewdly.
   c. It is a nipping and an eager air.
3. a. A depression travelling in south-westerly direction is moving on to Ohio and will be accompanied by rain and gale force winds, with thunder and lightning.
   b. Blow, winds, and crack your cheeks; rage! blow!
      You cataracts and hurricanes, spout
      Till you have drench'd our steeples, drown'd the cocks!
      You sulphurous and thought-executing fires,
      Vaunt-couriers to oak-cleaving thunderbolts,
      Singe my white head! And thou all-shaking thunder,
      Strike flat the thick rotundity o' the world!
                                            King Lear, Act IV.

TELLING SPEECH

Those readers who have studied psychology will be familiar with word-association tests which may reveal emotional factors in the testee's experience. In fact, the case is now becoming quite clear that words are often highly charged with emotional significance. This was true of course, long before the sciences of psychology and psychiatry existed.

All who would sway the conduct or beliefs of others have used words tellingly,[4] whether in attempting to produce religious conversion or for brainwashing, or merely to stir up an emotion needed for a purpose. Think for instance, of the simplicity and directness of the recorded sayings of Jesus, or remember:

> But when the blast of war blows in our ears,
> Then imitate the action of the tiger;
> Stiffen the sinews, summon up the blood,
> Disguise fair nature with hard-favour'd rage;

which Shakespeare's Henry V says before the siege of Harfleur. And thus has spoken many a football coach, in less poetic speech, but equally charged with emotion, before and during a big game. The words may *even* be in the form of a prayer, though why God should favour one team rather than another is an interesting speculation. Not only do the words used and their associated meaning evoke feeling, but even the sound, the inflexion, and the rhythm (some of Edmund Burke's most telling speeches in the British Parliament, when analysed, can be shown to be almost in blank verse) all operate on the hearer.

NUMBERS ARE WORDS TOO

It is nearly impossible to speak numbers or formulas with any emotional overtone. Imagine trying to sway another person's emotion by saying 3.142659 or $S = \frac{1}{2}gt^2$, or $CuSO_4$, in any manner whatever.

Occasionally numbers do have an emotional meaning—the figure $64,000 has, or rather had. Here the number was a symbol of power on the one hand and of mass anxiety about whether there would be success or not on the other; later it became a symbol of payola! At one time $64 was enough to interest people in who would win, but later a greater stimulus[5] was needed. And indeed millions throughout the land became emotionally entangled with the situation. Children were allowed out of bed unreasonably late (bad physical education), so as to see and hear the fate of someone they did not even know, except as an

---

[4] For instance, in Camel-sponsored TV and radio programmes the word *lucky* is not allowed to be used (Packard, *The Hidden Persuaders,* New York, McKay, 1957).

[5] The need for the greater stimulus may be a physiological one akin to the principles of the Weber-Fechner law, *q.v.*

image. And in this case, as in many others, the hidden factor operating insidiously, but consciously forgotten, is the promotion of some product. So too, pinball machines used to score in a range from 1 to 100. Now the range may be from 10,000 to 100,000. Perhaps one day it will be 10^7 to 10^{15}.

AUXILIARY PERSUADERS

Many extra nonverbal stimuli are used to sway our judgement too; the catchy tune associated with a commercial, the lady in relative deshabille, irrelevantly but effectively enforces the caption pushing a cigarette. The ordinary onlooker, if asked, claims not to be affected by the advertising; he enjoys the show, the picture, the girl, the gimmick. But it is certain, and experiment showed this long ago, that not only does it pay to advertise, but it pays to pay heavily for advertising, and is catastrophic not to do so.

HEADLINES

So too in the press, banner headlines, the playing up of sex, violence, fear, and hate, by giving prominence to items involving these factors sells a newspaper, and sometimes with it a line of political policy. Headlines or news flashes involving the noble sentiments of the Gettysburg address, or the Declaration of Independence, would never sell a paper. Even the funnies would influence us more. A revealing study of the physiology and psychology of conversion and brainwashing which has recently appeared indicates that no one is more suggestible than the hearty extrovert, the healthy prototype, which by many is regarded as a desirable norm, and very frequently found in our profession.[6]

ESCAPE TO JARGON

Aware of the power and the dangers of words then, their repercussive emotion-swaying effect, some workers in serious fields have sought refuge in two ways—either in numbers (which are of course, essential in some forms of evaluation), or in a sort of dry polysyllabic pedantic

[6] W. W. Sargent, *Battle for the Mind,* New York, Doubleday, 1957; A. M. Meerloo, *Rape of the Mind,* New York, World, 1956 (published in England as *Mental Seduction and Menticide,* London, Cape, 1957).

jargon which is not only dull to read but exhausting to plough through, and lacking in crispness and succinctness. There is nothing wrong with long words in themselves. Life would be impoverished if we all spoke and wrote only the basic English of the late C. K. Ogden, with its initial vocabulary of 800 words only. But to use long words which are no more accurate than short ones, to use generalised terms rather than words which trigger concrete images, fogs meaning.

PITHINESS, NOT FLOSS

For example, in the previous sentence, instead of "fogs meaning," which is condensed and pithy, evoking (it is hoped) a visual memory-image of unclarity, this phrase could have been used, "interferes with the valid elucidation of the semantic content intended by the employer of the phrase hereintofore mentioned." These eighteen words say no more than the two actually used, and valuable time is wasted in reading them and sorting them out. There is also a point from experimental psychology to be noted here. Attention, concentration, full awareness of what is being read, tires easily and fails, if the same sort of stimulus continues without variation. The "appetite cloys" as a poet has said (in two words). There is recent evidence from several sources in North America[7] that fatigue is essentially related to continual use without variation of the same group of receptors. We all find concentration difficult, but it is easier if there is a variety of stimuli—as every advertiser and radio or TV programme organiser knows. Wordiness without imagery appreciable through the senses and feeling is exhausting to all but a few. Concrete images, sensible in their meaning—smellable, touchable, tastable—make meaning clearer.

A TEST

Consider the following passages:

Physical education experiences which produce an extroverted objective flow of consciousness are more to be desired than those which turn the individual upon himself through an introverted development. (28 words)

Activities which direct the consciousness away from self and onto an external object or goal, such as a ball, a mountain, the design of the dance or

[7] See the works of D. O. Hebb.

the welfare of the opponent, are more to be desired developmentally than those which emphasize *my* muscles, *my* weight, *my* fitness score or *my* ability. (53 words)

It might be thought that these were by different writers. The first one is condensed, generalised thinking. On twelve readings the writers of this book and some others only half-understood it. The meaning of the second sentence is quite clear on a first reading. It also emerges that it says clearly what the first sentence was trying to say. The surprising thing is that both these sentences came from the same page of the same book and in the given order. The reason the second sentence is more comprehensible is that it immediately makes the ideas concrete in terms of one's senses.

Another Test

Or take the following pair:

Experiments are described which demonstrate that in normal individuals the lowest concentration in which sucrose can be detected by means of gustation differs from the lowest concentration in which sucrose (in the amount employed) has to be ingested in order to produce a demonstrable decrease in olfactory acuity and a noteworthy conversion of sensations interpreted as a satiety associated with the ingestion of food. (72 words)

Experiments are described which show that a normal person can taste sugar in water in quantities not strong enough to interfere with his sense of smell or take away his appetite. (31 words)

Rather less than half the words make the facts clearer and retain all the meaning. "Brevity," as Polonius says, "is the soul of wit." But it depends on the kind of brevity, as the first example shows; more words sometimes produce greater clarity.

Words of Action

It is odd that in physical education particularly, where short words are so common in the vocabulary of action, that we escape into complexity in our writing. Snap, jump, puck, sprint, drive, bunt, slog, pitch, ball, tee, club, bat, net, spike, run, shoot, clinch, jab, punt, hipe, stunt, kip, flick, pike, leap throw, swim, dive, goal, and many other monosyllables are the language of our practice, and possibly many of our profession are happiest among these dynamic words. But when it comes to convincing others of the wisdom of our goals, these words are not enough. We must reason well, pick words with exact meanings, arrange them in a good order, and not waste time by vagueness or circumlocution. Many of the things we wish to do can only be described in words. Numbers, in some of them, have almost no contribution to make. Our main influence will be through our words. Others will evaluate us by the way we speak and plead our claims, and that means we must continually evaluate our own powers of expression.

THE TERSE CASE

If we wish to make a plea for introducing more social dance in our programme, for mainly social reasons, we must marshal our arguments and put a case. The briefer and clearer that case, the more likely is a busy administrator, supervisor, or school principal to listen to it and understand. If we are to address a home-and-school association about parental help in matters of health education, we must be crystal clear in stating our aims, and the particular way in which parents can help. Contrast these two approaches to the above problem:

Parental supervision and co-operation of certain objectives in the health education curriculum is highly desirable. Within the limit of the sphere of jurisdiction of the school, there are certain problems of interpersonal relationships, which the teaching authorities, through the powers delegated to them, are insufficiently equipped and so are disadvantageously placed to deal with in the most effectual manner. Concomitant with these aforementioned deficiencies is the insufficiency of time-allotment during the pedagogical schedule for promoting more than a limited number of extracurricular ancillary services to the pupils, who, after evaluatory procedures are demonstrated, manifest certain psycho-social needs. (100 words)

We want your help. Some children, we find after testing and observation, need extra help in learning how to get on with other people. We teachers have only limited time and training, and surely this is a job you and we can do together. (44 words only, but count the syllables saved)

THE DEBASEMENT OF LANGUAGE

There are very few occasions when a spade should be called anything other than a spade, surely. An era of loose wording has caught us up in the flood of verbosity and word trickery. Catchwords such as "un-American" or "egghead" creep in, but bear little close examination. Ball-point pens were sold by the hundred thousand at a 1000 percent profit, by saying they would "write under water" (and this was before skin-diving was popular)—only meter readers working in the rain would want to write under water.

In spite of the negative findings of the very thorough investigations of the common cold in the Harvard experiment of Salisbury Plain, millions upon millions of bottles of antihistamines were and are sold in the States as a cold remedy. It is as well for the moment to ponder how clever use of words affect health education. We know, for instance, that aperients are very rarely necessary, and should really only be used with a doctor's advice. The laxative-manufacturing king knows this, but he knows too that the public is infinitely gullible. There is almost no limit to people's credulity and their guilt about their bowels. The advances of science have, if anything, made this worse by creating mystery around the scientific phrase, as advertisers know only too well. No longer are cosmetics merely to beautify, but they will provide vitamins and hormones as well. People know vaguely that certain vitamins affect the health of the skin; they know, too, that hormones affect femininity. What they do not stop to question is whether these important items can be pushed through the epidermis—an almost impossible feat. Nor do they consider the question of dosage, which is all important.

The verbal ingenuity of auto manufacturers and copywriters must be extraordinarily effective. An auto is of course, no longer merely a convenient means of getting from place to place rapidly and comfortably. A car has become an extension of one's body image, just as clothes, or a baseball bat or golf club, become extensions of the body image.[8] The car has become a symbol of the person in it and, just as we must (by social pressure) have new clothes more frequently than is reasonable in terms of wear,[9] so now we must "wear" a new car, and feel thereby more important and more up to date. And so cars have got bigger and bigger,[10] less functional, and so fast that they can only be driven at a

[8] A teacher in Detroit told me she had to have eleven different outfits to wear at school.

[9] As this book is written, the wisdom of having the small car is developing.

[10] Exosomatic appendages, according to P. B. Medawar, *The Future of Man: the B.B.C. Lectures (1959),* London, Methuen, 1960.

fraction of their potential speed, if the law is to be obeyed. (Is it un-American to break the American law?) And what has built up this mania for inflating the ego—as with Aesop's bullfrog, the clever use of words (and, of course, pictures) operating on the dismal inability of the common man to evaluate verbally. Galbraith, in *The Affluent Society* has suggested that this sort of thing is a major factor in keeping the American budget balanced.

HAVE WE COMMUNICATED SUCCESSFULLY?

Read any report of the proceedings of a physical education conference. Echoed again and again is the cry for more status, time, equipment, and money.

When a President was shocked by a report on fitness, who was sent for? The physical educationists who have among them members who have carefully studied physical fitness over many years? No, on the whole, people who had never *studied* fitness as such. And one of the reasons is that the physical education profession had never made itself clear, had not been articulate, had not established powers of verbal evaluation which were acceptable. Granted political expediency, which often operates, was our fairly large profession the one authority that sprang to mind as having something clear to say on this issue? Did we make clear comment on the validity of the tests or clear statements on the nature of fitness?

NUMBERS CANNOT REPLACE WORDS

Physical educationists in America have been deep in tests and measurements for years. A great deal of statistical information has been accumulated, but has this been reduced to simple verbal statements that busy politicians and administrators can grasp and use? Science involves measurement, but it also involves verbal interpretation. For ever and a day we shall have to persuade people of what we want by verbal argument. In a democracy the committeeman knows nothing of "significance at such and such a level of confidence." He knows "that a good ball team builds the reputation of his high school, and he is going to give them new bleachers and an electronic basketball scoreboard"—when, in fact, educationally speaking, the school may be des-

perately in need of more activity space, more equipment for the
ordinary child.

Our Aims Could Be Simply Expressed

The ordinary citizen can learn to understand that the children who
need the most help in physical education (as in many other subjects)
are (1) a much greater proportion of the school population than those
in the teams, and (2) those whose natural sports ability is low.[11] Figures may be useful to exemplify the differences in ability, but the real
skill in evaluating such a misplaced emphasis in education, and even
more, persuading parents and education authorities of the error of
present ways, is a verbal one.

Good Argument Is Necessary

The capacity to state one's aims and arguments clearly in simple language, is of great importance if things are to be changed. This book
assumes that change is necessary. It assumes that the present emphasis
on the gladiatorial aspects of sport, the cultivation of the few in general
at the expense of the many, is educationally unsound in a democracy,
and that two main tasks each involving verbal skill and evaluation, are
laid upon us. First we must be able to show why the present pattern is
not good, and second, we must be able to state, with justifying reasons,
why another pattern would be better. This is not a question of panic
about a fitness scare, or anxiety about graft in college sport. It is a
matter of first clarifying our own thoughts, marshalling the clear argument about the present situation, and making crystal clear what we
would wish to substitute for the present emphasis. This will require,
above all, ideas expressed in simple, forthright language, entirely in
terms understood by the layman. There is virtually nothing in the
Research Quarterly we can use in such a situation, excellent though
some of its contents may be, for those of us interested.

Is Our Position Secure?

The present emphasis may change through the public's becoming

[11] Maybe the unrealistic view that all boys could get on the team if only they
tried hard enough or were taught well enough is akin to that part of the American dream which sees all newspaper boys as future William Randolph Hearsts.

sick of it, by a gradual seeing of the light, or by the impact on people's consciousness and their awareness of evil practices. We may have nothing to do with it. Like the exposure of payola or the realisation of the virtues of the small car, it may come out of the blue or gradually. When a general feeling develops that change is necessary, we, because of our assumed uncritical association with sport in education, may be swept out too. As Dean Arthur Esslinger, in a speech in October, 1958, pointed out, "Sputnikitis" might lead to a greater emphasis on academic subjects, and something would have to go to create more time. We need not be complacent about the security of our position. Nor will numbers, numerical evaluation, at least that such as done so far, rescue us, though it may help a little. It will be our verbal ability to stand up to the powers-that-be, whose emotional and rational arguments will be strong. We could argue that in the Soviet Union, more time is given to physical education than in the United States, but that argument might produce a hollow laugh. The argument for physical education *here* for the *ordinary child* is the important one, and the one where verbal strength will count.

This is not to say that our dialectic capacity is our greatest tool. People may or may not respect us as personalities; they may or may not respect our scientific experiments. Yet, while both our personalities and our scientific achievements may be competent, we can take no risks with our verbal skill.

SUMMARY

To summarise then, although this is not a book on English, semantics, or logic, we feel that these studies should be compulsory for those who study physical education. There seems little doubt from general observation, or as is shown in part by specific studies (such as one done at the University of Indiana), that our profession:

1. Tends to be unskillful in the use of words.
2. Needs all the support it can get from those who do excel in the use of words.
3. Needs to clear up its own thinking.
4. Needs to attract to it those who by their skill in words can clarify our thinking and strengthen our arguments.

5. Needs to balance its increased skill in using scientific techniques, with better philosophical and practical thinking.
6. Needs critical minds operating in all forms of human communication, not just the scientific ones.

Drawing freely on the work of Stebbing, Gowers, Jepson, Thouless, Denys Thompson and others in England, Chase, Hayakawa and others in America, and W. J. Scott in New Zealand, we give later, with examples, some of the forms of "crooked thinking," which are apt to creep into our verbal statements, both spoken and written, together with some exercises in verbal evaluation.

Accuracy with Words

Even numerical accuracy is a relative matter, as we stress in a later chapter. One might go further and say that all accuracy is relative. The flexibility of word use, word order, and word meaning is almost limitless. But there are words with meaning which is quite exact in some usages. Something is *unique* or *not unique*. There are not degrees of uniqueness. In contrast, *excellent* is an inexact word unless one has some scale of values to which it is related, unless one knows the competence of the person using the word, or unless one knows how the rating was made in relation to other judgements—and probably other factors too. It requires a hard discipline to remember these factors about word value, and we certainly have slipped up at times in this book.

So too, the purely verbal statement, "In a right-angled triangle, the square on the hypotenuse is equal to the sum of the squares on the other two sides," is an accurate and valid one—as valid as a geometric or algebraic statement of the same idea. On the other hand, examine this statement: "Teachers spend twelve hours a day searching for truth and the other twelve hours searching for error."[12] Can you come to any conclusions about its real meaning, its accuracy, or its relation to truth?

The Poet and the Scientist

It is common to contrast the ways of the poet and the ways of the scientist, but this creation of what is called a false antithesis ignores

[12] *The Physical Educator,* XVI, no. 1, 11.

many things. We feel that had Shakespeare written today, as he did at the end of *A Midsummer-Night's Dream:*

> The lunatic, the lover and the poet
> Are of imagination all compact:

he might have added the scientist to his group of people with heightened awareness. Just as poets have been known to spend many days or months refining even a short poem, so a scientist will repeat an experiment again and again to get it right (for instance Paul Ehrlich in his search for Salvarsan).

SCIENCE USES WORDS

Not all scientific discoveries can be reduced to mathematical terms. In biochemistry some of the most important factors in all living matter —enzymes, vitamins, viruses, and trace-elements—are only partially understood, and it has been essential to have words to describe these factors until their exact chemical structure can be defined in a formula. The same is true in physics, a science in which measurement avowedly plays a major part; as more and more is discovered about the inside of the atom, new names have to be coined to describe the observed and sometimes measured subatomic entities. So the neutron, the neutrino, the anti-neutrino, the proton, the positron, the meson, and all the other components have to be given word names to describe them. In fact, numbers are very limited as to what they can describe. Some symbols such as π, 22/7, or 3.142859, etc., are invaluable short cuts. It is also quite true that when we say we did a round of golf in seventy-two strokes, we are more exact than if we say we did a pretty good round. But despite many examples that can be given of satisfactory numerical evaluation, there are many jobs which words do better.

THE SEARCH FOR TRUTH

Let us finish with the poet and scientist by saying that they both have to be very good observers, and that they have to have prepared minds—the poet with a usually good vocabulary, and the scientist with a framework of basic knowledge, and a means of measuring, and like the poet, an overwhelming desire to find the truth and nothing but the truth, and to express it accurately. This prepared mind is what allows these seemingly accidental scientific discoveries to be made. When Alexander Fleming observed, in 1929, that a Petri dish on which he was culturing some staphylococci had been contaminated by a mould, he did not, as one with an unprepared mind and little imagination might have done, discard the dish. He suddenly saw more than the contamination. He saw areas of germ culture where the growth was markedly less, less than in the uncontaminated parts. It flashed into his mind that there was some pattern of cause and effect in this. He had seen thousands of cultures growing before, thousands of contaminating moulds too, and this mould, *Penicillium notatum,* often enough too, but the end result of his imagination and prepared mind in this instance—a result developed later by Sir Howard Florey—was that millions of lives have been saved. True, measurement was used to check the findings, and in many later ways to develop, use, and check the use of penicillin, but the crucial observation, the fundamental evaluation made, was not a numerical one. So too, we owe our initial knowledge of radium to the doubts that crossed Mme. Curie's mind when she found a fogged plate in a drawer and deduced possible causes.

THE POET AS PROPHET

The poet too, sees sometimes more clearly than others have seen, or as when Shakespeare made Othello say:

> Farewell, the plumed troop and the big wars
> That make ambition virtue! O farewell!
> Farewell the neighing steed, and the shrill trump,
> The spirit-stirring drum, the ear-piercing fife,
> The royal banner, and all quality,
> Pride, pomp, and circumstance of glorious war!

This was not only Othello's views on his own future as a soldier, but a profound comment by Shakespeare on the complex nature of war, observations which in 1608, when this was written, were centuries ahead of their time. How penetrating is an evaluation such as "the big wars that make ambition virtue!"

SOME COMMON ERRORS

Let us examine some, and some only, of the common classes of error into which our profession may fall. Many of the examples will tend to contain more than one type of error; only the most obvious is indicated. See if you can find the others. Some examples are drawn from actual experience and our literature. Some have been adapted to stress the point.

Egocentrism. Regarding oneself as the norm to which other people are compared—a fault to be expected in youth. Its disappearance is a sign of maturity, but regression in all of us is common.
1. "I've never got a kick out of volley-ball, it's a lousy game."
2. "Look at me. I've played big-time sport: I haven't got a paunch."
3. "Smoking is just weak-willed; I never smoke!"

Ethnocentrism. Regarding one's own country or racial group as the norm or ideal of human group behaviour. Regarding those of different skin color, clothing, customs, or manners as inferior because they are different.
1. "Football is a red-blooded American sport."
2. "College football is the greatest bulwark we have against communism" (Radio commentator from New York, November, 1958).
3. "Pehr Henrik Ling, a sort of 19th century Swedish Bernarr McFadden" (*Life,* August, 1959).
4. "Of course, all young people neck."
5. "All Chinese smell!"
6. "Americans today are healthier, live longer and break more athletic records than any generation of their ancestors. If and when the actual facts are ever known, it is a reasonable guess that American children and adults will be found physically equal to any people on earth" (*Physical Education,* XIV, no. 1, 6).
   (In fairness to this example, it may be said that it is the peroration to an otherwise carefully reasoned article. How tempting are perorations!)
1. "That old American institution, the circus" (Heard on the radio, 1958).

Sectocentrism. Regarding one's own religious faith or viewpoint as normal and all others as misguided.
1. "———— University uses questionable methods in basketball. Typical Catholics!"
2. "The Buddhist just isn't a sportsman!" (English journal)

Sentimentality. Endowing inanimate objects or animals with feelings which are in fact in the mind of the speaker. Unreal emotion. This is, of course, the basis of much advertising and many popular songs. Several competent observers have remarked that sentimentality is surprisingly common in America, a country which is proud of throwing off the yoke of European tradition,

Sentimentality is often combined with anthropomorphism, or the assumption that animals, birds, and insects have emotions and reactions similar to those of human beings.

1. "My budgerigar just loves watching basketball on T.V."
2. "While no terrifying raging flames are presently licking at the timbers of our society, the Nation, if it responds to what is not a false alarm but a healthy alert, may avert a six-alarm fire" (*The Physical Educator*, XVI, no. 4, 128; the syntax of this sentence is also confusing).
3. "Throughout Forest Lawn the spirit of Youth—its hopes, its dreams, its innocence—is told in almost human sculptures, the glowing colours of stained glass and classic poetry" (Advertisement in a theatre programme).

Emotivation. The use of emotion-provoking words in a situation where calm and detached reasoning would give a more accurate picture. Disguising or distorting the truth with such words. For example, "Be a real he-man: buy Gole-Hi, the scent that rates with dates."

Post hoc ergo proper hoc. Attributing causality because one situation happened and succeeds another, or one is preceded by another.

1. "Americans have spread basketball round the world. Only an American could have invented such a game!" (In fact, it was invented by a Canadian.)
2. "If the sun had not come out at half-time we would have won."
3. "Once Korycbzki was injured there was no possibility of winning."

False or Weak Analogy. Using an analogy (particularly a striking one) to suggest a parallel situation, when in fact there is no, or only partial, parallelism. Some old ones frequently cited not only are false analogies but are hallowed by tradition.

1. "A chain is as strong as its weakest link."
2. "Where there is smoke there is fire."
3. "A special committee set up to bring this impressive step to fruition has already gone into action" (This is, of course, a mixed metaphor too).

The worn phrase. The repetition of a phrase as a comment, or in an attempt to conclude an argument, which is itself at best a half-truth, at worst an unproved generalisation.

1. "History repeats itself."
2. "You cannot change human nature."
3. "Women drivers!"

Exaggeration. Deliberately distorting the proportions of factors operating in a situation, in order to create a viewpoint or sway a situation.

1. "Balkan Sobranie is more than a name; it is a philosophy of living."
2. "A thinking man's filter and a smoking man's tobacco."
3. "THINK BIG, PLAN BIG and ACT BIG and from this gathering of proven dedicated fitness leadership could come a snowball, that might well move the mountain of passivity and sedentary habits" (*The Physical Educator*, XV, no. 3, 85).

Wishful thinking. Altering an argument to fit an emotional "set," either by omission of contrary factors or exaggerating supporting factors.
1. "Mom thinks I look just like Ingrid Bergman, so I'm going to be a movie actress."
2. "Americans and Canadians are just like brothers, living next door to each other with no fence between." (This may seem a phony example, but to one who has visited Canada several times, there seems no doubt that such a view is certainly not held in Canada—in fact rather the opposite. Canadians dislike being mistaken for an American.)

Rationalisation. Inventing reasons and an argument to justify a course of action or a decision which was initially an emotional choice, generally a pleasure-giving one.
1. "If I take Jane to that movie tonight it'll freshen me up for that assignment I gotta do when I get back."
2. "I'll have just one more for the road."
3. "Football makes you a regular guy."

Polysyllabism. Using long complicated words where short ones would convey just as much meaning. Using long words to bolster up a weak argument.
1. "Traumatic intervention induced bilateral ecchymosis and nasal epistaxis," meaning "He got a couple of black eyes and a bloody nose."
2. "Associated with the growing emphasis placed upon interscholastic athletics has been the effectiveness of communications media in developing an informed citzenry," meaning "More school sport has meant more public awareness of sport."
3. "An edentulous female septuagenarian of repellent appearance," meaning "A toothless old hag."

Euphemism. Using indefinite respectable words to disguise something about which there is a sense of shame.
1. "Approved comfort stations."
2. "At this stage of the busy journey, the Queen was given an opportunity to wash her hands."

Genteelism. Using a more respectable-sounding word of exactly the same meaning, to sound more impressive and increase one's status socially.
1. "Commence!" (for "Begin!")
2. "Keep your posteriors down."
3. "Remove your footwear!"
  (See Nancy Mitford's work on "U and Non U in England.")

Generalisation. Concocting a general principle from a single example, often from one's own experience. Making a general statement of a strong kind where in fact no general statement can be made, because there is a distribution of tendencies, a continuum, or no supporting evidence.
1. "Teamgames' players are more co-operative people than players of individual sports!"
2. "Field hockey is too rough a game for girls."
3. "He was a typical square-headed Kraut."
4. "Guess it was too formal for us" (Said by an eminent American professor as an explanation as to why Americans were not present at the Second World Lingiad; besides being a generalisation, it was an ignorant remark).
5. "Everyone agrees that the person who has physical fitness enjoys a healthy mental outlook" (*AAPHER Journal,* September, 1956).

Redundancy. Stating the obvious to such an extent that it reflects on the intelligence of the reader. Redundancy seems very common in some of our practical literature. For example:
The server in tennis aims to:
  a. Hit the ball with the racket.
  b. Hit the ball in the middle of the racket.
  c. Hit the ball over the net.
  d. Hit the ball into the correct receiving court.
  e. Hit the ball in such a manner that the receiver cannot return it.
  f. Be accurate.
  g. Be consistent.
  h. Not to step on the back-line.
  i. Be sportsmanlike.
  j. Be ladylike.
    Etc.
  (Some of these aims are of course irrelevant too. Most of them are surely self-evident to anyone who has watched tennis for five minutes.)

Other common errors are well described and exemplified in many books, including those listed at the end of this chapter. Examples of errors would be:—

The common syllogism
Suggestion by repeated affirmation, use of a confident manner, prestige
Prestige by false credentials, pseudo-technical jargon
Oversimplification or tabloid thinking
Vagueness and ambiguity
Mistaken inference
Half truths
Red herrings
Circular arguments
False antithesis
Argumentum ad hominem
Padding
Begging the question
Confusing ends and means

Examples of all these can be found in our periodical literature and in many of our published books. It could be amusing for interested persons to collect examples of these and other ways of crooked thinking. The authors would certainly be glad to receive examples culled from our literature. It would probably sharpen the evaluatory power of members of our profession if they occasionally deliberately spent time on just such a task. We need to be eternally vigilant with words.

RECOMMENDED READING

Beardsley, Monroe C., *Thinking Straight*, Englewood Cliffs, N.J., Prentice-Hall, 1950.

Chase, Stuart, *Guides to Straight Thinking*, New York, Harper, 1956.

Chase, Stuart, and M. Tyler, *Power of Words*, New York, Harcourt, Brace, 1954.

Evans, Bergen, and Cornelia Evans, *A Dictionary of Contemporary American Usage*, New York, Random House, 1957.

Fearnside, W. W., and W. R. Holther, *Fallacy*, Englewood Cliffs, N.J., Prentice-Hall, 1959.

Gowers, Ernest, *The Complete Plain Words*, London, Her Majesty's Stationery Office, 1954.

Hayakawa, S. I., *Language in Thought and Action*, New York, Harcourt, Brace, 1949.

Jepson, R. W., *Teach Yourself to Think*, 4th ed., London, English Universities Press, 1943.

Jepson, R. W., *Clear Thinking*, 4th ed., New York, Longmans, Green, 1948.

Laslett, P., ed., *The Physical Basis of Mind*, New York, Macmillan, 1950.

Miller, Clyde R., *The Process of Persuasion*, New York, Crown, 1946.

Potter, Stephen, *The Theory and Practice of Gamesmanship*, New York, Holt, 1948.

Potter, Stephen, *Some Notes on Lifemanship*, New York, Holt, 1951.

Potter, Stephen, *One-Upmanship*, New York, Holt, 1952.

Sherrington, Sir Charles S., *Man on His Nature*, 2nd ed., London, Cambridge University Press, 1952.

Stebbing, L. Susan, *Thinking to Some Purpose*, Baltimore, Penguin, 1939.

Thompson, Denys. *Between the Lines; or How to Read a Newspaper*, Toronto, Saunders, 1939.

Thompson, Denys, *Voice of Civilization; an Enquiry into Advertising*, Muller, 1943.

Thouless, Robert H., *Straight and Crooked Thinking*, 5th ed., London, English Universities Press, 1943.

Whiteside, Thomas, *The Big Puff*, London, Constable, 1955.

EXERCISES IN VERBAL EVALUATION

1. Comment on the quality of word use in the following captions in a well-known American book.

   a. A photo of some fully dressed 10-year-old children in a gym. Some are walking on a 6-foot-high balance beam 8 feet long; others are using tins with rope handgrips as stilts.
   Caption. "Play periods should be of adequate length to enable the children to have sufficient exercise."

   b. A photo shows four teen-aged youths, in sports clothes, playing ping pong, while four others are playing shuffleboard. All the youths are highly mesomorphic.
   Caption. "The skills that youth acquires will determine to a great extent how their leisure time will be spent."

   c. A photo shows a 12-year-old doing a rather untidy Western Roll over a bar 2 feet from the ground. Eighteen boys stand watching, 20 yards away. The teacher is 40 yards away.
   Caption. "Practice must be meaningful."

   d. A photo of a young man in long pants, with another young man on his shoulder, holding a 6-year-old boy above his head.
   Caption. "Good leaders will guide youth in the right way of living."

2. Go into a drugstore. List the titles of the glossy paperbacks and also tabu-

late the means by which your attention is drawn to the book. See if the cover has any relevance to the content.

3. Examine the advertisements in some popular magazine.

    a. List under headings those concerned with some aspect of health.

    b. Take each advertisement in turn and decide which emotion or value is played on to catch your attention, and how an attempt is made to convince you of the quality of the product.

    c. List the products under three headings: (1) essential to health; (2) contributes to health, but not essential; (3) deleterious to health.

4. During any one day, note on a card or in a pocket book how many times:

    a. You make evaluatory statements (1) in words; (2) in numbers.

    b. Those whom you meet make such statements.

    Classify these statements into valid and not valid ones.

5. Listen to, say, twenty commercial radio or television plugs. Analyse them.

6. Measure the percentage given on each page of a daily paper to advertisements. Analyse the type of advertisement and the persuasive devices used.

7. Examine the following passage and analyse its thinking in detail. There are at least twenty serious errors in it.

"Physical Education is now beginning to affect the fates of nations. As a result of the medical rejection figures for World War II—showing that about 35% of our men are unfit for military service—there is now a great public upstirring of support for the obvious solution to this problem: more sport for all. The increasing public enthusiasm for the World Series matches is yet another sign of widespread support for our cause—worthwhile exercise, otherwise physical education. The figures for mental ill-health in this country also give cause for concern. One in twenty persons at some time of their lives is treated for mental ill-health. Here again we must play our part. Aristotle's old saying, '*Mens sana in corpore sano*' never was more true. If we are to have healthy minds we need first healthy bodies. Let the educationists give their attention less to the frills like art, music and social studies, and more to the honest healthy exercise of our playing fields. Some of the money spent on scientific apparatus—most of it meaningless to the children—might well be diverted to the purchase of trophies, cups and shields, on which our fine young children could see their names blazoned for evermore, as a tribute to the healthy foundations laid for them in their youth. Obviously it is the games-playing youth who is fittest in mind and body. America is a sporting country, but it is evident that we still have 35% who need more sport—the other 65% are well catered for in this fine outdoor young nation."

chapter 4

SENSORY EVALUATION

Give me the ocular proof!
Othello

My heart leaps up when I behold
A rainbow in the sky;
Contrariwise my blood runs cold
When little boys go by.
OGDEN NASH, "Song to be Sung
by the Father of Infant Female Children"

OBSERVER AND OBSERVED INSEPARABLE

IN ALL problems involving observation and perception both the observer and the observed must be considered. The drunken man see two keyholes or presses the brake too late. In evaluation, because that which is observed tends to be thought of as more important than the observer, the idea that a mechanical error-free method of observation is best tends to dominate. And with the development of machines which cut out certain types of error in human judgement, such as the photo-finish camera, there has been a tendency in educational testing to down-write the human being as an accurate observer of his environment. Some clearer thinking in this area is needed.

56

ERROR AND SUCCESS

Obviously human judgement is prone to error. Man continually makes mistakes—takes up the wrong career, marries the wrong spouse, or merely misses the crucial putt or the foul shot at the basket. But man also makes some remarkably accurate judgements, as are shown by the voyages of Captain Cook, the exploration of America, the prophecy by H. G. Wells of the atomic bomb or the foresight of Aldous Huxley in *Brave New World,* or anything so mundane as mother threading a very fine needle. Let us examine briefly the means, as far as we know, by which man makes direct judgements, and also the sort of error that is likely to creep in. Later we can apply this to the field of testing generally, and then to evaluation in our own field.

THE FIVE PORTS OF KNOWLEDGE

Man perceives his environment through his senses, some of which are obvious and understood, some not so obvious but quite definable and partially understood, and some which we may presume to exist but cannot at present explain.

The more obvious senses are the five well-known ones, "the five ports[1] of knowledge," as Sir Thomas Browne called them in the seventeenth century. The receptor organs in the nervous system for these are easily observed and described by the anatomist and physiologist. Sight, hearing, taste, smell, and touch should have been studied in part, either in physiology, psychology, or both. There is no need to deal with them in detail here, beyond saying that each of them is still the subject of scientific investigation. For instance, a recent President of that most famous and select of scientific bodies, the Royal Society of London, Lord Adrian, the leading English physiologist, has devoted much time in recent years to the question of the sense of smell.

INVESTIGATING THE SENSES

Because age, illness, or failures in development affect the crucial communicative senses of sight and hearing, these have been particularly carefully examined by the scientist, but there are still many puzzles left about these well-known senses, even in just their receptive function.

[1] Gates.

When it comes to the whole problem of learning and memory, the capacity of a function to improve by experience, there are still many factors only partly understood. The physiology of a quite simple nervous system, such as that of the sea anemone, can be a lifetime study, and when it comes to anything so infinitely complex as the human nervous system, it is small wonder that there is still much to learn. In spite of this, leaps forward in knowledge sometimes come through the vision and judgement of a master mind—and Sherrington's, early in this century, is probably the mind whose light has shone more clearly than any other onto the nervous system. He demonstrated the way the nervous system reacts as a whole, and that its action is integrative. He showed that the effects of a simple stimulus radiate, through synapse after synapse, into quite distant and seemingly irrelevant parts of the infinitesimally complicated nerve network, and that we react as a whole not just locally. In spite of this step forward, and the thousands of highly trained workers devoting their lives to this field of study, the sheer complexity, the enormous number of interacting variables, brakes any rapid development of further understanding.

In the present age youth, and sometimes adults, may worship the wonders of the guided missile, space travel, television and the electronic computer, with its quarter-million valves, or transistors,—all the products of man's cerebral ingenuity. In spite of these remarkable developments, it is as well to stop and realise that all these intricate machines are nearly as simple as David's sling when compared to the intricacy, just in terms of mechanical and electrochemical complexity, of the human brain. It was once calculated that to run an electronic computer as complicated as the human brain would take all the electric power generated by Niagara Falls, and all the water of the Falls to cool it (the invention of the transistor, replacing the valve, to some extent modifies this comparison).

The Remarkable Accuracy of Our Senses

So at the level at which we are thinking here, let us be humble. We are only beginning to understand these senses of ours. We have to rely mostly on empirical observation, not on the ultimate in measurement. However the degree of accuracy to which it is certain that some of our senses can work need give us no cause for despair. But before going into that, let us consider senses other than the five obvious ones, always remembering that no sense operates in absolute isolation, one sense modifies or reinforces another, and indeed, as the psalmist says, we are fearfully and wonderfully made. Sense receptors which react mostly from stimuli outside the body are sometimes usefully called exteroceptors, though this in itself is only a convenient but artificial idea (as are many kinds of classification). We see the light through the pinhole in the gloom and "the gay motes that people the sunbeams," or we are blinded by the unacceptably large stimulus of the atomic bomb exploding. Our eyes are in fact more capable of distinguishing differences in light intensity than any photographic device so far invented.[2] We smell a faint trace of leaking gas in the air and look for a leak, or we hold our nose to inhibit reception as we pass the skunk. We listen, directing the megaphones of our ears, for the sound of the baby waking several rooms away, or we clap hands to our ears as the crawling, exploring baby turns up the radio full blast. We feel with feather-light touch of our finger tips for the flaw in a polished surface (our brain has more nerve network connected, in a sense, with our thumb and finger tips, than there is for the whole of our buttock and thigh), or we jerk our hand away from the hot stove. We sample our environment for minute stimuli or protect ourselves from too great ones.

ESP

Over and above these well-known five types of exteroceptors, there is very probably at least one that does not make sense, because, although its operation can be observed, at present there is no acceptable explanation of its *modus operandi*. This type of exteroception is known as extrasensory perception, or ESP, in which scientifically controlled experiments, where every other causative possibility is, so far as we know, ruled out, seem to indicate that there can be communication of simple ideas at a distance between people, cut off from each other in terms of the known and understood senses. The classic (i.e., the crucial) experiments have been done at Duke University, with a selection of cards having various unusual markings on them. One individual, guarded, sealed off from all possible contact direct or indirect, turns over one by one, a deck of mechanically shuffled cards. The re-

[2] The human eye is sensitive enough to pick up a match being struck 50 miles away, though of course experimentally this would be very hard to demonstrate.

cipient, a person chosen for his extrasensory receptivity, some miles away and also guarded, makes a record of the order of the cards, as they are turned up. The results, when the experiment is repeated many times and analysed by automatic machines, show a far greater degree of coincidence than can be explained by chance. As is explained in a later chapter, how chance operates (if that is not a contradiction in itself) is well understood, and it is possible to eliminate chance as a possible explanation in a properly designed experiment. It should be mentioned that some subjects seem devoid of ESP, while others are markedly sensitive. This has been suggested literally for a long time. The Highland woman with the "gift" known to our forebears, perhaps was extremely sensitive in ESP. This is not the time nor the place to discuss ESP further but its existence should be mentioned. It seems probable we shall begin to understand interpersonal relationships more when ESP is more fully understood, and many more convincing demonstrations have been made.

Personal Influence

If we pause to think of our own education—the influence on the part of one teacher or the lack of it on the part of another; the benign impact of some personalities, and less so of others—these are all real phenomena, even if we do not understand them. It has been posited that *suggestion* plays as big a role in teaching as *methodology*. G. P. Meredith, Professor of Psychology at Leeds University, has suggested that "excitement" by the teacher in his subject is a major factor in effective teaching, and this idea cannot be dismissed. We have seen in popular entertainment or in clinical psychotherapy how potent a force deliberate hypnotism can be, but we know next to nothing about that interpersonal influence which might be called unintentional quasi-hypnotism. We do know that in nearly all known abilities there is a wide range in a given group of people; in fact, the later parts of this book will be concerned with just these factors of the distribution of abilities. Is it too much to postulate that sensitivity—capability of receiving—will also be a markedly variable factor, in these unknown, unmeasured, and observed, but not understood, phenomena?

Why are these more abstract and ill-defined subjects mentioned here? Because it would be an incomplete picture to describe exteroception only in terms of the known factors. More still because we feel that ESP and other little-understood forms of interpersonal communication must ultimately be shown, in part, if not in all of their impact, to act through some receptor factor in the complex of the human nervous system.

Exteroceptors are sometimes divided into teleceptors (perception from a distance) and nociceptors (literally "perception which harms" —the proverbial pin prick)—a subdivision which does not bear close examination. The Indian fakir who stares at the sun until his eyes are burnt blind is using teleceptors as a form of nociception, for instance. But whatever deficiencies in classification there may be, or in knowledge of the *modus operandi* of perception, we become aware of an *external* environment through these various parts of our nervous system, each of which is potentially a field for lifetime study.

How We Know of Our Internal Environment

But what of other senses within us which tell of our internal environment and its relationships with the external one? Proprioception (literally "reception from oneself") is the general term given to such perception. Without going into much detail here it can be shown that many parts of the human body operate through a series of mechanisms of the "feedback" type, known in technology as servomechanisms. A typical feedback mechanism we all understand in daily life is the thermostat. Our car has one, our water heater has one, and our pop-up toaster and our central-heating systems have them. The thermostat in daily life generally operates through changes in temperature causing expansion or contraction in a metal component, which makes or breaks an electrical circuit. It is obvious too that human beings must have extremely good thermostatic controls, since the body temperature remains obstinately round about 98.6° F., although the external temperature may vary from below zero to 140° F. or more in the sun. Surgeons can deliberately lower the human temperature, at least into the low 50's, for certain types of treatment, and during illness temperatures have been known of about 112°; but in normal life this is a human factor which is remarkably consistent from individual to individual, from community to community, no matter the climate.

HOMEOSTASIS

It can be shown clearly that life consists partly of the constant restoration of equilibrium in the body, or homeostasis, as it is called. The sodium-potassium balance in the blood plasma and blood corpuscles is of major importance to comfort and that harmonious working of the total organism and capacity for adjustment which is the major part of health. So, too, the sugar level in the blood is maintained constant. Changes in these chemical balances cause acute discomfort, which is designed presumably to make us do something about restoring the balance. The effects of salt deficiency have been mentioned earlier. How important this can be is exemplified by a personal experience of a scientific friend in Kenya in 1928. A sack of salt rested on the ground while native servants were paid their wages in cupfuls of salt. In less than half an hour the sack was empty and removed. Even a fortnight later the salt-hungry cattle were still licking the spot where the sack had stood! Hunger and thirst are generally indications from our internal feedback mechanisms that equilibrium is in need of restoration, but this does not mean that what we choose to eat is quantitatively and qualitatively the best answer to the call for action. Appetite is a phenomenon only partially related to need, and is certainly a mischievous guide, as is evident when we look around at our fellows, especially some of the powerful ex-athletes.

KINESTHESIS

The proprioceptive functions most important to the physical educationist are those concerned with kinesthetic sense—awareness of where the body or parts of it are in space—for this sense is one which is much involved in motor learning problems, and indeed continually, whenever we rise from a horizontal position and challenge the ever-present force of gravity. The kinesthetic sense is a compound one built up by several feedback mechanisms. Some of these are in the muscles, and interesting work has been done recently by Hunt in America, Granit and Leksell in Finland and Sweden, and others, in showing exactly how these special small-nerve efferent fibres, the fusimotor fibres, as it were "tune" our muscles so that even tiny movements of a limb or digit in space cause a feedback of information. These special nerves play their part in the *total* picture of information feedback. Other special nerve endings pick up information about pressure, whether in joints or subcutaneously in the sole of the foot, and which feed us such important information about the firmness and evenness of what we stand on. Try walking on a pebbly beach after paddling in cold water and see how the feedback information fails. We all know, too, the total body reaction and feeling of elemental fear that occurs when on going down

FIG. 4.1. Sensory learning and discrimination in a pachyderm—an example of amazing subjective evaluation. The blindfolded elephant moves sideways popping the balloons, steps over the girl, and rests his foot lightly on her face. To make this movement with a leg weighing as much as a man his only guides are his touch receptors and the many proprioceptors which feed back information from muscles and joints. (*Sunday Pictorial,* London)

stairs in the dark we put our foot on a landing that is not there; the unexpected 6-inch drop (although of no danger whatever, were we aware of it), because the expected message from the foot sole does not arrive, causes the whole body and mind to react to the primitive fear of falling. This fear *when* falling—not the fear in conscious anticipation of falling, which is different—appears to be innate rather than acquired, since it is found in newborn babies. It may of course have been acquired *in utero.*

THE INTEGRATION OF THE SENSES

The example given from everyday life serves to show that the kinesthetic sense is not a simple one. The eye makes a contribution, the balance-checking mechanisms in the inner ear contribute to it, other parts of the brain, including the parietal lobes as has been shown recently by Denny-Brown in Boston, play their part. Mental processes may affect it, either through emotion evoking muscle tension which interferes with clear feedback information, or through too intensive confused thinking about a movement. For instance, anxiety-produced muscle tension in muscles other than those required for carrying out a given action can, as it were, jam the clear reception of tension information from the relevant muscles. Modern work on posture and movement control indicates clearly that we have two main systems of control—one crude, operated through the more primitive parts of the lower brain and transmitting general impulses extra-pyramidally, and the other concerned with accurate learned movement control, operating through the cortex and the pyramidal tract. This latter *learnt* control is sometimes known as ideomotor control. It is also possible for thought, or conscious cerebration, to affect kinesthetic awareness by means which we do not fully understand. The mind can produce ahead of the action a mental image (sometimes called ideation) of the position about to be assumed, for example in a dive, or a ballet leap, and this, it would appear from tests by psychologists and physical educationists, and by the empirical experience of many who have made a practice of pre-picturing movements, seems to facilitate the production of the desired movement. It has even been shown that games-playing can be improved significantly by thinking and visualising games situations. Wordsworth's "inner eye"[3] besides being the "bliss of solitude" is also a fine device for improving learning.

REACTION AS A WHOLE

To sum up, then, kinesthetic sense is a product of multiple stimuli and serves as a cogent example of the integrative action of the total nervous system. We react as a whole to situations, and the impulses fed in at one point by a stimulus to one receptor organ, diffuse through

[3] "For oft, when on my couch I lie/In vacant or in pensive mood/, They flash upon that inward eye/Which is the bliss of solitude." (Wordsworth, "Daffodils")

many parts of the total nerve network. One effect of this diffusion, sometimes popularly called "spillover" effect, is that not only are parts distant from the stimulus involved, but learning processes take place in a not-to-be-expected manner. One phenomenon that is relevant to our field of work—cross-transfer—will illustrate this. The organic mechanism through which this happens is not fully understood, but it has been shown experimentally on several occasions that deliberately strengthening muscles in, say, one arm and ignoring the other produces not only clearly increased strength in the exercised arm but a statistically significant increase in strength of the arm not specially exercised (probably subliminal contractions operate). There can also be a cross-transferring of learnt skills. There are also as it were *built-in,* reflex connections between movements—an example of which is given at the end of this chapter.

MAN AND THE MACHINE

This excursion into a little much simplified neurophysiology has a purpose that is threefold. First, it is our general aim to attempt to emphasize that the human nervous system is the major physiological factor we must have in mind when considering problems of evaluation. Second, it must be realised and is often forgotten that the complexity, ingenuity, and creative capacity of the human nervous system is far more elaborate, far more important, and far more fundamental than any of the artifacts man produces in the way of tests and statistical techniques (all incidentally products of his nervous system, for whether mind and brain are separate entities or not, there seems no doubt that mind operates through brain). The third purpose, and this has been deliberately kept till last, is to emphasise and exemplify what a remarkably accurate and reliable evaluatory mechanism, in spite of all the aforementioned possible errors, a sensory mechanism can be. We reiterate the view that the worship of the machine, the dominance of the machine in our lives— useful and wonderful though it may be—has led to a down-valuing of our own capabilities, even in just a mechanical sense. Because the machine—man's invention—has transformed our lives, we unconsciously worship it, and it is beginning to control us. The machine can yield information of an evaluatory kind sometimes better than we can ourselves. Galileo and his telescope, Leeuwenhoek and his microscope,

Roentgen and his rays, and many others, have extended our powers of perception immeasurably, but we still retain, if we choose, the power to make amazingly fine discriminations with many of our senses, and, if we are aware of the sort of errors that may creep in, consistent ones. Our senses can make valid and reliable judgements on many matters, and we shall continue to depend on them in many crucial aspects of living.

REMARKABLE SENSORY DISCRIMINATION

Although the Borgias always had a taster to sample their meals before eating, lest one of their ambitious friends were trying to poison them, all of us most of the time dispense with tasters, not only because we control the sources of food hygienically, but because our relatively untrained tongues can detect some tastes that should not be there. It is easy to fool tongues deliberately, we know, but in ordinary life they provide some sort of safeguard in judgement. However, we would class most people's tongues as unrefined testing devices. Consider, however, those who use their tongues and noses professionally—for example, the teataster, on whose valid and reliable, accurate and consistent judgement, sales and gradings of hundreds of tons of tea depend. The teataster's working day, for which he is well paid, consists of tasting (and then spitting out) about 10 cc portions of tea. On his judgement, the economy of the tea industry hinges. We laymen in this matter might be hard put to it to distinguish the cheapest of bulk poor-quality teas worth 20 cents a pound from the most expensive Darjeeling worth 10 dollars a pound. Sometimes as much as $150,000 may depend on a teataster's evaluation of *one* mouthful of tea. So far no scientific device is as good as a trained taster.[4] The wine industry is also dependent on trained tasters, with even more economic significance involved than tea and possibly more subtle shades of taste. We however are not trained for such purposes; our tongues are blunt instruments, often the blunter through smoking. The tea or wine taster cannot smoke at his work, nor must he sully his taste with anything that from its strength or spiciness decreases the sensitivity required in tasting the delicate shades (with their huge economic significance) of various teas or liquors.

[4] Information courtesy of Mr. John Brooke, of Brooke Bonds, Ltd., who obtained detailed opinions from several parts of the world for us to illustrate this point.

SOME PRINCIPLES OF DISCRIMINATION

Three principles arise from this example of tasting.

1. Discriminative skills have to be learnt and practised.
2. One sort of stimulus can interfere with perception of another sort of stimulus.
3. Overstimulation by maximum operation of a function can temporarily inhibit sensitivity to minor stimuli.

This last is the same phenomenon as is experienced when, immediately after a bout of violent whole-body exercise, we may find difficulty in making fine coordinations, such as threading a needle. It appears there can be after-images in our muscles. (A physiological law, known as the Weber-Fechner law, is relevant to these latter two points.)

These points are also, in general, true of machines. They must be calibrated and their accuracy checked. All clocks, all thermometers, all speedometers, must be tried, checked, and adjusted. In a sense a machine has to learn to evaluate, and requires checking in its accuracy and consistency.[5]

Exemplifying the second point, a chemical balance is useless in an earthquake. A radar device scanning for planes may have trouble with snowstorms or seagulls, or can be affected by fluctuations in the voltage of the circuit operating it. Most evaluating machines are disturbable by unwanted stimuli. For the third point, a radio broadcaster is controlled by a technician, so that his speech stays within a certain volume range of decibels. Sound volume above a certain level spoils the quality of sounds of less volume. This is particularly tricky when broadcasting or recording orchestras. So too, many machines have dampeners to offset stimuli over and above the stimuli expected. The shock absorber in the car is an example of this. Springs are necessary to save jolting, and shock absorbers are necessary to absorb the bounce movement of the springs. In human senses some of these adjustments are automatic—the response of the iris of the eye to changes in light intensity being one. In others there is only a little possible adaptation and a considerable time lag in its operation.

[5] Freudian psychoanalysts must be analysed themselves. This is in a sense a calibration of a whole person who will evaluate others.

The Superb Neuromuscular Skill of the Violinist

Let us consider now a *kinesthetic* skill in which the eye and ear check the accuracy of the mechanisms controlling muscle tension, which operate to a surprising degree of accuracy and from memory. The fingers of the violinist's left hand have to stop the four strings at specific intervals in order for the string to give a certain note when it is bowed or plucked. Some violins of the earlier centuries had marks or pieces of gut, known as frets, across the fingerboard to help fiddlers visually in finding the right space interval, and also to add an exact point for

Fig. 4.2. How accurate is a good violinist? The surprising answer is 1/200 of an inch. (*Otago Daily Times*)

pressure on the string. Modern violins have no such things. With practice a violinist learns to stop a string so that it plays the note dead in tune, i.e., exactly the right number of vibrations. He must not slide on to the note, or a discordant wail is produced; hence, his ear cannot check *before* he plays the note. He can stop the string with his eyes closed or on his music, so the only mechanism for getting the interval right is his kinesthetic memory, preserved in the proprioceptive memory of the muscles of his fingers, hand, wrist, forearm, etc., and in the tendon and joint organs, all contributing to the total memory of the learnt pattern of movement. How accurate is the fingering of a good violinist?

The surprising answer is to one two-hundredth of an inch[6]—a high degree of accuracy for anything outside precision engineering, or microscopy. What is more, this is done with so blunt and indefinite an instrument as a finger tip. Truly a quite remarkable fact of accurate evaluation. Learning to be so accurate takes much practice, and this possibly explains the shortage of really first-class violinists.

Of course, the making of a violin itself is an example of superb sensory judgement. The best violins are made entirely by hand, from about seventy pieces of wood of seven different species, and the modern Hoing instrument, which compares well with the famous old makes, the Stradivarius or Guanerius, is still made entirely by hand. Selection of the wood is by eye and ear, eye-hand co-ordination in the exquisite carving, continual ear-testing as the parts are adjusted, and the varnishes are applied. So too, with the more mundane craft of the watchmaker. The finished instrument is an objective and impersonal instrument for recording time, and adjusts automatically to temperature changes which would mar its accuracy. Parts are made by machinery, but the fundamental skills involved in assembly, adjustment, and repair are sensory ones.

SENSORY DISCRIMINATION IS THE BASIS OF CRAFTSMANSHIP

Sensory and nonmechanical evaluations are the necessary basis of many crafts, trades, and professions. Automation may diminish the number of component workers in a manufacturing process, but there will always be the need in some essential contributors to society for sensory judgement and purely intellectual judgement—both apt to be called subjective judgement by the authority on testing. Lawyers and judges, physicians and surgeons, teachers, artists, writers, actors, and musicians, as well as mothers and fathers, will always have to depend much of the time on subjective judgement and the development of their senses. So too, if a man can be landed on the moon he can tell us more than any machine.

OBJECTIVITY AND SUBJECTIVITY ARE NOT OPPOSITES

The distinction between objective and subjective evaluation tends to

[6] Personal communication from Mr. Maurice Clair, former leader of the Boyd-Neel String Orchestra.

be a false antithesis, and its overemphasis has caused much confused thinking. Some forms of satisfactory evaluation are best made by objective means (always devised by subjective skill.) The amount of wind blowing during a sprint race is best measured by an anemometer, because measuring wind velocity is not a task our senses can carry out accurately. On the other end of the scale, the selection of a president, a prime minister, a friend, or a wife will tend to be dominantly a subjective judgement. So too will the initial diagnosis by a doctor of an ill-defined trouble. His fingers, his eyes and his ears, and maybe his ESP will yield him essential information. This will perhaps be confirmed or modified by objective diagnostic techniques later, but surgery and nursing will always be primarily subjective skills. Judging dives will always be dependent on the human eye. Devices will be brought in to minimise prejudice, but even if the dive were filmed and projected, there would ultimately have to be a human decision.

Between the two extremes of mainly subjective and objective, there will be many forms of evaluation that are part one and part the other. Instead of antithesis, black and white, we have really a spectrum mostly grey. It is obviously important in certain judgements to try to minimise personal bias, but it is just as important in other evaluations to allow it full rein. The contributions to our thinking and to the enrichment of our lives of Leonardo da Vinci, Michelangelo, Dante, Goethe, Shakespeare, Milton, or Plato, Aristotle, and the great philosophers, or the great religious leaders have been dominantly subjective. Objective assessment of their influence or essential value is almost impossible.

So we must maintain respect for the capacity of the senses (and the intellect) to evaluate. And let us not be slavish followers of the doctrine of making divisions where none in fact exist.[7] There are differences in degree, but few of kind. There will always be basketball referees, car drivers, teachers, doctors, and artists who make essential, subjective sensory judgements. We can learn to recognise the likely sources of error— the types of error that will occur, our own particular prejudices, our evaluatory ineptitude—but let us strive towards the goal of making skilled judgements, whether they be dominantly subjective, objective, or as most judgements are, a mixture.

[7] We suspect in fact that *objectivity* has become a "blessed" word, hung on to gratefully by those who have not thought through the complexity of the issue.

RECOMMENDED READING

Adrian, E. D., *The Physical Background of Perception,* Toronto, Oxford University Press, 1947.
Bell, Clive, *Civilisation,* New York, Harcourt, Brace, 1928.
Hebb, D. O., *The Organization of Behavior,* New York, Wiley, 1949.
Katz, David, *Animals and Men,* Baltimore, Penguin, 1953.
Lorenz, Konrad, *King Solomon's Ring,* New York, Crowell, 1952.
Riesman, David, *Individualism Reconsidered,* New York, Anchor, 1955.
Walter, W. Grey, *The Living Brain,* New York, Norton, 1953.
Young, J. Z., *Doubt and Certainty in Science,* New York, Oxford University Press, 1951.

EXPERIMENT IN SENSORY EVALUATION: A BUILT-IN REFLEX

1. Arm yourself with a pencil and a pad of paper.
2. Stand with your left side against a table, on your left leg. (If left-handed vice versa.)
3. First rotate your right leg in a clockwise circle, making your toe move round about a 1-foot circle. Keep this movement going smoothly.
4. Holding the paper in your left hand write on it the figure 8 about 1 inch high. Write it with a continuous smooth action and keep your leg going in the clockwise circle. Did you leg behave itself?

chapter 5

NUMERICAL EVALUATION

Forsooth—a great arithmetician.
Othello

I believe that mathematics is judged by subjective standards.
The standards vary in detail from person to person and country to
country, although certain over-riding features may stay constant.

D. B. SAWYER, PROFESSOR OF MATHEMATICS,
Inaugural Address, University of Otago

NUMBERS ARE NOT NECESSARY TRUTHS

THE learned Schoolmen of the fourteenth century debated seriously
how many angels could dance on the point of a needle, but long before
this more valid enumeration had been used to make important and real
calculations. Pythagoras, 1400 years before (although like some of the
Schoolmen in that he believed in the transmigration[1] of souls), evolved
what to all except the professional mathematician appears to be an
eternal truth, a perpetually valid evaluation concerning the square on
the hypotenuse of a right-angled triangle. The clause, "what appears
to be," is inserted as a caution, for so-thought final truths even in
mathematics or science are sometimes found not to be final. Many of
Newton's ideas seemed to be final truths for two and a half centuries,
until Einstein showed them in certain ways to be inadequate. In the

[1] CLOWN: What is the opinion of Pythagoras concerning wildfowl?
MALVOLIO: That the soul of our grandam might inhabit a bird.
Twelfth Night

mathematical world a special type of thinking and language is used, and there is often difference of opinion about the nature of mathematical truth. It is not the purpose of this book to enter this particular field of philosophy, which requires a degree of special ability and training, not likely to be found among our profession. Addition, multiplication, etc., is probably responsible for our tendency to believe that all numbers indicate truths. Five fives are twenty-five and ever more shall be so. All our early training in arithmetic includes the idea of a final and right answer. This blind acceptance of numerical statement as veracity leads us to unconscious respect for numbers, even though in fact they may be used to mislead us.[2] Maybe too, the difficulties we overcame in remembering tables, the rewards and punishments, pleasure or pain, associated with early training in sums, have built up an inevitable association in the neurones of our brain and body that numbers and truth go together. Whether this fallacy can be exorcised in all the members of a democracy is unknown, but there is little doubt that specious numerical arguments are used by politicians, salesmen, and other propagandists continually, in order to sway our judgement. As with verbal epithets, where emotional reactions are evoked which may cloud our judgement, so by a rather more subtle mechanism, we can be misled by numbers. And because calculation has produced such wonders, essential in science, industry, and medicine, numbers are part of the make-up of the golden calf of today—or the sacred cow of science (which is no reflection on the beliefs of the Hindu).

SOME OF THE LIMITS OF NUMERICAL EVALUATION

Let us therefore consider what numbers can and cannot do, at our level of understanding, and what they can do better than words.

Take for instance the game of golf. Assuming[3] an ability to count, honesty, and no cheating, numbers can tell us exactly, finally, and indisputably, how many strokes a player takes to do a hole or a round. This same score of strokes can also give us *relative* information. It can be compared with a previous score, that of another player, or with a norm or an ideal, such as the par-score for the course.

Numbers can also tell us the length of the holes. This is an absolute

[2] D. Huff, *How to Lie with Statistics,* New York, Norton, 1954.
[3] In most judgements there have to be assumptions. How often we forget this.

figure, though the scale used is *relative*. If it is given in yards, it means that the distance is a multiple of a standard against which our measuring device has been directly or indirectly checked. The original official yard is kept in London and is the distance between two plugs of gold sunk in a bar of platinum which is kept in the Exchequer Offices, at a temperature of 62° F. The original distance chosen is traditionally that of the length of the arm of Henry II of England.

This is most of the ultimate truth about yards. It depends, of course, on other knowledge about measuring temperature, and the coefficient of linear expansion of metal. As far as our golf hole's length is concerned, we give a round figure and omit fractions. There is also a possible, or probable, error (a concept we must study carefully later) of a few feet, because the hole may be moved on the green or the driving line on the tee may be moved backward or forward.

Some Odd Inconsistencies in Units

Yards are the same length in all counties, as are metres. However, there is not always this consistency about units. A *billion* yards in the United States is one-thousandth of the same distance in England, as the word *billion* has two different meanings, being a thousand million in the United States and a million million in England. This verbal inconsistency is little realised.[4] Other measuring units too are not consistent in their meaning—*gallons* for instance. A billion gallons of gasoline in the United States is much smaller than a billion gallons in England, since the U.S. gallon is again smaller than the British. In Canada a billion gallons is different again, since there they use the U.S. billion and the British gallon. All of this indicates that before a unit is meaningful it must be quite clearly specified what unit is being used. In a shrinking world with greater international exchange of all kinds, this identifying of units becomes increasingly important, and emphasises the need for all to know the metric system. The confusion that exists in track and field results, with two main unit systems operating, is already well known (to say nothing of confusion created by different hand and electronic timing systems). *International* democracy, in the Olympic Committee sense, uses the *metric* system, while *national* democracy in the United States and Britain has used the *foot-pound-*

---

[4] *Time* magazine for instance has been known to quote English billions in conjunction with U.S. billions without differentiating.

second system. Thus the particular *demos,* or people concerned, must be defined when dealing with measurement.

Reverting to our golf game, the weight of the ball must be enumerated, as lying between certain limits—again a relative measurement. The length of an individual stroke can be measured. The system of handicapping can give an indication of the expected normal prowess of a player. In fact we can pin down many factors with numbers, and do this accurately. But there are limits, here as always, to what numbers can do. Numbers cannot tell us why a putt was missed or what Sam Snead's score will be tomorrow. Numbers cannot explain the effect of our opponent's comments on our less successful shots. Numbers cannot evaluate the effect of that second helping of pie which we ate just before playing, nor the impact of an astonishingly gaudy golf jacket our opponent wears, nor that irritating itch behind our left ear, nor the blister on our right thumb, nor can they evaluate the pleasure we got from that number 2 iron shot, from that hanging lie on the rough at the sixteenth hole, nor the remarkable beauty of the view from the seventh tee. Each of these factors is a reality, but cannot be evaluated satisfactorily by numbers. True, as mentioned before, rating scales can be contrived to fit many situations, but who in his right mind would describe a foozled shot with a percentage instead of a silent or audible cuss word.

ACCURACY

This example from everyday experience shows that numbers may describe certain sorts of truth, that relative factors nearly always come into the matter, and that in some cases numbers are well nigh useless for evaluation. But still someone will say numbers are more accurate than words. In certain situations where numbers are the best device for describing differences, this is true—but let us examine the word *accuracy* more closely. It is not such a final term as might be thought. In softball or baseball an *accurately* pitched ball travels over the plate and between certain specified levels. One too high, too low, or not over the plate is inaccurate, and significantly so, for it is a "ball" and not a "strike." We could at this stage discuss man's capacity to judge truthfully and consistently such differences between balls and strikes. He is of course, thrown back entirely on his sensory perceptive mechanisms, his eyes in particular. And as with other discriminatory skills, no doubt practice improves judgement, although this is offset eventually by age changes impairing acuity of vision. That evaluations of pitching are extremely important is clear. It is also clear that pitchers, batters, catchers, coaches, and fans do not always accept an umpire's evaluation. It would be possible to design a laboratory pitch-registering mechanism that sorted out strikes and balls, against which an umpire's capacities could be calibrated, but even when the more accurate umpires had been sorted out, errors would creep in—sometimes in fact, and probably more often in the minds of those watching with a vested interest.

Accuracy Is Always Relative

A really excellent pitcher could probably pitch fairly consistently through a ring of smaller aperture than the full strike rectangle, though it seems doubtful if any one could learn to pitch through a 3-inch hole consistently. Even the most accurate pitcher would fail in consistency at some level. On the other hand, any good archer could hit regularly a 3-inch bull's-eye at the pitching distance. If a rifle were used, the target could be reduced to the size of a nickel. If the rifle were held in a vice, the target could be reduced further still, and the consistency would depend more on the bullets than the gun. Thus we have a scale from an invisible target, and the normal errors of a pitcher and umpire, to a fixed, consistent rifle and a fixed, observable target. The moral of this is that accuracy is a *relative* word and not an absolute one.

A score expressed in numbers *generally* means more, tells more truth, than one expressed in words. If a marksman is known to have scored 987 out of a maximum possible of 1000 in target-shooting, we know more than if we are just told he is an excellent shot. How much relevance this has to his capacity to shoot bear or wild fowl is questionable, but it may have some.

Significant Accuracy

But numbers, while they may tell us more truth than words, only do up to a point. There is always a limit of sensible accuracy, of significant meaning. The Olympic record for the broad jump at the time of writing is still Jesse Owens 1936 figure of 26 feet $5\frac{5}{16}$ inches. Here is a figure expressed to one-sixteenth of an inch. Are we sure Owens did not jump 26 feet $6\frac{7}{16}$ inches or 26 feet $6\frac{1}{4}$ inches? No, of course we cannot be sure, for measuring broad jumps has to be an *approximation*.

There is apparently no way of measuring the actual take-off point, and so the front edge of a board is used; beyond this margin the jumper cannot take off and still have his jump scored. Hence, it results that some jumps are from well back on the board, or even from behind it, and the extra distance jumped is discounted as not measurable—or more accurately because the rules do not include the increment. At the landing end there is also a problem of relative accuracy. The distance from the take-off board is measured to the furthest back *mark* made in the pit by the jumper. A first-class pit has a flat surface (again *relatively* flat when compared with a billiard table), and is of a mixture of sand and other components which it is hoped will give a clean break, when the surface is interrupted by a jumper landing. However, the humidity of the air the size of pit-mixture particle, the angle of entry of the jumper's feet—all or any of these may affect the mark left. With a certain degree of cohesiveness of the jumping-pit material, there will be a little erosion behind the actual entry mark. With a dry pit and fine particles, a jumper may lose more than an inch, due to trickling down from the back edge of his landing mark, thus making it apparently nearer the take-off board and shortening his jump. So in fact it is not possible to measure broad jumps with more than a certain degree of accuracy with present methods. The man who claims to have jumped 22 feet, $5^{37}/_{64}$ inches is not talking more accurately than the man who says he has jumped 22 feet $5\frac{1}{2}$ inches. He is merely inventing a degree of supposed accuracy which in fact is impossible in the circumstances. There is a point beyond which figures are no longer *significant*—that is, they cease to add any extra meaning. The man who claims his intelligence quotient is 121.05263684 is demonstrating a lack of knowledge (or intelligence) about IQ's and mathematics. Percentages are often used in this way. Perhaps forty-seven people are tested in something not very susceptible to accurate assessment, and then the results are expressed in percentages to four places of decimals. In fact it is often more truthful to say "about half" than 48.7359 percent. Giving over-detailed and impossibly overcalculated figures as results is one of the errors of which all amateur calculators must be wary.

MANY FACTORS ARE INVOLVED IN SIMPLE ASSESSMENTS

Returning to the broad jump, let us consider one other factor so far not mentioned. For a record to be regarded as valid, the jump must be in relatively still air—specifically there must not be a wind of more than 2 metres per second, and this must be measured with accurate anemometers. The basic assumption here is that a following wind may help a jump, and we presume this is true. Therefore the influence of wind must be regarded as an unfair advantage when it comes to record-making. But what evidence is there, and how was it obtained, that in fact winds of more than such and such a rate do help which jumpers? The sciences of aerodynamics and ballistics enter here and suggest that the weight of the jumper, his speed, his shape in the air, and his angle of take-off are all related to the amount of wind which will affect him. Aerodynamics experience also suggests that taking off against the wind may increase height, but of course wind may speed the run-up, and in that way give more "boost" to the jumper. The exact effect of wind direction and force on a given weight, speed, angle of take-off, and shape of jumper is at present untested. In such cases an outside figure which covers all possible cases is needed, and possibly testing would show that the present upper wind-speed limits is a wise one.

A PROBLEM IN ASSESSMENT

Significant accuracy is not only a matter of *relative* size, i.e., a small fraction, as the following problem shows. Imagine a circular steel band made to fit tightly around the equator. (Some imaginations will reject this, and quite rightly, as an impossibility. Some will say that you can-not fit a band on water, and in any case there are excrescences which would make the band not circular. For the purists then, imagine a steel band—of Invar, the steel alloy which does not expand or contract with temperature change, if you like—fitting closely round a globe 25,000 miles in circumference.) The band is then sawed through and an addi-tional piece of band 10 feet in length is let into the band. Thus the band is now 25,000 miles, 10 feet long, an increase of a minute frac-tion—to be precise an increase of 1/13,200,000 in length—insignificant it might be thought. Now let us imagine further that this second very slightly larger band is concentric with the sphere, that it fits more loosely than the previous band did. How much looser is it in fact? A detectable amount? Could one perhaps slip a cigarette paper between the band and the sphere, or would something much thinner be needed? Or, on the other hand, could one walk between the band and the sphere, or creep through? Common sense of course suggests that the gap would be very narrow indeed. After all, a difference of such a minute fraction would be barely detectable. Calculation would however give us the correct answer, and you can work that out. (The answer, which is surprising to most nonmathematicians, is given with the calculation at the end of the chapter.)

CONSTANTS AND VARIABLES

This example illustrates that common sense (whatever that elusive quality may be) is not a safe guide to significance in calculation. It serves to introduce the ideas of *constants* and *variables*. In many problems there are both constants and variables, and one of the essentials in understanding a problem is the way in which these two types of factor are operating. The relationship of the length of the radius of a circle to its circumference is a consistent one, and is expressed finally by a formua, $C = 2\pi r$ where C is the circumference, r is the radius, and π is a constant, expressed as a fraction $22/7$ or $3\frac{1}{7}$, or in decimals as 3.143, etc.—though if greater accuracy is needed, more decimal places can be used, $\frac{1}{7}$ never finally working out is a repeating decimal (0.142857).

Circumference and radius are *variables*, but they are always related by a constant. Similarly, the squares of the sides of a right-angled triangle are *variables*, but have a *constant* relationship, discovered by Pythagoras. All triangles can, by drawing one line, be split into two right-angled triangles, and on this the science of trigonometry is built.

Other *variables* may not have the advantage of being related by a constant to one other. Pythagoras must have found this when cogitating on the transmigration of souls, or due to that curious capacity of the human mind to think in one way on one occasion and another way on another, he perhaps never thought of triangles and souls in the same mood or manner. Even three hundred years ago Shakespeare could make clear his doubts about Pythagoras by having Gratiano say to Shylock:

> O' be thou damn'd, inexecrable dog!
> And for thy life let justice be accus'd.
> Thou almost mak'st me waver in my faith,
> To hold opinion with Pythagoras,
> That souls of animals infuse themselves
> Into the trunks of men. . . .
> > *The Merchant of Venice*

Mathematicians have no monopoly on truth, nor scientists either, but their methods of dealing with those problems which lend themselves to calculation and numerical evaluation are such that they have the capacity to express certain sorts of truth about *constants,* the relationships of certain sorts of *variables,* and as will be shown later, *causality, relationship,* and *tendency.* They are also interested in *probability* at a level far beyond our comprehension.

MATHEMATICAL METHODS ARE VERSATILE

It is important to realise two things. *First,* many more problems lend themselves to mathematical evaluation than might be realised—and this includes many problems in the field of physical education. *Second,* mathematical argument is not always dissociated entirely from *emotional reaction,* when the topic being considered is one about which people feel strongly. Reactions to the famous Kinsey Reports on human sexual behaviour exemplify this. These statistical analyses of intimate human behaviour produced marked emotional reactions, which in many cases were not detached examinations of the evidence produced by Kinsey and his colleagues. Rather, they were statements—sometimes wrapped up in scientific jargon—of prejudice by reviewers, whether supporters or antagonists of the view of Kinsey.

Dr. Clyde Kluckhohn, Professor of Anthropology at Harvard, could write of the second Kinsey book in *The New York Times Book Review,* ". . . this is science, serious science and science in the grand style," but of course other scientists reacted in an entirely hostile manner, casting doubt on Kinsey's scientific methodology. This is not to say that when emotions come in at the door, calculation flies out of the window, but it is a note of warning that although true mathematical reasoning is devoid of emotional content, the reaction to numerical evaluation, whether it is valid or not, can be strongly emotional—and emotional viewpoints can be expressed by means of figures.

Pseudo-Scientific Persuasion

One of the perils of an age of pseudo science, when millions have a smattering of scientific phraseology, is that there is a mystery attached to ideas expressed in numbers. It is the function of this book to try and clear some of the fog from this field. There is nothing necessarily bogus about emotion, feeling, sensory reaction, and all the associated neural and biochemical changes that go on internally and externally. In fact, man's emotional reactions are real and apt to be more truthful than much of his ingenious reasoning and rationalisation. The mistake is to think that we generally think without feeling and that we feel without thinking. As was pointed out before, in the psychologist's jargon *cognition* and *affect* are not generally separable. In fact, we often experience both at the same time, and the problem is to understand how much and in what way one process affects the other. The evidence from neurophysiology and endocrinology can tell us why.

USES AND LIMITATIONS

Numerical evaluation can be properly applied to situations which some people would regard as unlikely. For instance, it is possible to measure with a sensitive instrument that in ordinary daylight there is a range of intensity of tone and colour in a given landscape in the order 1 to 500. It is also possible to show that the range of intensity and colour obtainable from the use of oil paints is in the range of 1 to 50 on the same scale. From this it can be seen that to depict nature's light variables as they are is impossible, and some compromise in tone values has to be made. While this explains to the artist the difficulty he faces, and may even suggest a way of approaching light values, no calculation can tell an artist how to treat his subject or what to include or leave out. Science can tell us that our depth of clear focus is very short with near objects. A simple experiment will show this. Hold one finger up in a direct line with a clock at least 7 feet away. It is impossible to see both the finger and the clock sharply in focus at the same time, though one can see objects in line ten and twelve feet away, respectively, in focus at the same moment. Similarly, our cone of clear vision increases its area as the square of the distance from the eye of an object seen. With one eye closed, look at the middle of an unknown page of a book, without moving the other eye at all, from a distance of say 9 inches. Have someone else check that you do not move your eye—the tendency to scan and search with the eye is strong (in fact, modern neurophysiology suggests that when awake we "scan" with all our senses in a way somewhat similar to radar). Only a few words will be seen clearly. At 18 inches many more will be seen, at 3 feet more still, though acuity may fail soon after this distance.

These limitations of focus and zone of clear vision, both capable of numerical evaluation, should perhaps affect an artist's treatment of his subject, but numerical assessment can neither guide the hand of a Botticelli, an El Greco, or a Jackson Pollock nor the judgement of those who would appreciate their work. However, although the eye cannot see near and distant detail at the same time, many painters provide equal definition at all distances.

Variables Are More Common Than Constants

Calculation can tell us things which are surprising about the growth[5] and behaviour of living organisms, and insofar as natural forms are used in design, these can often be numerically evaluated. But the main difference between calculation used in assessing life functions or shapes and that used in our elementary mathematical training is that the former concerns the subtle relationships of *variables,* rather than the behaviour of *constants.* We cannot count the number of angels that can dance on the point of a needle, but we can find out and calculate a large number of things about human beings—the way they move and live and have their being. This type of calculation and numerical evaluation will open a new world of ideas to those who look beyond the mechanical processes. Even though it is only applicable to some problems, an understanding of elementary statistical reasoning and method can affect our whole quality of thinking on many problems both inside and outside our profession. *This effect on the quality of our thinking is by far the most important outcome of studying statistics.* It matters little whether we can calculate a standard deviation or use factor analysis, if we cannot apply the principles of thinking learnt in this field to other situations than the ones where we are asked to use them.

> Sure, he that made us with such large discourse
> Looking before and after, gave us not
> That capability and god-like reason
> To fust in us unused.
>
> *Hamlet*

Laziness of mind and complacency are the enemies of the spirit of evaluation. Suitable numerical, sensory and verbal ability, and constant application of these to all manner of situations, are some of the signs of

[5] See D'Arcy W. Thompson, *On Growth and Form,* London, Cambridge University Press, 1917.

the man being educated, as opposed to the man whose education has stopped.

THE PROBLEM OF PUTTING A BAND AROUND THE EARTH

Solution. Given the new circumference of the band (25,000,000 miles plus 10 feet) we want to find the new radius.

We know the formula relating circumference and radius is

$$C = 2\pi r \ (\pi = 22/7) \quad \text{or} \quad r = \frac{C}{2\pi} \quad \text{or} \quad Cr = \frac{7}{44}C$$

Therefore, the radius is approximately 1/6 (7/42) of the circumference, and any increase in the circumference will be accompanied by an increase of approximately 1/6 in the radius.

In our problem, the increase in circumference is 10 feet. Therefore, the increase in radius is approximately 1/6 of 10 feet, or just over 1 foot, 6 inches, which is enough to *creep* through.

The fastidious may complain that we have made no exact calculations. They can work it out the long way, if they wish. Approximations can often save a lot of hard work and produce an answer of sufficient validity.

chapter 6

THE WORLD PICTURE

I'll put a girdle round about the earth in forty minutes.
A Midsummer Night's Dream

NEW FRONTIERS IN SCIENCES

ON THE whole, until very recently, knowledge in certain fields, medicine and science for instance, has known no frontiers. A common world pool of tested knowledge has been added to gradually by workers far apart in latitude and longitude, of different colour and nationality. The whole fabric of chemistry or physiology is the result of putting together scraps of related knowledge springing from the experiments and thoughts of people often with no language in common. Even when there was free trade in knowledge, this created problems, and these were overcome by two main means, interchange of visits, with interpreters when necessary, and by translation in full or abstract form. In a rather different and more tolerant world in 1813 Michael Faraday and Sir Humphry Davy, two Englishmen, could visit Paris to discuss scientific problems with leading French scientists when England and France were officially at war. It is as well to remember that this was not in other ways entirely a tolerant time—sheep stealers were hung or deported to the Colonies, and minor crimes were heavily punished. Rather earlier, when Robert Boyle (whose law is part of the international property of chemistry) was appointed to teach chemistry at Oxford, he was preached against in the university pulpit for bringing such a mundane and artisan subject into the intellectually hallowed precincts of a university.

New Problems for Scientists

Though there was severe conflict between religion and science, until after the beginning of this century, there was no international conflict or reserving of information within science. This is a new phenomenon, aggravated by the use of science in warfare, and brought about largely as the result of the combined operations of many scientists working in different countries, whose efforts over many years brought us to the point of releasing and harnessing atomic energy. When Lord Rutherford succeeded in first splitting the atom in 1922, a friend wrote to him asking him if he had no fears of the possibilities of the effects of such forces. In his reply, he wrote, "You need not be alarmed about any possibilities of any atomic disintegration; if it had been feasible, it should have happened long ago on this ancient planet. I sleep quite soundly at nights."[1] How differently we think now! How differently we think now! How man has become divided against man even in the world of science. Even in the healing arts it was deemed necessary to reserve information about penicillin from the enemy during World War II. Scientists have been faced in the middle of this century with new ethical problems. No longer can they just find out and publish what they find.[2]

The Fragmentation of Knowledge

But this is not the only change. Not only is there fragmentation of matter but also of knowledge. A chemistry professor, as late as 1910, could well be aware of almost all that was going on in the chemical world—who was working on what and why. Only forty years later by 1950, such a professor might not be able to grasp fully all that was going on in his own department in one university. Similar examples could be drawn from other sources. Scientists can now be very lonely and isolated specialists.

Our Own Field is More Complex

And what about us in the middle of the twentieth century? Physical education is an eclectic subject—part science, part art—drawing for substantiation of its ideas on many sources. How have these profound

[1] Personal Letter to Arthur Smithells, F.R.S.
[2] See the publications of the Committee on Science and Freedom.

changes affected us? We have been called by critics within our own ranks sciolists,[3] rather than scientists, and we must admit the possibility; however, we fight the tendency to be regarded as dilettantes with a smattering of scientific jargon with which to dazzle the multitude— little better than the mountebank selling his pills and salves at the fair.

We can, however, say some things with certainty. In the 1960s we are interested in *more* sciences than we were in 1900. Obvious examples are social anthropology, social science, psychology, and statistical science. We can say also that the fragmentation of knowledge in sciences generally has made our task more difficult. It is a deal harder to become a well-informed physical educationist in 1960 than it was even twenty-five years ago. We can say too that physical education itself, that is, conscious and intentional emphasis on the subject, reaches much further afield now than earlier. Apart from isolated primitive groups, there must be few major accumulations of people where the influence of our subject does not occur. Workers from both sides of the Atlantic have found themselves advising whole countries new to general public education on physical education. In the last twenty-five years our subject has become nearly as international as arithmetic, but not so much as medicine, religion, or trade. The Coca-Cola bottle or the Bible can be found in Pacific island stores, whereas yet no physical educationist's foot has trodden or indeed may ever tread there.

Few Real Limitations for Us

Have we too, been affected by the clamps put on the spread of knowledge in science? Very little as regards to potential war. It is, of course, conceivable that some country might hit on some new way of training people to get fit rapidly for military purposes. In wartime this might remain a military secret, but in peacetime we seem to share such information if the opportunity arises. Anyway, the sort of fitness associated with most previous wars, since the internomadic battles or caveman days, through the Crusades, the American Civil War, and the two world wars—that sort of fitness may not now be the main problem; though however, much cerebration will dominate in future wars, some psychophysical fitness will be needed. In interwar phases at a time of mutual distrust, problems of fitness are much more subtle and often

---

[3] K. A. Schrecker, "Scientific Physical Education?" *Journal of Physical Education,* XLIV, 133.

concerned basically with morale. The radar observer, scanning an almost continually empty screen, isolated in the snowy wastes of the Distant Early Warning Line or even the Pinetree Line, is faced primarily with a problem of morale—and of course, keeping reasonably fit in a situation of limited mobility.

OUR RELATIONS WITH SPORT

Turning to our mores frequent activities in peacetime, what can we say of our involvement internationally? Physical education is associated inevitably, whether we like it or not, with sport. And sport in the last half-century has not only spread further but has changed, it would seem, in nature. The game basketball, invented by the Canadian Naismith while at Springfield, has spread far and wide. Soccer, which was predominantly a British game, has become the major international team game, played from Helsinki to Hongkong to Tierra del Fuego, although making little impression on the North American continent. Lawn tennis, in contrast to real tennis, which has almost died out, in a hundred years has spread far and wide. Certain games, like American football and baseball, English rugby and cricket, and Finnish Pasopallo have remained rather more static. Some games such as hurling, jai alai or pelota, Australian rules football, or the Eton Wall game, have remained entirely local (see Chapter 19).

What other changes have come with the spread of sport? Has this spread of activities, which once existed for fun and exercise, continued to maintain the atmosphere of sport and sportingness? Has the much-vaunted team spirit—often supposed to be a by-product, a concomitant learning of indulgence in team games—led to an increase in international good will? Or perhaps, has sport become more earnest and serious, sometimes even bitter? Has the old idea of a clear difference between amateur and professional sport remained, or was it a myth in any case?

IMPORTANT NEW STUDIES

Two recent publications, *Britain in the World of Sport,* by the staff of the Birmingham University Physical Education Department, and *Sport in the Cultural Pattern of the World,* by Jokl, Karvonen, *et al.,* are interesting and relevant reading on these topics. The social scientist, David Riesman, has analysed the development of American football in

Individualism Reconsidered;[4] this is a fascinating study of the cultural diffusion of a game (see the section on sport ethnograms). Have we through sport learned to love our enemies? Have the high ideals of Coubertin for the Olympic Games retained their relation to reality? In some countries, including the United States and Britain, sport has become a major industry. How has this affected its nature? These are questions we cannot evaluate here; in fact, we would be hard put to it to evaluate them at all. But they are surely questions which must be asked! One of the early attempts at such evaluation at an international level by sampling opinion from various countries is the UNESCO publication *The Place of Sport in Education* (1956).[5] This is a thought-provoking document which all physical educationists should read, even though neither the States nor Britain replied to the questionnaire sent out. Much of its contents would make good material for debate and discussion. It is to be hoped that other international studies with a bearing on our field will be made.

INTERNATIONAL COMMUNICATION

This raises a point to which we must give some attention: the available means of international exchange of information. Before bringing down the focus on evaluation itself, we must look at the larger picture. How in fact have ideas about physical education spread? There would seem to have been *before* recent times three main ways. X visited Y to study with him and then returned to his own country. A classical example would be the visit of Pehr Henrik Ling, of Sweden, to Franz Nachtegall, in Denmark, in 1804. Or later, the influence of Springfield College on such leaders as Gunna Hoh in China (now in Formosa) or Dr. Ferenc Hepp, another Springfield man, in Hungary.[6] Such personal visiting has gone on for a long time at various levels. Sometimes it has had profound effects. A leader has come back to his own land inspired with new ideas, or perhaps looking at his old ones in a new way. Indeed, the writers of this book would not be writing if one of them in 1938 had not been stimulated by the late C. H. McCloy. This is still

[4] New York, Anchor, 1955.

[5] Obtainable from UNESCO Publications Center, 152 West 42 Street, New York 36, N.Y. See also *Sport and the Community*, CCPER, London, 1960.

[6] Formerly head of the Royal College of Physical Education in Budapest, and editor of a multilingual *Dictionary of Sport and Physical Education* (in preparation).

one of the best means of international exchange, provided language is
not an insurmountable problem.

Another more complex form of this personal visiting is the visiting
of demonstration teams or groups showing practical work. This can be
very misleading, as two examples will suffice to show. To many American or South African minds the mention of the term modern Danish
gymnastics would conjure up the name Nils Bukh, as indeed is shown
by summaries of national histories. It is true that Bukh was one of the
leading figures in Denmark in the period 1920–1950. But he was only
one of them. To anyone who knows Denmark, the names of Knudsen,
Lindhardt, Braa Hansen, Junker, Agnete Bertram, and Asmussen, are
probably more important, and indeed Bukh's work was forbidden[7] in
Copenhagen (which houses one third of Denmark's population)
schools. Bukh was a good publicist and took abroad many teams, which
gave polished demonstrations purporting to represent typically Danish
gymnastics, when in fact they only represented one branch of it.

A similar distortion about physical education in Sweden has occurred, through the narrowness of one or two Swedish leaders. There
are ideas current in many places that Swedish gymnastics are stiff,
formal, and undemocratic and are the only real items in Swedish
physical education. Some Swedish touring groups have been stiff and
formal, but others, in particular Maja Carlquist's Sofia Girls, and the
Idla Groups, led by Ernst Idla, a refugee from Esthonia, are as rhythmical and relaxed in movement as could be imagined, and often quite
informal as to class arrangement and lesson plan. But aside from gymnastics, Sweden is in a participant way a major sporting nation, with
huge numbers of yachtsmen, skaters, skiers, tennis players, track and
field athletes, tented campers, canoers, soccer and handball players,
and varp[8] throwers. It seems probable that Sweden has a higher participation rate in sport than has the United States.[9]

Thus the personal visit to see what really goes on is needed to check
what appears in print, and what is given the name of typical physical
education by touring groups. Language may well be a barrier, but
there are few countries where interpreters who speak English cannot be

[7] Personal communication from Col. Lang Kilde, Chief Inspector of Physical
Education in Copenhagen schools (1934).

[8] As a test of your investigatory powers, find out what a varp is!

[9] If one includes the amazing National Walk Championships between Sweden
and Finland, with five million competitors from 8 to 80, the point is emphasised.

found, and physical education, since it deals with concrete visible situations, can often be understood, in part, without words. Just as the rhythm of rock 'n roll might promote movement in the Solomon

Fig. 6.1.   The Swedish Sofia girls trained by Maja Carlquist. (By permission of Maja Carlquist)

Islander, so watching, say, volleyball, would make it apparent to every observer what was happening and why it was fun. Though Riesman points out that there are national groups who cannot get the hang of game-playing. He also makes the very nice point that some folk pastimes are essentially a form of international language, and cites the advice given to American servicemen stranded in isolated places among potentially hostile natives—sit down and start making cat's cradles with a piece of string![10] The same could be said, of course, about cricket or American football to some observers; both seem odd games except to their local fans.[11]

[10] Riesman, *op. cit.*

[11] Dean Seward Staley, who has studied games far and wide, confesses to being completely baffled by cricket!

DISSEMINATION THROUGH COLONISATION

Another spread of ideas in sport and physical education has come through colonisation, whether imperialistic, protective, or political. Contrary to popular idea, the game of horse shoes was not spread by the Roman camp-followers at the time of the Roman Empire, because horses at that time were not shod. However, undoubtedly the Indians of India play cricket because the British took it there, and New Zealanders play rugby because they are of British stock. The spread of a game like field hockey is more puzzling; while in the nineteenth century it was spread in the British Empire, it had done much wandering on no clear pattern for several centuries before that. Something like hockey was played in ancient Greece. Polo probably originated in Persia or further east. However, many cases illustrate a reverse traffic in sport in the imperial picture. Dr. Carl Diem, who visited the East in 1955–1956, has recently compiled a study on horseback games played in eastern countries.

FIG. 6.2. An international language of friendship—a Maori girl and a visiting supervisor play string games. (Photograph by P. A. Smithells)

THE BOSTON CONFERENCE

The United States represents a later postcolonial type of development. The yoke of Britain was cast off in 1776, and the States have since developed several sports of its own, modified European forms, and itself become a major exporter. Also, as a country grown together from many groups of differing national and social backgrounds, it has benefited much by the internal exchange of ideas from subgroups within its own culture. But this has not been without its difficulties too, because subgroups coming from countries with some strongly established line in physical education have attempted—on the whole unsuccessfully—to convert this vast new country to the way of thinking of their original mother or grandparent country. One thinks of enthusiastic German turners remembering Father Jahn; American Swedes, such as Baron Nils Posse, following rather narrowly some ideas of "Father" Ling (and only some, for Ling had a very broad outlook); or American Czechs setting up "Sokol" groups in memory of "Father" Tyrs. And of course, there is still British cricket of a sort, in Pennsylvania and California, at least.

To read seventy years later the report of the famous Boston Conference on Physical Training of 1889 is illuminating. It was a great occasion for peddling certain European lines, by emphasising their special virtues and by ingenious special pleading, but it also led to the birth of American physical education proper.[12] Although today pressure groups pushing European national ideas still exist, the rejection by American physical educationists of systems from Europe is more or less nationwide. This was probably an essential move, for several reasons, and the wisest answer to warring factions; but there are some who are now beginning to feel that the rejection was too total, and that some useful babies went out with the unacceptable bathwater (see Chapter 17). In particular, it has been sad to see the poor communication and low rate of exchange of ideas between people—the States and Britain—whose tongues are nearly the same, but where the Atlantic gap is still considerable.[13]

The International Traffic of the Mind

But what of evaluation in this picture of the spreading of ideas and practices in the last seventy-five years? Evaluation is not a system of gymnastics, a sport, or even an aim or objective. It is a means to all of these. Science, whether in Omsk, Buenos Aires, Natal or Chicago, uses much the same means of evaluation. Balances weigh in micrograms, star distances are calculated in parsecs, small lengths are measured in Ångstrom units throughout the world. True, room temperatures may be Fahrenheit, centigrade, or even Reaumur, but science sticks to centi-

---

[12] It is also noteworthy how poor were evaluating tools at that time.
[13] P. A. Smithells, *The Atlantic Gap—A Plea for Better Understanding in, Physical Education,* Dunedin, N.Z., 1948.

grade. Wherever psychology is studied there is, in spite of the babel of teams in this young science, some common approach, say to intelligence testing. Sphygmomanometers may be used on Eskimos or Trobriand Islanders. Even anything so elusive as a culture pattern can be looked at in fairly standard ways—kinship patterns, taboos, totems, group dynamics, etc. The Oedipus complex, by Freud in modern Vienna, out of Homer and Aeschylus in ancient Greece, can be found in Patagonia or Siberia. Food values can be assessed in Pasadena, Timbuktu, or Springfield on the same calorie or vitamin scales. In many scientific and subscientific fields there are international standards. In medicine, there are International Units, as in vitamin classifications, or penicillin doses. Whereas at one time almost each individual hospital had its own system of classifying drug dosage, gradually there have come national pharmacopoeias and the International Pharmacopoeia, which make for clearer cross-understanding. The good sense of such moves in a shrinking world is of course borne out in the work of the numerous international agencies working on the health scene, branches of the UN organisation, such as WHO, the UN Observer Groups, UNESCO, international police units, or local aid plans, such as the Colombo Plan.

HAVE WE ANY INTERNATIONAL STANDARDS?

But what of us? Is there any international physical fitness index, or recreational efficiency unit, or even anything so simple as an international strength index? The Kraus-Weber pantomime was a comment on our lack of such things. Is there any satisfactory way in which we can relatively evaluate the merits of this, that, or the other way of doing something, teaching something, ranking objectives in order of priority, or gauging the effect on group dynamics of what we do? Certainly there were no such criteria at Boston in 1889, but if we met at the Azores or Hawaii for a world conference on standards in physical education in 1962, where would we be and what would we be doing? To start with, it might be guessed, we would each be rooting hard for some pet bit of evaluation done in our own country, or even an individual might be blowing his own particular evaluatory trumpet. Only a handful of those present would have any international understanding and be aware of the important work done in countries other than their own. To some, the difficulties may sound insuperable. But worse difficulties have been overcome. Those bent on establishing the International Pharmacopoeia were up against similar difficulties, and even more frustrating ones, such as the confusions over trade names and scientific names, and the time lag before patent problems were sorted out. The general public is unaware of these extra difficulties; they think of aspirin as a scientific name, when in fact it was the proprietary name of one firm for acetyl salicylic acid.

The Desire Must Come First

We shall only get international understanding when we want it sufficiently, and sufficient numbers of our profession have, as it were, the basic grammar and language for discussion. We need to come to agreement about two equally important things: First, standardization of the meaning of terms used and, second, the much easier problem of common statistical language. The emphasis so far has been perhaps on statistical language, for numbers are always more international than words; in any case, statistical method has no particular relationship to physical education, being an evaluatory device we borrow from mathematics.[14] Even so, there are signs of national one-eyedness, as is pointed out in the section on factor analysis, p. 222.

Reaching international agreement on basic terms used in evaluation may be for us the more important step, and there are several considerable difficulties we have to face.

What Will We Spend Money On?

The first is financial in outward aspect, but springs from much deeper sources. It would be easier to arrange for a tour of twenty players of some game for three months in, say, ten adjacent European countries, than it would be to arrange for as few as six real experts in physical education evaluation to meet for a month together, at some central place, say Paris or London, to think out this basic problem. But it is an urgent need. It is useless to try and deal with such a problem in the pell-mell rush of international conferences, where too many people try to deal with too many things in too short a time. As a profession, we are prepared to spend considerable sums of money on research projects,

---

[14] Distinguished mathematician friends are sometimes found to be very sceptical of our uncritical use of statistical techniques.

but it might well be in our general interest to sacrifice one project in each of half a dozen interested countries in order to subsidise such a long-overdue basic discussion as that envisaged. It sounds relatively simple when described, but the financial difficulties, while superficially the greatest, are probably of secondary importance. How many of us are prepared to lose possible prestige from a research project in order to undertake what would be a rather undramatic task, and for which no personal glory would emerge?

The public might support a sports tour because of the national prestige it might bring. Crowds would pay to see international games, partly because they are willing to pay for skill, and partly because they hope to see someone win or be beaten. But have we in general in our profession shaken off the attitudes prevalent in sport? Many of us have been successful athletes. Our success in motor skill may have been the main motive for our taking up physical education, or being prompted to by someone else successful in this field. In youth the struggle for success in physical prowess was of importance to our ego. We had to be determined to win. In adult life determination to find out, the obsessional drive, is necessary for a scientist, an evaluator. But is this the same as the will to win of the athlete? Bunsen gave his burner to the world, making nothing from it. No scientist or doctor is regarded as acting within the accepted ethics of his field if he deifies himself or tries to form a monopoly around some process or substance of his own discovering.

Is perhaps the hostility between leaders in our profession, which is sometimes evident in young middle age and later, a carry-over from the sort of rivalry in sport of our youth? This attempt to evaluate our own profession is dealt with more fully in another chapter, but the idea is mentioned here as a possible contributory difficulty to this sort of international co-operative enterprise.

Is National Prestige A Handicap?

There is also another difficulty—that of national prestige. This is of course, a major factor in sports promotion. The team playing a game (which in itself has no serious meaning), becomes a symbol of national sovereignty, and the crowd too becomes emotionally involved. A water polo match between the U.S.S.R. and Hungary at the Melbourne Olympics in 1956, became a symbolic occasion which affected players and crowd. Certainly on other occasions this national rivalry is healthy and friendly, but depending on basic relationships between two countries, a game can be mere fun and healthy rivalry, or a symbolic gesture of hate. For example, there is little doubt that South Africa and New Zealand are regarded as two of the most formidable and skilful players of the English game of rugby. Both of them have beaten England at this game often, and this in a sense may be related in spirit to what July Fourth is in America. But the most intense rivalry is now between the two countries themselves. New Zealand visited South Africa in 1949, and lost most of the matches. In 1956 the South Africans visited New Zealand and were soundly beaten for the first time as a touring side. Neither tour was noteworthy for the good spirit of the games; in fact, in 1956, many New Zealanders were ashamed of the state of their favourite game. But it is not impossible that behind this bitterness and hostility was another factor concerned with a way of life. New Zealand has an indigenous minority coloured race, the Maoris, whom she is proud to treat with complete legal and political equality. Normally the New Zealand team has several Maori players, but it was felt impossible to take Maori players to South Africa on tour in 1949, because of the prevailing colour bar in that country. Between the two tours in 1949 and 1960, Apartheid in South Africa developed considerably, and it is conceivable that unconsciously the rugby struggle became symbolic of difference in the way of life—and one charged with considerable emotional tension, as any American knows from the differing views above and below the Mason-Dixon line. Indeed, in 1960, when a further tour to South Africa was planned, there were protests from all religious groups and trade unions against the exclusion of Maoris from the New Zealand side.

So, too, the magnificently organized and staged 1936 Olympics, while the work of a non-Nazi, the revered Carl Diem, took on somewhat the prevailing international tensions of the day.

This is in a sense the story of the Boston 1889 Conference in modern sports dress. The protagonists of German and Swedish gymnastics then were not only trying to sell ideas they believed in gymnastically; there was still the tendency for minority groups to push their way of life via the medium of social, recreational, and educational patterns.[15]

[15] For a penetrating study of Jahn's political influence, see I. McIntosh et al., Landmarks in the History of Physical Education, London, Routledge, 1957.

A PLETHORA OF INTERNATIONAL BODIES

And this picture of national prestige is still observable in the field of international relationships in physical education proper today. There are several international bodies in physical education and no entirely dominant or supranational one, with world coverage. There is not even a satisfactory international body comprising the English-speaking world.

FIEP

The main existing bodies are the Fédération Internationale d'Education Physique, the oldest of the bodies, with membership of some sixty countries. This was originally founded in the 1920s as the Fédération Internationale de Gymnastique Ling, by Major J. G. Thulin and his colleagues. Major Thulin has been the most encyclopaedic of writers about Swedish gymnastics, having published many books translated into other languages. The FIGL, later the FIEP, has always had a basically Scandinavian background, although its leaders have wished it to be truly international; its government is now centred in Portugal. The fact that Ling's name was associated with it earlier of course militated against enthusiastic following by the worshippers of Jahn and Tyrs, and also against American interest in the body. There is little doubt that Ling was a remarkable man of international stature and not, as *Life* described him in 1949, "a sort of nineteenth-century Bernarr Macfadden." Ling was a philosopher, poet, historian, and educator, and a member of the select Swedish Academy, and he has no modern equivalent. But surely however great a man may be, no international body must be associated in title with a person whose reputation is associated predominantly with one country. Even such truly international names as Nansen, Smuts, or Schweitzer could not be wisely used in an international body. This the FIGL was made to realise in 1951 at the Ankara Conference when it became le Fédération Internationale d'Education Physique (FIEP) (but the head of Pehr Henrik Ling remains on its crest.) Nor was this particular association free of the tendency to be Scandinavian-dominated in its writings. This is probably due to the proximity of Scandinavian workers to its long time headquarters in Lund, South Sweden, than to any wish on the part of its leaders. The change to Portugal may be fortunate. Although there has been a steady increase in membership of this today, this is not necessarily due to a change of heart in major countries so much as the joining of countries who are taking up physical education seriously for the first time, and particularly those who adopt Scandinavian methods. It is sad to relate that the FIEP has very few members indeed in the United States, Canada, Great Britain, Germany, France or Russia—in fact in some of these countries there is either complete ignorance of its existence or fairly open hostility. Major Thulin—who is one of the few physical educationists with an honorary Doctorate in medicine, is an old man of over 80, who has striven for a high ideal and has devoted many thousands of dollars of his own money to this end—has never ceased to hope that this would become the main international forum in physical education.

LIGYMM

A more recent development has been the Liga Internationale for Moderne Gymnastik, which appears to be a Central European group attempt to bring together those workers in physical education who were using Austrian, German, Esthonian, and modern Finnish types of rhythmic gymnastics as a basis for the movement side of physical-education teaching—partly as a reaction to the Scandinavian domination of FIEP. It was founded in 1950 after the 2nd World Lingiad, and its headquarters are now in Munich. The chief figures in it are Hinrich Medau, Ludwig Bode, and Hilma Jalkanen.

IAPESGW

Mention must be made also of the international activities of the International Association of Physical Education and Sport for Girls which, under the dynamic leadership of Dr. Dorothy Ainsworth, has held several international conferences—three, at least, in Europe and one in Connecticut. Realising the difficulty Europeans may have in procuring dollar exchange, this body has often arranged its meetings in European centres. It brings together workers in the field of women's physical education for conferences and exchange of views. These have no doubt done much to improve human relationships in the profession, and particularly transatlantic ones, for the United States members of these conferences have had to put their hands deeply in their pockets in order to bring themselves to European meetings.[16]

The disadvantage of this body is of course that it is for women only, although men have been permitted to attend deliberations and take part. Second, its international activities are intermittent, and in contrast to the FIEP and the LIGYMM, which both publish periodicals in more than one language.

ASSOCIATIONS IN THE EAST

There are also possibly other international associations in the non-English-speaking world and it seems probable that India, China, and Indionesia and other states in this area, will collaborate internationally before long. The linguistic difficulty there may be increased, and it is conceivable that the only international language usable may be English, which of course would be of great advantage to those in America and the British Commonwealth, and the European and South American people who have English as a first foreign language.

Already active interest in international cooperation in physical education has been shown by Professor A. K. Vaidya of Amravati, whose Shree Hanvmar Vyayam Prasavak Mandal (Institute of Physical Education) is doing important research in malkhamb, lezim, and lathi (indigenous forms of Indian physical education).

TWO NEW INTERNATIONAL BODIES

It has become customary in the middle of this century to hold international physical-education conferences at the time of the Olympic Games, which of course are held every four years. These have sometimes been arranged by the host country. For instance, it was Australian physical educationists who sponsored and organised a significant international conference at Melbourne University, in November 1956, which was well attended. During the informal discussions associated with such conferences, there seemed to be a felt need for a new international body. This idea had also been much discussed behind the

---

[16] It has sometimes, albeit unfairly, been accused of pushing the American way of life. This impression may have been gained from the vitality of its American leaders, whose sheer dynamism may have been mistaken for chauvinism.

scenes at the Copenhagen Conference of the International Association of Physical Education and Sports for Girls and Women, in July 1949, and the Second World Lingiad and Congress at Stockholm, which was held immediately after the Copenhagen Congress. Several meetings had been held at Copenhagen and Stockholm on this topic, but there seemed even then to be some divergence of aim between United States leaders and those from other countries, particularly in the British Commonwealth.

It was during this period after the war that the great ancillary bodies of the United Nations grew in strength, particularly, from our angle, UNESCO and WHO.

Even in 1956, no international physical education association had consultative status with UNESCO or WHO. Several experienced leaders visiting Melbourne felt we would have to found a nonpartisan, truly international body, which would act as a channel of communication to the two UN bodies. So, after the conference, a small representative group nominated by the conference, met in the presence of an observer from WHO to think out the best form for a new international body. A provisional committee under the presidency of Dr. Fritz Duras of Melbourne University was set up, with well-known leaders from some twelve widely distributed countries. Further meetings were held in Paris, in September 1958, and in Helsinki, in August 1959, with UNESCO observers present.

ICSPE

This body had now given itself the provisional title of the International Council for Sport and Physical Education (ICSPE) and an Englishman, as secretary, appointed Mr. William Jones, working at the UNESCO Youth Institute, at Gauting in Munich, Germany. Naturally the process of sorting out aims and ideals, and drafting a constitution, were the subject of much argument, and at times there were strong differences of opinion, but by the time of the 1959 Helsinki Meeting, the plans of ICSPE were fairly clear, and, as had been the intention since the initial gathering at Melbourne in 1956, the founders of ICSPE wanted to make no final move until their plans could be ratified at a widely representative world congress to be held at the time of the Olympic Games in Rome in 1960. This ratification occurred at

Rome, and the Rt. Hon. Philip Noel-Baker, a distinguished internationalist and athlete, was elected President.

But meanwhile, in 1958, the old division that had interfered with sound planning at Copenhagen and Stockholm in 1949, turned up again. For various reasons, sincerely believed in by one of the original Melbourne Committee, an American felt that the new body was not being planned in the best possible way, and started independent negotiations with another international body, WCOTP—the World Confederation of Organisations of the Teaching Profession—a powerful organisation which already had consultative status with UNESCO. This side action caused some perturbation in 1958 and 1959 among those trying, under great difficulties, to push through the plans of ICSPE. It would be pointless here to trace the detailed negotiation, beyond saying that the present writer[17] was opposed to the WCOTP move, insofar as it ran counter to the long-laid plains of ICSPE and, above all, for a reason that surely should be appreciated in America.

Within the teaching profession as a whole, it would be a brave person who said our status was high (an act of self-delusion perhaps). It was felt by several of us that our status in a huge international teachers' organisation was not likely to be any higher, nor would we have independence of action or effective contact with those interests of physical education not dealt with by teachers. But the rift was there, and just before the ICSPE Planning Committee met in Helsinki in 1959, a comference under the auspices of WCOTP was held in Washington, D.C.

ICHPER

Another new body was formed as the International Council on Health, Physical Education and Recreation, which, although it may provide a useful bridge between AAHPER and WCOTP, does not have the same functions or purposes as ICSPE. ICHPER is now established under the presidency of Dr. Arnsworth, with headquarters in Washington, and has a full programme planned.

Writing unofficially, but as in fact a council member of FIEP, LIGYMM, and ICSPE, and as a member of the Foreign Relations Committee of CPEA, the author[18] must express the hope that Americans interested in the international exchange of ideas in physical educa-

[17] P. A. Smithells.
[18] P. A. Smithells.

tion, will join actively in ICSPE, as well as by supporting ICHPER. As has been stressed before, Americans have counted little so far in the field of international consultation, except on the women's side.

To conclude the story of ICSPE, a conference was held at Rome, in August 1960, when the constitution of ICSPE was ratified, on the vote of a widely representative group of 123 delegates from 37 countries, including some of the most famous names in modern physical education. At the conference there were representatives of 33 international organisations specialising in physical education, sports, and allied fields, from both sides of the Atlantic and both sides of the Iron Curtain, and from Eastern and Western countries. These included delegates from FIEP, ICHPER, and ICSPE. Also they set up a formal Executive Board with members from over twenty countries (including the United States) and a Research Committee, with members from eighteen countries. At last, in 1960, after long travails, it can be said that there is a major international forum for physical education with direct consultative status with UNESCO. This event marks a stage in our maturity as a profession. Let us hope that—in this world of initials —FIEP, LIGYMM, IAPESGW, ICSPE, and ICHPER learn to work together. We give below the research programme (already in action) of ICSPE.

Research Programme of the ICSPE

First, investigation of the problem of *physical education in schools* is planned. It is considered imperative that a comprehensive model experiment be initiated to yield evidence on the issue in its entirety, providing for the assemblage of didactic, developmental, physiological, clinical, psychological, sociological and administrative data, wherever possible in quantitative form. The results are to be correlated so as to provide concise information on responses to exercise curricula in respect of selected sectorial combination patterns, and on the nature and scope of immediate and delayed transfer effects of training between different personality sectors. In the interpretation of the material its relevance within the framework of the major short- and long-term aims of general education will thus become amenable to evaluation.

Second, it is proposed to follow up the recently communicated clinical and pathological observations on the inhibitory influence of sustained physical activity upon the *aging process*. The threefold differentiation of the problem insofar as it manifests itself in a decline of form, of function, and of health necessitates a correspondingly differentiated methodological approach. The three phenomena in question will be analyzed against the established effects upon aging of heredity and nutrition. The favorable morphological status of physically active workers and of trained athletes in age groups of 30 to 70, and even older; the conspicuously high performance standards of subjects conditioned through training, and the morphologically and functionally superior cardiovascular findings which collectively distinguish the latter, will be placed in juxtaposition to the diametrically opposite results obtained from physically inactive men or women. J. N. Morris' researches will receive special attention in this context. Small sample analyses as well as large-scale investigations will serve as statistical patterns of study, which also pertains to the question of longevity of athletes, as recent reports by Paul White in the United States and by Karvonen in Finland indicate.

Third, *rehabilitation* is to be subjected to intensive research. On empirical grounds, rehabilitation today is considered a complex issue. Its surgical, orthopedic, social, educational, and administrative aspects are commonly viewed as if each represents a categorical equal among partners whose combined resources, once they are pooled, will bring about this new discipline of medicine which is currently evolving. Against such a view, it is of considerable scientific importance to extrapolate for special study the exercise factor. The latter is the most important single physiological component of therapeutic significance in medical rehabilitation, and is the most decisive modifier causing functional adjustment in rehabilitative treatment. Remedial training for physically substandard school children; remedial training for the injured and crippled; restitution of functional abilities of older persons; and active treatment of a variety of further categories of patients will have to be subjected to an analysis. These studies are expected to yield information from which elaboration of new techniques of physical training, as well as application of the underlying principle, will be possible on a much wider basis.

Fourth, the *cultural significance of sport and physical education* will be given further study. The analysis of the published data collected at the 1952 Olympic Games in Finland suggests that the world-wide quest for international understanding allows effective canalization into the co-operative procedures of athletics and sport and play. The common aims and ideals which motivate large numbers of men and women of all nations to indulge in and enjoy organized physical activities engender a social situation which carries superior qualities of interpersonal and intergroup relations. Here, idealistic goals, such as trends towards greater "individual freedom" and "universal peace," become amenable to active pursuit, and with it, to a purposively directed policy based upon knowledge of sport, of planning, and of large-scale administrative measures.

Fifth, a special effort will be made to clarify the *inherent linkage of dif-*

ferentiated motor acts with such introspective events as motivate and accompany them, representing, as they often do, their decisive facets. "Aesthetic" and "emotional," "artistic" and "phenomenological," elements of individual experience are bound to the physical realities of varied exercise situations, such as those ubiquitously encountered in sport and physical education. The physical components of motor acts though most readily demonstrable in "purely scientific" studies, are but one aspect of the event in its totality. The development during recent years of philosophical and psychiatric concepts, such as those elaborated by Erwin Straus in his study, *The Upright Posture,* or by Buytendijk in his book, *Das Spiel des Menschen und der Tiere,* have opened new vistas for the examination of exercise as a holistic problem. Because of the unique variability of motor performances of man, sport and physical education are eminently suited to extend our insight into the compact nature of "Geschehnis und Erlebnis," or the mechanics of movements, as against the way they are experienced in their entirety.

RECOMMENDED READING

Bibliographie und Dokumentation der Leibesübungen, J. Recla, Institut für Leibeserziehung der Universität Graz, Graz, Austria.

Bulletin de la Fédération Internationale D'Education Physique, Antonio Leal d'Oliveira, R. das Amoreiras 22, 2º Lisbon, Portugal. (French and English)

The Department of Ergonomics, University of Bristol, Bristol, England.

Index and Abstracts of Foreign Physical Education Literature, Epison Kappa Fraternity, 3747 North Linwood Avenue, Indianapolis 18, Indiana. (This gives the best list of world journals, but unfortunately, no Russian journals are listed. It is written in English.)

International Council on Health, Physical Education and Recreation of WCOTP, various publications. 1201 Sixteenth Street, N.W., Washington 6, D.C.

Internationale Zeitschrift für Angewändte Physiologie, Springer Verlag, Neuenheimer Landstrasse 28–30, Heidelberg, Germany. (This journal includes the old *Arbeitsphysiologie.*)

The Journal of Physical Education, Physical Education Association of Great Britain and Northern Ireland, Ling House, 10 Nottingham Place, London W1. (This journal is little known in the U.S. Free specimen copies will be sent on application. See also *The Physical Education Yearbook,* published at the same address.)

List of Institutions, Research Centres, Persons and Periodicals in the Field of Physical Culture, Institute for Research in Physical Culture, Marymoncka 34, Warsaw (1961).

Proceedings of the College Physical Education, AAHPER, 1201 Sixteenth
Street, N.W., Washington 6, D. C.

Le Travail Humain, Presses Universitaires de France, Départment des Pério-
diques, 1 Place Painlevé, Paris V^e. (French)

Wissenschaftliche Zeitschrift der Deutschen Hochschule für Körperkultur,
Friedrich-Ludwig Jahn Allee 59, Leipzig C 1, East Germany.

part ii

BASIC METHODS

chapter 7

POINTS OF APPLICATION

EVALUATION, MEASUREMENT, TESTING

THE current educational concept—*evaluation*—is of relatively recent origin. It is concerned with measuring both *what* educational results and progress are achieved, and *how* this progress is being made. It is not a static concept. It thus assesses the effectiveness of our objectives, being, as Wrightstone points out, "a relatively new technical term to designate a more comprehensive concept of measurement than is implied in conventional tests and examinations."[1] The width of this concept is stressed by Ross when he writes, "As distinguished from measurement, evaluation is often used to refer to the process of appraising the whole child, or the entire educational situation."[2] This we have attempted to stress throughout our book.

EVALUATION

Thus, evaluation in educational fields gains information about:

1. Programmes, facilities, equipment, materials, and buildings
2. Attitudes, interests, and activities of pupils
3. Aptitudes, abilities, and achievements of pupils
4. Classification, grading, and grouping of pupils
5. Physical characteristics
6. Leadership qualities, personality, and social and character traits of pupils

[1] J. W. Wrightstone, "Evaluation," in W. S. Monroe, ed., *Encyclopedia of Educational Research*, New York, Macmillan, 1941.

[2] C. C. Ross, *Measurement in Today's Schools*, 3d ed., Englewood Cliffs, N.J., Prentice-Hall, 1954.

109

7. Relationship of teacher, parent, neighbour, and friend and other environmental influences on pupils
8. Participation of pupils in programmes and curricula
9. Methods of learning and teaching
10. Administration, time-tabling, and organisation in schools
11. Any feature or school situation where appraisal is involved

Measurement

Measurement, on the other hand, involves the use of "a precise quantitative value, which can be placed on a physical property or outcome of instruction."[3] Unlike much evaluation, measurement enumerates in units and scales of time, distance, and mass, allowing ready statistical treatment. Direct physical measurement of height, weight, and other physical dimensions of humans are obvious examples, while strength, speed, endurance, and other physical abilities can be measured less directly, and less accurately.

But measurement is also a term used in education for gaining information about intelligence, special abilities and aptitudes, and educational achievement, especially by tests using numerical scales. Such measurement is of course, by no means as *precise* as most direct physical measurements.

Testing

Testing is the process of measurement or evaluation in education, the process of trying someone out or putting a person to the test. Tests, as we have shown, are widely used in everyday life—in science and in industry. In education, tests have come specifically to mean statistically standardized evaluation devices and examinations, though by no means all tests used are standardised.

Evaluation, measurement, and testing are educational tools to improve the work of the school, to assist teaching and learning. They can help us to determine the best teaching content, the most suitable teaching method, and what the results of our teaching are. The development of sound techniques for each of these three stages of education should help to reduce the large amount of trial and error in teaching and learning.

[3] W. J. Micheels and M. R. Karnes, *Measuring Educational Achievement,* New York, McGraw-Hill, 1950.

SPECIFIC PURPOSES OF EVALUATION

The purposes of evaluation in physical education will vary with each school and each situation, but even if conditions are quite primitive, evaluation can play a part. Teachers should accordingly be aware of the purposes to which evaluation techniques can be put. A glance at textbooks on education reveals a remarkable similarity in their views on the purposes of evaluation. One wonders whether great minds think alike, or whether they digest each other's textbooks. It would seem the appeal to authority, which science usually eschews, is rather prevalent in educational writings.

It should be first observed that the purposes of evaluation are found to fall into two broad categories: *research*, to increase knowledge; and *application of knowledge* in schools, to improve instruction. This is parallel to the rather misty distinction between pure and applied science.

If we may refer to existing authorities, the first six texts listed at the end of this chapter all outline the *purposes* of evaluation. The frequency of the stated purposes in these standard texts are as follows:

1. For research (five times)
2. To improve instruction:
   a. Diagnosis (six times)
   b. Placement, grouping, or classification (five times)
   c. Progress, achievement, or results (four times)
   d. Guidance or counselling (five times)
   e. Motivation (six times)
   f. Methodology, improvement of instruction, or as part of teaching (three times)
   g. Prognosis (once)

RESEARCH

From a long-term point of view, the main function of evaluation in education is both to increase knowledge and to improve techniques. As a result, suitable tests and measurements might be devised to apply this knowledge, using statistically sound techniques, standardisations, and norms.

This sounds all very fine, but several snags to research in physical education are at once apparent. First, this function of research begs the question of whether education lends itself fully to the scientific method, that is, whether the children and their teachers should receive the same sort of treatment as do rocks and fossils, periodic tables and triangles. This brings us to the question of whether education is an art or a science, or a blend of both. If education is to be considered a science, then research in it should follow the pattern of scientific investigation. If education is to be considered an art, then research must compromise with the unpredictable human and biological complexities, and the ever-changing social dynamics of the shrinking world. Physical education is a subject, we feel, which should include an admixture of the artistic and the creative, with the scientific, the logical, and the semantic. It is, in fact, part art, part craft, and part science.

Second, in physical education, we are dealing with total people and whole situations. We know from psychological study that the individual responds as a whole in behaviour situations. Research in physical measurement, and in skills of running, jumping, throwing, climbing, and swimming is reasonable if it limits itself to the effects of those skills. But we must be cautious in claiming that a test battery of four items each measuring a football skill would in the aggregate provide a valid and reliable measure of football ability. The skills themselves, as measured by the test, may be quite artificial as far as the game is concerned. Results of tests may contribute towards our knowledge of the game and of its players' ability, along with total impressions gained subjectively. But even if some test items were identical with parts of the game situation, the whole would still not be the sum of the parts.

RESEARCH FACILITIES

Third, our plea for research carries with it the implication that research facilities with almost complete coverage of our school system should be established, to distribute evaluation research evenly, with the express purpose of promoting the development of scientific and suitable programmes at all levels of education. The sheer machinery of such a setup would be tremendous. Research centres would be needed to co-ordinate evaluation on a national and international scale. All teachers would need special courses to enable them to use evaluation techniques and tests correctly and with discrimination. They would need extra time and help from counsellors to carry out evaluation and individual guidance, as well as, inevitably, smaller classes.

Counsellors, clerks, and administrators; computers, apparatus, and equipment; gymnasiums, laboratories, and clinics—all these would need to be at hand. School timetables and organisation adapted for maximum flexibility, to allow continual regrouping of pupils for different activities, would need to provide elective courses, to make individual physical education most effective, as a result of the information gained by extensive evaluation programmes.

The cost of such a programme on a nation-wide scale, would be prohibitive, and not likely to come into being in our time. Instead, careful surveys should be made to establish which areas and levels of education merit such research, and resources should be allotted accordingly. There is a need for reorientation of thinking about research in physical education. The authors favour a swing in emphasis towards the infant and elementary-school level, and particularly the junior high-school level, where most physical education schemes are empirically built up. They now tend to be largely *recreational* during a formative period which calls for *conditioning* and *developmental* physical education of the most enlightened kind possible. Large-scale research into the physical education needs of *growing* children is the most important area of all. There is also, we think, a case for finding out what experience and information are best for those just leaving school. Do we know the following, and educate accordingly?

1. What is the maximum and optimum, strength and stamina that can be developed in children at various ages, so that they might attain the fullest realisation of their physical potential when mature? A study of the conditioning schedules over the years of Jon and Ilsa Konrads, and other child prodigies makes interesting reading. There is a marked difference from one country to another in the physical demands made on young children.

2. How do the health, posture, and physical fitness of children in one country compare with criteria acceptable to the medical profession generally, and with standards in other countries? The Kraus-Weber saga underscores the need for further intercultural research into these topics.

3. Are our children taught the skills of swimming early enough and

well enough in relation to water safety? When is the most suitable age to teach swimming, cycle-riding, skating, skiing, and so on? The pressure downwards in the age groups in America and elsewhere for "itty bitty football," etc., is a new phenomenon for mankind, and one we do not understand. Maybe it is desirable that certain adult skills should be taught early and others deferred till late adolescence. We do not know.

4. What proportion of our young children attain sufficient motor and rhythmical ability, within their own limits, to reach a level of reasonable skill and social acceptability?

If these and similar questions have not been tackled fully, and the physical education of the youngsters enriched accordingly, then all the thousands of dollars allotted to research amongst university students could well be better spent. Inevitably there is an intellectual gap between graduate research and the elementary school, but the practical gap could be closed, or at least narrowed.

RESEARCH TO AID CONTINUITY OF PROGRAMMES

Again, the widest possible research into physical education at the elementary and junior high level would be conducive to smooth continuity into appropriate high-school programmes, and eventually physical education at all levels of schooling could be built up on the soundest possible footing.

This is not to decry research at more advanced levels, or isolated research by individuals, whether they have elaborate resources at their disposal, or are working with the most meagre facilities. But it is significant, we think, that a very large proportion of texts on evaluation in physical education deal predominantly with evaluation at the college and university level.

Lastly, we make a plea for more research in the schoolroom and gymnasium as an integral part of improving teaching and learning, and the physical well-being of our youngsters, rather than merely in the laboratory or library of the university.

This leads us to a study of the purposes of evaluation to improve instruction in the schools themselves. We are glad to see such experiments as the AAHPER Youth Fitness Project, and the California and other local projects,

THE IMPROVEMENT OF INSTRUCTION

DIAGNOSIS

Diagnosis is an essential evaluative procedure in education, and, as in medicine, constitutes the assessing of symptoms, their causes, and remedies. In education and physical education, diagnosis involves the analysis of components of a skill or topic, in order to discover weaknesses and strengths. Of course, diagnosis is of little value without subsequent remedial work or therapy to reduce or eliminate such weaknesses.

Most teachers informally diagnose their pupils' work from time to time. In basic subjects, such as spelling and arithmetic, systematic and objective diagnosis is possible using standardized tests, which are concerned with just those elements of the activity being analysed. In contrast, achievement tests generally seek to assess pupils' relative ability in a whole field or activity.

In physical education, standardised diagnostic tests are rare, and this is an area little developed. Yet subjective diagnosis permeates our teaching when we point out and correct individual and group faults. There is a definite need for sound diagnostic tests of basic abilities. Tests of strength, power, speed, endurance, agility, balance, control, and rhythm, associated, of course, with appropriate remedial practice or therapy, might enable teachers to detect incipient weaknesses in children early, and help each child to develop strengths and abilities up to their potential.

The same need is apparent with the teaching of classes and squads, in that steady improvement and progress in any course will depend on sound diagnosis and suitable practices. This applies particularly to the weak or beginning teacher. Experienced physical educators can usually spot common faults, and effectively reduce or eliminate them.

For example, a possible diagnostic test in swimming might be based on the assumption that arm action and leg action each generate about 50 per cent of the forward drive in the breast stroke. Get the pupils to swim a width of the pool using leg action only, then a width using arm action only. Count the number of leg strokes, then the number of arm strokes, and compare these with your previously established norms. Relatively more leg strokes, or more arm strokes, required to propel the swimmer across the pool would indicate a weakness in that component of the stroke, and would suggest a need for more coaching and practice in that component—though there may be some swimmers who because of body build are dominant in either legs or arms.

Prognosis is the predicting of the course of future events or developments. It is a form of evaluation gaining considerable use in education with aptitude and readiness tests, and is also a feature of testing in vocational guidance, industry, military service, and sport. Prognostic tests aim to predict the ultimate level of achievement in any activity. When valid measures become available, much wasteful teaching will be eliminated, and the possibilities of more effective teaching to the upper limit of pupils' capability will be increased. Unfortunately this branch of testing is still at the pioneer stage.

A few prognostic tests in physical education are available, but their validity is only fair. Tests of motor educability and of aptitude in certain sports would be examples. If such tests provided a highly valid and reliable measure of prediction of future achievement in physical skills, teachers and coaches could plan appropriate teaching and training schedules, give individuals effective guidance, and, in fact, plan years ahead.

Such a prospect sounds most exciting, but valid and reliable tests require years of research with large samples, using the longitudinal approach. And the unpredictable human being, the changing and changeable individual, will offset high validity and reliability coefficients.

One example of a prognostic test is in the area of *motor educability,* the ability to learn motor skills easily, quickly, and well. Revisions of the Brace Test by C. H. McCloy, at the University of Iowa, include items of the stunt type. The results of these tests were found, for example, to correlate positively with track and field athletics, but there has been little evidence that they *predicted* future motor skill of subjects.

Classification, as a function of evaluation, is the arrangement of people into groups according to specified criteria. It has been shown that effective group learning usually occurs where the groups are fairly homogeneous as to the abilities of that particular learning situation. This grouping should take into account both potential and realised ability, and should, as far as possible, occur for each subject or activity being taught. But rarely are pupils reclassified into appropriate groups for every session, and usually only one classification basis suffices for all schoolwork in high schools. This tends to be the age group, or the stream or course of academic work, which the pupil enters.

Pupils need not be grouped solely on the basis of ability. They may be classified according to interests, physique and size, condition, age, and leadership. To take an obvious example, the flyweight boxer is classified in a separate division from the heavyweight.

In physical education, classes or squads grouped according to criteria other than physical ability render effective teaching more difficult. The standard aimed at is usually that of the average performer, so that the talented pupil is not always extended, and the weaker pupils often cannot keep pace.

Similarly in sport, it is not much fun for the skillful player to always be in the same team as the "dud," while the awkward player will soon dislike a game in which he is always being shown up as incompetent.

One might visualise a day when more homogeneous grouping is possible in all subjects, by classes and within the class. Elective groups will assist this trend, but extremely flexible timetables would of course be necessary.

MOTIVATION

Motivation, the force acting on a body so as to cause it to move, has a valuable function in education. It can stimulate pupils' learning and provide incentive to all-out effort. In education, it has been widely admitted that school examinations are designed to motivate pupils to greater efforts in their studies.

In physical education, motivation is especially important. In 1934, Cozens wrote: "Competition is the spice of the physical education activity, and this of course applies equally well to competition against one's own previous record, and to competition against the record of one's fellow pupils."[4] In sport (especially in golf), most of us are aware

[4] N. P. Neilson and F. W. Cozens, *Achievement Scales in Physical Education Activities for Boys and Girls in Elementary and Junior High Schools*, New York, Barnes, 1934.

of the motivation to beat our own previous best, but how many teachers capitalize fully on this first principle stated by Cozens?

Cozens found that one of the best ways to motivate individuals and classes was by means of "achievement scores," that is, objective measures or norms, from which the pupils could determine their own level of ability. Pupils became very eager to improve their own performances, and were able to compare their scores in different activities.

Because likes and dislikes are very closely connected with success and failure respectively, care must be taken that some early success can be tasted, by pupils of every ability, in schoolwork. As each pupil improves, there should be further challenges to motivate him to reach and master a series of attainable goals, each progressively more advanced.

Achievement scales, consisting of norms or standards, are in effect just this, a series of goals ranging from easy to difficult. The motivating effect of achievement scales is high in, say, gymnastics and games skills, swimming, and track and field, especially if all the stages of the course or schedule are clearly set out and attractively mounted on the notice board of the physical-education department. Pupils know what to aim for, and what progress they are making.

Further motivation can be promoted by tests, by achievement awards, such as badges or stripes, for the various levels or stages of achievement reached in the various courses taken. Competition between pupils, too, stimulates enthusiasm and effort, though one has to devise safeguards so that the less able pupils are not unduly discouraged by emphasis on competition for the best pupils only.

An example of the type of test with a high motivating quality is the motor-ability circuit, or obstacle course, of the type conceived many years ago by Dorothy Humiston.[5] Revisions of the Humiston Circuit, say, in the form of a ten-item test, with emphasis on the main elements of physical ability appropriate to the class, can be exciting and stimulating, as well as providing a measure of motor ability. We have tried out several. The test is performed individually against time, and pupils are encouraged to beat their previous best time.

ACHIEVEMENT

Achievement is the attainment of the individual of status or perform-

[5] Dorothy Humiston, "Measurement of Motor Ability in Women," *Research Quarterly*, VIII, no. 2 (May, 1937).

ance, in reference to previous performance. *Status* is the term which usually refers to initial achievement or condition—the state in which the teacher finds his new class, as far as a given activity is concerned.

The evaluation of achievement is a very old idea, being recorded more than two centuries before Christ in the form of tests for Chinese civil servants. Much more recent is the evolution of school examinations. Although one of their traditional purposes has been to classify pupils for promotion or placement, they have always claimed to measure achievement, improvement, or status. To this day, most school examinations are designed to measure pupils' achievement.

In physical education, achievement usually refers to improvement in skill or condition or knowledge. Such improvement signifies a change in status, and a basic definition of education is to promote change. Achievement testing differs from diagnostic testing in that the field is usually comprehensive, sampling all the major skills of the course, although the score is often a composite one.

Yet, some achievement tests may be used diagnostically, for, from the results, the effectiveness of the course can be assessed, faults in learning and teaching diagnosed, and future programmes and practice modified. Again, the scores from achievement tests are often used for classification and promotion, and it is quite proper for them to have this additional function, because the composite score obtained could provide a suitable basis for ranking pupils.

Achievement tests in physical education usually assess:

1. Performance in activities, or mastery of physical skills
2. Knowledge, rules, principles, tactics, and theory
3. Condition: physical, postural, nutritional, etc.
4. Hygiene: knowledge of health and safety
5. Growth and development: physical, social, etc.
6. Any specific objectives of the programme

POTENTIAL AND REALISED ABILITY

It should be made clear that ability is considered in two senses: potential and realised (or actual) ability. Prognostic tests are concerned with potential ability, and deal with such concepts as capacity, aptitude, latent ability, potential, etc. Diagnostic and achievement tests are concerned more with actual or realised ability, and deal with such concepts as status, attainment, progress, improvement, and knowledge.

Our knowledge of potential ability is scant, and confined largely to guesswork, but we are on surer ground with actual and realised ability, being able to measure many of its manifestations with a fair degree of validity.

RECOMMENDED READING

Bovard, J. F., F. W. Cozens, and E. P. Hagman, *Tests and Measurements in Physical Education,* Philadelphia, Saunders, 1949.

Cureton, T. K., Jr. *Physical Fitness, Appraisal and Guidance,* St. Louis, Mosby, 1947.

Larson, L. A., and R. D. Yocom, *Measurement and Evaluation in Physical Health and Recreation Education,* St. Louis, Mosby, 1951.

Lindquist, E. F., *et al., Educational Measurement,* Washington, American Council on Education, 1951.

McCloy, C. H., *Tests and Measurements in Health and Physical Education,* New York, Appleton-Century-Crofts, 1954.

Micheels, W. J., and M. R. Karnes, *Measuring Educational Achievement,* New York, McGraw-Hill, 1950.

Research Methods Applied to Health, Physical Education, and Recreation, Washington, AAHPER, 1949.

Ross, C. C., *Measurement in Today's Schools,* New York, Prentice-Hall, 1954.

Scott, M. Gladys, and Esther French, *Evaluation in Physical Education,* St. Louis, Mosby, 1950.

Stroup, F., *Measurement in Physical Education,* New York, Ronald, 1957.

chapter 8

STATISTICAL MEASUREMENT

MANY of us take fright at the mere mention of statistics, or the sight of statistical symbols and formulas. How unnecessary and unfortunate this is, because for our purposes in general education and physical education, the statistical techniques needed for the proper treatment of the results of tests and measurements are very simple. In fact, the algebra and arithmetic taught at the junior high-school level are sufficient for the calculation involved in everyday statistical measurement, as used by practising teachers. For the small minority of physical educators who advance to do full-time research, advanced statistics can become intensely fascinating, involving more complicated mathematical techniques, but these are not the concern of this book.

When the student is aware that the mathematics and techniques of elementary statistics are simple and easily mastered, it makes a world of difference in his approach and enjoyment of the subject. He will find that, by using techniques no more difficult than deriving a square root, he can adequately deal with much of his evaluation data, organise it so as to bring out more significance, and then express the results with understanding and confidence. Then he will find that he will be able to *use* the results of his evaluation programme, and to *improve* his teaching courses and his work with pupils. These, after all, are the main aims of evaluation in a school.

THE PRINCIPLES OF MEASUREMENT

In physical education, as has been pointed out, we are constantly applying techniques of measurement to our work; or maybe we are evaluating activities. Where suitable, these techniques of testing or measurement should be based on scientific methods, both at the stage of collecting the information, and of treating it. The usual scientific way of dealing with or organising information so as to utilize it fully and bring out its real significance is known as *statistical method*. This method is essentially the same as methods used in social science, such as education, psychology, sociology, and anthropology, and has developed in turn from the techniques used in mathematics and physical sciences. There are differences between measurements in the physical and social sciences. In the physical sciences, we deal predominantly with constants and variables which can be isolated. In the social sciences we deal mainly with variables which are not easily separable from each other. Again, in the physical sciences, we can measure exactly to a millionth part of a gram (a microgram) in weight, or to a thousandth of a milli-metre (a micron) in length. But in the social sciences, measurement is almost always an approximation of tendencies or behaviour, rather than direct measurement which can be used to frame a *scientific law*. A scientific law is not always absolute, but indicates the state of confirmed theory—for the time being.

STATISTICS

The term *statistics*, to the layman, refers to figures about facts. In one year, National Motors made so many thousand autos, and the next year, so many more. Or Puncher Pancras fought a hundred fights, won eighty and lost twenty, gaining twenty-five knockouts, and being knocked out ten times.

Such statistics occur every day in every newspaper, in most political speeches; they are in fact ubiquitous. What few people study carefully is the interpretation of figures about facts, and ways of collecting and expressing figures about facts. Some politicians, advertising agents, and crusaders for causes (such as antifluoridation) often interpret figures to suit their case. The methods of some of these "men with a mission" are apt to be largely guesswork and are also apt to include a measure of wishful thinking. On the other hand, statistical method, which arranges and treats figures by a detached objective process, aims to prevent guesswork, misinterpretation, and bias, and to bring out any significant meaning inherent in figures about facts. Statistics is simply the science of interpreting data in the precise language of mathematics. It has been applied for centuries in that subject, and later to measurements in chemistry, physics, astronomy, and biology. It is more recently used a great deal in economics (industry and commerce), and is being increasingly applied to the measurement of human and animal characteristics in such new fields of study as demography, biophysics, ethology, cybernetics, and logistics. In our fields, statistics has two main forms: (1) descriptive statistics; (2) sampling statistics.

DESCRIPTIVE STATISTICS

Descriptive statistics, the better-known form, treats figures about facts as a *whole;* i.e., describes the facts themselves, about a whole situation. The Census shows us how many people live in the United States, or how many cattle there are in Texas, or how much rain fell in Eugene, Oregon, each day last year. Compiling such statistics involves counting according to some plan, and presenting the figures in an orderly way. Sometimes the counting is easy, as with the compiling of the school roll or register. Sometimes it is laborious, as with the counting of the people in a large country. Some people are born and others die before the counting is finished and the figures published.

Thus, descriptive statistics on a small scale may be quite accurate, as with the school roll. On a very large scale, as with the Census, some accuracy may be lost, although in proportion to the total figures, errors should be extremely small.

Descriptive statistics forms the basis for a great deal of local and national government policy and administration, and also for most businesses and occupations. The newspaper reporter, the attorney, or the detective who says "I just want the facts"[1] is typical of an approach in many walks of life. From facts obtained over a period of time, the trends operating can be assessed. From graphs showing these trends, the future facts can sometimes be predicted by extrapolation. Such predictions become less accurate as they extend further into the future, because of unknown influences not affecting the present known trends.

SAMPLING

In statistically describing some data, the counting method is not possible. Descriptive statistics cannot be applied to the counting of grains of sand on a beach, or of the number of blood corpuscles of an

---

[1] "Comment is free, but **facts** are sacred" is the stated credo of some newspapers.

anaemic child. Luckily there is a short cut in such problems. This is a technique called *sampling*.

If we know the area and depth of the sand on the beach, and if we find by looking at samples from different parts of the beach that the grains are of about the same size and dryness, then we can select a small but typical sample of dry sand (say one cubic centimetre). By weighing this carefully, taking say a thousandth of this weight of sand, and counting the grains in this 1/1000 cc, we can then multiply our result by a thousand times the number of cubic centimetres of sand on the beach. This should give us an approximation of the number of grains of sand on the whole beach.

SAMPLING STATISTICS

To count corpuscles, we could draw off a small quantity of a child's blood, dilute this say a hundred times, and select one drop of this solution. By using a microscope slide with a graticule of fine squares etched on it, we could count through the microscope the number of corpuscles on a typical square, and by multiplying again, obtain an estimate of the corpuscle count in the child's blood. The general process which uses this sampling technique is known as *sampling statistics*. It studies data by sampling a *part* of a particular population. The term *population* is used to denote the whole of what we happen to be studying, and *universe* could describe the complete total existing in that region, country, or world. In the sand example, the amount of sand on that beach could be termed the population, and the amount of sand in the whole region or world could be termed the universe.

The knowledge gained from studying a *part* is then used to generalise about the *whole* population. In studying the intelligence of eighth-grade schoolchildren for instance, we could select a small cross section for a sample, obtain the desired information, and then draw conclusions about *all* eighth-grade schoolchildren in the country.

Sampling is not always as difficult as the examples given, but they do serve to emphasise the care and forethought necessary. In any experiment, we must be sure that the sample is really typical of the whole population. For example, one could attempt to sample the total water in a swimming pool by filling a bottle at the edge. But can we be sure that the water at the edge, near the surface, is the same as the water in the middle and at the bottom? Again, the bottle must be clean, and free from *extraneous* matter. Pathologists who analyse specimens of urine often find completely foreign matter in the samples, because old medicine bottles were used.

It can be appreciated that to find out about a total situation, by studying a part, we must be sure that the part accurately represents the total. The sample has to be *typical,* that is, a cross section of the population. The sample of blood was taken on the assumption that it was fairly typical of all the blood in the child's body, which is the case in all limbs in a healthy person. There are even techniques now for sampling blood in the different chambers of the heart, and these have made a great difference to diagnosis in cardiac troubles.

But to select one eighth-grade class, on the assumption that the children are typical of all eighth-grade children in the country would not be justified. After all, they might be a bright class, a rural class, an old class, a female class, or a science class. None of these is typical of the whole population. A sample which includes a cross section of the whole population would be required. All eighth-grade children with surnames beginning with B from a city and a rural county would provide a more representative sample, from the point of view of being typical eighth-grade children, from all over the country—except that there might be local ethnic groups in the United States which would distort the sample. So, too, western children seem to grow faster than children from eastern States.

The nearer in size the sample is to the whole population, the more typical it will tend to be, and the closer sampling statistics comes to descriptive statistics. The advantage of sampling statistics is simply one of convenience: the saving of time and effort. After all, some accuracy is bound to be lost if the whole population is not studied. Yet quite useful results can be obtained by the careful study of small yet typical samples. We must make sure that our sample is adequate in quality and in numbers, for the *levels of confidence* which we can achieve in our results will partly depend on these. (The statistical techniques for determining *levels of confidence* is dealt with in Chapter 9—briefly it is a measure of likely validity.)

SAMPLING STATISTICS IN EVERYDAY LIFE

Sampling statistics are widely used in everyday life. The TV weather man in developing his weather forecast map has been given data about weather from a sample of observation posts. Consumer councils may test a random sample of, say, every thousandth product turned out by a factory or bought at different retail stores.[2] Public opinion experts might sample the views of residents by quizzing every tenth household of every tenth street, or telephoning the top number of each page of the telephone directory. Industrial chemists analyse the contents of processed foods at regular intervals, based on sound sampling.[3] Randomising samples may prove to be very difficult, since human beings rarely make choices, even at very young ages, of a random kind. It has been shown that when persons are asked to write from random a list of numbers or words there is in fact almost always a pattern in these which negates their true randomness. Professor John Cohen at Manchester University, in studies on luck and randomness over several years, has shown that our minds tend to act as "implicit and unwitting calculators."[4] It is therefore best to use a mechanical method of randomising.

THE PATTERN OF STATISTICAL METHOD

Statistical studies generally conform to a pattern with these stages:

1. Planning the investigation
2. Collecting the data
3. Treating the data
4. Interpreting the data and expressing results
5. Drawing conclusions, and, where appropriate, applying results

Planning the Investigation

This is often the most neglected phase of a research project. It begins with the consideration of a broad topic, and the focusing down on a part of the topic to be investigated. This should be specific enough to

[2] The Consumers Union, which gives carefully determined ratings on all manner of retail products, never buys its goods for testing from wholesalers. See *Consumer News* or *Consumer Reports*.

[3] Colour-matching, with yarns and materials, so that a product is constant involves sampling. The trained eye is still better at this than any mechanical device—another example of fine sensory discrimination.

[4] "The Psychology of Luck," in *The Advancement of Science*, XVI, no. 63. The British Association for the Advancement of Science, 18 Adam Street, Adelphi, London WC 2.

be well within the resources of the investigator, who should think through the problems likely to be met, and set out clearly the objectives of the study. Acquaintance should be made with relevant research and literature all the while, because these can affect the whole pattern of the investigation. This does not mean one should take Tom Lehrer's advice and plagiarise, but simply that other investigators may be on the same track.

Forethought is required too in planning ways of obtaining any required data. Appropriate evaluation techniques should be developed, to be applied to the most suitable and representative sample available. Plans should be made to record the data so that it can be easily collated and treated. Agreement should be reached with all persons sponsoring and assisting the project, with a time schedule drawn up for the various stages of the investigation.

The measuring devices should be thoroughly prepared and tried on a small 'pilot' sample, so that weaknesses and unsuspected snags can be eliminated—even if several dummy runs with pilot groups become necessary (see Chapter 11).

Statistical method is a branch of scientific method, the slogan of which could be "the truth, the whole truth, and nothing but the truth." The research worker should maintain a dispassionate honesty in the handling of his data. The scientist always looks for negative evidence, never assuming he is right until he has checked beyond reasonable doubt that he is not wrong. He may have a "hunch" about something, which may be verified in an experiment, but he should examine his findings ruthlessly along with other scientists, to make sure that no other interpretation can be made, before he publishes his conclusions. Complete dedication to truth-seeking is needed from the planning to the publication stage, and it is here that informed colleagues can guide the research worker. There is always the danger of the fanatical research worker letting wishful thinking and ambition drive him into publication, having ignored some slip in calculation or some negative evidence. We suspect that our own eager profession has to watch itself particularly in this matter.

COLLECTING THE DATA

Data can be collected in a great variety of ways, and care should be taken to choose the most effective means available and to make the best use of it by thorough preparation and presentation of the collecting medium or method. Studying the action of the polio virus merely by asking the victims how they felt would be ineffectual, although their answers might contribute in part to such a study. Again, it would hardly be appropriate to assess the suitability of potential immigrants from foreign countries merely by giving them tests written in English, although knowledge of English might contribute towards their suitability; a genius might fail in this. A questionnaire to school principals roughly handwritten or poorly mimeographed, without adequate sponsorship, is not likely to bring a ready and sympathetic response. It may be important before coming to final conclusions about a survey to sample those who did not reply to see whether there was a common relevant factor in their noncompliance. A clear understanding of the objectives of the study, coupled with careful and thorough planning, are essential before ways and means of obtaining data can be determined.

In education, data can be collected by standardised interviews; by observation; by tests, measurements, or experiments; by photography, recording, and other electrical and mechanical devices; by questionnaires; by conferences of informed people; by letters; and from books, periodicals, and research abstracts. In physical education, the same media are used. Obvious places where information might be obtained are the school and classrooms; gymnasium; pool and camp; track and sports fields; library;[5] office and clinic; home, neighbourhood, and church; and workplace and playground or club.

It must be emphasised that the collecting of data about human beings can be very time-consuming. The zoologist or physiologist can take his rabbit out of its cage when it suits him. He does not have to consider the rabbit's viewpoint. The chemist has his material in bottles around him. However, the education research worker is dealing with beings who have ideas and plans of their own, and are not at hand very often. In a school, one's main duty is teaching, and we should not interrupt this unduly by testing. Our collecting techniques should therefore be well organised and rapid, and where possible, used with groups, even though some clinical procedures can be carried out only with individ-

---

[5] In New Zealand there is a comprehensive interlocking library service with a national catalogue. This means that if a book, microfilm, microcard, or journal is in any New Zealand library it can be borrowed by an enquirer in a different place on what is called *Interloan*.

uals. Tests wherever possible should be interesting to the children so that the learning process goes on as much as possible. It is also a truism that, in general, individuals perform better in a test when they know how they are doing, than if kept in the dark about results; discretion in this is needed, of course, e.g., with intelligence tests.

Thus we should try to obtain the most suitable data easily collected. We must consider fully how valid these data are likely to be, and whether the collecting process, administration, scoring, and recording are appropriately objective and reliable (see Chapter 11)—and worth the trouble.

Prior planning can reduce to a minimum any extraneous factors, i.e., data extra to, and not relevant to, what is being investigated. Much research loses in quality and validity by being cluttered up with material which does not bear directly on the topic being studied, or because it partially measures the desired factor, mixed up with a number of other factors, and therefore does not measure it accurately.

TREATING THE DATA

This involves first the arrangement of the data in some workable form, and is largely a mechanical process. Scores are first picked up in random order (raw scores) and are often placed in order of highest to lowest (ranked scores), or tabulated according to score and frequency (frequency tabulation). This first stage is essentially a tidying, sifting, and simplifying stage, somewhat like picking up a used deck of cards and sorting them into neat piles according to their suits and spots. Unwanted data are put aside, and the information is reduced to workable size, perhaps in one summary, or in several tabulations, each referring to a separate test or to a different aspect of the topic. We are now ready for any mathematical or graphical treatment, which, for the ordinary physical education teacher, need not be difficult. As said earlier, only simple arithmetic is involved, with nothing more complicated than the square root, which can always be found from tables anyway. (These mathematical processes are dealt with in Chapters 9 and 10.)

Advanced statistical techniques, such as factor analysis and non-linear correlation, do use more difficult mathematical concepts, but such work lies beyond the scope of this book. Our aim is to bring simple research methods into the school situation. The university research worker may use some advanced techniques, or avail himself of the consultant services of the statistical laboratory. Normally, data are mathematically treated to indicate such things as:

1. The way scores are distributed, e.g., the distribution of heights of college basketball players
2. Averages and spread of scores in such distributions, e.g., mean and range of scores in a health-knowledge test
3. Comparative position and value of single scores, e.g., how Bob scored in diving and long jump
4. Relationship between two or more abilities or factors, e.g., whether boys who skate well are also good at skiing
5. Direction of change in people's abilities or characteristics, e.g., whether children of 12 are taller now than in 1900, and if so, how much so

Interpreting the Data and Expressing Results

Once data have been treated, they are usually in a form which allows us to interpret the information meaningfully, referring back to our sample and the evaluation carried out. After all, there is no guarantee that another sample would have provided the same answer, although, as explained later, there are ways of assessing the statistical *significance* of the answer as it might apply to other samples.

The interpreting of the information calls for judgement, imagination, and that elusive quality we call common sense, as well as scientific integrity and mathematical accuracy. It is essentially a cautious phase, during which trends should be discussed and analysed with experts. The trends may not be what was expected or hoped for. In all branches of science there are disappointing experiments and investigations. He who would evaluate must expect this. He may neither prove nor disprove something, but he will gain from the experience of scientific enquiry.

There are four main ways of expressing results visually.

1. The verbal or linguistic form expresses results in words
2. The tabular or numerical form expresses results in tables, or columns of figures
3. The graphical or cartographical form expresses results in graphs, maps, charts, plans, sections, etc.
4. The pictorial form expresses results in pictures, diagrams, cartoons, photographs, models, etc.

Results can be expressed in other ways. Auditory media include recordings, tapes, film tracks, and other sounds (the impulses from an electromyograph can be fed onto a tape to give a rising and falling note or volume).

WORDS

Words are the commonest medium for expressing information (see Chapter 3).

"Thirteen-year-old children put on more weight during the first half of a semester than during the second half . . ." might be a purely verbal account of a result. While words are extremely useful for summarising findings, and provide the best shades of meaning in qualitative descriptions, they are not generally as exact as numbers, where quantitative expressions and comparisons are to be made.[6] For example, yesterday's weather of "fresh northerly winds, cloudy with occasional showers, and cool temperatures" summed up the situation adequately for a single day's report. Certainly, numerical readings of wind strengths, amount of cloud cover and precipitation, air temperature and pressure, and humidity would have enhanced the verbal report.

NUMBERS

Numbers these days are used almost as often as words in expressing information, particularly in education. The advantages of numerical expression, with its brevity and precision, become greater as more data have to be expressed.

A summary of the weather over a month can be given verbally. For example: "April was generally cloudy, cool and windy, although rainfall was only average. The heavy rain of the first week was followed by changeable weather, and in the last fortnight mainly cloudy or fair weather prevailed, except for the two-day storm on April 27–28th, and the cold showery weather which followed." This could be the sort of verbal description we would use in writing to a friend overseas, but it is hardly systematic, precise, or detailed enough to be used as the official weather record. Such qualities enable numerical expression in the form of tables to come into its own.

A table, giving day-to-day figures to show wind speed and direction,

---

[6] But words are not symbols and most numerical results have to be interpreted back into words finally.

hours of sunshine and cloud amounts, minimum and maximum temperatures, air humidity and pressure, amount and kind of precipitation, and similar data, would provide a full and exact record of April's weather in one page of about thirty lines. Tabulations constitute excellent means of expression for this type of information, and can be easily read and analysed by most laymen.[7]

But would such a tabulation be appropriate for expressing weather over a year? On the above basis, day-to-day records would require columns extending to 365 lines, rather lengthy and unwieldy. While day-to-day records would still be necessary, the data could be summarised into fifty-two weekly records, or twelve monthly records, with averages for each weather feature. This "grouping" of data (see below in this chapter) causes a loss in accuracy of detail for daily situations, but the weekly or monthly trends for the year would be at once apparent.

GRAPHS

Graphs could express these weekly or monthly summaries even more clearly, because there would be no need for the reader to make mental calculations to find the wettest month, the sunniest week, and so on. The mere size of the bar in a bar graph, or direction of line in a line graph would create a direct visual impression of bigness or smallness, and of up or down. In many instances, it is often easier to express information vividly by graphs, charts, or pictures than by words or tabulations. Weather data, such as the mean temperature or the monthly rainfall over a year lends itself admirably to expression in, say, a bar graph, or in a line graph (Fig. 8.1).

Again, wind speed and direction over a year could be an important consideration in deciding the way an athletic track should lie on a particular site. These could be drawn on a chart of the site, and the track could be orientated in the most suitable direction. Such a chart, giving pictorial expression of information, might make a stronger impression on the planning administrators than a list of figures or a string of words (see Figure 8.2).

---

[7] Although the effectiveness of communications may depend on the sophistication of the receptor. The Kinsey Reports were relatively meaningless to those who knew no statistics.

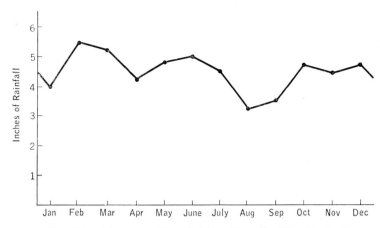

Fig. 8.1. Mean monthly rainfall at Dunedin, New Zealand.

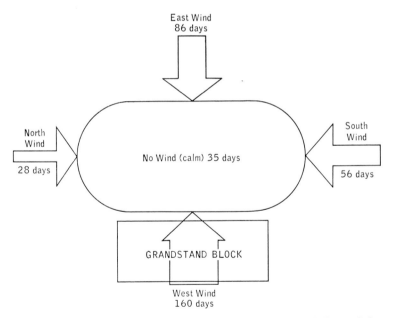

Fig. 8.2. Plan of proposed track to show frequency of days of four prevailing winds.

BASIC CONCEPTS OF TABULAR EXPRESSION

When collating a large number of scores or measurements, they first must be rearranged, and reduced to a workable form. Rearranging raw scores is usually done by ranking them in order from greatest to smallest, just as the sergeant-major does when he orders, "Tallest on the right, shortest on the left, fall in!"

GROUPING DATA

Reducing is done by grouping the score units, or the raw scores into suitable intervals. Thus instead of say a hundred score units, we might have twenty intervals of five units each. This will enable the information to be tabulated more succinctly and simply.

This system of grading into groups is used for instance in selling eggs. A thousand eggs might have a thousand different weights, but for selling purposes small differences do not matter. They are therefore graded by a machine into say six grades, from extra-large to very small.

The grouping of score units into intervals will vary with the data. For most tabulations, up to about twenty intervals, called "class intervals" or "step intervals," make a convenient grouping. Where smaller divisions are required for statistical treatment, such as T-scales (see Chapter 10), about forty class intervals are desirable. With weather data, score units of days might be grouped into intervals of weeks or months; measurements of length, e.g., the long jump, from inches into feet; and so on. With scores in tests, it is usual to group them into class intervals of five each, or of ten each.

With very large numbers in a sample, this grouping becomes necessary to avoid cluttering up the work with too much detail, and to save time and effort. If we measure the intelligence of high school boys and girls, tabulations of say 500 boys' scores and 500 girls' scores in long lists would be most difficult to work with. The 1000 raw scores all mixed up would be an almost meaningless jumble of figures. Merely separating boys' scores from girls' scores is a form of grouping. And ranking each set of scores would be a further refinement.

The grouping of score units in class intervals of five units would produce tabulations for boys and for girls, each with about twenty class intervals. Of course, each individual score loses its identity when it is placed in a class interval, and some slight accuracy is lost, but this is negligible with large samples. The saving of time and effort, and the ease of interpretation of grouped data in tabulations more than off-set it. You can still refer to Jim's or Bob's score by referring back to the original records of the test.

Intelligence Quotient Scores of 500 High School Boys

Intelligence Quotient	Tallies	Frequency f
155–159	/	1
150–154	//	2
145–149	///	3
140–144	++++	5
135–139	++++ //	7
130–134	etc.	10
125–129		15
120–124		20
115–159		35
110–114		50
105–109		80
100–104		90
95– 99		80
90– 94		50
85– 89	etc.	30
80– 84	++++ ++++ ++++	15
75– 79	++++	5
70– 74	//	2
		$N = 500$

STEPS IN DRAWING UP A FREQUENCY TABULATION

1. From the raw scores, find the highest to lowest, i.e., the range. In our case, 156 was the highest IQ and 74 was the lowest, the range being 82.
2. Within this range, work out a suitable number of class intervals, aiming for about 10 to 20 intervals or roughly 15 class intervals. Dividing the range by, say, 15, then will give an idea of the size of each

class interval. In our case 82/15 gives us about 5 score units as a suggested class interval.

3. Write the class intervals in a column, with the highest at the top, e.g., 155–159, 150–154, etc.

4. Record each score beside its appropriate class interval, by a tally mark in the form of an oblique stroke thus: /. As the tally marks increase, it is a good idea to make each fifth one a line through the four oblique strokes, thus: ////. This makes it very easy to count the scores after they have all been entered beside their class interval.

5. Add the tallies within each class interval, entering the total in column *f* which stands for the frequency.

6. Add the frequencies in the *f*-column to give the total number of cases, *N*.

The *frequency tabulation* is very useful as a means of expressing data. It makes a simple summary of the scores, it can be converted easily into a graph, and it can be used for calculating averages and other statistical concepts. It allows for quick interpretation of the nature and pattern of the score distribution.

BASIC CONCEPTS OF GRAPHICAL EXPRESSION

The mathematical principles of constructing graphs apply in our field as in other subjects. A graph consists initially of two lines intersecting at right angles, called *coordinate axes*. These two coordinate axes form four *quadrants*. The intersection of the axes is called the *origin* (*O*). Scores at the origin are zero, and increase *towards the right along the horizontal axis* (*OX*). Another set of scores could be placed on the graph, starting with zero at the origin, and increasing *upwards along the vertical axis* (*OY*). These measures to the right of, or upwards from the origin are always *positive,* that is, carry a plus (+) sign. Any measures which are *negative,* or carry a minus (—) sign, would be placed on the left of the origin, starting from zero, and increasing as they move *to the left along the horizontal axis* (*OX'*). A second set of negative measures could be placed on the graph, starting with zero at the origin, and increasing downwards along the vertical axis (*OY'*).

THE GRAPH AND THE MAP COMPARED

A graph thus has room for two sets of scores or measures. Each set of measures can have both negative and positive scores, but in practice most graphs show two sets of positive scores, and therefore use only the northeast or $(++)$ quadrant.

The set of scores first graphed is usually that to be placed along the horizontal axis. Then the other set of measures is placed up along the vertical axis. It is the same when working from the graph to find certain measures. Like the human infant, you start horizontal, and then

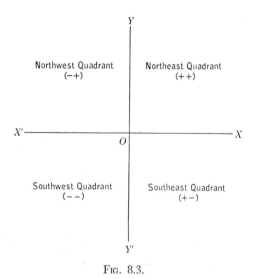

FIG. 8.3.

try the vertical. A good example of this sequence is finding a map reference, when using a map with squared grid lines. These grid lines are the same as lines on a graph. "Eastings" (from an origin or the left-hand side of the map) are read first, towards the east horizontal grid lines; "northings" (from an origin or the bottom of the map) up the vertical grid lines are read second. Thus a map reference *129 045* would be found from the map below to be Conical Peak.

The ideas of map and compass directions can assist us in understanding the principles of graphical representation. The cartographer's principle, of working towards the east to begin with, is the same as the mathematician's principle of working along the horizontal axis first, and having scores increase as they move east from the origin. Again, we call the horizontal axis used first the $X'OX$ axis, and the vertical axis used second the YOY' axis.

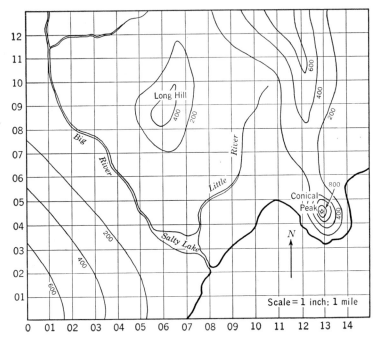

FIG. 8.4.   Map of Salty Lake Area, showing grid reference.

We can continue the map and compass analogy with the four quadrants formed by the axes. We can call the top right-hand quadrant the northeast quadrant, and we know that both variables will be positive in this quadrant. The opposite quadrant, where both variables will be negative, is the southwest quadrant. The top left-hand quadrant, where the first (horizontal) variable is negative and the second (vertical) variable is positive, will be the northwest $(-+)$ quadrant. And the bottom right-hand quadrant, where the first (horizontal) variable is positive, and the second (vertical) variable is negative, will be the southeast $(+-)$ quadrant.

The score value along the first (horizontal) axis is known as the *abscissa* and the score value up the second (vertical) axis is known as the *ordinate*. Thus in Fig. 8.5, point *B* has an abscissa (hours taken) of 2, and an ordinate (miles covered) of ½. The rate of the tortoise's whole journey could be graphed by plotting a series of points, of which *B* is only one.

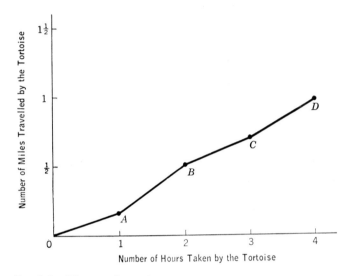

Fig. 8.5. The tortoise and the hare—graph to show the rate of the tortoise's journey.

STEPS IN CONSTRUCTING A GRAPH

The two most common types of graph are the line graph and bar graph. The first steps for these are the same.

1. Construct a frequency tabulation.
2. Draw two coordinate axes, intersecting near the bottom left-hand side of the graph paper.
3. Take two more than the number of class intervals (grouped data) or scores in the frequency tabulation, and divide this total into the number of squares along the baseline of the graph. The dividend (disregarding fractions) will tell you how many squares you can use

for each class interval. For example, in graphing the IQ's of the 500 boys in the last tabulation, one would take the number of class intervals, 18, plus 2, which equals 20, and divide this into, say, 110, if there are 110 squares to accommodate the class intervals along the baseline. We see that there will be 5 squares available for each class-interval, since $110/20 = 5\frac{1}{2}$.

4. Mark in the class intervals accordingly. If the smallest class interval is not zero, leave one space next to the origin, and show that the scale of scores here are not regular, by a *break*, thus:

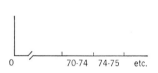

Of course, score values should rise as they move to the right, away from the origin.

5. Use the same procedure to mark in the frequency scale up the vertical axis. Find what number of squares per frequency unit will allow the greatest frequency to be accommodated on the page. As these start at zero, no break will be needed.

6. Aim to have the graph about three-fourths as high as it is wide, because this roughly conforms with the shape of the normal probability curve (see Chapter 9).

7. The procedure from this point varies for either the line graph or the bar graph.

The graph is now ready for plotting in the scores, for the units of the scale are marked along the baseline, and the units of the frequency scale are marked up the vertical axis.

LINE GRAPH

From frequency tabulation, using the same example:

1. For each class interval, mark in the appropriate frequency, by a cross midway along that interval, and opposite the frequency for the class interval.

2. Join each of these crosses by straight lines.

3. The two extremities, i.e., the crosses at each end, should now be joined to the baseline at the midpoint of what would have been the next class interval.

This type of line graph is called a frequency polygon—the statistical name for a line graph which shows the distribution pattern of scores for any sample. The scores are marked in along the baseline, and the frequencies are marked in up along the vertical axis. This frequency polygon is so called because it appears as a many-sided figure, or polygon, expressing frequencies. It is used especially to show several distributions on the same graph, using different colours, or types of lines. Bar graphs do not lend themselves as readily to this function.

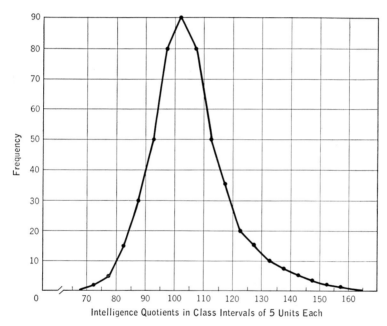

FIG. 8.6. Frequency polygon—intelligence quotients of 500 high school boys.

BAR GRAPH

From frequency tabulation, using the same example:

1. For each class interval, mark in the appropriate frequency by a horizontal line above the whole of that interval, and opposite the frequency for the class interval.
2. Make vertical columns, by joining the ends of the horizontal lines with vertical lines.

3. The two extremities, i.e., the horizontal lines at each end, should now be joined to the baseline by vertical lines.

This type of bar graph is called a column diagram, or histogram. *Histogram* is the statistical name for a bar graph which shows the distribution pattern of scores for any sample. The scores are marked in along

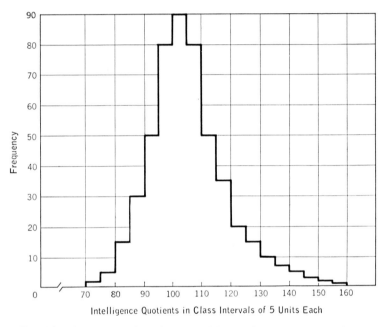

FIG. 8.7.   Histogram—intelligence quotients of 500 high school boys.

the baseline, and the frequencies are marked in up along the vertical axis. This column diagram is so called because it appears as a diagram of columns, each one expressing frequencies. Each interval is presented by a rectangle, the sides of which are not usually projected down to the baseline. Each of these rectangles has an area directly proportional to its frequency, compared with the area and frequency of any other rectangle. The area of the whole column diagram is similarly directly proportional to N, the total number of cases, compared with the area and frequency of any single rectangle.

Thus the column diagram is a mathematically true representation of the distribution pattern, and is more commonly used than the frequency polygon for graphing single frequency tabulations.

TYPES OF GRAPH

LINE GRAPH

This is used very frequently in many walks of life, because it is simple to draw, and gives a quick, vivid impression of the nature of the data or the trend of the measures. Nurses use them in hospitals for recording the trends of a patient's temperature. The line graph lends itself to the plotting of several sets of data on the same graph. Because of its continuity, it allows the use of marking devices, such as pens, on paper-

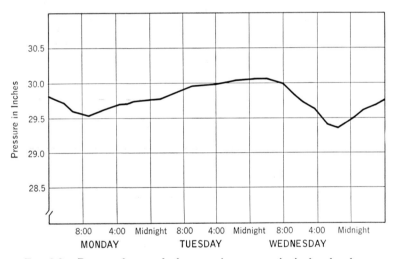

FIG. 8.8.   Barograph record—barometric pressure in inches by days.

covered drums, which revolve very slowly, such as once in twenty-four hours, or once in a week. For example, the barograph is a measuring device which records atmospheric pressure (measured by an aneroid barometer) on a time scale mounted on a drum which revolves once in a week. When removed, the time scale appears as a line graph, showing atmospheric pressure trends during that week.

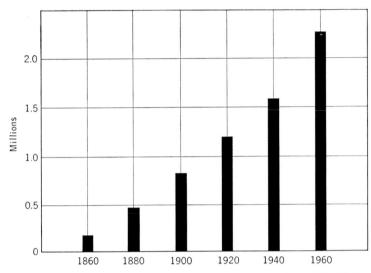

Fɪɢ. 8.9A.   Simple bar graph—New Zealand population, 1860–1960.

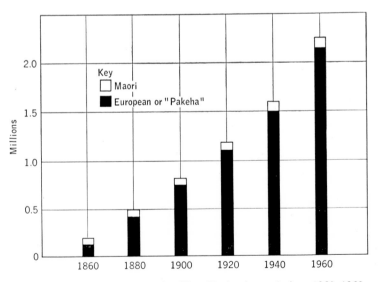

Fɪɢ. 8.9B.   Sectioned bar graph—New Zealand population, 1860–1960.

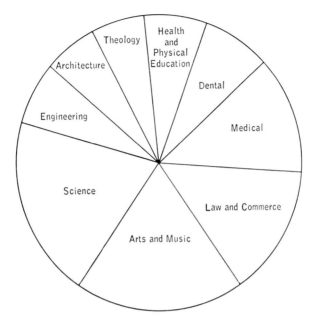

FIG. 8.10. Sector or pie graph—departments at a university.

BAR GRAPH

Many types of measures can be represented by the use of a bar for each different measure, with the frequency or amount determining the length of each bar. This technique is resorted to a great deal in geography, in industry, in economics, and similar fields. It often shows data about population, production, exports and imports, resources, weather, and the like. The bars can be simple, representing one quality only, e.g., population, or *sectioned*, representing several qualities in the one bar, e.g., males and females.

SECTOR GRAPH OR PIE GRAPH

When proportions of some quantity or concept are to be represented graphically, the most appropriate type is usually the sector graph, the angle subtended by each sector being directly proportional to the amount of that measure. That is, each sector shows "the slice of the pie" for that measure.

This method is commonly used to express types of export out of the total exports of a country, types of imports, of industries, places, etc. In education, it may be used to show the choices or activities of various proportions of a sample of people.

SYMBOLIC GRAPH AND CARTOON GRAPH

Many unusual, vivid, and animated ways of expressing information are used today. They are often based on one of the previously mentioned types of graph. These can show information in a very attractive and eye-catching manner, but often it is only approximate, and sometimes the cartoon method tends to complicate, rather than simplify, the

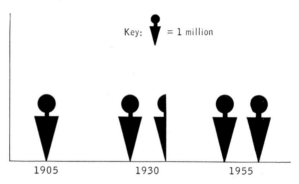

Key: = 1 million

1905   1930   1955

Fig. 8.11.   Symbolic or cartoon graph—population increase in New Zealand from 1905–1955. Note in this graph the symbol units are repeated rather than increased in size.

expression of the information. This form of graph communication has been very highly developed by Marie Neurath, and her father, the founder of the Isotype Institute. So distinguished a scholar as Lancelot Hogben (*Mathematics for the Million; Science for Everyone*) considers the isotype development as an important educational medium.[8]

[8] Lancelot Hogben, *Cave-Painting to Comic Strip*, New York, Chanticleer, 1949.

RECOMMENDED READING

Garrett, H. E., *Statistics in Psychology and Education,* New York, Longmans, Green, 1953.

Huff, Darrell, *How to Lie with Statistics,* New York, Norton, 1954.

Lindquist, E. F., *et al., Educational Measurement,* Washington, American Council on Education, 1951.

Stroup, F., *Measurement in Physical Education,* New York, Ronald, 1957.

Tate, Merle W., *Statistics in Education,* New York, Macmillan, 1955.

chapter 9

MEASUREMENTS AND THEIR
DISTRIBUTION

CHANCE

You have all heard of the law of averages. But what does it mean? If we toss a coin four times, and each time heads comes up, what would we expect for the fifth toss? If the coin is evenly weighted and not a "double-header," and if it is spun sufficiently in a high toss, then we can expect a one-to-one chance at any toss. That means that there will be an even chance of heads or tails on the fifth toss, or any toss, no matter what the previous score of heads or tails. Uneven weighting of the coin, or a consistently spun toss will naturally affect this even chance.

By a similar principle, the likelihood of a newborn baby being a boy or girl is about even, although here, certain genetic factors and hereditary tendencies will affect this even chance. And before long, we may be able to defeat chance and choose the sex of a baby. In chance distribution then, we have two main considerations: the pattern of chance distribution itself, and the presence of factors which will disturb or distort this pattern.

Chance Distribution Expressed Numerically

Let us return to coin-tossing and examine the principles of chance distribution. If we toss one, two, three, or more coins a sufficient number of times, a pattern of distribution will begin to emerge. With one coin, the chances or probability of heads to tails will be one to one. With two coins, the chances will be this pattern: one of both heads, two of heads and tails, and one of both tails. In numerical expression of ratios then we have for one coin: 1:1; for two coins: 1:2:1; for three coins 1:3:3:1; and so on. This is in fact the mathematical expression of the ratios of probability, expanded binomially.

We could express these principles of chance or probability by a diagram, building up the diagram into a pyramid, by adding an extra coin at a time to our coin-tossing experiment and working out the probability ratios. The diagram would appear like this:

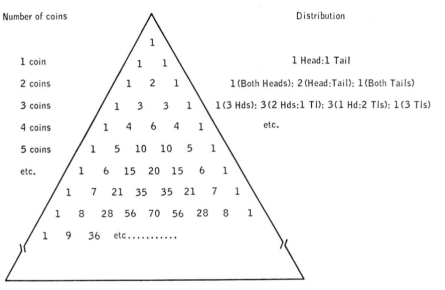

FIG. 9.1.   Part of Pascal's triangle of probability ratios.

This triangle or pyramid can be extended downwards indefinitely. It is known as Pascal's Triangle, after the great French mathematician, Blaise Pascal. A Belgian, Baron Quetelet, developed this principle, as applied to human characteristics, but did not systematise it as did Sir Francis Galton around the turn of the last century.

CHANCE DISTRIBUTION IN EVERYDAY LIFE

There are many examples of such distributions in everyday life. One of the best known is that of plant and animal breeding, and the acquisition of hereditary characteristics. The Mendelian laws of breeding follow these principles. The characteristics of peas have usually been quoted by biologists, but these principles apply also to humans.

Of course these are only the ratios of probability, and therefore the chances lie this way; but the presence of extraneous factors may distort the chances.

The Normal Probability Distribution

The pattern of probability ratios, expressed as chance distributions, is known as the "normal probability distribution." As Garrett says, in *Statistics in Education and Psychology,* "Measurements of many natural phenomena, and of many mental and social traits under certain conditions, tend to be distributed symmetrically about their means, in proportions which approximate those of the normal probability distribution."[1]

This normal probability distribution is the pattern which results from the distributions of measurements, marks, or scores of samples in biology, anthropology, psychology, education, botany, zoology, astronomy, and other sciences. It also occurs where chance factors operate in industry and commerce, in ballistics, in chemistry and physics, and in gambling sports.

THE NORMAL PROBABILITY DISTRIBUTION EXPRESSED GRAPHICALLY

Let us measure the heights of 10,000 adult men. With a very large random sample of adult men, these should be distributed approximately according to the normal probability distribution. If we wanted to see how the 10,000 cases would appear in graph form, we could imagine that they were to be lined up in files according to height in inches along the runway of an aerodrome. We would use the same method as in drawing up a frequency tabulation (see Chapter 8). First we would find the range, which might be, say, 20 inches, from 4 feet 11 inches to 6 feet 7 inches. Of course there would be very few men of such extreme shortness or tallness as these, since most would be around an average height of say 5 feet 8 inches. If we put in pegs every 5 yards across the runway, with successive heights each an inch different, then our 10,000 men could each line up across the aerodrome according to his height. Each man who was 4 feet 11 inches tall (to the nearest inch,

[1] H. E. Garrett, *Statistics in Psychology and Education,* New York, Longmans Green, 1953.

i.e., taller than 4 feet 10½ inches, but shorter than 4 feet 11½ inches) would line up beside the 4 feet 11 inch peg. Each "5-footer" would line up beside the 5 feet 0 inch peg. Each man who was 5 feet 1 inch tall would line up beside the 5 feet 1 inch. And so on through the heights right up to the tallest men of 6 feet 7 inches.

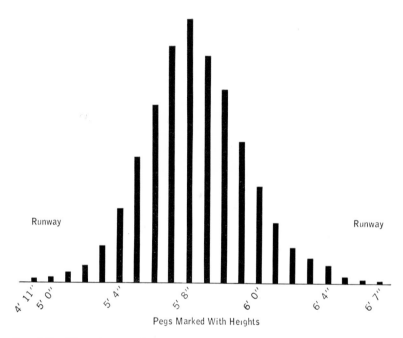

Pegs Marked With Heights

FIG. 9.2. View from a helicopter of 10,000 men, lined up according to height on an airport runway.

As we arranged the men, we would find that most would be lining up beside the middle pegs, and few would be lining up beside the end pegs. Now let us go up into the control tower or a helicopter and look down on the 10,000 men. From above, they would look something like the pattern formed in Fig. 9.2.

FREQUENCY TABULATION OF PROBABILITY DISTRIBUTION

If we counted the number of men in each line, we could draw up a frequency tabulation of the distribution of the heights of these 10,000 men. It might work out something like this:

Frequency Tabulation: Theoretical Distribution of Heights
of 10,000 Adult Men

Heights (to Nearest Inch)	Frequency
6' 7'' (or taller)	28
6' 6''	30
6' 5''	50
6' 4''	100
6' 3''	150
6' 2''	200
6' 1''	350
6' 0''	550
5' 11''	800
5' 10''	1100
5' 9''	1300
5' 8''	1500
5' 7''	1350
5' 6''	1000
5' 5''	700
5' 4''	400
5' 3''	200
5' 2''	100
5' 1''	50
5' 0''	25
4' 11'' (or shorter)	17
	$N = 10,000$

It can be seen that most men are between 5 feet 6 inches and 6 feet. The further the pegs are from these middle heights, the fewer men there are. If we draw a line between each furthest man from each peg, a curve is produced. This is, of course, the same procedure as constructing a frequency polygon. The greater the number of cases (N), and the greater the number of class intervals (here we took 21 class-intervals, 1 inch apart), then the smoother does this curve become. It approximates the shape of a bell, seen from the side. In our example the bell-like curve is not quite symmetrical, for reasons which will be discussed later.

PROBABILITY DISTRIBUTION EXPRESSED AS A GRAPH

If we constructed a graph from a frequency tabulation of the heights

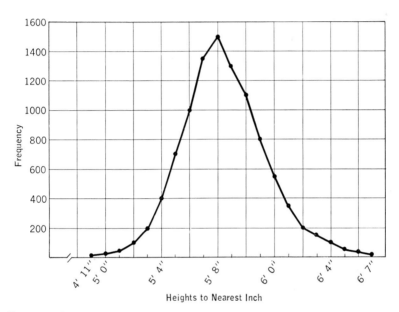

Heights to Nearest Inch

FIG. 9.3.   Frequency polygon—theoretical distribution of heights of 10,000 men.

of these 10,000 men, we would get a similar-looking result (see Fig. 9.3).

Let us once more go back to the coin-tossing experiment. If we tossed 8 coins about 250 times, the frequency tabulation we drew up from the way they fell should be, according to Pascal's triangle, as follows:

Eight heads	1
Seven heads: one tail	8
Six heads: two tails	28
Five heads: three tails	56

Four heads: four tails	70
Three heads: five tails	56
Two heads: six tails	28
One head: seven tails	8
Eight tails	1

Fig. 9.4 is a graph constructed to express this distribution.

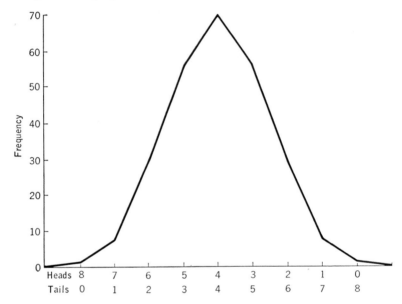

Fig. 9.4.   Theoretical distribution of fall of 8 coins 254 times.

But of course things never work out in practice quite like they should in theory. If you tried this experiment, you might get a pattern not quite like the theoretical distribution. We found that from tossing 8 coins 254 times we actually got the pattern shown in Fig. 9.5.

This pattern is, of course, not quite the symmetrical smooth bell-like pattern that is the theoretical result. This theoretical pattern is called the "normal curve of distribution," or the "normal probability curve" or the "Gaussian curve." It is merely the graphical expression of the normal probability distribution (see Fig. 9.6).

The normal probability curve is symmetrical; that is, its highest point is halfway along it, or occupies the midpoint of the total range of scores of measurements. This highest point represents the greatest frequency or concentration of scores: it is the most popular measurement, and is the mode. Towards each end of the curve, the scores or measurements are not as frequent or concentrated, but become more scattered

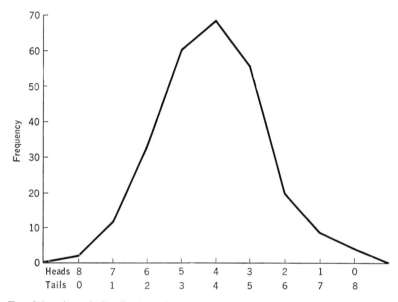

FIG. 9.5. Actual distribution of fall of 8 coins 254 times in an experiment.

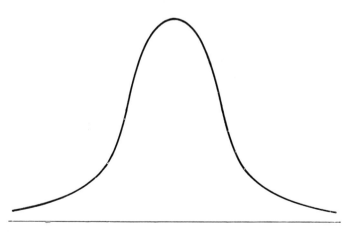

FIG. 9.6. Normal probability curve or normal curve of distribution.

or dispersed. At the very ends of the curves the scores become so infrequent that they eventually are not achieved at all in the sample, and they disappear.

It can be seen then that the height of the curve above its baseline is directly proportional to, and represents the frequency for, that particular score or class interval. Where the curve is highest, there is the greatest frequency; where the curve meets the baseline, there is no frequency at all. The measures at these two ends must have been so extreme that no one in the sample of men was short enough or tall enough to be able to qualify for such an odd height. In the coin-tossing example, of course, more extreme scores than were recorded are impossible with eight coins. One would immediately suspect a fall of nine heads with eight coins!

Let us go back to the example of the heights of 10,000 men. Why was their distribution not symmetrical, yet in the coin-tossing experiment the distribution was symmetrical? In the first place, with chance distributions a perfect curve is never achieved, because there is never a perfect experiment with a perfect sample and no extraneous factors. This applied equally well to our two experiments. But with the heights of men—or any physical measurements—there is usually the tendency for extreme cases to extend further in a positive direction from the mode than in a negative direction (except of course where abnormal pathological cases occur). After all, men in the United States have grown taller during the last half-century, and it is conceivable that extreme tallness is more likely than extreme shortness. Also it is harder to approach zero in physical measurements than to extend a similar distance above the most popular measurement. If the anterior-posterior thickness of a man's body at waist level is 9 inches, we all know it is easier to add 6 inches and have a 15 inch "spread" than to take away 6 inches and to measure only 3 inches through the waist.

This tendency seems typical with anthropometric measurements, especially girth and weight, and to a lesser extent with height. Such a tendency also occurs in some sports: for example, if the average golf score for men players is 80, it is much easier for scores to range more than 20 strokes higher than 80, that is, 100 or more, than it is for scores to range more than 20 strokes less than 80, that is, 60 or less.

Such distributions of measurements or scores from actual experiments are therefore never quite identical with the normal probability curve, and are rarely even symmetrical. If the normal probability curve is not achieved—and it never is quite achieved in practice—the curve or line graph yielded will not be symmetrical, and will be skewed. Even if it were symmetrical, it would probably be different in shape from the normal probability curve, because it might be flatter or higher, or have more than one hump or mode.

Variations From the Normal Probability Curve

POSITIVELY SKEWED CURVE

One of the most common variations is the one we have been discussing—where the curve is skewed in such a way that scores are more

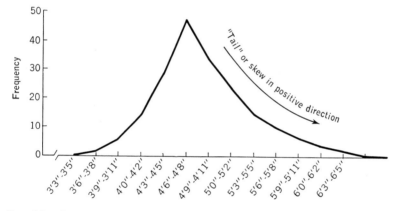

Fig. 9.7.   Positively skewed distribution—high jump scores of 200 physical education freshmen.

extreme at the positive end of the distribution. This type of distribution produces a *positively shewed curve*. Here the greatest freqeuncy is before the mid-score of the total range of scores, and a *"tail"* extends in a positive direction, to the right of the graph. It occurs with most physical measurements and with scores resulting from physical abilities, especially measures of strength and power such as the standing long jump, the vertical jump, and dynamometrical strength tests. It occurs, too, in distributions of golf scores.

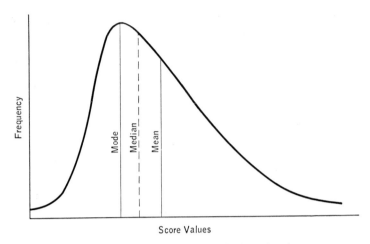

Fig. 9.8. In a markedly skewed distribution, the three measures of central tendency may be well separated. The median is least affected by extreme scores or freak distributions, and is often preferred with such conditions.

With educational tests, it occurs where the test is too "difficult" for the class, where the class is not bright enough for the test, or where maybe the marking has been too hard. Or the class may be atypical to start with—it may contain mostly dull children whose scores bring down the mode. With tests in track and field, in the case of a class not specially trained in an event, the presence of a few students who have been given special coaching in an event, e.g., the high jump, will produce a positive skew or "tail" in a positive direction (see Figs. 9.7 and 9.8).

NEGATIVELY SKEWED CURVE

The reverse of this type of distribution is, of course, the *negatively skewed curve.* Here the greatest frequency is higher than—or after—the middle score of the total range of scores, and a "tail" extends back to the left of the graph, in a negative direction. It occurs in sorts of situations opposite to the positively skewed examples: where the test is too easy for the class, the marking has been too easy, or the class is too bright for that test (or at least the majority of the class are bright in an atypical group). This pattern is very common with examination results, in which most students pass.

The next type of distribution is also very common. This has two "humps" or modes, although one mode is usually higher or more pronounced than the other. Very rarely is this *bimodal curve* symmetrical (see Fig. 9.9). It occurs where the abilities or measurements of the sample are sharply divided, such as where boys and girls are included in the same sample, when scoring physical abilities, or taking anthropometrical measurements. It is often true of undergraduate university physical-education classes—which contain some who are merely passing the time there, whose main goals are athletic performance, while others will go on to the doctorate level. Or perhaps half the sample have had special training in a given field, while others have not. Or it may be an ability in which some of the class are naturally more experienced, for instance the case of a mechanical-ability test with a mixed sample of boys and girls. What happens, of course, is that each of the two groups in the sample has its own mode when the scores are graphed, and the resulting curve is bimodal.

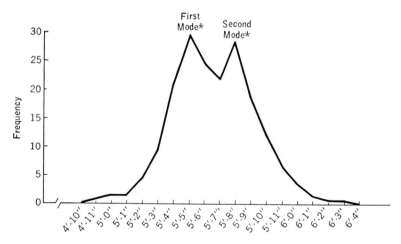

FIG. 9.9. Bimodal distribution—heights of 200 men and women physical education freshmen.

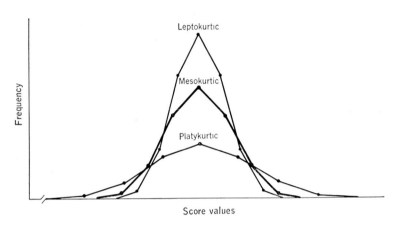

FIG. 9.10. Kurtosis—while most distributions in educational measurement tend to be mesokurtic, homogeneous groups tend to yield leptokurtic patterns.

KURTOSIS

Still another variation differs not so much in symmetry as in shape from the normal probability curve. The distribution has a marked feature, either "peakedness" or "flatness," compared with the normal curve. This aspect of a curve is known as *kurtosis* (see Fig. 9.10). The normal probability curve is called *mesokurtic*. A steep high curve is called *leptokurtic*. It occurs usually with very homogeneous groups, that is, groups which are highly selected, where all have similar measurements, or gain similar scores. For example, members of a tennis club would produce a more leptokurtic distribution of scores in the Dyer tennis test (see Chapter 18) than a random sample of the population. Or the heights of members of a basketball league in which a minimum height is 6 feet 2 inches would be more leptokurtic than the heights of a random sample of men.

A flat, wide, shallow curve is called *platykurtic*. This is not so common. It might occur with samples that were widely differing in ability or measurements—that is, with unusually heterogeneous groups. Of course, apparently leptokurtic or platykurtic distributions could be artificially produced by inappropriate class intervals, or proportions to a graph, when plotting the distribution of scores or measurements.

J-CURVE OF CONFORMITY

Other distributions are possible, especially with abnormal groups, or measurements of unusual traits. One is the *J*-curve, usually found when such traits as conformity to accepted social or community behaviour are measured. For example, the filing of income tax returns or entries for a competition before the closing date will produce the greatest frequency on that date, and the few days just preceding it (see Fig. 9.11).

U-CURVE OF DICHOTOMY

Another example is the *U*-curve, with strongly dichotomous tendencies in the sample, such as would happen with political loyalty in a

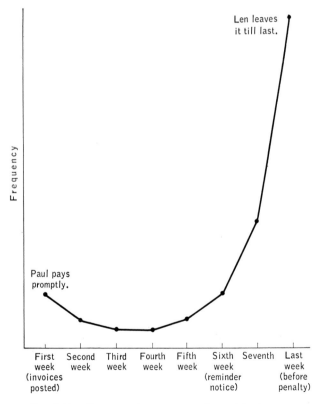

FIG. 9.11. J curve—the payment of municipal taxes.

two-party political system (see Fig. 9.12). The majority of people will be strongly one way or the other, with the resulting high frequencies at the ends of the graph; the smallest frequencies towards the centre will

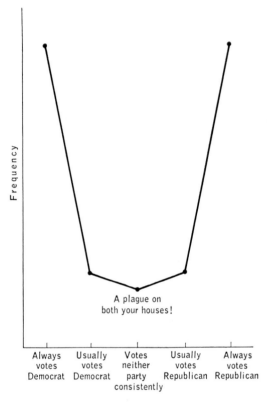

Fig. 9.12.   U curve—political loyalty in a two-party system.

be occupied by cases which have indefinite or not so strong political bias or preference. This group is known as the "swinging vote."

The distribution of scores or measurements that approximates to the normal probability curve has two main features. First, there is a concentration of scores around the highest point of the curve, which is called the *mode*. Second, there is a scatter of scores away from this point, with fewer cases the further away we go. These two features are known statistically as *central tendency* and *dispersion,* respectively.

MEASURES OF CENTRAL TENDENCY

Only with a symmetrical distribution, as in the normal probability curve, do measures of central tendency coincide at the highest point or *mode.* The symmetrical normal probability curve naturally has the greatest frequency at the top of the "hump." But it also has an equal number of scores or measurements on either side of the mode. Therefore, the score or measurement with just 50 percent of cases on either side of it, is, in the normal probability curve, the case at the very top of the hump, or one of the cases within the class interval occupying this position. This case is known as the *median.*

There is a third measure of central tendency with which we are all familiar. That is the arithmetical average, or *mean.* It is the one used most often by ordinary people. It is also one that may be very misleading.

Measures of central tendency have a twofold function: (1) The measure of central tendency represents *all* scores in the distribution, in order to describe the sample's performance or quality as a whole; and (2) The measure of central tendency, indicating the "typical" performance of the sample, enables us to compare two or more groups or samples in terms of this "typical" performance.

Mode

The mode (Mo) is the measurement or score that occurs most often in a distribution. It is the commonest or most popular score—and this is the meaning of the word in everyday life: the mode is the fashion, and à la mode means in the fashion. The mode in a distribution is found by inspection, both with a frequency tabulation and with a graph; it is in fact the largest score in the frequency tabulation, or the highest peak in the graph.

Example: How to find the mode

Collar sizes of 200 men's shirts sold during May were:

Size (Inches)	Numbers Sold (f)
19	1
18½	1
18	3
17½	5
17	13
16½	21
16	32
15½	49
15	34
14½	23
14	11
13½	4
13	2
12½	1
	$N = 200$

By inspection, the largest score in the frequency tabulation is 49, being the number of 15½ inch collar size shirts. Therefore the mode, or most popular size, was the shirt with the 15½ inch collar.

Median

The median (Md) is that point in a distribution which has half the cases on either side of it. It is found by ranking the scores and finding the middle score. This score is the median. With grouped data, the median will be hidden within one of the class intervals.

steps for calculating the median

1. Find the total number of cases (N).
2. Rank the scores, highest to lowest.
3. Apply the formula:

$$\text{Median (Md)} = \frac{N + 1}{2} \text{ th score}$$

4. Find the score or measurement at that point, working from either end of the distribution.

Example: Calculation of the median

The mathematical marks of a class of twenty-three high-school boys were:

Name	Mark (Raw score)	Name	Ranked Scores
Alan	79	Colin	100
Bob	36	Ian	95
Colin	100	Ken	90
Don	75	Paul	85
Eric	55	Fred	82
Fred	82	Henry	80
Gary	64	Alan	79
Henry	80	Jim	77
Ian	95	Don	75
Jim	77	Tom	74
Ken	90	Neil	72
Lou	46	Mike	70
Mike	70	Stan	66
Neil	72	Gary	64
Owen	0	Ray	60
Paul	85	Eric	55
Quentin	51	Quentin	51
Ray	60	Lou	46
Stan	66	Bob	36
Tom	74	Uriah	25
Uriah	25	Wayne	15
Victor	10	Victor	10
Wayne	15	Owen	0
	$N = 23$		

1. Find total number of cases: $N = 23$.
2. Rank the scores. This is done in the right-hand column.
3. Apply the formula:

$$Md = \frac{N + 1}{2} \text{ th score}$$

$$= \frac{23 + 1}{2} \text{ th score}$$

$$= \frac{24}{2} \text{ th or 12th score from either end}$$
$$\text{of the ranked scores}$$

$$Md = 70 \text{ (mark scored by Mike)}$$

If there are an even number of cases, the steps are the same. Supposing there are 22 in the class (omit Owen's score of zero), then the median is now the $(22 + 1)/2$th case, or the 11.5th case from either end. This would lie halfway between Neil's 72 and Mike's 70 marks, and by interpolation would be 71.

MEAN

The mean (M) is the arithmetical average of the scores in the distribution. It is calculated by adding all the scores and dividing by the total number of cases.

STEPS FOR CALCULATING THE MEAN: UNGROUPED DATA

1. Find the number of cases (N).
2. Add up all the scores of measures (m) to give $\Sigma\, m$.
3. Divide the total sum of the scores (m) by the total number of cases (N), that is, apply the formula:

$$\text{Mean (M)} = \frac{\Sigma\, m}{N}$$

EXAMPLE: Calculation of mean

The weights of 15-year-old boys at a rural high school were as follows. (How do these boys compare in weight with 15-year-olds throughout the country, whose mean weight is 130 lb.?)

Name	Weight in Pounds m
Alfred	150
Ben	140
Claude	135
Dan	130
Evan	125
Frank	125
Ron	120
Sam	115
Tim	110
Will	100
	$\Sigma\, m = 1250$

1. Find the number of cases: $N = 10$.
2. Add all the scores: $\Sigma \, m = 1250$ lb.
3. Divide the sum of the scores $(\Sigma \, m)$ by the number of cases (N), that is, apply the formula:

$$M = \frac{\Sigma \, m}{N}$$

$$= \frac{1250}{10}$$

$$M = 125 \text{ lb.}$$

These boys have a mean weight of 125 lb., 5 lb. lighter than the national average of 130 lb. for 15-year-old boys.

STEPS FOR CALCULATING THE MEAN: GROUPED DATA

1. Find the number of cases (N).
2. Draw a frequency tabulation.
3. Multiply each score or measure (m) by its frequency (f). (Where scores are grouped within class intervals, take m to be the midpoint of that class interval and multiply it by the frequency of that class interval; repeat this for each class interval.)
4. Add these products (fm) to give $\Sigma \, (fm)$.
5. Divide this by the number of cases, that is, apply the formula:

$$\text{Mean } (M) = \frac{\Sigma \, (fm)}{N}$$

EXAMPLE: Calculation of the mean for grouped data

What is the average number of strokes per hole required to reach par figures, when par figures for each of the 180 holes on 10 golf courses are:

Par Figures "Bogey" m	Number of Holes f	fm
6	5	30
5	40	200
4	85	340
3	50	150
	180	720

$$M = \frac{\Sigma \ (fm)}{N}$$

$$= \frac{720}{180}$$

$$M = 4 \text{ strokes per hole}$$

STEPS FOR CALCULATING THE MEAN: GROUPED DATA (SHORT METHOD)

1. Find the number of cases (N).
2. Draw up a frequency tabulation.
3. Assume a mean, as near the centre of the distribution as possible. With class intervals, the assumed mean (A.M.) will be taken as the midpoint of the selected class interval.
4. Find the deviation x of each class interval from the selected class interval. Indicate whether each deviation is positive or negative.
5. Multiply each class-interval deviation (x) by its frequency (f), putting it in a $+ fx$ column if positive, and a fx column if negative.
6. Add each fx column and find the algebraic sum, $\Sigma \ (fx)$, by subtracting the sum of the $- fx$ column from the sum of the $+ fx$ column.
7. Divide the sum $[\Sigma \ (fx)]$ by the number of cages (N); multiply this result by the size of the class interval (C.I.); Add this product to the assumed mean, taking into account the sign. Thus, the formula is:

$$M = \text{A.M.} \pm \left(\frac{\Sigma \ fx}{N} \times \text{C.I.} \right)$$

EXAMPLE: Calculation of mean, by the assumed mean method

The scores of 200 high school girls in a knowledge test were as follows. What was the mean score?

Scores (Class intervals of 5 points)	Frequency f	Class Interval Deviations x	$+ fx$	$- fx$
90–94	1	+8	8	
85–89	1	+7	7	
80–84	4	+6	24	

Scores (Class intervals of 5 points)	Frequency f	Class Interval Deviations x	$+ fx$	$- fx$
75–79	6	+5	30	
70–74	10	+4	40	
65–69	16	+3	48	
60–64	30	+2	60	
55–59	36	+1	36	
50–54 (assume $M = 52$)	30	0	0	0
45–49	20	−1		−20
40–44	16	−2		−32
35–39	10	−3		−30
30–34	8	−4		−32
25–29	6	−5		−30
20–24	4	−6		−24
15–19	1	−7		− 7
10–14	1	−8		− 8
	$N = 200$		+253	−183
			$= + 70$	

1. In the example above, we have drawn up the frequency tabulation of 200 scores.
2. We assume a mean, at the midpoint of the central class interval, which includes the marks between 50 and 54. The midpoint of this class interval is the 52 mark. The assumed mean is therefore 52.
3. The deviations of each class interval from the assumed mean class interval are listed in the column marked x.
4. Each deviation is multiplied by its frequency, and the result put in the $+ fx$ column if the deviation is positive, and the $- fx$ column if the deviation is negative.
5. These columns are added, and the algebraic sum of fx is $253 - 183$, or $+70$.
6. Apply the formula:

$$M = \text{A.M.} \pm \left(\frac{\Sigma \ (fx)}{N} \times \text{C.I.} \right)$$

$$= 52 \pm \left(\frac{+70}{200} \times 5 \right)$$

$$= 52 + 1.75$$

$$M = 53.75 \text{ marks}$$

Using Measures of Central Tendency

THE MODE

This is the quickest measure of concentration to find, but it is only a rough estimate, and may be quite misleading in freak cases. It is valuable especially when the score recurring most often is sought. Accordingly it is used in industry and commerce, in education and in some sciences for this purpose; it is not much used in statistical research.

THE MEDIAN

This is not quite as easy to find, because it has to be computed by counting or calculation rather than by mere inspection. It is especially valuable when rank order, i.e., scores in order of merit, is the basis of expression of test results. Occasionally it is desirable to quote the central case, rather than the arithmetical average; and sometimes the median is chosen because further statistical treatment involves concepts which refer to the median, such as the *quartile deviation*. It is not as liable to give as distorted an impression as the mode.

THE MEAN

The mean, or arithmetical average, is the measure of central tendency most commonly used. Since it gives equal weight to each measure, it does not lend itself to giving distorted impressions, even in unusual distributions, and it is therefore dependable. Accordingly, it is used a great deal in research, and is the basis for further mathematical treatment which may be required. Several statistical techniques begin with the mean as the basis; these include *standard deviation*, and *product-moment correlation*.

These measures do not adequately describe distributions of scores, because they merely indicate concentration or central tendency. In addition, if we are to compare means, we need to know how the scores are spread, scattered, or dispersed in either direction. Aristotle knew the dual concept of mean and extreme. Having found the mean, we shall now look at the extremes—the variation or dispersion in a distribution of scores.

FOUR MEASURES OF VARIATION OR DISPERSION

THE RANGE

The *range* (Ra) is the difference between the greatest and smallest value, i.e., between the highest and lowest scores. The range embraces all the measures, and shows merely total spread. In this sense it is often unsatisfactory, because one very high or very low measure might give a false impression of the general dispersion.

Yet it is the measure of dispersion used most frequently in everyday life. Temperatures in a particular district are said to range from 55° F to 85° F. The range of prices in a shop is said to be very reasonable. Some models of autos are described as in the moderate price range. Bids at an auction sale of wool may range from 35 cents to 80 cents per pound (a range of 45 cents).

The range is found by simply subtracting the lowest score from the highest score. Sometimes a really exceptional lone score at one end may be discarded, if a misleading impression is likely to result, but of course this would not be mathematically correct. A judgement must be made as to whether an isolated lone score is the result of an error in scoring or not. For instance in a 100-yard dash, if four out of five watches gave a range from 10 seconds to 10.3 seconds, and the fifth watch gave 9 seconds—an error could be presumed.

THE MEAN DEVIATION (M.D.)

This is the "average of all the deviations from the mean." It is not much used, being superseded by the *standard deviation*. The latter is mathematically sound, while the mean deviation suffers from an apparent mathematical weakness of disregarding positive and negative signs. Perhaps for this reason it is little used.

STEPS IN FINDING THE MEAN DEVIATION

1. Find the mean.
2. Find the deviation of each measure from the mean (x).
3. Add these deviations $(\Sigma\, x)$.
4. Divide the sum of the deviations by the number of cases, that is, apply the formula:

$$\text{M.D.} = \frac{\Sigma\, x}{N}$$

The Standard Deviation (S.D. or σ)

This is really an extension of the mean deviation, in that it takes into account a greater number of cases, and appears mathematically more sound. It is less affected by sampling errors, and is customarily used in research. Mathematically, it is "the square root of the average of the squares of all the deviations from the mean." With ungrouped data, it is calculated as for mean deviation, but with two extra steps.

The standard deviation, when used with reference to the mean of a series, indicates the dispersion or spread of scores around the mean. Many research articles use this method of describing a distribution of scores in a test.

STEPS IN FINDING THE STANDARD DEVIATION: UNGROUPED DATA

1. Find the mean.
2. Find the deviation of each measure from the mean (x).
3. Square each deviation (x^2).
4. Add the squared deviations $(\Sigma\, x^2)$.
5. Find the average of the squared deviations by dividing by N.
6. Take the square root, that is, apply the formula:

$$\text{S.D. or } \sigma = \sqrt{\frac{\Sigma\, x^2}{N}}$$

Example: Calculation of standard deviation, grouped data

Find the mean and standard deviation of the weights of 15-year-old boys at a rural high school.

Name	Weight in Pounds	x	x^2
Alfred	150	$+25$	625
Ben	140	$+15$	225
Claude	135	$+10$	100
Dan	130	$+ 5$	25
Evan	125	0	0
Frank	125	0	0
Ron	120	$- 5$	25
Sam	115	-10	100
Tim	110	-15	225
Will	100	-25	625
	1250		1950

$$M = \frac{1250}{10} = 125 \text{ lb.}$$

$$\text{S.D.} = \sqrt{\frac{\Sigma x^2}{N}}$$

$$= \sqrt{\frac{1950}{10}}$$

$$= \sqrt{195}$$

$$\text{S.D.} = \pm 14 \text{ lb.}$$

The standard deviation of the weights was thus almost exactly 14 pounds (or 1 stone). We might now compare this with the standard deviation of weights of 15-year-old boys throughout the country, which is, say, 16 pounds.

We can therefore say that the weights of our small sample of boys were less dispersed (having a smaller measure of dispersion) than the national sample. In other words, the weights of our boys were more

174   PRINCIPLES OF EVALUATION IN PHYSICAL EDUCATION

concentrated around the average or mean than the national samples.

Linking this with our example of finding the mean, we can conclude that our ten rural high-school 15-year-olds, weighed less on the average (having a mean 5 pounds less than the national average), and their weights were more concentrated around this lower average than the national sample (because our standard deviation was only 14 pounds in comparison with the national standard deviation of 16). Put another way, 15-year-old boys throughout the country are heavier, with a (greater tendency to extremes in weight than our rural sample.

STEPS IN FINDING THE STANDARD DEVIATION: GROUPED DATA

With grouped data, the simplest way of finding the standard deviation is to multiply each squared deviation by its corresponding frequency, before adding them. Thus the steps are as follows:

1. Find the mean, having drawn up a frequency tabulation, with frequency column f.
2. Find the deviation of each measure from the mean (x).
3. Square each deviation (x^2).
4. Multiply each squared deviation by its corresponding frequency $[f\ (x^2)]$.
5. Apply the formula:

$$\text{S.D. or } \sigma = \sqrt{\frac{\Sigma f(x^2)}{N}}$$

EXAMPLE: Calculation of standard deviation, grouped data

What is the mean height, and the standard deviation of heights of these 40 women students majoring in physical education? Compare the results with women's national norms of 5 feet 4½ inches in height, ±2 inches S.D.

Height	Frequency f	Height Above 5 Feet m	fm	x	x^2	$f(x^2)$
6' 0"	1	12	12	+6	36	36
5' 11"	2	11	22	+5	25	50
5' 10"	0	10	0	+4	16	0

Height	Frequency f	Height Above 5 Feet m	fm	x	x^2	$f(x^2)$
5′ 9″	2	9	18	+3	9	18
5′ 8″	3	8	24	+2	4	12
5′ 7″	8	7	56	+1	1	8
5′ 6″	9	6	54	0	0	0
5′ 5″	6	5	30	−1	1	6
5′ 4″	4	4	16	−2	4	16
5′ 3″	2	3	6	−3	9	18
5′ 2″	0	2	0	−4	16	0
5′ 1″	2	1	2	−5	25	50
5′ 0″	1	0	0	−6	36	36
	$N = 40$		240			250

$$M = \frac{\Sigma (fm)}{N}$$

$$= \frac{240}{40}$$

$M = 6$ inches over 5 feet

$$S.D. = \sqrt{\frac{\Sigma f(x^2)}{N}}$$

$$= \sqrt{\frac{250}{40}}$$

$$= \sqrt{6.25}$$

$$S.D. = \pm 2.5 \text{ inches}$$

We now can describe the distribution of heights of the women physical education students. The mean height was 5 feet 6 inches, with ±2.5 inches S.D.

We can therefore say that those in our sample were taller by 1½ inches than the national norms, and also that the heights of our samples were more spread or dispersed than women of their age (as shown in the national norms). Thus, our physical-education majors were taller, and more heterogeneous in height than women generally (as shown in national norms).

There are other techniques available for large samples. References on statistics, such as those listed at the end of this chapter, usually include more advanced formulas for grouped data.

Education authorities or associations often provide special charts based on the scattergram principle (see the following chapter), which enable research workers to calculate means, standard deviations, and correlation coefficients quickly. The assumed mean method is generally favoured, and appropriate formulas are set down to allow for the calculation of these measures, where very large samples are involved. Computers and calculating machines are also playing their part in reducing mathematical drudgery, as well as susceptibility to error.

Before embarking on statistical work of the kind described in this and the next chapter, the student should ascertain what resources are available for making the calculations which may be involved. He may thus save a great deal of time and work, and be sure of correct answers.

The Quartile Deviation (Q)

This is half the distance between the upper and lower quartile points in a distribution of scores. It is thus a measure of dispersion. It is sometimes known as the semiinterquartile range.

When ungrouped scores are ranked, the *median* is the point with half the scores on either side of it, that is, with about 50 percent of scores above and about 50 percent of scores below it.

The median can thus be regarded as the point with two-quarters of the scores above it, and two-quarters of the scores below it. If we divide the ranked scores into four equal groups, the median then becomes the second or middle *quartile*.

Median

Lowest Score	Lower Quartile (25th Percentile)	Middle Quartile (50th Percentile)	Upper Quartile (75th Percentile)	Highest Score

Each quartile is a quarter of the way along the ranks. The lower quartile, or twenty-fifth percentile, is known as Q_1. The upper quartile, or seventy-fifth percentile is known as Q_3.

These two *interquartile* points of an order-of-merit list are important, since they mark off the limits of the middle 50 percent of the distribution. The difference between the score at the upper quartile (Q_3) and the score at the lower quartile (Q_1) is known as the *inter-quartile range,* and is found obviously by the formula:

$$\text{Interquartile Range} = Q_3 - Q_1$$

Half of this interquartile range marks off 25 percent of the distribution. It is called the *semiinterquartile range,* or *quartile deviation,* and is found by the formula:

$$\text{Quartile Deviation } (Q) = \frac{Q_3 - Q_1}{2}$$

This is, of course, a measure of dispersion which refers to the median, because it refers to the dispersion of 25 per cent of the scores on either side of the median.

STEPS IN FINDING THE QUARTILE DEVIATION

1. Find the range and rank the scores.
2. Find the upper quartile, by the formula:

$$Q_3 = \frac{3 \ (N + 1)}{4} \text{ th score}$$

3. Find the lower quartile, by the formula:

$$Q_1 = \frac{(N + 1)}{4} \text{ th score}$$

(Just as we find the median by the formula $(N + 1)/2$th score which locates the midpoint of the ranked scores halfway along the distribution, so we find the upper quartile by a formula which locates the point three-quarters of the way up the distribution. And we find the lower quartile by a formula which locates the point one-quarter of the way up the distribution.)

4. Subtract the score at Q_1 from the score at Q_3.
5. Divide the result by two, that is, apply the formula:

$$Q = \frac{Q_3 - Q_1}{2}$$

Example: Calculation of quartile deviation

The mathematics marks of a class of twenty-three high school boys were ranked thus:

Name	Ranked Score
Colin	100
Ian	95
Ken	90
Paul	85
Fred	82
Henry	80
Alan	79
Jim	77
Don	75
Tom	74
Neil	72
Mike	70
Stan	66
Gary	64
Ray	60
Eric	55
Quentin	51
Lou	46
Bob	36
Uriah	26
Will	15
Victor	10
Owen	0

The upper quartile is found by the formula

$$Q_3 = \frac{3 \ (N+1)}{4}\text{th score from the lowest in the distribution}$$

$$= \frac{3 \times 24}{4}\text{th score}$$

$$= \text{eighteenth score from bottom}$$

$$= 80 \text{ mark (Henry)}$$

The lower quartile is found by the formula

$$Q_1 = \frac{N+1}{4} \text{th score from the lowest in the distribution}$$

$$= \frac{24}{4} \text{th score}$$

$$= \text{sixth score from bottom}$$

$$= 46 \text{ mark (Lou)}$$

We now apply the formula

$$Q = \frac{Q_3 - Q_1}{2}$$

$$= \frac{80 - 46}{2}$$

$$= \frac{34}{2}$$

$$= \pm 17 \quad \text{mark}$$

The quartile deviation (Q) is always used with reference to the median. In the above case, we found earlier in the chapter that the median was a 70 mark. We can therefore express the median and quartile deviation as Md. 70 mark, with $Q \pm 17$ marks. The quartile deviation here is rather large, indicating a widely scattered distribution of marks. It should be noticed that the limits of the quartile deviation will coincide with Q_3 and Q_1 only in a symmetrical distribution. In a skewed distribution such as the above, they naturally will not coincide.

COMPARING THE FOUR MEASURES OF DISPERSION

Fig. 9.13 shows approximately the proportion of scores covered by each measure of dispersion, in a normal distribution. One quartile deviation covers 50 percent of all scores, or about 25 percent either side of the median. One mean deviation covers 57.7 percent of all scores, or about 28.85 percent either side of the mean. One standard deviation covers 68.26 percent of all scores, or about 34.13 percent either side of the mean. The range covers 100 percent of all scores.

If the distribution is skewed, or the sample is small, the measures of dispersion will not always mark off these exact proportions of cases.

HINTS ON INTERPRETING MEASURES OF DISPERSION

1. A *large* measure of dispersion indicates a widely scattered distribution of scores, or the presence of one or more very extreme cases. If the measure of dispersion is large, the sample is heterogeneous, as far as the results of that test are concerned. A graph of the scores would tend to be platykurtic, bimodal, or markedly skewed.

2. A *small* measure of dispersion indicates a concentrated distribution of scores, and probably no extreme cases. If the measure of dis-

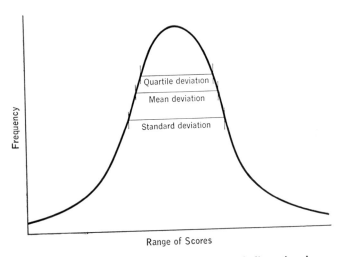

FIG. 9.13. Comparing the four measures of dispersion in a normal distribution.

persion is small, the sample is homogeneous, as far as the results of that test are concerned. A graph of the scores would in this case tend to be leptokurtic and symmetrical.

3. In a fairly normal or symmetrical distribution of scores, with a large sample, the standard deviation value will be about a fifth or a sixth of the range. In our example with grouped data, the S.D. of 2.5 inches was almost exactly one-fifth of the Ra. of 12 inches. On a bell-shaped frequency polygon, approximating the normal curve of distribution, the limits of one standard deviation occur just about where the

shape of the curve changes direction, that is, where the concave shape of the lower extremes becomes a convex shape as it rises towards the mode (see Fig. 9.14).

4. Similarly, in fairly normal distributions with large samples, the mean deviation value will be about one-seventh of the range. With small samples, this proportion would tend to be higher.

5. Again, in fairly normal distributions, with large samples, the quartile deviation value will be about one-eighth of the range. With small samples, this proportion would tend to be higher. In our example, Q of 17 inches was only a sixth of the range, being much higher than

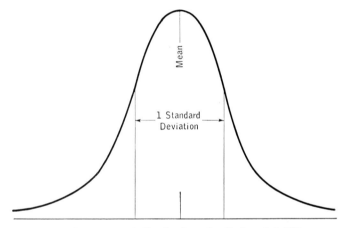

FIG. 9.14. In a normal distribution, the limits of 1 S.D. occur about where the curve changes direction.

one would expect in a normal distribution, and reinforcing the conclusion (already made because of the large value of Q) that the marks were widely scattered.

WHEN TO USE EACH MEASURE OF DISPERSION

The range is used when the data are few, and when other measures are not justified. It is a quick estimate of dispersion, when just the total spread needs to be indicated. It can be found by inspection.

The mean deviation is not used often, except when it is desired to weight all deviations according to actual size. It is used with reference to the mean.

The standard deviation is used most frequently. It is the measure with the highest reliability, and the accepted measure of dispersion for research purposes. It weights deviations slightly more heavily than the mean deviations, so that it has the advantage of allowing extreme scores to influence its value. It is always used with reference to the mean. It lends itself to further mathematical treatment. And it can also be the basis of coefficients of correlation, of measures of reliability, etc.

The quartile deviation provides a fairly quick measure of dispersion. It has the advantage of not being influenced by extreme scores at either end of the distribution. Therefore, where there are scattered, odd, extreme measures, particularly with small samples, it is usually advisable to use the quartile deviation. The quartile deviation is always used with reference to the median.

Percentiles, Deciles, etc.

Just as we can find the quartile points in a distribution of ranked scores, so we can also find points at any other proportion along the ranks. A common interval is hundredths, i.e., in terms of what percentage of scores are above or below a particular score. No matter how many scores there are in a distribution, a score which is halfway along the ranks will be 50 percent of the way along. Thus we can compare scores in different tests, in terms of the *percentile rank* which each score occupies in its own distribution.

The percentile rank of a particular score expresses the percentage of scores *below* it in that ranked distribution.[2] For example, a score with a percentile rank of 90 has 90 per cent of scores below it (and 10 per cent of scores above it). A score with a percentile rank of 55 has 55 per cent of scores below it, i.e., is just above the median (50 percent) score. A score with a percentile rank of 4 has only 4 per cent of the scores below it, and is of course one of the lowest scores in the distribution.

---

[2] Some sources reverse this, considering a percentile rank of a particular score to express the percentage of scores *above* it, in a ranked distribution.

1. Rank the scores.
2. Draw up a frequency tabulation of score units.
3. Count the number of scores below the score in question.
4. Divide this number of scores by N, and multiply by 100, that is, apply the formula:

$$\text{Percentile rank of a score} = \frac{100 \ (\text{lower scores})}{N}$$

EXAMPLE: Calculation of percentile rank of a score, ungrouped data

In the standing broad jump, measured in inches, forty boys scored as follows. What are the percentile ranks for 79 inches and 73 inches?

Inches	Tallies	Frequency
96	/	1
95		0
94		0
93	/	1
92		0
91	/	1
90		0
89		0
88	/	1
87	/	1
86	//	2
85	/	1
84	//	2
83	/	1
82		0
81	/	1
80	//	2
79	///	3
78	////	4
77	//	2
76	///	3
75	///	3
74	//	2

Inches	Tallies	Frequency
73	/	1
72	//	2
71	/	1
70		0
69	/	1
68		0
67	/	1
66	/	1
65		0
64		0
63	/	1
62		0
61		0
60	/	1
		—
		$N = 40$

1. The ranked score units, with frequencies, are listed above.
2. Count the scores below 73; 8 boys scored below 73.
3. Apply the formula:

$$\text{Percentile rank of a score} = \frac{100 \ (\text{number of lower scores})}{N}$$

$$= \frac{100 \ (8)}{40}$$

$$73 = \text{20th percentile}$$

4. Count the scores below 79. Assuming that the scores are evenly distributed throughout each class interval (for 79 inches is theoretically a class interval of 78½–79½ inches) we would choose the median score of the three scores of 79 inches. *One* of the scores in the 79-inch interval would therefore be included as *below* the chosen score. Including *one* of the scores in the 79-inch interval, there are 24 scores below the chosen score.
5. Apply the formula:

$$\text{percentile rank of } 79 = \frac{100 \times 24}{40}$$

$$= \text{60th percentile}$$

1. Rank the scores.
2. Draw up a frequency tabulation in score units.
3. The reverse is now applied, compared with the previous example.
   Apply the formula:

$$\text{Score} = \frac{\text{Percentile} \times N}{100} + 1$$

EXAMPLE: For the 20th percentile

$$\text{Score} = \frac{20 \times 40}{100} + 1$$

$$= (8 + 1)$$

$$= 9\text{th score from lowest}$$

$$= 73 \text{ inches}$$

EXAMPLE: For the 60th percentile

$$\text{Score} = \frac{60 \times 40}{100} + 1$$

$$= (24 + 1)$$

$$= 25\text{th score from lowest}$$

$$79 \text{ inches}$$

It will be noticed that the formulas for percentiles have the same basis as those for median and quartiles.

In a similar way, *deciles* can be found by using 10 instead of 100 in the formulas. Thus, the second decile in the above example is again 73 inches, and the sixth decile is again 79 inches.

A school principal may ask to see examination papers of pupils occupying these positions: top, ninth decile, upper quartile, median, lower quartile, first decile, and bottom. These points in a distribution involving fairly large numbers of pupils can provide school administrators with a good idea of the range of achievement throughout the sample.

STEPS IN FINDING THE PERCENTILE RANKS: GROUPED DATA

1. Draw up a frequency tabulation of the grouped data, to show frequency for each class interval.

2. Starting from the bottom, construct a cumulative frequency total, thus: beside each frequency, write the total scores below it. In the example which follows, there are no scores below the lowest class interval, so 0 is written in the t column. There is one score below the 70–79 class interval, so 1 is written in the t column. There are two scores below the 80–89 class interval, so 2 is written in the t column. And so on, until the top of the column is reached. Here the cumulative total plus the frequency for that class interval should equal N. To check the cumulative totals, the sum of the highest f and t entries should be written in a space above the t column, and should be the same as N.

3. These t totals mark off the cumulative frequencies at the bottom of each class interval. For instance, the total 12 in the t column opposite the class interval 100–109 represents those scores in all the class intervals *below* 100 feet. To adjust each t entry so that it truly represents the midpoint of each class interval, we must naturally add half the frequency for each class interval to its t entry. Thus, the third step is to write down half the frequencies in the next column, which is labelled $\frac{1}{2}f$.

4. Next, add each half-frequency to each t entry, to provide a cumulative frequency total which truly represents the midpoints of each class interval. This column is the $t + \frac{1}{2}f$ column.

5. To scale these measures so that they represent a hypothetical 100 cases, we now multiply the $t + \frac{1}{2}f$ column entries by $100/N$ which in our example is $100/400$ or $\frac{1}{4}$. Thus we divide by 4 to obtain percentile ranks.

EXAMPLE: *Calculation of percentile ranks,* grouped data

Find the percentile ranks for these scores of 400 high-school boys in base ball throw for distance. (See table on p. 187.)

THE RELIABILITY OF MEASURES AND STATISTICAL SIGNIFICANCE

We should now consider how significant any measure of central tendency (e.g., the mean) or of dispersion (e.g., the standard deviation) really is.

Distance in Feet (Class Intervals)	Frequency f (N = 400)	Cumulative Total t (N = 400)	Half-Frequency ½f	Total Adjusted to Class Interval Midpoints t + ½f	Per-centile Rank
310–319	1	399	0.5	399.5	99.875
300–309	1	398	0.5	398.5	99.625
290–299	2	396	1	397	99.25
280–289	2	394	1	395	98.75
270–279	6	388	3	391	97.75
260–269	8	380	4	384	96
250–259	8	372	4	376	94
240–249	8	364	4	368	92
230–239	16	348	8	356	89
220–229	16	332	8	340	85
210–219	24	308	12	320	80
200–209	32	276	16	292	73
190–199	24	252	12	264	66
180–189	32	220	16	236	59
170–179	40	180	20	200	50
160–169	32	148	16	164	41
150–159	28	120	14	134	33.5
140–149	24	96	12	108	27
130–139	20	76	10	86	21.5
120–129	24	52	12	64	16
110–119	24	28	12	40	10
100–109	16	12	8	20	5
90–99	8	4	4	8	2
80–89	2	2	1	3	0.75
70–79	1	1	0.5	1.5	0.375
60–69	1	0	0.5	0.5	0.125

Let us return to the example used earlier in this chapter, in which we found that the mean weight of ten 15-year-old boys at a rural high school was 125 pounds. Any single measure such as this mean (or the Standard Deviation of ± 14 lbs.) is called a *statistic,* and refers just to this sample of ten boys tested. We can now ask how typical our sample is, in relation to the whole population of 15-year-old boys of which it is a very small part. We could also ask how the mean of our sample compares with the true mean of that particular population. This true mean is a measure referring to the whole population. Such a measure is known as a *parameter*.

Of course, the true mean or parameter is unknown unless we test the whole of that particular population, and this would take too much time and labour. But we can indicate with a certain degree of confidence the limits within which the true mean might be expected to lie.

We have already pointed out in Chapter 8 how our sample should include a cross-section of the whole of that population, that is of all the 15-year-old boys in the country. Our 10 country boys certainly do not constitute a representative sample!

Supposing a large scale experiment involving a large representative sample of 15-year-old boys found that the mean weight was 130 pounds. How reliable is this mean?

The reliability of the mean depends on three factors: (1) the impartiality of the sample—it must be representative; (2) the number of cases—obviously the nearer the number of cases approaches the total of that population, the more reliable any statistic will be; and (3) the standard deviation—with a small standard deviation we can be fairly certain that unmeasured cases not in our sample would tend to fall close to the obtained mean.

Thus, we can state that the reliability of a mean will be greater if the sample is representative, N is large, and the S.D. is small. The last two make up the components for the formula which is used when assessing the reliability of the mean. This measure is called the standard error of the mean, and is found by this formula (when the sample is fairly large):

$$\text{Standard Error of the Mean (S.E.}_m) = \frac{\text{S.D.}}{\sqrt{N}}$$

Because the standard error of the mean indicates the *reliability* or *stability* of the mean, it can be used to determine the degree of confidence we can have that the standard error of the mean embraces the true mean of the whole of that population. This principle is elaborated in many standard statistical texts, and deals with such statistics as the mean, the standard deviation, the coefficient of correlation, and so forth.

This brings us to the concept of *levels of confidence* and *confidence limits*. These are best illustrated by the *difference* between two statistics. Our example could be the mean of 130 pounds in the large sample of 15-year-old boys, and the mean of 125 pounds for the 10 rural boys. How significant is this difference, in which the country boys are 5 pounds lighter? How confident can we be that similar experiments would show the country boys to be lighter? Or was our difference just due to fluctuations in sampling?

One technique for determining such confidence in our difference is known as the *null hypothesis*. This assumes that there is *no* significant difference between the means of the two samples, unless proved otherwise. By using the properties of the normal curve of distribution, the likelihood of a *significant difference* can be proved.

Two *levels of confidence* are usually proposed. The 5 percent level of confidence indicates that there is only a 5 percent chance that the difference would not occur, i.e., in 95 experiments out of 100, rural boys would be found to be lighter than 15-year-old boys in general. The 1 percent level of confidence is much stricter, indicating a level of confidence that a similar result would occur 99 times out of 100 experiments. This 1 percent level is used most by statisticians. A difference which meets the 1 percent confidence limit is said to be a *statistically significant* difference (to the 1 percent level of confidence). These confidence limits can be determined by quite simple formulae, described in most statistical texts.

RECOMMENDED READING

Bloomers, P., and E. F. Lindquist, *Elementary Statistics in Psychology and Education,* New York, Houghton Mifflin, 1960.

Garrett, H. E., *Statistics in Psychology and Education,* New York, Longmans, Green, 1953.

Guilford, J. P., *Fundamental Statistics in Psychology and Education,* New York, McGraw-Hill, 1950.

Huff, Darrell, *How to Lie with Statistics,* New York, Norton, 1954.

McCloy, C. H., *Tests and Measurements in Health and Physical Education,* New York, Appleton-Century-Crofts, 1954.

Scott, G., and E. French, *Evaluation in Physical Education,* St. Louis, Mosby, 1950.

Vernon, P. E., *The Measurement of Abilities,* London University Press, 1949.

chapter 10

ABILITIES AND THEIR ASSESSMENT

TESTS or quizzes are scored and examinations marked with one of the following aims in mind:

1. To assess the subjects' performances in the same thing *at the same time,* e.g., measuring the heights of a class of boys, or marking a set of knowledge tests.

2. To assess the subjects' performances in the same thing at different times, e.g., measuring the growth of a boy *over a period* (that is, measuring changes through time), or marking examinations which can be compared with results of tests at the start of a semester, to assess progress at the end of the semester. For example, we might test intelligence upon entry into school, and look at this in relation to scores in math, English, history, etc., at the end of the first semester.

3. To assess subjects' performances in different things at the same time, e.g., testing strength and speed, or examining in English and mathematics, with a view to comparing relative ability in the two fields, or finding the relationship of one ability to the other.

4. To assess subjects' performances in different things at different times, for example, testing strength and speed over a period to assess relative progress in each factor.

The great majority of tests have the first aim, but many of these would be more purposeful if they were modified to have the second aim. It is usually of more value to have a measure of progress over a period, than to have but one measure of ability, even when it can be compared with measures of other individuals. It is more useful to know what is happening to Bill as time goes on, than to know how he compares with the rest of his class.

ASSESSING PERFORMANCE IN THE SAME THING
AT THE SAME TIME

There are five main methods of measuring, scoring or marking.

Direct Measurement

This is generally a highly objective form of measurement, and can be extremely accurate if the measuring device is sound, if it is correctly used, and if the thing being measured does not fluctuate. Examples of direct measurement are those of height, and of girth in inches, of speed in seconds, of weight and of strength in pounds. (Each of these, as with so many characteristics of living things, does vary slightly compared to the constancy of inanimate things, such as the specific gravity of lead, the atomic weight of hydrogen, etc.)

Count-Scoring

This type of measurement is also objective, since the scorer has only to count the number of strokes or repetitions. Examples of count-scoring are a round of golf, where the scorer counts the number of strokes required to propel a ball into the eighteen holes of the course; tests of ball skills, where the scorer counts the number of passes, throws, hits, or catches; archery or other target scores; short-answer examinations such as true/false or multiple-choice tests; or arithmetical sums, where the marker scores the number right. The possible errors may be due to lapses of concentration and other human failings, but are not inherent in the method.

This form of measurement usually involves one or both of two scoring principles: first, the *time* taken to finish a set task, e.g., the 100-yard dash, and the *performance* in set tasks, e.g., putting the shot. Often time and performance are combined, e.g., in rapid-fire rifle shooting, and most intelligence tests. These principles are often known as *rate* and *power*. Most examinations combine rate and power by imposing a time limit, and by including graded items from quite easy to quite difficult questions.

Variables in physical education lend themselves more readily to this type of measurement than assessments in most other subjects, because so much of our work in physical education involves direct measurement or count-scoring. It is easier to measure weight with scales, and to measure it accurately, than to assess intelligence with an intelligence test, or ability at English with an examination.

Even so, many physical-education activities aim for quality of movement. In dance, for example, where quality is an important feature, problems of assessment are presented, of similar difficulty to those encountered in English, history, music, art, etc., where quality is essential.

Direct measurement and count-scoring usually involve equal units of measurement, such as inches, pounds, seconds, or repetitions. In general the measured difference between 99 and 100 pounds *is exactly the same as* the difference between 120 and 121 pounds, or anywhere else in the scale. Also, these units may range from zero to any upper limit.

In a simple arithmetic or true/false test, also, each answer can be worth an equal mark, and a candidate can conceivably score zero. This assumes that each question is of equal difficulty, but of course they rarely are. But they are weighted the same, and the scoring progression is arithmetical.

But count-scoring is sometimes based on a different principle. The units of scoring may be the same, but the questions of tasks get more difficult. In golf, the beginner finds it much easier to improve from 150 to 140 per round, than does the expert to improve from 75 to 65. It would be more realistic to compare the improvement from 150 to 140 with that of from 75 to 70—in the category of a geometric progression. Even this is not quite accurate, for this lower geometric interval still represents a more difficult golf improvement than the higher one.

In a similar way, in the 100-yard dash, the difference between units of 1 second are by no means equal in the opinion of the sprinter. It is easier to improve from 11 to 10 seconds than from 10 to 9 seconds. In fact, although a generation ago the world record was 9.3 seconds, no runner today has had a time of less than 9 seconds officially recognised. And in such events, there is no zero time, or score, for the perfect contestant.

The fixing of approximately equal units and an arbitrary zero is even more difficult in mental tests and in examinations. For, though many a teacher may sometimes be tempted, he can hardly be certain that a pupil has exactly zero ability in any given subject.

All the same, despite these difficulties, count-scoring, with its high degree of objectivity, is an accurate method.

NUMERICAL ASSESSMENT

This method of scoring involves the assigning of marks, usually out of a set maximum such as 10, 20, or 100, for a performance or examination. This is an inferior type of marking, usually being very subjective and unreliable, and the validity suffers as a result. These represent major statistical weaknesses, yet the method remains a common one of marking examinations, despite the tremendous advances in statistical measurement during the past fifty years. There is no constant basis for comparing one performance with another, except that which is in the examiner's head.

Common examples of numerical assessment include assigning of percentage marks in examinations, by subjective scoring; subjective assessments of numerical scores for interview results; and scoring numerically in diving and gymnastic events. There are many weaknesses and idiosyncrasies of examiners in assigning numerical assessments. For example, the majority of examination results out of 100—when the pass mark is 50—show many scores between 50 and 55 and relatively few between 45 and 50. This is quite contrary to chance probabilities, even if the mode is well above 50. Again, in diving and gymnastic competitions, or in interviews, examiners have favourite marks, and marks which they avoid, such as 0, 1, 4, and 10 out of 10. Frequency distributions of such tests or interview scores often bear little resemblance to appropriate probability curves.

There are however, many ways of improving numerical assessments, to make them statistically more valid, reliable, and objective: use of more than one examiner or judge, use of "outside" judges unfamiliar with the candidates, combination of several separate tests rather than one examination, use of objectively scored items combined with subjective ones, and systematising of marking systems, so that a consistent basis of marking or scoring is achieved. For example, the criteria for scoring diving could be standardized, in terms of approach and take-off, execution of the dive in the air, and entry, so that each examiner at least begins by attempting to assess the same aspects of the performance. And the process could be (and is) taken further by setting up standards and criteria for each part of the dive, establishing certain marks for, say, deficient, inferior, fair, good, very good, etc. This would minimize the wide fluctuations brought about by "hard" or "easy" marking by different examiners or judges.

LETTER GRADING AND SCORING ACCORDING TO A SCALE

This is really an abbreviated form of numerical assessment, with the results expressed in words, or letters, or on a scale. Consequently, they are subject to the same eccentricities of examiners and the same errors of statistics. While being similarly subjective and unreliable, the system does not pretend to be able to discriminate between digits or units of a hundred or so marks. It merely classifies them into a few broad grades so that the susceptibility to error is at least less evident though proportionately no less real.

Examples of this system are:

1. *Letter Grades,* e.g., A, B, C, D, and E (five-point scale), or the same cloaked in the guise of classical respectability—alpha, beta, gamma, delta, epsilon. Sometimes this five-point scale in letter form is elaborated by the addition of a plus or minus for each letter, converting it to a fifteen-point scale. At other times a three-point scale A, B, and C is used, which, similarly, can be converted into a nine-point scale by plus or minus elaborations to each letter.

2. *Figures* in the form of a three-, five-, or ten-point scale, or even seven-, fifteen-, or twenty-point scales. An odd number is most common, so that the central number can be assigned to performances given a midscore.

3. *Words.* Often in school reports, performances of pupils are described in words, such as, Excellent, Good, Average, Passing, Failing.[1]

As for systems using letter grades, the distribution of scores in each category should usually conform roughly to the pattern of the normal distribution curve. For example, 80 students so graded would tend to be distributed something in the nature of 5 A's, 20 B's, 30 C's, 20 D's and 5 E's; or with words, 5 Excellent, 20 Good, 30 Average, 20 Passing, and 5 Failing. Exactly such a distribution would, of course, never happen, but a distribution quite remote from the normal distribution pattern would indicate abnormalties in the test, the sample of subjects,

---

[1] Including the almost meaningless term "Very Fair."

or the scoring system, *i.e.*, that the test, the class, or the scoring system, was not a usual one.

In knowledge tests and examinations in various school subjects, the popular scores for each grade are often: Excellent—90 plus; Good—80–89; Average—70–79; Passing—60–69; Failing—59 or less. This system appears a little flattering, since one would expect average scores to be nearer the midpoint of the scale. A more realistic scale, we believe, is the following one, used in New Zealand University examination marks: Excellent—75 plus; Good—65–74; Satisfactory—50–64; Failing—35–49; Inferior—34 or less. More people would fail with this score arrangement, but this would be expected in examinations where the passing standard is rather stringent.

The use of words in evaluation is dealt with also in Chapter 3.

Ranking

Ranking consists of putting the scores or marks in rank order, that is, in order of merit or attainment. This, of course, can be a further stage in the treatment of examination or test results that have been scored in any of the ways mentioned previously in this chapter, for any set of scores can be ranked (see Chapter 8). Often ranking is used as a method of scoring itself, for example, the ranking list on a club tennis ladder. The members are listed in order of attainment in tennis, and this rank order can be altered by play-offs between members in the ranking list. It is also common socially amongst hens who have a "pecking order," or among people who are conscious of social status. Again, it is sometimes used to assess written tests or assignments, such as essays. The examiner reads each essay, and places them in what he considers to be order of merit. He may or may not later assign marks to them, but may just put up the ranking list.

Examples of ranking are found in connection with ladders in club tennis, table-tennis, badminton, volleyball, curling, etc.; points tables at any stage in a season for football, baseball, basketball, etc.; seedings in tennis, track and field, or team sport, particularly as a basis for a national tournament; the "Top Ten Tunes of the Week/Year" (sometimes!)[2] and Hit Parades; first, second and third prize in a show or

---

[2] It is dangerous to assume that what is impressive statistically is necessarily honest.

country fair; "Sportsman of the Year"; "Top Ten Films of 1961."

Ranking is usually not very sound as a method of assessment, but may be the most suitable if count-scoring is not possible. It has definite weaknesses, but these are fairly obvious, and are usually taken into account, in contrast to the often-forgotten weaknesses of numerical assessment.

First, *position* only and not *score value* is taken into account. There is not a numerical scale of the usual type where cardinal numbers or score quantities are used, the units of which carry approximately equal weighting. The ranks are evenly spaced, and thus outstandingly good or bad scores do not show up as such, while any big gaps in numerical scoring are not apparent either.

Second, it is generally used only with a small sample, because it becomes unwieldy with large numbers. After all, with more than a dozen or so, it is difficult to rank accurately, especially with the middle cases of the distribution. Ranking from subjective marks or scores, with large numbers of cases, is highly suspect as a statistical device. Usually only the extreme cases are easy to separate out into their appropriate rank.

Thirdly, the number in the total group is an essential part of the expression of any rank. "I came fifth" sounds pretty good, but not if it is out of five. But "I came fifth" in a national examination, with 20,000 candidates, is worth writing home about. The rank is applicable only to that particular group, and to the size of the sample.

Lastly, ranking is based on *rectangular* distribution, because position only is taken into account. This is quite unlike the normal probability distribution, even though a graph of the actual scores of the same test might approximate a normal curve. For the last two reasons, comparing ranks in two or more sets of scores may give quite misleading results. For example, the fifth out of five should not be compared with the fifth out of 20,000 in a national examination.

PERCENTILE, DECILE OR QUARTILE RANKING

Using the method described in constructing a cumulative frequency table, the *percentile rank* of any score can be obtained. A person with a percentile rank of 90 knows that only 10 percent of the group scored better than he did. A person with a percentile rank of 25 (i.e., Q_1, or the first or lower quartile) knows that three-fourths of the group scored better, and only a quarter of the group scored worse than he did.

School principals or heads of departments, in order to judge a teacher's standards, may ask to see examination papers at the three quartiles (i.e., Q_3, median, and Q_1); or perhaps the best paper, those at the 90th, 75th, 50th, 25th, 10th percentiles, and the worst paper. These papers would provide samples of standards throughout the class, from best through intermediate levels to worst.

ASSESSING PERFORMANCE IN THE SAME THING AT DIFFERENT TIMES

This is commonly used as a means of evaluating progress in a subject or skill during any particular course, semester, or year. One has to make sure that the tests given at the beginning and repeated at the end are comparable, and that any "practice effect," or other known influence, is taken into account. Also the conditions for testing and administration of the tests must be as nearly identical as practicable.

Then again, it must be remembered that any improvement may be due to the process of time, in terms of maturation, development, greater enthusiasm, and incidental learning, rather than to the efforts of the teacher in that particular course.

To give a basis of comparison which allows for incidental learning, it is necessary to have two groups tested, each as nearly even as possible; one, "the control group," will be given no special instruction in whatever is being tested, while the other one undergoes the course, instruction, or experiment. This latter is the "experimental group." The tests are repeated at the end of the course, and usually improvement is found with both control and experimental groups. Any significantly greater improvement with the experimental group, can usually be attributed to the instruction or experiment, provided care is taken to note all other possible causes of difference.

A classical experiment of this type is the one done in 1959 at the University of Lexington, by Dr. Ernst Jokl. In a high school that previously had had no physical-education programme (only sport)[3] two parallel classes were chosen. Each child was given a thorough medical examination, a battery of four cardiac efficiency tests, performance tests, and psychometric tests. One class, the control group, continued

[3] We deliberately beg this question.

with no physical education; the other, the experimental group, had a period a day of physical education of a European kind. After a set period the children in both groups were tested in all the ways used in the pre-experiment examination. This is the most comprehensive experiment of which we have knowledge. There are also somewhat similar experiments done by T. K. Cureton at the University of Illinois, and in the Medford Study, by Harrison Clarke at the University of Oregon.

The problem often arises as to how to carry out such experiments without causing hardship to the control group, which gets none of the particular instruction during the period. This problem can be overcome in several ways.

Take the example of, say, 200 ninth grade girls. You are anxious to see what effect instruction in either dance or track and field has on them. The sample can be divided into two groups each of 100. Tests of both rhythmical ability and track ability are given to both groups. One group is instructed in, say, rhythm and dance, for the first semester, while the other group is given track coaching. The first group becomes the experimental group for dance, and the control group for athletics, while the second group becomes the control group for dance and the experimental group for athletics. At the end of the first semester both groups are retested in both rhythmical ability and athletic ability.

The next semester, the teaching content is reversed. The first group is instructed in athletics and the second group does dance and rhythm. The role of each group as experimental or control group becomes the reverse of what it was in the first semester. At the end of the second semester both groups are retested in both abilities. Now the three sets of results—those before and after the first semester, and after the second semester, can be assessed and compared. Any significant differential improvement in any experimental group compared with its appropriate control group can be attributed to the instruction in that subject, as long as all the results, and the conduct of the experiment, meet reasonable statistical requirements.

A second field where assessments at different times in the same thing are compared is in the growth and physique of children. The mere comparison of height and/or weight at the beginning and end of a period, as an indication of healthy growth is an oversimplification of the situation in a complex and subtle area. This question is discussed in Chapter 12.

There is a third situation where assessments in a test are compared with assessments in the same test administered at a later date. This is where the reliability or consistency of a test is being assessed. This process is discussed later in this chapter, when correlation is explained.

ASSESSING PERFORMANCE IN DIFFERENT THINGS AT THE SAME TIME

This situation is very common in evaluation. Teachers usually want to see how a class measures up, in midyear, or at the end of the course, and end-of-the-year examinations are fairly general in schools. Many methods of constructing tests are used, including some relatively sound ones and some not so sound. The construction of tests is discussed in the next chapter.

What concerns us here are the ways of assigning marks. Count-scoring, numerical assessment, letter grades, and ranking methods are all used, depending on what is being assessed. While some of the less objective and less valid methods of assigning marks are the best available in many circumstances, it must be realised that they limit the uses to which the marks can be put afterwards. They can be used in each subject or examination as a measure of achievement. But numerical assessments of a subjective type do not lend themselves to much sound statistical treatment. And this is particularly true if we wish to assess performance in several things, and then compare them, or add them. Scholarships and prizes in some places have been awarded in the past on the basis of the sum of several examination marks for each candidate, when the marks themselves were obtained on a not very sound basis, or when the marking system was not suitable for totalling marks on any statistically sound basis. There are ways of putting together marks, however wrongly given, but their limitations should be realised and admitted.

Perhaps the most useful of these devices is the *profile*, used to combine or compare several results. First, it should include a simple marking system, such as letter grades, or simple numerical scale, for instance, a five-point scale. Secondly, it does not produce a total aggregate mark, which in most cases would be statistically unsound, but rather a total visual impression of the several results.

The profile is generally constructed by using large-squared paper, so that there is a horizontal line for each assessment, and a vertical line, for each letter grade or point on, say, a five-point scale. The examiner writes the subjects or topics down the left-hand side, and puts a cross on the appropriate score for each subject, along the line. In the example below, the best scores (excellent) are on the left. The crosses are then joined to give a "profile."

Profile for Students Applying to Become Teachers

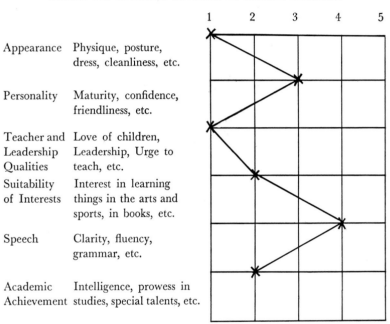

| | | 1 | 2 | 3 | 4 | 5 |

Appearance — Physique, posture, dress, cleanliness, etc.

Personality — Maturity, confidence, friendliness, etc.

Teacher and Leadership Qualities — Love of children, Leadership, Urge to teach, etc.

Suitability of Interests — Interest in learning things in the arts and sports, in books, etc.

Speech — Clarity, fluency, grammar, etc.

Academic Achievement — Intelligence, prowess in studies, special talents, etc.

1—excellent;   2—good;   3—satis-factory;   4—poor;   5—inferior.

Profiles are most useful for summarising several sets of scores, in order to show a complete picture of a series of tests. They are especially suitable as a basis for recording assessments during interviews, particularly because a person's strong fields tend to give a "halo" effect in an interview, and his weaknesses submerge. The subjective ratings of the examiner can be entered quickly on previously prepared forms, and the assessments for each candidate can later be compared. They are often used by selection panels interviewing candidates for positions, in talent contests, "Miss World" or "Miss Galaxy" competitions, and such, but not always in choosing Miss Alpha Theta Epsilon of 1965, or the Dream Honey of Palooka State High, or the "top tune!"

USES FOR PROFILES

The profile is not limited to subjective, simple assessments of the above kind. The method stands on its own merits as a useful graphical form of expressing results. It can accordingly be used on examination reports, and reports of pupils' schoolwork for parental perusal. It is often the method used on cumulative and other school-record cards of each pupil's progress through the school. A glance at the line joining the crosses shows the reader an immediate picture of total or aggregate score, and the nearer the whole line or "profile" reaches the excellent side of the graph, the higher is the assessment of that pupil's progress or achievement. It does require careful interpretation though, in two ways. Not all components of the profile may be equally important, and not all markers who supply the items mark with equal severity. A wise principal, director, or head of a department, learns to know who are the generous markers and who are the hard markers on his staff. In looking at the profile he is then able to make appropriate compensations.

Thus, the statistical weaknesses of the profile, which uses rough or subjective assessments, can be realised if we try to add and compare totals of test results as shown on the profile. This can be true also of examination totals in various subjects, if we try to add and compare the results of different individuals. And yet—as in the following example— unsound techniques are often used.

COMPARING AGGREGATE TOTALS

Suppose you have the task of finding the top scholar academically[4] of the school, from candidates' results in six subjects. The three best pupils scored as shown in the table on page 203 (their rank is in brackets).

These three boys each had an average rank of third in their six subjects, having two firsts, a third, a fourth, and two fifths each. Yet Alan

---

[4] In New Zealand, known as the "dux."

	Alan	Bob	Colin
English	65 (5th)	75 (1st)	70 (3rd)
French	60 (5th)	70 (1st)	65 (4th)
Mathematics	100 (1st)	90 (3rd)	80 (5th)
Science	95 (1st)	85 (4th)	75 (5th)
History	78 (3rd)	75 (5th)	80 (1st)
Physical education	82 (4th)	75 (5th)	85 (1st)
Total	480	470	455

scores a higher total of points. This is due to the fact that he is the only candidate to score more than 90 in any subject. Admittedly he comes first in these subjects. Bob and Colin came first in two subjects each; yet they could score only between 70 and 85 for first place. You might argue that this is an unusual case, but it so happens that the subjects in which Alan scored over 90 were math and science. Generally, it is easier to score the possible 100 percent in these two subjects, because the data consist of factual problems which, if the candidate gets them right, score the full mark. But in other subjects, particularly English, languages, and discursive subjects, where expression and interpretation are essential, it is very difficult to score a nearly full mark (unless questions are purely factual, and this type of question may defeat the purpose of the subject, as discussed in Chapter 11). It is usual for top marks in science and math to be close to 100 percent, and in languages to be nearer 80 percent. If the marks in each subject are merely added, obviously students excelling in math and science would gain the highest totals.

To give each candidate an equal chance, each subject should be *weighed* or *scaled*.

SCALING TO A RANGE

If you are faced with a number of different marked items from different scores, there is a quick method of making all the sets of scores have about the same range. It is unfair to those with extreme marks, but offsets an easy or hard marker. Say the scores were:

	(Miss X) Hygiene	(Miss Y) Posture	(Miss Z) Punctuality	(Mr. A) Sociability	(Mr. B) Sportsman-ship
Bridget	40	50	20	84	92
Diana	42	53	32	82	5
Marlene	53	64	49	75	63
Greta	25	66	51	83	37
Deborah	60	72	27	95	70
Jean	51	74	11	78	26
	—	—	—	—	—
Ra = 25–60		50–74	11–51	75–95	5–92

Inspection would tell you that Mr. A was easier to please than Miss Z. It might tell you that too, Miss X's scores are the most normal sort of distribution, though lacking in high scores. However, you could to some extent offset all their biases by arbitrarily deciding to fit each of these marks to a range of 35 percent to 80 percent. This is done by a simple device, using graph paper, useful for converting scales and ranges to each other.

On the vertical scale mark 35–80 and on the horizontal 1–100. In actuality, the graph can start horizontally at the lowest score of the

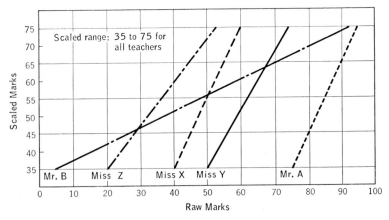

Fig. 10.1.   Graphic method of scaling to an agreed range.

lowest marker—provided it is less than your desired lower mark. In this case it is Mr. B's mark for Diana's sportsmanship.

These are usually constructed so that each set of marks conforms closely to a theoretical normal curve of distribution, since most sets of scores in education with large samples are distributed roughly according to this pattern. It is therefore a useful basis for setting up a "universal scale." With it, we can compare any performance in any test with any performance in another test whose scoring is based on the same scale.

There are three well-known standard scales, based on the properties of the normal curve of distribution, known respectively as the Z scale, the S scale, and the T scale. While Z scores are the simplest, they are unwieldy, because they nearly always involve fractional quantities and are therefore not popular. S scores have been devised to assist in working out grades in school subjects. T scores are the most popular standard scores used in physical education, being versatile and easily understood.

CONSTRUCTION OF A T SCALE

In terms of the normal distribution pattern, the T scale is based on Standard Deviation units above and below the mean.

The advantages of the T scale are that all scores are positive, that they use equal units and do not involve fractions, and that an average score is worth 50 points, (or halfway along a hundred-point scale).

Standard Deviation Units

−5 S.D.	−4 S.D.	−3 S.D.	−2 S.D.	−1 S.D.	0	+1 S.D.	+2 S.D.	+3 S.D.	+4 S.D.	+5 S.D.

T *Score Units*

0	10	20	30	40	50	60	70	80	90	100

It can be seen from the above tabulation that each standard deviation is worth 10 T scores. Working either way from the mean (worth 50 T scores), a scale of 0 to 100 in T scores represents a range from —5 S.D. to +5 S.D.

We saw in Chapter 9 that fewer than one case in a million falls outside plus or minus 5 standard deviations from the mean, and therefore the T scale range of 0 to 100 accommodates virtually all possible scores. In actual practice, the range of 20 to 80 embraces most scores, as just over one in a thousand falls outside the plus or minus 3 standard deviation range.

STEPS IN CONSTRUCTION OF A T SCALE

1. Draw up a frequency tabulation of the scores, as shown in Chapter 8. It is better in this case to have more class intervals than usual, say about 40 to 50, otherwise the scale will fail to discriminate between the persons with rather similar scores. To achieve a regular distribution with this number of class intervals a sample of at least 100 and prefer-

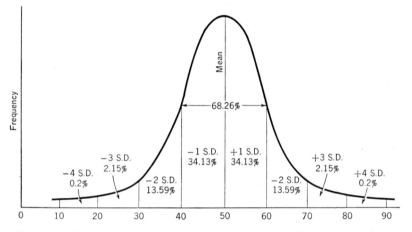

Fig. 10.2.   The normal distribution curve in terms of S.D. units, percentages of cases within each unit, and T score values for S.D. limits.

ably over 200 pupils should be tested. Total the frequencies in the column marked F.

2. Starting from the bottom, construct a cumulative frequency total, T. The way to do this (as described in finding percentile ranks, Chapter 9) is to write, beside each frequency, the total scores *below* it. In the example on page 187, there are no scores *below* the lowest class interval, so 0 is written in the T column. There is one score below the 70–79 class interval, so 1 is written in the T column. There are two scores below the 80–89 class interval, so 2 is written in the T column. And so on, till the top of the column is reached. Here the cumulative total plus the frequency for that class interval should equal N. To check the

cumulative totals, the sum of the highest F and T entries should be written in a space above the T column, and should be the same as N.

3. These T totals mark off the cumulative frequencies at the bottom of each class interval. For instance, the total 12 in the T column opposite the class interval 100–109 represents those scores in all the class intervals *below* 100 feet. To adjust each T entry so that it truly represents the midpoint of each class interval, we must naturally add half the frequency for each class interval to its T entry. Thus, the third step is to write down half the frequencies in the next column, which is labelled $\frac{1}{2} F$.

4. Next, add each half-frequency to each T entry, to provide a cumulative frequency total which truly represents the midpoints of each class interval. This column is labelled the $T + \frac{1}{2} F$ column.

5. To scale these measures so that they represent a hypothetical 100 cases, we now multiply the $T + \frac{1}{2} F$ column entries by $100/N$, which in our example is $100/400$, or $\frac{1}{4}$.

Thus we divide by 4 to obtain percentile ranks.

6. Convert the percentile ranks into T scores by using the chart at the end of this chapter. Merely read the T-score value for each percentile rank, and write in the T-score column. Use the nearest whole number or nearest half of a T score, and interpolate where necessary.

7. The T scale is now complete. It is based on approximate standard deviation values, that is, the percentage of scores which lie within 1, 2, 3, 4, or 5 S.D. from the mean. From Chapter 9, we found that 34.13 per cent of the cases lie on either side of the mean; that is, the upper limit of 1 S.D. occurs at the 84.13 percentile, and the lower limit of 1 S.D. occurs at the 15.87 percentile. Because the T scale is based on 10 T scores, representing 1 S.D., either side of a mean of 50, we would expect that a T score of 50 is an average score. In our example, a throw of 170–179 feet is average.

A T score of 60 is 1 S.D. above average. In our example, a throw of 220–229 feet is 1 S.D. above average. A T score of 49 is 1 S.D. below average. In our example, a throw of 120–129 feet is 1 S.D. below average.

Extending the T scale further, a T score of 70 is 2 S.D.'s above average. In our example, a throw of 270–279 feet is 2 S.D.'s above average.

EXAMPLE: Calculation of T scores (see page 187)

Draw up a T Scale, to show T scores for these four hundred high-school boys' results in a baseball throw for distance.

VALUES OF T SCALES

1. Raw scores of different tests can be converted into standard units for *comparing results* of one test with another.

2. Such scores are *meaningful* to students, teachers, and administrators, because they know that in all sets of scores, 50 is average, above 50 is better, and below 50 is worse.

3. The *student* can work out his relative ability in a single test, and compare it with his results in other tests. For example, a test battery in field hockey may have four tests, in which a student may gain T scores of, say, 43 in dribbling, 56 in goal shooting, 60 in field and drive, and 62 in push pass. According to the test battery, he is much the weakest in dribbling, and can use this knowledge by concentrating on his weak skills.

4. Teachers and administrators can use T scores in different tests by adding them to obtain a single composite score. In this way students' examination results can be treated to decide the top scholar of a school, the awarding of scholarships and prizes, or the top all-around athlete.

5. In track and field, the T-scale principle is used to compare performances in different events, for diagnostic and prognostic purposes. Also, decathlon and pentathlon points systems can be constructed by using standard scales of this type. At a high school, the champion in track and field can be decided by using T scales for each event. Pupils can elect, say, four events, including at least one running, one jumping, and one throwing event. The pupil with the highest total score from his T scores in each of his four events is the champion.

6. Similar procedures can be carried out in aquatics, where achievement is swimming, diving, lifesaving, synchronised swimming, etc. can be measured in T-scale units. Relative strengths and weaknesses in aquatic skills become more obvious, giving guidance to pupils and teachers for individual practice and schedules. Composite scores can be the basis of awarding credits, badges, etc.

7. Performances in games and sports lend themselves readily to measurement with T scales. Relative skill and weakness both in the techniques of one game, and between one game and another, can be

indicated, and appropriate programmes determined. It may be possible one day to select teams from T-score results if valid tests can be constructed to predict performance in games. To do this, test batteries would need to sample all the main skills, and in addition, performances would need to approximate those of the real game situation. Individual sports, such as skiing, lend themselves to this approach much more than team games, such as football; target sports, such as archery and riflery, are more suitable than field sports, such as hockey, with court games, such as volleyball, somewhere in between. Such a technique would enable a school or group to see its own *local* winners in terms of *general* standards.

8. Gymnastics, callisthenics, and dance generally do not lend themselves readily to T-scoring, because quality of movement, rather than performance which can be quantitatively measured, is sought. At the same time, achievements charts using many activities in these fields can be constructed, based on the T-score principle. These charts can be of value in providing incentive to pupils in physical-education lessons.

CORRELATION

A second main function of assessing performances of groups in different things at the same time occurs when we wish to know the relationship of one ability to another. Much of our knowledge in general education and physical education has been extended and enriched by the measurement of relationships between variables. This is particularly true of human variables and abilities.

The relating of one ability to another is known as *correlation*. Correlation is an expression of "going-togetherness," the tendency for one ability to vary along with another ability.

For example, anyone with experience in track and field knows that most good sprinters tend to be good long jumpers, in contrast to other athletes such as high jumpers, shot putters etc. It is apparent that sprinting and long jumping have something in common, probably connected with running speed. But it does not necessarily mean that one ability causes the other. All it means is that the two abilities have common elements: that sprinters are likely to be good long jumpers, that long jumpers are likely to be good sprinters, and that high jumpers and shot putters, etc., are not likely to be as good at either sprinting or long jumping. It is important to realise the basic principle that *correlation does not necessarily mean causation*.

While we suspect that sprinting ability and broad-jumping ability have something in common, we do not know how much, unless we use a measuring device, and have a large enough sample of athletes.

An easier quality to measure and compare might be height and weight with adult men. Again we would suspect that the taller men are the heavier ones. This is indeed true generally, and there is some going togetherness between hight and weight. This going togetherness of qualities or abilities is the essence of the concept of correlation (see Chapter 12).

Correlation is implied when people say such things as: "Faster drivers have more accidents"; "Champions in sport are usually weak in schoolwork"; "Short men are the most aggressive"; and so on.

But correlation, as was said before, need not mean causation. A good example of the caution needed in interpreting apparent relationship is the lung-cancer and cigarette-smoking question of the past decade. It is true that there has been a high mathematical correlation between the incidence of lung cancer and cigarette-smoking. But there has been some lack of agreement even amongst the foremost scientists as to whether this relationship is causative, or whether some other factor, common to both, has been influencing the situation.[5] This has been one of the first great public statistical controversies, with all kinds of emotional overtones operating. No wonder the layman is confused.

To anyone in the education profession, an understanding of this concept of correlation is basic to the business of analysing and comparing human abilities. The relation is not always positive; that is, one set of figures does not always rise with the other set, as it does when comparing height and weight. One set may go up, while the other set goes down. Examples of this are found in many sciences, especially physics. For instance, as the altitude increases, the boiling point of water decreases. Again, as pressure on a gas increases, its volume decreases. These two are examples of negative correlation (in science sometimes known as an *inverse variation*). And, of course, there is often no *significant* relationship between abilities, such as weight-lifting and play-

---

[5] WHO has studied the mass of evidence on this question on a world basis and has recently come out strongly against smoking.

ing chess, or the redness of hair compared with basketball skill. Even if those of the All-American team have red hair in one year, it means nothing. It can be seen that we can have two extremes—perfect positive correlation (like direct proportion in mathematics) and perfect negative correlation (like inverse proportion in mathematics). There is a range of possibilities in between.

The commonest and simplest technique for calculating correlation uses a simple mathematical expression for its degree:

1. Two sets of scores can have perfect positive correlation. This is called a coefficient of +1.
2. Two sets of scores can have perfect negative correlation. This is called a a coefficient of −1.
3. Two sets of scores can have no significant correlation, with a coefficient of about zero (0).

An example of perfect positive correlation is the relationship between diameters and circumferences of circles. The larger the diameters, the larger the circumferences.

An example of perfect negative correlation is the relationship between the length of baselines and heights of rectangles of the same length. The greater the length of baseline, the smaller the height.

The range of possibilities between these extremes can perhaps be best illustrated by examples of low, medium, and high correlation. Take the statement. "People who are good at languages are good at mathematics." There is probably a slight or low positive correlation here, because the most intelligent people will tend to be good at both, and both tend to be subjects taken by bright students.

Again, "The greater the height of men, the greater their weight." This has been found to be of medium or moderate positive correlation, since taller people tend to be heavier, though not always (see Chapter 12). Or again, "The students who do well in class in one year will do well the next year." This is usually of high positive correlation, because only a few students in a class are likely to change their rank from near the top to near the bottom from one year to the next—however, we must learn to tolerate and investigate these changes when they do happen. The cause may be important. Dropping a child for a team, or punishing him for a fall-off in customary performance level is educationally unsound.

In a similar way, there are possibilities of negative correlation being low, medium, or high. "The higher the latitude of a place, the lower is its average daily temperature," is an example of low or medium negative correlation, since many other factors other than latitude are operating on temperature, such as altitude, distance from the sea, effect of warm or cool ocean currents, etc. "The higher the altitude, the lower the air temperature." This is an example of high negative correlation, because it is nearly always so, except in such cases as an *inversion* in atmospheric temperature.

And lastly there are the thousands of cases of little or no correlation, either positive or negative. For example, the relation between latitude and longitude in a random selection of places in the world. The relation

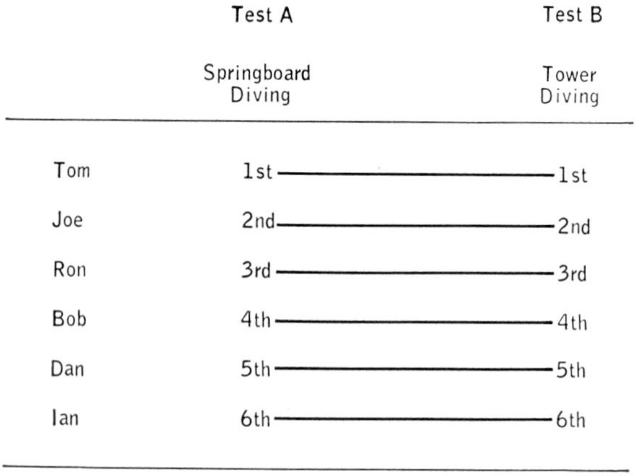

	Test A	Test B
	Springboard Diving	Tower Diving
Tom	1st ——————————————— 1st
Joe	2nd——————————————2nd
Ron	3rd ——————————————— 3rd
Bob	4th ——————————————— 4th
Dan	5th ——————————————— 5th
Ian	6th ——————————————— 6th

Fig. 10.3.   Perfect positive correlation.

between weight and intelligence of adult women. The relation between license number of a car and its mileage reading.

Thus, correlation, expressed as a mathematical coefficient, can range from $+1$ and never less than -1.

Let us look again at these extremes, by working with hypothetical examples.

Example 1.   Perfect positive correlation

Six college athletes were given tests in springboard diving and in tower diving. Their rankings in each test were correlated.

Tom was best at springboard diving and at tower diving. Joe was second best at both, Ron was third at both, Bob was fourth at both, Dan was fifth at both, and Ian was worst at both springboard and tower diving.

This is an example of perfect positive correlation. Such perfect "going-togetherness" is in practice very rare, but let us examine such a relationship between these two tests.

Let us connect each first placing with a straight line, similarly with each second placing, and so on. The pattern formed by these connecting lines can indicate the correlation. The more nearly the lines are parallel, the higher will be the positive correlation. In this case, as we would expect, the lines are perfectly parallel, and the correlation is a perfect positive one. The coefficient of correlation would be $+1$, as we shall show later.

The second example will be to see the relationship between the ability at springboard diving and basketball, with our six athletes.

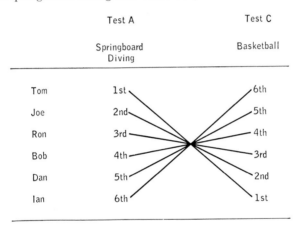

Test A   Test C

Springboard   Basketball
Diving

Tom   1st   6th
Joe   2nd   5th
Ron   3rd   4th
Bob   4th   3rd
Dan   5th   2nd
Ian   6th   1st

FIG. 10.4.   Perfect negative correlation.

EXAMPLE 2.   Perfect negative correlation

Six college athletes were given tests in springboard diving and in basketball. Their rankings in each test were correlated.

In this example, Tom was best at springboard diving, but worst at basketball. Joe was second at diving, but second-last at basketball. Ron was third at diving, but third-last at basketball, and so on. The rank order for diving is the reverse of the rank order for basketball.

This is an example of perfect negative correlation. Again, such an opposite relationship is in practice quite rare, but the features of perfect negative correlation become clearer if we examine the pattern of ranks.

By connecting each first placing with a straight line, each second placing, and so on, we get a very different pattern. The more nearly the lines intersect the centre of the pattern, the higher will be the negative correlation. In this case, as we should expect, the lines intersect exactly at the centre, and the correlation is a perfectly negative one. The coefficient of correlation would be —1, as we shall show later.

EXAMPLE 3.   Near zero correlation

Six college athletes were given tests in springboard diving and in archery. Their rankings in each test were correlated.

In this example, Tom was first at diving and fourth at archery; Joe was second at both; Ron was third and fifth; Bob was fourth and sixth; Dan was fifth and first; and Ian was last and third. An irregular pattern such as this would usually emerge from a random selection of athletes.

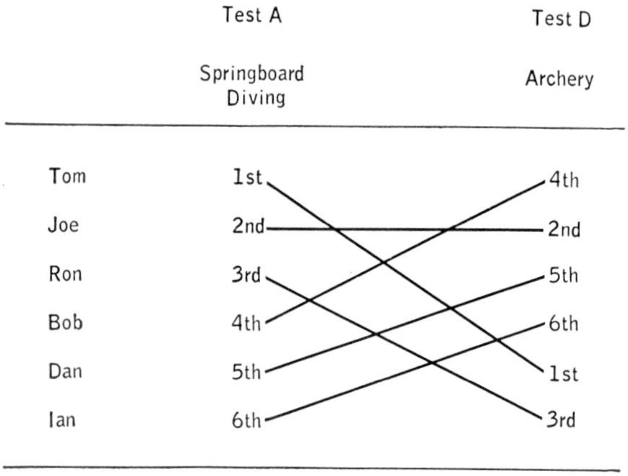

Test A

Springboard
Diving

Test D

Archery

Tom	1st	4th
Joe	2nd	2nd
Ron	3rd	5th
Bob	4th	6th
Dan	5th	1st
Ian	6th	3rd

FIG. 10.5.   Near zero correlation.

Let us again connect first placings with a straight line, second placings, and so on. When connecting lines show no systematic trend, there will be little correlation either way. So, in this case, we should expect a coefficient of correlation to be close to zero, or either slightly positive or negative.

CALCULATING THE COEFFICIENT OF CORRELATION

RANK DIFFERENCE METHOD

There are several ways of working out the mathematical coefficient, and there are slight variations with each method. We shall consider first a simple method for use with small numbers; it deals with the differences in ranking of measures in each set of scores. It was developed largely by Charles Spearman, and is called the Spearman Rank Difference Method, or sometimes just Rank Order Correlation.

STEPS IN THE RANK DIFFERENCE METHOD (CALCULATION OF RHO OR ρ)

1. List the two series of scores so that each individual's two scores are beside each other (usually the first series is listed in rank order).
2. Beside each measure in each distribution, write its rank.
3. Find the difference in rank between each score in the first distribution and its corresponding score in the second distribution. These rank differences could be termed d.
4. Square each of these rank differences, in the column d^2.
5. Add up these squared rank-differences, giving the sum $\Sigma (d^2)$.
6. Apply the formula

$$\text{rho} = 1 - \frac{6 \, \Sigma \, (d^2)}{N \, (N^2 - 1)}.$$

Let us use this method of calculating a coefficient of correlation with our three examples.

EXAMPLE 1

Name	Test A Springboard Diving		Test B Tower Diving		Rank Difference	
	Score	Rank	Score	Rank	d	d^2
Tom	42	1st	40	1st	0	0
Joe	39	2nd	38	2nd	0	0
Ron	35	3rd	33	3rd	0	0
Bob	30	4th	31	4th	0	0
Dan	26	5th	24	5th	0	0
Ian	21	6th	20	6th	0	0
						—
						0

Applying the formula:

$$\text{rho} = 1 - \frac{6 \, \Sigma \, (d^2)}{N \, (N^2 - 1)}$$

$$= 1 - \frac{6 \times 0}{6 \, (36 - 1)}$$

$$= 1 - \frac{0}{6 \times 35}$$

$$= 1 - \frac{0}{210}$$

$$= 1 - 0$$

$$\text{rho} = +1$$

This result, a coefficient of correlation of $+1$, means that there was perfect positive correlation between the two sets of scores. If the sample had been a very large one, we might have concluded that, because there was perfect positive correlation between tower and springboard diving with our athletes, all athletes who are good at springboard diving would be good at tower diving, and all athletes bad at one will be bad at the other.

The second example should give us the opposite result.

Example 2

Name	Test A Springboard Diving		Test C Basketball	Rank Differences	
	Score	Rank	Rank	d	d^2
Tom	42	1st	6th	5	25
Joe	39	2nd	5th	3	9
Ron	35	3rd	4th	1	1
Bob	30	4th	3rd	2	1
Dan	28	5th	2nd	3	9
Ian	25	6th	1st	5	25
					—
					70

Applying the formula:

$$\text{rho} = 1 - \frac{6 \, \Sigma \, (d^2)}{N \, (N^2 - 1)}$$

$$= 1 - \frac{6 \times 70}{6 \, (36 - 1)}$$

$$= 1 - \frac{420}{210}$$

$$= 1 - 2$$

$$\text{rho} = -1$$

This result, a coefficient of correlation of —1, means that there was perfect negative correlation between the two sets of scores. If the sample had been a very large one, we might have concluded that, because there was perfect negative correlation between tower diving and basketball with our athletes, all athletes good at springboard diving would be bad at basketball, and all athletes bad at springboard diving would be good at basketball. This, of course, would never happen, but if there was a tendency that way, found from many correlation experiments with large samples, then we could look for causes. For example, divers are usually fairly short, and basketballers need to be tall, so that those excelling in diving will probably not do well at basketball.

Let us work out the third example: Will it be exactly zero, or slightly more or less?

EXAMPLE 3

Name	Springboard Diving Test A Rank	Test D Archery Rank	Rank Differences d	d^2
Tom	1st	4th	3	9
Joe	2nd	2nd	0	0
Ron	3rd	5th	2	4
Bob	4th	6th	2	4
Dan	5th	1st	4	16
Ian	6th	3rd	3	9
				——
				42

Applying the formula:

$$\text{rho} = 1 - \frac{6 \, \Sigma \, (d^2)}{N \, (N^2 - 1)}$$

$$= 1 - \frac{6 \times 42}{6 \, (36 - 1)}$$

$$= 1 - \frac{252}{210}$$

$$= 1 - 1.2$$

$$\text{rho} = \quad - 0.2$$

This result, a coefficient of correlation of —0.2 means that there was slight negative correlation between the two sets of scores. If the sample had been a very large one, we might have concluded that, because there was slight negative correlation between springboard diving and archery with our athletes, there would be a slight tendency for athletes who are good at springboard diving to be bad at archery, and the reverse.

PRODUCT MOMENT METHOD

Another method of working out the coefficient of correlation—usually called the *product-moment method*—involves the product of the first moment about the mean of each series of scores, divided by the product of the second moment about the mean of each series. (Moment[6] in this sense refers to the "power" of each mean.)

This method is sometimes referred to as the Bravais-Pearson technique, after the scientist Karl Pearson, who refined the methods of Bravais. This procedure of calculating the correlation coefficient is used much more frequently than the rank difference method, especially in research, because it is particularly suitable for use with large samples, and can be adapted readily for grouped data, as well as for ungrouped.

Greater accuracy is obtained by the Product Moment method, as it takes into account the actual score values, instead of merely their rank order.

STEPS IN THE PRODUCT MOMENT METHOD (CALCULATION OF R)

1. List the two series of scores so that each individual's two scores are alongside each other (usually the first distribution is in rank order).
2. Calculate the mean of each series (Series X and Series Y).
3. Find the deviation (x) of each score in the first series (X) from the mean of that series, noting each time whether the deviation is positive or negative.
4. Similarly, find and note down the deviations (y) from the mean in the second series (Y).
5. In a double column XY multiply each deviation X by its corresponding deviation y, taking into account the signs. In recording them, put the positive products on the left-hand side of the double

---

[6] There is some parallel with "moment" in mechanics: in this case, mean and fulcrum are synonymous.

column, headed $+XY$, and the negative products on the right-hand side of the double column, headed $-XY$.

6. Find the algebraic sum of the XY column, by adding up all scores, the $+xy$, and all the $-xy$ scores, then subtracting the sum of $-xy$ from the sum of $+xy$, to give $\Sigma \, xy$.

7. In a single column X^2, square each x. In another single column, Y^2, square each y.

8. Find the totals of the X^2 column ($\Sigma \, x^2$), and of the Y^2 column ($\Sigma \, y^2$).

9. Apply the formula:

$$r = \frac{\Sigma \, xy}{\sqrt{\Sigma \, x^2 \, . \, \Sigma \, y^2}}$$

THE PRODUCT MOMENT METHOD USING GROUPED DATA

With large samples and grouped data, a modification of the product moment method just described is used to calculate the correlation coefficient r. If the two series of scores were plotted on a graph, the pattern emerging would indicate the nature and amount of correlation.

1. Draw up frequency tabulations for both series of scores.

2. Write the class intervals of the first series (X) along the horizontal or x axis; and the class intervals of the second series (Y) down the vertical or y axis.

3. Plot the score of each subject in the appropriate cell or square of graph paper, according to the x and y value. Use tally marks as shown in Chapter 8.

4. The resulting graph is known as a scattergram. Special forms are obtainable, which provide the formulas for working out the exact correlation coefficient.

5. An approximation of the coefficient can be estimated by inspecting the pattern formed by the tally marks:

    a. A narrow, cigar-shaped pattern running northeast/southwest indicates high positive correlation. The broader the pattern the lower the correlation, an oval or egg-shape representing low positive correlation.

    b. A narrow, cigar-shaped pattern running northwest/southeast indicates high negative correlation. The broader the pattern, the

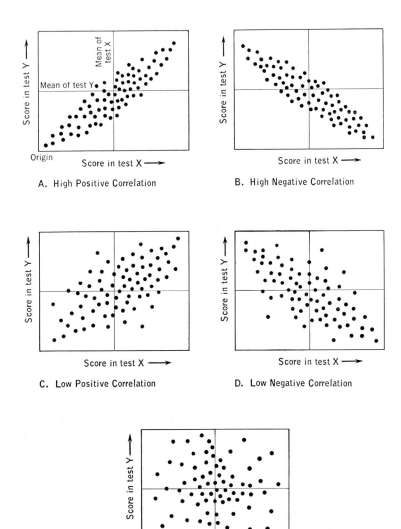

A. High Positive Correlation

B. High Negative Correlation

C. Low Positive Correlation

D. Low Negative Correlation

E. Zero Correlation

Fig. 10.6. Scattergrams.

lower the correlation, an oval or egg-shape representing low negative correlation.

c. A circular pattern with no particular direction indicates little or no correlation either way.

USES OF CORRELATION TECHNIQUES

1. The correlation technique is the basic tool of educators for determining the relationship between abilities or qualities.

2. If two abilities or skills have a very high positive correlation between them, then a test which validly measures one of the abilities should also measure the other.

3. Correlation is helpful in assessing the validity of a test. If it correlates highly with another test which is well established in terms of validity, or with expert ratings, or other appropriate criteria, then the first test will tend to have qualities similar to the criterion with which it correlates.

4. Correlation can be used to determine the reliability or consistency of a test. If a suitable sample is tested at two different times with the same test, and the two sets of results, when correlated, yield a high positive coefficient, then the test from the point of view of retesting, is reliable or consistent.

5. Correlation can indicate the objectivity of test-scoring systems. If the pattern of scores of one judge is correlated with the pattern of scores of a second judge, and a very high coefficient is yielded, it will indicate that the two judges scored the test objectively.

6. Correlation is used for many statistical purposes, and is one of the most frequently used research techniques. The research method known as factor analysis is only one well-known technique which uses correlation procedures.

7. Correlation has many forms, and the linear correlation described is only one. Other correlation techniques and their uses are mentioned below.

ADVANCED CORRELATION TECHNIQUES

The following correlation methods have more specific purposes. The procedure for calculating correlation by these methods and the formulae used can be found in most advanced statistical texts.

1. The Coefficient of Determination is used for comparing two co-efficients of correlation.
2. Partial Correlation.
3. Multiple Correlation.
4. Tetrachoric "R"
5. Chi square
6. Biserial "R"
7. Curvilinear Correlation

Factor Analysis

It has already been stated that tests which correlate highly with one another tend to measure the same quality or ability. Insofar as a test correlates with other tests, it measures some common factor or factors; this is referred to as the *communality* of the test. Insofar as the test fails to correlate with other tests, it measures something specific or unique, referred to as the *specificity* of the test.

A large number of tests applied to a large sample, when inter-correlated, can indicate the number and amount of common factors. Depending on the mathematical treatment, different factor patterns can be produced. However, it is now clear that there is a *hierarchy* of communality, in that some factors overlap more than others. And most studies show that after taking out a major common factor mathemati-cally, there are residual correlations which indicate overlapping between factors with lower *saturation* than the major common factor.

Thus we can postulate factor patterns of human abilities as a result of analysing test results by correlation into common factors. This tech-nique is known as *factor analysis*. Factor-analysis research began with the work of Charles Spearman around 1904, and has been used ex-tensively with both mental and physical abilities for nearly half a century. Factor analysis has been one of the most important techniques used in improving intelligence tests and vocational guidance tests dur-ing the past generation, and is likely to play a major role in future development of our understanding of human abilities and techniques of measuring them. It will, however, require more research for valida-tion. There is a wide measure of disagreement on methods and in-terpretation between individuals and research groups on both sides of the Atlantic.

THE STRUCTURE OF HUMAN ABILITIES

Factor-analysis studies have tidied up our empirical ideas on the structure of human physical abilities, but as already pointed out, factor analyses tend to show ONLY *proportion* and *amount*—and sometimes the *number* of major factors that can be isolated in a research study. Factor analysis cannot *identify* and name factors beyond question; it cannot reveal human abilities, but rather *isolates* and *classifies* them.

Furthermore, the results of factor-analysis studies depend for their validity on the quality of the tests used, the samples involved, and the statistical and research procedures carried out. All these have their limitations and weaknesses. In fact two different research treatments of the same data have been shown to produce two quite different factor patterns, because of different mathematical technique or interpretation.

Again, as pointed out in other chapters, any research dealing with humans deals with living organisms—each one different from another, each unique, especially with such a highly differentiated organism as *homo sapiens*. In the light of factors common to all humans, only generalisations can be made. In any case, the human being is a living entity and, usually, in one sense an integrated personality. To say that as a result of research techniques we have isolated any factor or ability is no modest claim, particularly since our present techniques and tests do not pretend to measure abilities in isolation, but must consider extraneous factors. Also, most tests measure the manifestations or products of abilities, rather than the abilities themselves.

It can be appreciated that those who worship at the shrine of objective tests might well be worshipping false gods. And those who outline an arbitrary pattern of the structure of human abilities have a very difficult case to defend.

The following patterns showing the possible structure of human abilities are accordingly purely hypothetical, although certain schools of thought, backed by considerable research, hold fast to one pattern, others believing in a different one.

PATTERN OF SINGLE GENERAL FACTOR

One general factor runs through all tests. In mental tests it may be general intelligence; in physical tests, it may be general motor ability, often referred to as G. In addition, minor specific factors are present in each test. This was an early theory, originally held by Spearman, Thomson, and Burt, and others in England.

TEST	general	specific
1	X	X
2	X	X
3	X	X
4	X	X
5	X	X
6	X	X

Fig. 10.7. Theoretical analysis of human abilities: pattern of a single general factor.

TEST	group factors a	b	c	specific
1	X			X
2	X			X
3		X		X
4		X		X
5			X	X
6			X	X

Fig. 10.8. Theoretical analysis of human abilities: pattern of multiple group factors.

Pattern of Multiple Group Factors

Several major factors run through some tests. In mental tests, they may be verbal, number-space factors, etc.; in physical tests they may be strength, speed, dead weight, etc. In addition, minor specific factors are present in each test. This is a later theory, developed mainly by Thurstone and associates in America.

Pattern of Hierarchical Group Factors

A general factor runs through all tests, and several major group factors run through most tests as well. As above, in mental tests the general factor might be general intelligence, and the major group factors might be verbal, number and spatial factors, etc.; in physical tests, the general factor might be general motor ability, and the major group factors might be strengh, speed, dead weigh, etc. In addition minor specifics are present in each test.

This is a later theory also, developed first by Burt and later by Vernon and associates in England.

Of particular interest to physical educators are the two group factors involving muscular coordination and skills. *Psychomotor coordination* is considered to be a type of motor ability involving fine muscular skills and discriminations. Group factors such as manual, finger, and other dexterities, and perceptual speed and hand-eye coordinations have been yielded in factor-analysis studies.

These fine muscular coordinations are largely manipulative in nature, and have been found to correlate slightly more highly with general intelligence than gross muscular coordinations or whole body movements.[7] Neither yields more than low correlation coefficients, however.

Physical or athletic ability, involving large muscle groups, has been isolated in factor-analysis studies, and variously termed general motor ability, motor ability, athletic ability, motor educability, and dynamic gross motor ability. In tests involving physical skills, group factors consistently emerge. McCloy found in his earlier experiments that strength, speed, and dead weight were factors.

TEST	general factor	group factors a	b	c	specific
1	X	X			X
2	X	X			X
3	X		X		X
4	X		X		X
5	X			X	X
6	X			X	X

FIG. 10.9. Theoretical analysis of human abilities: pattern of hierarchical group factors.

Higher intercorrelations have been found in analyses of physical tests than in manipulative tests, suggesting that there is some justification for postulating a general physical or athletic ability.

One of the most comprehensive surveys of factor-analysis studies was made by Howard Steven Brown,[8] who compared twenty-six different

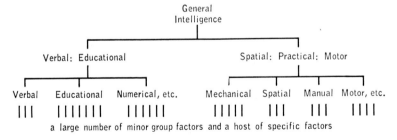

FIG. 10.10. A hypothetical classification of human abilities, based on a hierarchical factor pattern.

[7] There is possibly a neurophysiological explanation why this might be so.
[8] H. S. Brown, "A Comparative Study of Motor Fitness Tests," *Research Quarterly,* XXV, no. 1 (March, 1954), 8.

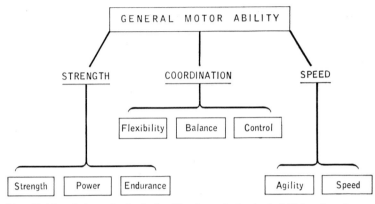

FIG. 10.11. A hypothetical classification of physical abilities, based on a multiple group factor pattern.

factor-analysis studies. Again, he found that strength was yielded most frequently, with speed or velocity, and dead weight next in order. Other factors yielded consistently were power, endurance, coordination, control, body structure, and, in certain types of study, agility and balance. From a careful investigation into relevant studies on factor analysis, it is possible to put forward two versions of the structure of physical abilities. These two diagrams illustrate what could be the structure of athletic ability, the first following a hierarchical pattern, and the second a multiple group factor pattern.

RECOMMENDED READING

Bloomers, P., and E. F. Lindquist, *Elementary Statistics in Psychology and Education,* New York, Houghton Mifflin, 1960.

Garrett, H. E., *Statistics in Psychology and Education,* New York, Longmans, Green, 1953.

McCloy, C. R., *Tests and Measurements in Health and Physical Education,* New York, Appleton-Century-Crofts, 1954.

Research Quarterly, articles on factor analysis studies, Washington, AAHPER.

Stroup, F., *Measurement in Physical Education,* New York, Ronald, 1957.

Thomson, G. H., *The Factorial Analysis of Human Ability,* London University Press, 1939.

Vernon, P. E., *The Structure of Human Abilities,* New York, Wiley (and London, Methuen), 1950.

CONVERSION TABLE OF PERCENTILE RANKS INTO T SCORES
(Based on Approximate Standard Deviation Values)

Percentile	T Score	Percentile	T Score	Percentile	T Score
99.9	80	67	54	31	45
99.75	78	66	54	30	44.5
99.5	76	65	53.5	29	44.5
99.25	75	64	53.5	28	44
99.0	74	63	53	27	44
98.5	72	62	53	26	43.5
98	70	61	52.5	25	43
97	69	60	52.5	24	43
96	68	59	52	23	42.5
95	67	58	52	22	42
94	66	57	52	21	42
93	65	56	51.5	20	41.5
92	64	55	51.5	19	41
91	63	54	51	18	41
90	62.5	53	51	17	40.5
89	62	52	50.5	16	40
88	61.5	51	50	15	40
87	61	50	50	14	39
86	60.5	49	50	13	38.5
85	60	48	49.5	12	38
84	60	47	49	11	37.5
83	59.5	46	49	10	37
82	59	45	48.5	9	36
81	59	44	48	8	35
80	58.5	43	48	7	34
79	58	42	47.5	6	33
78	58	41	47.5	5	32
77	57.5	40	47	4	31
76	57	39	47	3	30
75	56.5	38	46.5	2	29
74	56	37	46.5	1.5	28
73	56	36	46	1.0	26
72	55.5	35	46	.75	25
71	55	34	45.5	.5	24
70	55	33	45.5	.25	22
69	54.5	32	45	.1	20
68	54.5				

To construct a T *scale:* Find percentile rank of each score (with ungrouped data, or of each class-interval mid-point with grouped data (see p. 187). Read off the "T" Score corresponding with each percentile rank (see p. 207).

chapter 11

TESTS AND THEIR USES

TEST REQUIREMENTS

Any test or measurement should be purposeful, suitable for the purpose, and challenging. Its results should be usable and, if possible, it should continue the educational process.

Suppose you are given a test which is quite meaningless to you, which you do not enjoy very much, and of which you are not told the results afterwards. If you are wondering what it is all about, does the test really challenge you to do your best; afterwards would you feel it was worth while, not knowing how you performed?

Consider the Subject's Viewpoint

A teacher should always consider the subject's point of view when giving a test. As suggested above, a test may not be very sound educationally, nor purposeful. Yet many such tests are given in schools. A good question for deciding whether a test is justified is: "Will this test be of greater benefit to the pupils and their education than the same time spent on purposeful teaching or learning of new skills?" This involves viewing the test both from the point of view of the teacher and the pupil. Another criterion is suggested by the question, "Would an enlightened but critical school administrator approve of its educational soundness?"

Other Basic Considerations

The teacher should consider further: "Is the purpose of this evaluation programme really to improve teaching and learning, for this and

228

other classes? If so, will the results be usable and used, or will they be filed indefinitely—so much lumber-room data? In addition to benefiting the pupils, will the use of the results later save teaching and learning time?"

As a result of such examination, are you satisfied that your evaluation program is purposeful and worth while, and the results likely to be used to good effect? If so, then you are in a position to determine whether suitable tests are available or will have to be made up, whether you have the administrative facilities and equipment to carry out the tests, and whether you have the time and personnel available to enable the tests to be constructed, administered, scored, and recorded, and the results processed for the purposes to which you intend to put them.

Further, you should decide as realistically as possible just how much time you can spend on evaluation in proportion to the total physical-education time at your disposal. A good working rule might be that no more than about one-tenth of teaching time should be devoted to formal testing. Such tests should conform to the criteria of purposefulness just discussed, and they should also conform to statistical requirements of effective tests.

Requirements of tests are of three main kinds: *statistical, administrative,* and *motivational.* Before tests are selected and used, their requirements, implications, and possibilities for the particular situation should be carefully considered. It would be foolish to select tests that were statistically sound, but administratively impracticable; and it would be equally foolish to use tests that were administratively suitable, in which the subjects would not co-operate fully or give of their best.

STATISTICAL REQUIREMENTS

Statistically, the tests should be as objective, valid, and reliable as possible for their purpose.

OBJECTIVITY

To be *objective,* a test may be administered to the same group by different individuals and still obtain the same results or scores. This depends partly on administration and partly on scoring methods. The administration of the test should be such that conditions are virtually identical for the subjects every time the test is given. Wherever possible, the scoring system should be objective, that is, the same score would be given, no matter who was the scorer. This is easier in some activities than others. Golf is scored objectively, boxing rather subjectively. No matter who scores a golf round there is rarely any dispute over the scoring, but there are often disputes over the scoring in boxing rounds.

BOTH OBJECTIVE AND SUBJECTIVE TESTS

Most tests in physical education are designed to have objective scoring systems, although tests in gymnastics, dancing, diving, etc., where quality or "form" is assessed, have, in general, subjective scoring systems. These can be improved to some extent, by using several judges, agreed scoring criteria, and consistent scoring systems, but they are still subjective in that different scorers or judges award different scores for the same performance. There are those who argue that skilled subjectivity by a competent, experienced, and shrewd judge is the most valid method in some cases; indeed, it is the basis of selection for most team games. While this remains true for such activities as those just mentioned, where objective scoring systems have not yet been devised, techniques are improving, and it is likely that the objectivity of scoring will be increased, even with activities where quality rather than quantity is being assessed.

An example of an activity in which measurement is claimed to be objective is the 100-yard sprint; yet there are many errors possible of a subjective kind, as where different timekeepers will show different times. Human reaction time varies greatly, occasionally by even as much as a second. The timekeeper may watch for the smoke rather than the flash of the pistol, or may wait for the sound to reach him. He may hold down the knob of the stopwatch and affect its mechanism. He may anticipate the runner reaching the finishing tape, or his position at an angle to the tape may involve parallax, or the stopwatch may not be accurate. He may be too close to the track to have sufficient depth of focus to see all runners clearly. The cumulative total of all possible errors such as these could be one of several seconds! And yet for world and national record purposes hand-timing and machine-timing are put together!

But even so, such an extreme error, of 20 or 30 percent, is seldom if ever reached, and the usual one is less than half a second—or 5 percent in the 100-yard dash—and less, the longer the distance. In sports where the scoring is subjective, the error may be 50 or even 100 percent. In the 1956 Olympic Games at Melbourne, the ratings of divers' performances by experienced judges varied tremendously. Prejudice in judges might cause one judge to award three points, and another judge might award eight out of ten points. Such disparity is minimised by the technique of discarding extreme scores and averaging the remainder.[1]

VALIDITY

To be *valid* a test should measure accurately that which it sets out to measure. Subjective scoring may of course reduce validity, but no matter how accurate the scoring, the test itself may not be valid. In the field of testing, the validity of a test often depends on the quality being assessed. For example, the quality sportsmanship can be assessed only approximately, but weight can be measured fairly accurately, using scales. Generally, tests of personality and character have relatively low validity compared with measurements of strength, height and weight, etc. When assessing personality, or even intelligence, only the "products" or manifestations of the quality can be measured. When measuring height and weight, the characteristic itself is being measured. Thus the scales measure accurately what is intended to be measured, namely weight (see Chapter 13). However, the intelligence test measures only the products of intelligence, while the measuring device itself is not as precise.

So far, in personality and intelligence testing, we have found no perfect criteria of validity, as we have found in tests involving direct measurement. What is usually done is for the test to be compared with a well-established test, proved to be sufficiently valid to measure reasonably well what it sets out to measure.

Again, it is often not possible to isolate the quality we are trying to measure. This is, of course, true of physical activities as well as personality and intelligence. We may, in measuring handgrip strength,

[1] Though Franklin Henry has suggested dangers in this practice (*Research Quarterly*, 1952).

be measuring arm strength, and body strength as well.[2] The less the quality to be measured can be isolated, the less valid the test of it is likely to be.

Lack of motivation can affect test performances. If the subject's grandmother has just died, or if he is tired, hungry, or uninterested, he may not do his best. The importance of rapport between tester and subject, and of providing incentives for the subject to make the maximum effort he is capable of, is obvious; otherwise the test will not accurately measure the quality it sets out to measure, and the validity of the test will suffer. This in part explains the extraordinary variability in strength measurement of the same individuals noted by several observers.

VALIDITY VARIES WITH THE TYPE OF TEST

We can consider different fields in the light of the validity possible in testing.

1. *Measurements of time, distance and mass* tend to be highly valid, depending on the accuracy of the measuring devices and their operators. Height, weight, and speed can be measured with a high degree of validity.

2. *Measurements of strength, power, and endurance* tend to be of fairly high validity, provided that the instruments and operators are accurate; however, sound criteria of what constitutes the particular kind of strength, etc., being tested may vary. Static strength can usually be measured more accurately than power and endurance. But strength tests can only measure the *output* from potential strength—parallel to performance in intelligence tests.

3. *Measurements of bodily condition* vary greatly in their validity. Cardiovascular and respiratory tests may diagnose one aspect of a condition, but it may not be directly related to the condition itself. The question of what is a good criterion for bodily condition is involved. Validity of single tests may be only fair, but the use of a battery of tests will tend to improve validity.

4. *Measurements of physical and mental skill and ability* again vary in validity. When we test for, say, motor ability, we assume that what we are measuring is primarily that ability. This means that we are

---

[2] In fact, the Sherringtonian concept of the integrative action of the nervous system shows such isolation is impossible.

assuming that we agree as to what motor ability is, and can measure it in isolation. Neither assumption is absolutely true, but research in factor analysis and other directions is helping us in our attempt to measure such abilities with a higher degree of validity.

5. *Measurements of applied motor skills,* such as sports skills, produce similar difficulties and loss of validity. The inability to define and isolate the skill decreases validity. Tests of sports skills should involve situations similar to the game itself, should involve the main skills used by all players, and should not be influenced unduly by the use of opponents differing in skill. It is the problem of devising sports tests similar to the sport, where an opponent is involved, that makes their construction so complex. Two factors crop up which often decrease the validity of tests: *Social and temperamental dynamics* exist in team sports such as softball. This social atmosphere is hard to create in a test. *Tactics* are the second influence that are hard to incorporate in a test. Nevertheless, there are many practical uses of sports tests that might make them worth while as educational tools and motivators, even though their validity is only fair (see Chapter 19).

6. *Measurements of personality and character* present so many problems of measurement that validity is often quite low. Often there is not complete agreement on what is being measured, it is very difficult to isolate the quality, and it cannot be measured objectively, although many personality tests have objective scoring systems. Again, research is causing the field to develop rapidly, and along with this, measurement techniques are improving.

RELIABILITY

To be *reliable,* a test should be consistent. Repeating the test later on the same group should achieve approximately the same result—the same performers should in general do well each time, and those who did badly the first time should in general do badly when it is repeated. This requirement in a test, known as reliability, is easy to measure, by comparing the pattern of results of the first administration of a test with a second test later. This is known as the "test-retest" method. For example, in measuring the heights of a class of boys, those found to be tallest on the first measuring in general would be found to be tallest also on the second measuring. Measurement of height should be reliable or consistent with each measuring, as far as the distribution pattern of heights is concerned (with variations for growth rates).

Reliability varies with different situations. Objective scoring systems tend to produce more reliable results than subjective marking. Yet highly trained judges of, say, poultry or dogs produce scores that correlate well (see Chapter 4). Highly valid tests tend to be more reliable than those with low validity. It can be appreciated that some extraneous factors which reduce validity, such as nervousness, lack of motivation, or fatigue, will also reduce the consistency of reliability of results.

The repeating of a test usually results in an all-around improvement in scores. This is known as "practice effect." It affects the reliability coefficient of the test, especially when some individuals improve relatively more than others.

ADMINISTRATIVE REQUIREMENTS

The teacher should next consider whether the tests contemplated are practical administratively, while still meeting statistical requirements. Can they be given within the normal framework of the physical-education program, using the organisation, facilities, equipment, and personnel usually available? The most suitable tests can be given during a normal class period. They should be simple, with a minimum of equipment and no special expensive apparatus. They should be easy to administer, without undue preparation and explanation. They should be easily understood by the teacher and the pupils. Complicated tests take a long time, and often do not produce results that justify the trouble taken.

Tests should be straightforward in their scoring and interpretation. They should have alternate or parallel forms, particularly if there is a marked practice effect. They should be standardised with norms if possible, or desirable. If special score cards and instructions are needed, these should be supplied with the test.

These are general requirements, which may have exceptions. However, often a standardised test is not suitable or available. Teachers should be prepared to modify an existing test, or construct a new one to meet their special needs, realising that existing norms may no longer be appropriate. Most teachers have not much in the way of elaborate facilities for testing, such as administrative assistants, clerical staff, computers, and the like. They are as a result thrown on their own resources with their testing programmes. Remembering what was said earlier about not spending too much time on formal testing, the teacher should endeavour, where possible, to incorporate testing procedures in his normal lesson routine, so that he can gain information without interfering with teaching time. There are many possible opportunities for informal testing. Before and after some lessons, some individual evaluation can be carried out. When some groups or squads are practising skills learnt during the lesson, one or more groups can perform simple tests of physical strength, speed, and skill. Early in the lesson, stunt-type tests can be carried out, with the whole class performing at once, in teams, or in pairs. By careful planning before the program begins, a great deal of information can be gained in these ways, and opportunities to get to know each pupil can be made during individual testing and measuring.

For the few tests which are more formal and require a whole period devoted to them, preliminary planning and organisation can ensure that they are carried out correctly and quickly, so that no more extra teaching time is used than possible. The use of the most suitable formations, such as pairs, groups, or teams, for appropriate testing procedures, will also ensure that they are carried out quickly and efficiently.

MOTIVATIONAL REQUIREMENTS

We must try to develop the incentive for each pupil to give his best in every test. Without this motivation, the results of tests will lose much validity, and the attitudes of the pupils will suffer. There are several ways to ensure that tests will be sufficiently motivating. Some tests, by their very nature, present a challenge to the pupils, and hence are self-motivating. Others require skilled administration by the teacher.

The most important need is to establish rapport with the subjects, to accept them personally, and to be accepted by them. A natural, yet purposeful relationship should prevail, and the teacher should hope to inspire his pupils to perform well. An enthusiastic, business-like, yet sincere, approach usually gets the pupils interested, and an atmosphere of trust and confidence should result. Students who are too nervous, who are upset by the conditions, or who find the work unpleasant, are not likely to give a performance in keeping with their ability. An artificial or too formal approach may instill strain. On the other hand, too informal an approach may induce sloppy performances.

Students should be told whenever possible what is the purpose of the test, what it involves, and how they can help with the education program by co-operating fully. They should afterwards be able to see their own individual results, if, as is sometimes desirable, class scores are not posted or read out. If you let the students in on the purpose of the work to be done, they usually appreciate it and become interested.

Therefore tests must be meaningful, and worth doing for their own sake. For boys, they should present a challenge to at least their strength and skill, and for girls, to at least their skill and form in movement. When appropriate, care should be taken to ensure that in any test, players using good form will be able to score higher than players using poor or incorrect form.

ADMINISTRATION OF TESTS

Tests of course, should be carefully planned before they are administered to avoid waste of time. There are two main types of tests: pencil-and-paper tests, and performance tests. Here are some hints for administering such tests.

Pencil and Paper Tests

1. Become absolutely familiar with the test and its administration beforehand. Try it out on yourself, or with a "pilot" sample.
2. The room should be light and warm; there should be no distractions. Desks should be well spaced to avoid the possibility of subjects looking at each other's answer forms. Seats should be comfortable.
3. Distribute test papers and equipment before the subjects enter. Papers face down. Equipment such as clocks, etc., should be

checked and adjusted beforehand. See that every subject has a
pen or pencil and an eraser.

4. Two administrators are usually best—an examiner, and an assistant, who may be a senior student.

5. The examiner should try to create an atmosphere free from any
feeling of strain or strangeness. With older children, explain the
purpose of the test, or make it into a quiz or puzzle; with young
children treat it as a game. At the same time, emphasise effort
and good use of time.

6. Administrative directions and conditions should be strictly adhered to, and the instructions to subjects should be read slowly
and clearly, making sure all children understand them. Treat
written instructions similarly.

7. At the beginning, the examiner and assistant should move quietly
around the room, to see that all children are doing the test as instructed. If any child has misunderstood, and is not doing so, explain the proper procedure to him, giving no other assistance beyond
that allowed in the test directions. Otherwise, avoid too much moving about.

8. When the subjects begin, the examiner should write down the exact
starting time. He should allow the exact time given in the test
directions.

9. When subjects finish before the allotted time, they should check
their work. With young children, early finishers might be given
silent reading. When papers are completed they should be placed
face down on the subjects' desks, or handed to the assistant near
the door as they leave. If early finishers are allowed to leave, they
should do so without distracting those still working.

10. When repeating the test at a later time, to compare results, measure progress, or assess test reliability, allow exactly the same conditions for the retest as for the original one.

Performance Tests and Tests Involving Physical Activities

1. Preparation
   a. Decide whether it is justified, of sufficient purpose, and the re-
      sults likely to be worth while.
   b. Have the test adequately sponsored, with the approval of the

school authorities (this may be automatic, or special permission may have to be obtained).

   c. Be absolutely familiar with the test and its administration beforehand. Try it out on yourself or on a "pilot" sample.

   d. Draw the layout of the test area on the blackboard beforehand, to help you become familiar with the test, and so that pupils can refer to it.

2. Equipment and testing area

   a. Equipment and marking should be prepared beforehand. Instruments such as watches, dynamometers, and spirometers, etc., should be checked and adjusted.

   b. As many sets of targets, markers, obstacles, etc., as possible should be laid out, to have the maximum number of pupils active, to reduce time, and to avoid bottlenecks. Have extra equipment in readiness for bottlenecks and breakages. Plan to use space and walls to best advantage.

   d. Use ground and floor markings of chalk and tape to the best advantage.

   e. Consider what part of the available area is to be used, and how, by those not actually being tested at a given moment.

3. Organisation

   a. Some tests can be done by the whole class at the same time, with teacher or student demonstrating.

   b. Other tests can be best done using a partner arrangement in two lines; one line does the activity, with partners marking, then the second line performs, partners marking.

   c. Where only a small group can be tested at a time, the remainder of the class can be doing group or squad practices, or having a lesson, while one corner is being used to test each group at a time.

   d. Another arrangement is for several activities to be tested at the same time, one for each squad area. This requires familiarity with the items, or the use of assistants at each area. The whole class or squad leaders may have to be briefed beforehand, or instructions may have to be posted at each area. Usually, teams move to the next area all at the same time, although by using individual instruction and score cards, each pupil can move from activity to activity in his own time. Some tests, especially of strength and endurance, have items which should be performed in a certain order, and the arrangement decided upon should allow for this.

4. Assistants (assistants, scorers, and recorders are sometimes needed)

   a. Assistants should be briefed at a preliminary meeting, unless the class can be profitably occupied at the beginning of the session. Printed or mimeographed instructions may be helpful. If they have been through the tests themselves previously, the assistants will be more familiar with their administration.

   b. Scorers will need score cards which should be clear and simple, with instructions and briefing. Thin cardboard for durability or a clipboard with pencil provided are best. In some events, such as throwing and batting tests, spotters are needed to mark distances reached by the ball.

   c. Recorders may be needed instead of or as well as scorers, if results of the whole class are being recorded on one page. These should be mounted on stiff board backing sheet. Spare pencils, erasers and pages should be provided, and the tasks of the recorders, as well as where they are to position themselves, should be made clear to them.

5. Presentation

   As with most tests, the teacher should establish rapport with the subjects, describing the procedure—using a blackboard diagram, if necessary—and encouraging them to do their best. Yet the class should not be forced into doing activities which may be dangerous or beyond their powers. The test should suit their age and stage, avoiding activities which might cause undue stress or strain. Some preliminary training, and certainly warming up, may be desirable. Limbering-up activities might include some items of the test, to familiarise subjects with them; however, care must be taken that all children have the same amount of practice, and that where standardised tests with norms are used, no items where practice effect could affect scores are included in the warm up.

   Get the class to carry out the test as best they can. Procedure should conform exactly to instructions with standard tests, and keep the conditions uniform for each class.

6. Results

   The class should, wherever possible, be told of the purpose of the test beforehand, or at least when the test is completed; results should be given, usually to the whole class, or to individuals if some are likely to be upset by poor relative performances. In some tests the pupils may be told their raw scores, but not their significance. As with intelligence-testing, there may be a need for not labelling a child in his own mind. Always keep neat and permanent records of results in filing cabinets, since the information may be needed in the future, or be used by other teachers. It is a good idea to make a schedule before the test, of the purpose, scoring, recording, interpreting, and using of the results. The extent to which this plan can be carried through to its conclusion is a good indication of the value of the test.

TYPES OF TEST

Tests and measurements in physical education are of three main kinds: physical measurements, pencil and paper tests, and performance tests involving manipulation or physical activity.

Tests may be constructed as single items, or combined into a battery of items with an aggregate score, or have the items linked into one continuous task, with an aggregate score or time.

Administratively, tests can be given to individuals, for example, physical measurements, or to groups, for example, pencil-and-paper tests.

1. *Physical measurement* includes anthropometric measurements, such as height, weight, girth, and somatotype; medical examinations of some kinds; and physiological tests and measurements.
2. *Pencil-and-paper tests* include achievement tests (of intelligence and other abilities), aptitude tests, diagnostic tests, knowledge tests, attitude and interest inventories, personality tests, questionnaires, anecdotal and interview records, case histories, records of observation, self-appraisals, and check lists.
3. *Performance tests* are of three main types.
    a. Sensory tests of sight, hearing, reaction time, threshold of touch, etc.
    b. Manipulative tests of finger and hand dexterity, reaction time, perception of relations, etc.

c. Physical tests of motor ability, condition and fitness, and specific abilities, skills, and achievement.

THE CONSTRUCTION OF TESTS

Many teachers wish to carry out an investigation which will involve the constructing of a test or other evaluation device such as a questionnaire. It is especially important for the amateur researcher to delineate and consider carefully the topic or problem, and decide on the appropriate methods of collecting and interpreting the data which will help him solve the problem. Suggestions for constructing tests and questionnaires are offered for three areas: physical performance, general knowledge, and specialized knowledge.

Constructing a Physical Performance Test

It has already been stressed that most physical activities and characteristics lend themselves readily to measurement and evaluation, especially where data of a quantitative nature are being sought. Physical growth, type, and condition (sometimes) can generally be measured directly. Physical skill and fitness can often be measured by instrument directly, and by objective tests, using count-scoring.

More and more the attention of nations is directed to the physical status of youth, and the role of measurements and tests becomes important—even essential—to the assessment of present position and to improvement.

Physical tests of performance involving activity have been devised for all sorts of situations and conditions, particularly during the past generation. Some tests have been discarded as not meeting with statistical and other requirements; others have stood the test of time. Techniques have improved greatly, and it can be claimed today that tests for nearly all situations can be devised which will measure the required variables with a fair degree of validity, reliability, and objectivity. Where quantity is the essential ingredient of the variables, the techniques of measurement can be accurate; however, where quality is sought, the situation is more difficult, and it may well be that—as in the criticism of music, painting, sculpture, and dance—words, with their tremendous flexibility, are the best medium of evaluation.

Some techniques involve expensive apparatus, administration, and scoring and recording procedures; yet most physical characteristics can be measured accurately by a simple approach, using a minimum of complicated equipment and procedure.

The steps in constructing a physical performance test are as follows.

1. *Consider the particular topic or problem.* For example, you might be interested in the relationship between leg kick and arm action in breast stroke swimming. A good way to start is to formulate a question —for instance, "Is the relative number of leg kicks, arm strokes, and complete strokes required to get across a swimming pool a good test of breast stroke swimming?"

2. *Investigate the main ideas, activities, and skills pertaining to the topic.* Now we break the topic down into its more obvious components, etc. "Breast stroke swimming involves both style and speed, produced by arm and leg action. What is the relationship of the main skills of *arm stroke drive* and *leg stroke drive* to the complete stroke?" (You might even break it down to include length of glide as well.)

3. *Study the relevant articles and literature to see what tests and research have already been done in this field.* What were the tests designed to do? What were the main purposes of the research? Has your problem already been studied? Have suitable tests been devised to measure what you are trying to find out? Are such tests statistically sound? Are suitable norms applicable to your intended sample available? Are such tests feasible in your own situation, as far as equipment, facilities, personnel, and time are concerned? This is a crucial question sometimes overlooked in the general enthusiasm. If not, perhaps you can begin in a small way, and gradually build up towards more ambitious and advanced testing. A test such as the swimming example could be conducted in any school with a pool.

You will probably find that tests you encounter in your reading do not exactly meet your needs, but they may clarify your problem, trigger ideas, indicate errors to avoid, and provide a working basis. You may be able to use existing tests, or modify them, before drawing up new norms, or you may need to construct a new test and new norms. Let us assume that we are going to construct a swimming test to analyse the relation between the complete breast stroke and its main components, arm drive and leg drive.

4. *Procedure for constructing a test.*

a. *Analyse the activity* to see what skills are involved. A good test should be concerned with important skills used by all participants. In our example, arm and leg drive are essential skills.

b. *Work out activities* involving these skills. These activities should be measurable objectively, or able to be rated by experts—observers trained with set criteria. Our activities could include one width of arm action only, one width of leg action only, and one width of complete breast stroke.

c. *Set up a scoring system.* We could count the number of strokes per width of the pool. The scoring system could discriminate effectively between participants yielding a pattern of scores approximating the appropriate curve of distribution. Avoid "ceiling effect"—the tendency for many subjects to gain the best possible score—and "basement effect"—the tendency for many to achieve the worst score level—by adjusting the difficulty of the items or the scoring system so that most subjects gain intermediate scores.

d. *Try out the test* on a small group of subjects—a pilot sample —and modify the items for difficulty and administrative ease. Adjust the scoring system. Eliminate unsuitable items.

e. *Draw up the test,* and work out clear descriptions, instructions, equipment and markings, number of trials, and scoring and recording systems. In our case, brief explicit instructions on the three methods of swimming the width of the pool, with scoring directions, would be compiled.

f. *Prepare score cards* and recording and summary forms. A class list with four columns would suffice: (1) for names, and number of strokes taken to swim a width, (2) using arm action, (3) using leg action, and (4) using the complete stroke.

g. *Choose the most suitable available criterion of validity.* For example, in the breast stroke test, two criteria could be used, length of time to swim the length of pool using the breast stroke and expert ratings by three judges for breast stroke style. Work out a suitable rating basis for the judges, e.g., 20 points, of which 5 each are allotted to correct and legal stroke, easy and relaxed style, good leg and arm drive, correct timing and breathing. Your score card should make it easy for the judge to break down the components of the movement.

5. *Collect the data.* Try out the test on a pilot sample, say at least fifty subjects, who should be typical of those to whom you will be giving the test. For instance, do not use your school swimming team for pilot-testing for the whole school. Also, usually later, carry out the validating time trial and judges' ratings. Make any improvements and adjustments that appear desirable, and repeat the test some days later.

6. *Interpret the data.* Correlate the test results with those of the validating criteria, to give validity coefficients. (Both the validating criteria could be correlated together, as could the rating of Judge A, with Judge B, with Judge C, etc.) Correlate the results of the test, with those of the retest, to give a reliability coefficient. (See Chapter 9).

7. *Draw conclusions and apply them.* If the validity and reliability coefficients are reasonable, if the test has proved interesting to pupils and has not been too difficult to administer (there may be "bugs" that need consideration), then begin to put the test to use, recording results carefully, neatly, and permanently. If possible establish norms for the different types of subjects involved. Use the results, group and individual, and the norms, to modify and improve your program.

Further statistical treatment can, if you wish, be applied, and this is dealt with in texts on research. However, the practising teacher will find that the steps outlined in this chapter will take considerable time, and they should be sufficient for his purpose. Further treatment would depend on time, personnel, and resources available. If you have neither the time nor enthusiasm to construct such a test, why not try the use of achievement charts.

Achievement Charts

USES OF ACHIEVEMENT CHARTS

1. When posted on the physical-education notice board, the charts show minimum to maximum requirements of that part of the course. Pupils can appreciate just what is expected of them, and can grasp the outline of the course as a whole. They can see their own level, and see a series of graded goals before them related to their own ability.

2. Charts are a good means of motivation, challenging pupils to beat their own record and to improve steadily in the skills of the course.

3. They assist the teacher with the planning of the course, and at any

stage enable him to evaluate the progress of individuals and classes, with reference to the beginning status, and the intended level of achievement at the end of the course.

4. Being kept up to date from week to week, they are always topical, and tend to enthuse and interest both pupils and teacher.

5. They can assist with diagnosis of weaknesses and observation of unusual talents of individuals and groups, so that appropriate action can be carried out. Exceptional potential ability can be spotted quickly.

6. They can be used for individual, team, class, and school competition.

7. They can assist with team selection.

8. They can be the basis of potted or tabloid sports of the decathlon or battery type.

9. They can be the basis of end-of-course assessment and reports, and subsequent planning.

10. They can be used for comparison of individuals and classes.

11. They provide a basis for research and the drawing up of norms.

CONSTRUCTING ACHIEVEMENT CHARTS

1. Analyse the activity or sport, and decide on the important skills or events. (See the previous section for details of most of the following steps.)

2. Carry out a preliminary survey with a pilot sample to find out in what class grade, or at what age, the required proportion of students can master the skill or reach a specified standard in the event. Depending on the purpose of the charts, the need for motivation, etc., different proportions might be required. School records, and results of previous track meets, should assist with the selection of standards.

3. Post this on the notice board at the beginning of the course. It is a guide and pointer. It should show the main outline of the course, but should be flexible and not adhered to too rigidly.

4. Explain to the students the standards that are to be aimed at during different stages of the course. Prepare individual achievement score cards, or arrange your chart so that individual progress can be marked in.

5. Each student has his achievement level recorded on his card. Work

may be done in pairs or in groups, with the leader demonstrating and recording, or with the teacher and recorders. It may or may not be wise to post individual performances up on notice board, because poor performers may be discouraged. The purpose of improving individual performances or beating one's own record should be emphasised, rather than aiming to be the best in the class. It is educationally difficult to decide when it is wise to let someone know his status and when to tell him and his group.

6. Keep a running score of mean performances and best performances in each event, without mentioning the names of the performers. This indicates to the students the standards being reached by the class.

7. Record results each year; adjust and revise standards and establish new norms.

QUESTIONNAIRES

The questionnaire is widely used in educational research. It has been found by surveys that nearly a quarter of investigations in educational fields use the questionnaire method of collecting data. Why is it so popular? Because it provides information about educational matters and programs that is not available from the usual sources of literature —libraries, documents, tests, school records, etc. It is also a simple and inexpensive way of collecting much information or many answers within a reasonably short time. It is in some ways a lazy method, but it may be the sequel or climax to extensive and very thorough study of a topic. It may enable an investigator to clarify and summarize the main points arising from his research. On occasion it may occur at a time when the investigator needs outside ideas on the topic, and so usefully supplements his own personal interpretations with the opinions of a wide circle of experts in that particular field.

The questionnaire then, can be a most useful evaluation technique, particularly in fields where measurement and testing are not very effective or appropriate, and where subjective information and opinions are sought. Such areas as organisation, programmes, attitudes, opinions, interests, preferences, undocumented procedures, and personal experiences provide a rich source of educational information, about which the questionnaire can discover a great deal. Occasionally, if, say, schools or principals are peppered with a continuous stream of questionnaires, they can become understandably irritated. It is as well to see before issuing questionnaires whether the proposed group to be sampled is in a willing mood.

REQUIREMENTS OF A GOOD QUESTIONNAIRE

1. It should be on a sound educational topic, worthy of study.
2. It should seek data available only through the questionnaire method. Nothing annoys people more than to have to find data for people which are already available by some other means.
3. It should be sponsored by the correct authorities, who should be asked not only to give permission for the questions to be answered but also asked to encourage answering.
4. It should be as far as possible meaningful and interesting to respondents; simple, neat, and attractive in appearance; and not too lengthy, with clear and unambiguous questions well arranged and set out.
5. It should be reasonable, both in regard to the respondents' answers, and in the time and arrangements necessary for replying. The inclusion of a stamped and addressed return envelope is a courtesy, and also motivating.
6. It should be as objective as possible, both in the unbiassed framing of questions, and in the asking for simple, direct answers, e.g.:
   a. Yes/No
   b. Ratings on a 3-, 5-, or 7-point scale, such as Excellent, Very Good, Satisfactory, Fair, Poor
   c. Quantities or proportions, such as 30 children per class—75 percent can swim, half are taught to swim
   d. Checking or underlining answers, such as Always, Often, Sometimes, Occasionally, Never
   e. Ranking in order of preference or of importance, such as *Oliver Twist, Treasure Island, Tom Sawyer, Little Women, Uncle Tom's Cabin*
   These may need to be substantiated by opinion and qualifying comments, e.g., some unforeseen view, for which space may need to be provided.
7. It should be preceded or accompanied by a letter, stating the

purpose, safeguarding the anonymity of respondents, and promising a genuine summary of results.

8. It should be preceded by thorough study of the topic, and questions should be checked by several experts, including the sponsors. It should in fact, be very carefully constructed (many are not).

9. It should be completed by a sufficient proportion (usually at least half) of the most suitable random sample, using follow-up letters if necessary.

10. It should lend itself to adequate statistical treatment of answers. Some questionnaires are so constructed that it is virtually impossible to analyse the answers.

STEPS IN CONSTRUCTING A QUESTIONNAIRE

Again the main stages of statistical procedure mentioned in Chapter 8 apply: (1) define problem and objectives; (2) collect the data; (3) treat the data; (4) interpret results; (5) draw conclusions; (6) apply results.

1. Defining the Problem

a. First consider the selected broad topic or problem. Begin to study and analyse it; discuss it with others, especially experts on the topic.

b. Read around the topic, in relevant articles and research. See what other investigators have found out and begin to clarify and limit the problem you wish to tackle. Nearly all beginners want to find out too much about too wide a topic.

c. Consider whether the problem is likely to be educationally significant and worthy of investigation, both from your point of view, and from the point of view of others who may become involved. Is it likely to interest educators? Is there an easier, more suitable way of approaching the problem, or is the questionnaire the only alternative? How will the collection of data produce worth-while results—or at least clarify the issues—so that further fruitful study and research might be promoted? Keep discussing ideas with experts, for it would be foolish to commit yourself and others to hundreds of hours of work which might be wasted.

2. Collection of Data

a. Decide on who is best fitted to provide the particular information you need. Begin to select a wide random sample which is likely to yield comparable data. Aim at quality in respondents, rather than mere quantity, and at the same time assess whether it is reasonable to ask such people the sort of questions you are proposing. Will they co-operate? Are they too busy? Can they provide answers without extra research or consultation on their part?

b. In consulting with experts, try to obtain the highest appropriate authority to sponsor the questionnaire, approve the project, and permit respondents to fill it in. It has been found by investigators[3] that higher-authority sponsorship is a primary factor in gaining satisfactory responses to questionnaires.

For example, if students or teachers are asked to respond to a questionnaire issued by a university, then (1) the principal or superintendent of schools should approve, and (2) the dean concerned should sponsor, as a general rule.

c. Prepare the questionnaire with a view to the highest possible standards of technique, and at the same time, a minimum of expense, time, and labour. The questionnaire should ask for the particular information which will actually meet the needs of the study and lend itself reasonably well to statistical treatment. To satisfy this requirement, the investigator should think through the problem and anticipate the possible outcomes. Many questionnaires fail to produce the sort of information required to fulfill the objectives of the study, because the problems were not thoroughly explored, the questions badly framed, the positive possibilities not sufficiently anticipated. In some cases questionnaires have provoked hostility, with far-reaching effects.

The questionnaire should be *complete* and *valid,* designed so that it will find out what it seeks to find out. It should conform to the questionnaire requirements outlined earlier in this chapter. It should be tried out on a *pilot sample* of respondents similar to those who will be in the main sample. Improvements in wording and setting out can be made accordingly.

d. The revised final questionnaire should be attractively printed or mimeographed in typescript, preceded or accompanied by a letter of explanation and/or sponsorship. These should be sent to each selected respondent, or in the case of sampling schoolchildren or students, to

[3] R. A. Davis and E. L. Barrow, "Critical Study of the Questionnaire in Education," *Education Administration and Supervision,* XXI (February, 1935), 137–144.

the appropriate authority—with a stamped, addressed return envelope, and a spare copy of the questionnaire for his own files. A record should be kept of the respondents, so that follow-up letters can be sent to those who do not reply within a reasonable time.

3. Treatment of Data

a. A check should be kept of returns, for follow-up letters, and for calculating percentage of replies, etc. The first step is to collate and summarise the responses to each question. The form of the questions determines the ease of statistical treatment. Frequency tabulations can be drawn up to show the frequency of answer to each choice in a question. For example:

Do you brush your teeth after breakfast?	Yes:	160
	No:	40

How often do you brush your teeth after breakfast?	Every day:	90
	Most days:	40
	Quite often:	10
	Occasionally:	15
	Never:	45
		——
		200
		——
	(Qualifying comment) I chew an apple	80

b. A record should be kept of qualifying comments, and these too should be classified according to the shade of opinion expressed. Unusual, particularly significant, and humorous comments should also be recorded.

4. Interpreting Results

a. When all information is summarised, the trends for each response should be studied. These should be interpreted in consultation with experts. It is dangerous to interpret ideas or to draw conclusions on one's own, and prone to error.

b. The limitations of the questionnaire should be kept in mind and noted on paper. The data gained are only as sound as the quality of the investigation has permitted.

5. Drawing Conclusions

a. Conclusions should be drawn and described. Care should be taken to keep faith with respondents, by keeping information confidential and anonymous.

b. A summary of the whole investigation and its findings should be compiled. The limitations and statistical significance of findings, and suggestions for further research should be included.

c. This should be sent, possibly in abbreviated form, to respondents, and the press if desirable. It is wise to consult relevant higher authority before letting the press in. The full study should be published in the appropriate periodical, or as an abstract or thesis—if it is the sort of study for publication. It may be just a study for finding information to improve your program in a school.

6. *Applying Results*

a. Suggestions for further research, if any, should be followed up, if possible, by the appropriate research centre or by individuals.

b. Modifications to programs or teaching methods, or to educational procedures, should be undertaken in the light of the findings of the investigation.

c. Any worth-while norms or summaries which can be drawn up should be used, and also sent to any appropriate educational authorities.

KNOWLEDGE TESTS

Knowledge tests have similar functions in physical education to written examinations in other subjects. They can be administered at the beginning of a course to assess *present status,* or *achievement,* and thus determine the needs of students for that particular course. They can also be used as a means of classification into various ability groups for a course of instruction. During the course, they can be used for the *diagnosis* of weaknesses in learning and teaching, with a view to giving remedial practice, or to modifying teaching methods. At intervals, knowledge tests may be used for the purpose of providing *motivation* to students to review earlier work and learn new work.

THEIR MANY USES

At the end of the course, knowledge tests can be used again to assess *achievement,* so that a comparison of results with those of the initial achievement tests might afford a measure of *progress* during the course.

It must not be thought that knowledge tests should be confined to theoretical branches of our craft, such as health and safety education, and the allied sciences, anatomy, physiology, and kinesiology. Physical-education teaching has swung markedly from the physical to the socio-educational during the last generation in the United States, and the emphasis is very much—perhaps too much—on knowledge teaching, as well as teaching and practice of activity. Such fields as the knowledge of rules and principles of games, the history and development of sports, the background of dance in its various forms, the therapeutic values of exercise and activities, the philosophy behind physical education and recreation in its many facets—all these have been introduced, and even to activity periods of physical-education programs.

USING STUDENTS' MINDS

As a result, our work, it is to be hoped, is becoming meaningful to the students, and the pupils' thinking, as well as their movement, is being stimulated. Their ideas, as well as those of the teacher, are contributing to the richness of the program. There is some danger that, in bringing in pupil participation in planning and pupil choice, hard work has diminished.

In consequence, there is greater scope for the judicious administering of knowledge tests, for purposes such as those just described. Most knowledge tests are spontaneous and original on the teacher's part, as few statewide or nationwide knowledge tests have been standardised.

It is therefore important for the practising teacher to be conversant with the most suitable types of test, and to know how to construct and administer them.

TYPES OF KNOWLEDGE TESTS

Knowledge tests can range widely in type. There are the extremely informal approaches: discussion with a student, quizzing a group of students during play or between physical activities, or merely asking questions of individuals during class sessions. These fairly prevalent forms of testing are valuable, but they do not lend themselves readily to adequate statistical treatment or recording of results, especially with large classes. Nevertheless, an astute teacher with a good memory, who has developed the habit of recording impressions, can utilize such data, especially when he is required to give an impromptu rating of students' ability or knowledge at any particular time.

Coupled with questioning and discussion is the technique of observation. Alert teachers are constantly observing, diagnosing, correcting, and reobserving during class and group activities. The more experienced teachers can even observe several performances of individuals, and thus are engaged in noting assessments of skill and knowledge as work proceeds. Such observation has other values—it also evaluates social and emotional manifestations, and behaviour qualities. Markedly atypical behaviour and maladjustment can be observed and appropriate action then be taken. These characteristics range widely, and include clumsiness, nervousness, fear, defective posture, inadequate strength, insufficient endurance, personality difficulties and many forms of maladjustment and malfunctioning. The teacher should develop the habit of noting down observations at the end of each lesson, and regularly recording such impressions, with the action intended or taken, in the individual student's dossier. Much atypical behaviour or activity can be tactfully dealt with on the spot, but if the cause is to be effectively traced and treated, subsequent further investigation, referral, or therapy will usually be necessary.

The type of knowledge-testing to which most research has been devoted is that of written tests. These are of three main types: (1) assignments, projects, and worksheets; (2) essay examinations and tests; (3) short-answer examinations and tests.

It is important to give some written knowledge tests at intervals during a course, partly to motivate students, but also to provide assessments of class and student progress and learning, as well as the effect of teaching methods.

From the results of written tests, the teacher is in a position to assess which topics or skills have been mastered, and which topics require revision or more attention. A measure of individual achievement is provided, to supplement ratings afforded by observation of and discussion with each pupil. If a student is absent during the period of written examinations at the end of the course, the level of attainment during the year can be more accurately assessed if results of written examinations held during the course are available. As a result of very satisfactory work during the year, he need not be unduly penalised, and may be granted an aegrotat pass, or credit.

ASSIGNMENTS, WORKSHEETS, AND PROJECTS

These written tasks are generally allotted during or after a topic has been dealt with in class, and the assignments form a follow-up study around the topic. Usually the student carries out the task in his own time, say for homework, but he is required to hand it in, or to file it in his workbook, when it is completed, within a specified period. This system means continuing teaching beyond the actual instruction period, and has much to commend it, because it might enable students to apply the skills or material of the lesson into further school situations, or real life. It also gives the chance to bright or industrious students to extend themselves and do extra work without deterring or upsetting the less able student, since such a happy state of affairs is not always possible during the actual class sessions themselves. It provides yet another opportunity for students to become familiar with the use of libraries and the techniques of original research and study. Typical assignments might be:

Choose any game or sport covered this semester, and write a short history of it.
Summarize at least three studies on leisure time recreation of teen-agers *or* juvenile delinquency.

Assignments usually have to be completed in students' free time, say within three to six weeks. They are generally in the form of an essay or report in note form. Typical projects might be:

With your buddy, devise an orienting course in the school grounds or park, sketching it on a large-scale map to show correct bearings and distances.
Make a wooden, plastic, or clay model of an athlete performing an athletic skill in good style.

Projects usually involve practical or manual work, and may be partly or wholly carried out during class, in a free-study period, or in the students' own time. These take varying times to complete, depending on the nature of the project, and usually one to six periods.

Typical worksheets may be charts, diagrams, summaries, or blank forms, which are to be filled in or completed before the next session. They are usually distributed towards the end of a session, and contain

material based on the session, to provide documentation or further application of the work covered. An example might be to "Construct
and draw a motor ability circuit different from the one just performed
(e.g., a Humiston-type motor ability circuit) using the same area, but
different arrangements of apparatus. State both its values and its
limitations."

ESSAY TESTS AND EXAMINATIONS

These—once worshipped as the complete measure of achievement—
have been for some time generally in disrepute, until recently, especially
since the so-called "new type tests" of the objective short-answer type
were developed over a generation ago. The cause of the fall from
grace of the essay test was that it was marked subjectively, and consequently results were unreliable. One examiner might award 80 percent and another 40 percent for the same essay. The weaknesses of
these tests were emphasized many years ago by Hartog and Rhodes[4]
in England, but a massive case had to be built up against them in the
form of investigations on both sides of the Atlantic, before the tradi-
tionalists, particularly in Britain, were swayed. In America, the essay
test was tried, found guilty of grave statistical shortcomings, and
virtually banished from the American educational scene (with dire
effects on the ability of children to write sustained and well-organised
prose). In Britain and Europe, more conservative educators, particularly at the higher levels of study, still cling to the essay on the
grounds of strengths other than statistical soundness. In the British
Commonwealth, there are mixed attitudes. It is probably best to adjust to the prevailing pattern in an institution in this matter.

Essay examinations usually have few required items, generally less
than six questions. They are easy to prepare, but very difficult to mark
accurately. They are usually scored by numerical assessment in the form
of a total percentage, which may be divided into proportions, e.g., 20
each for 5 questions. The resulting total percentage is often converted
into letter grades: A, B, C, D, and E, or their Greek equivalents. The
reverse is sometimes practised: each question is marked by letter grades,
which are later converted to numerical sums adding to a percentage
score. It can be imagined that the methods of converting from letters
to numbers vary!

[4] P. J. Hartog and E. C. Rhodes, *An Examination of Examinations,* 2nd ed.,
London, Macmillan, 1936.

There may be an important place for the essay test, in association with objective short-answer tests. The values claimed for the essay are that it requires the students to study a question, marshal his ideas about the topic, organise them in terms of the question, exclude irrelevant ideas, and express himself logically and fluently and with power, originality, and conviction in his written answer. The emphasis is not so much on fact-finding and recall, as on applying facts and ideas, and integrating them into a coherent, appropriate answer. Many educators neglect this important aspect of education. Concise, fluent, and accurate self-expression in answer to a carefully worded question has a vital place at the higher levels of schooling, and this is particularly true for the humanities and subjects with a strong philosophical flavour; the absence of writing ability mars much scientific writing, although there are classical exceptions.[5]

It is not suggested that essay tests replace objective tests in final examinations. But there might well be more essay-type assignments and tests at intervals during higher school and university courses.

Final examinations, if they are to be the only criteria of a final grading, should be largely objective in marking. But at the higher educational levels, and in the more discursive and philosophical aspects of our field, self-expression, application of knowledge, and the organisation and integration of ideas should be evaluated, along with the mere recall of facts. Suggested compromises in this testing situation are offered after the next section, and there is also a little-known one given which to some extent has the merits of the essay and the objective test.

OBJECTIVE TESTS AND EXAMINATIONS

These are of two main types, the recognition and the recall tests. In the recognition test the answer is chosen from among several choices, while the recall test demands memory and provision or completion of the answer.

1. *Alternate choice* such as Yes/No or True/False. In these, to a question or statement, the candidate must answer Yes, No, or I do not

[5] See a forthcoming anthology of the best scientific prose by T. R. Henn of Cambridge, or *A Book of Science Verse*, selected by W. Eastwood, London, Macmillan, 1961.

know; or indicate whether the statement is true, false, or doubtful. These tests are fairly easy to construct, but considerable care has to be taken not to make the answer obvious. They lend themselves readily to manual and mechanical scoring. They also allow for guessing, which demands some correction in the scoring, such as number right minus number wrong. It is thus theoretically possible to score less than zero!

An example of the alternate choice test is:

1. The most popular measure in a series is the mode.	T	F	D
2. The most reliable measure of dispersion is the range.	T	F	D
3. The larger the measure of dispersion, the more concentrated the series.	T	F	D
4. The quartile deviation is used with reference to the mean.	T	F	D
5. The median is the central case in a ranked series.	T	F	D

2. *Multiple choice* is a recognition test with several—usually three to six—choices to complete the stem of a statement. Again, the test is easy to construct, but care is needed, especially with grammar (singular and plural, past and present, capital letters of proper names, etc.), to ensure that the answer is not "given away." Questions should be in homogeneous groups in short-answer tests.

Here is an example of a multiple choice question:

1. The correlation between broad jumping and sprinting with a large sample of track and field athletes is:
   a. high positive   d. near zero
   b. moderate positive   e. low negative
   c. low positive   f. high negative
2. The measure of dispersion which includes all cases in a distribution is:
   a. range   d. probable error
   b. mean deviation   e. quartile deviation
   c. standard deviation   f. interquartile range

3. *A matching choice* question usually comprises two lists, each with between five and twenty statements. The first statement in the left-hand list matches or fits best with one statement in the right-hand list. The left-hand list usually contains the longer, or descriptive, statements, and the right-hand list may consist of names or words. Both lists are usually in alphabetical order, and the second list may contain several extra names to minimise the element of guessing by elimination.

Here is an example of a matching choice question:

In the parentheses beside the name of the school in the lefthand list, write the number opposite the name of the educator who pioneered or advocated that type of school:

( )	Academy	1.	Basedow
( )	Court School	2.	Comenius
( )	Folk High School	3.	Froebel
( )	Gymnasien	4.	Grundtvig
( )	Kindergarten	5.	Milton
( )	Philanthropinum	6.	Sturm
( )	School of Mother's Knee	7.	Vittorino da Feltre

This type of question is particularly useful for a factual type of information involving who, what, where, and when, but not suitable where interpretations and subtle shades of meaning are required in the answer.

WEAKNESSES OF OBJECTIVE TESTS

In the first place, these tests are too factual, encouraging rote-learning, and shallow, superficial knowledge. Second, they do not give scope for self-expression, the marshalling of ideas, and the application and integration of them into a fluent and logical answer. Nor do they give practice in sustained and planned prose. Third, they do not allow for qualification, showing penetrating understanding, and the subject with a half-grasp of the topic can often, undeservedly, score well.

SUGGESTIONS FOR IMPROVING OBJECTIVE TESTS

True/false tests can overcome some of their weaknesses by means of the following procedures: In addition to stating whether the statement is true or false, the subject is asked to give reasons. In another form (see example) the subject is asked to examine a phrase, to say whether it be true or false and why, and if it be partially true to say why. Experience suggests that a student's capacity to sort out the meaning of partial truths is valuable and demands critical acumen. Another variation leaves a space for the correct answer if the question is false; this the student must fill in.

Multiple choice tests in some fields are improved by the subject choosing the best-fitting match and the second best, stating his reasons in, say, four lines.

Matching tests can be improved by having a recall rider added to each question. In the example just given, the subject could be asked to state which educational school of thought each educator belonged to.

Recall tests can in some fields be improved by the subject being required to justify, or give reasons for, the term he has used.

It is not suggested that such modifications to short-answer tests will always improve them. Complete objectivity is lost as far as marking is concerned. For fields involving a philosophical basis, this loss might be more than compensated for by the deeper and more analytical approach required of the subject.

A compromise between short answer and essay type tests and assignments may be the most suitable approach in many fields. A typical program of tests and assignments in a course might be:

1. Short assignments requiring essay answers at regular intervals.
2. Short-answer tests at regular intervals during the course.
3. Short-answer and essay type in about equal proportion for final examinations at the end of the course. To avoid the slow writer or slow thinker being penalised, an extra half-hour for every three hours of examination time might be allowed.

CONSTRUCTION OF KNOWLEDGE TESTS

1. Knowledge tests should be comprehensive, sampling the whole field. Therefore, about a third or more of the test should be devoted to short factual answers.

2. Tests should at the same time allow scope for application, analysis, and integration of knowledge. Therefore, about a third or more of the test should give the chance to organise and express ideas.

3. They should be valid in that they measure knowledge in the given field, with irrelevant or extraneous factors and knowledge kept to a minimum.

4. They should, where possible, continue the educational process. (Final examinations do not usually allow this.) Candidates should in many cases go through their script papers afterwards, noting their weaknesses. The teacher should give remedial practices where applicable. In final examinations, the True/False and Yes/No type are not ideal, because they may leave an incorrect impression in the student's mind, and no subsequent steps are taken to correct it.

5. The test should be neatly printed or typed, with suitable rubric, and space for the candidate's name or code number. The date, time, and place of the examination should be posted well in advance, at least a month for important or final examinations. Rules for examination for all candidates to read should be posted well in advance too. These notices should be signed by the head of the department or school, not just the class teacher. A senior teacher or head should ensure that any class is not overburdened with too many tests coming close together, over and above assignments. A test should have a simple form and clear instructions; these must be straightforward and promote confidence and rapport. Deliberate traps and pitfalls should be avoided. Try out the test on several experts and colleagues to test the phrasing and meaning of the items. Revise any that are unsuitable.

6. The items should range from the very easy to the very difficult, generally in that order. Most items should discriminate between good and poor performers, yielding a fairly normal distribution of scores without exhibiting a marked ceiling or basement effect. Item analysis should show few items with a difficulty rating outside the 10–90 range.

7. The items should be grouped homogeneously in sections, each of which is not unduly long, and should provide a variety of tasks for the candidate. Generally, the shortest and simplest types, e.g., alternate response, are placed first, and the longest, subtler sections, such as essay questions, are placed last.

8. Allowance should be made when preparing the test items that slow writers and slow thinkers are not unduly penalised. Optional time extensions may need to be provided.

9. The test can be made permanent if it proves very satisfactory and meets statistical requirements; norms can then be established.

SCORING TESTS

Scoring Physical Performance Tests

Scoring should be as objective and reliable as possible. We have already pointed out that direct measurement and count-scoring, correctly using the best possible measuring devices, and experienced scorers, adequately prepared, constitute highly reliable and objective scoring systems, regardless of whether the test is valid or not. Unfortunately, many tests with excellent scoring systems are not highly valid, and despite the accurate scoring system are of little use.

Direct measurement and count-scoring methods can be used a great deal to measure physical performance, particularly quantitative performance in terms of distance, time, weight, and energy. Areas such as physical growth, track and field athletics, swimming, and most games and sports lend themselves readily to objective scoring.

In other fields, such as diving, dance, and gymnastics, highly objective and reliable methods of scoring are more difficult to devise, because quality is the main criterion of good performance. Yet subjec-

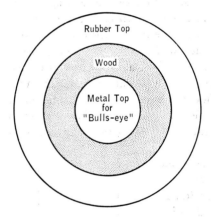

Fig. 11.1. Wall target for throwing tests. Each area has a different surface, producing different sound of impact; and each area is painted a different colour. Radii of concentric circles increase by 4½ or 6 inches (larger circles for junior pupils).

tive rating systems in some sports have improved greatly, and can be made fairly reliable.

EXAMPLES IN PHYSICAL PERFORMANCE TESTS OF OBJECTIVE SCORING OR
MEASUREMENT

1. *Throwing.* The measuring devices should be as accurate and yet as simple as possible for the particular situation. For example, *wall targets* (see Fig. 11.1) should have clearly visible yet thin dividing lines, or, better still, contrasting colours should be used. Again, sounds of impact can be made contrasting, by using different materials, such as wood, rubber, and metal, for each area. The score value for each area should be clearly labelled. The use of bright colours and auditory

stimuli also creates interest, increasing the motivating quality of the test. Liberal use of poster colours, coloured chalk or tape, ropes, poles, sticks, flags, and white or coloured lines on grass, concrete, or blacktop, to mark throwing zones—and similar aids—will promote interest and be conducive to effective measurement. When measuring throwing for distance, the marking of white lines at intervals is very time-consuming. A simpler way is to place sticks or markers down the line of throw, at say 10-yard intervals, with smaller markers in between, say, 10- to 15-feet intervals. A football grid comes in handy for such purposes. The class can be divided into teams or groups, with one group prepared for each, say, 100-yard dash, broad jump, and throw for distance (using football, baseball, softball, or cricket, depending on the prevailing sport of the school). Thus one group of about eight will be at the throwing area. Half of them have three turns each at throwing, while the other half are stationed well down the throwing line to retrieve and roll back balls, and to record distances. The spotter and recorder should stand at the side opposite the approximate distance of the throw. The spotter identifies the thrower and notes the length of throw to the nearest 10 or 15 feet, and passes the information to the recorder, who merely concentrates on entering the data on the recording sheet.

In this way, a whole class can be tested in throwing for distance and two or three other skills in a half-hour session, without needing outside scorers. Purposeful, brisk organisation coupled with adequate markings and equipment in the test layout stimulates the students to maximum effort and interested participation.

The same can be said about applied throwing techniques used in specific sports. For example, in softball and baseball, the pitching frame (width of the plate-knee to shoulder opening) is a useful aid to measuring accuracy of pitches of students (see Fig. 11.2). Several of these, with one to each pair of pupils, permit a rapid measurement and recording of this skill.

In cricket, accuracy in bowling can be

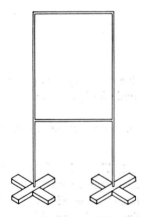

Fig. 11.2. Wooden softball pitching frame for pitching in pairs. The size of the opening is that of the average "strike" zone.

scored on a ground target, again using a partner system, one bowling and one scoring and fielding. The scoring system for each square of the target will vary according to length of bowl, and whether a straight bowl, an off-spin, or a leg-spin is required. These targets could be prepared on old roller blind or canvas, and stored away when not in use.

Scoring in throwing events with large balls, such as basketballs, volleyballs and the like, can be quite objective and valid in, say, shooting baskets, or throwing for accuracy or speed against wall targets, as measures of the skills involved. However, many skills in these games depend a great deal on teamwork between players. Tests involving pairs or groups of subjects are not highly valid because of the unpredictable element of the human opponent or teammate—although in a sense this makes the situation nearer to that of the actual game.

2. *Catching.* Tests designed to measure skill and speed in catching present similar problems. Catching in pairs does not yield a valid measure of the catching ability of either partner. Throwing and catching against a wall can be a more valid test, but is very limited in its scope. The use of ball ejectors, pitching machines, and mechanical devices of this kind can provide a constant means of propelling a ball, so that catching ability of fielders can be tested with a fair measure of validity. A ball-propelling machine can be made quite cheaply, or there are many on the market, and, while not as quick or consistent as a pitching machine, it can provide a fairly valid measure of small-ball catching ability, at various distances. The subject starts at, say 30 feet, moving in 3 feet at a time to 18 feet, then 2 feet at a time to 12 feet, then a foot at a time. Three trials at each distance score till all three trials are missed at two consecutive distances.

3. *Running.* Running distances for time present relatively few problems of scoring as far as objectivity, reliability, and validity are concerned. Administratively, however, such tests as the 100-yard dash, are awkward in that the start and finish are so far apart. The test should be controlled and recorded at the finish, with only the starter and competitors at the starting end. Timing, spotting and recording are thus all carried out near the finish line. The other method of noting distance run in a certain time, mentioned earlier, can also be used. Scores can be converted after.

To get over the distance problem, courses where the starting and finish lines are at the same point, offer alternatives with easier administration. Times on such courses cannot be compared with normal track norms involving straight courses, because of the varying distances round the turns. The simplest type is the "round the marker and back" course, of say 50 yards each way—a long shuttle run in fact. Another is the course around a softball diamond, which of course is a little less than 100 yards, even allowing for running outside the diamond.

Within the groups there should be a partner system. The timer uses a metronome or stopwatch, and calls out the seconds, as soon as a runner starts. The runner's partner notes the time called immediately after the runner arrives back at the finish. He, or the recorder for the group, notes the time. Four runners on a softball diamond can each start from a different base, and be timed together, with their partners scoring. Then they change about, and the other four run.

These systems are more suitable for junior and senior high-school pupils. For college students, the regulation track event may be preferred, if sufficient time and administrators are available for the more complex scoring system. For a large group the ingenious progressive circular relay is an excellent motivation for the dash, and also for evaluating the level of baton-passing efficiency.

Progressive Circular Relay is a running competition which gives sprinting and baton-passing practice to many boys or girls in a small area. It can be run on an athletic track, but a smaller circle or, better still, an oval about 100 yards long and 60 yards across is very suitable. Flags on sticks are placed around the perimeter at about 30-yard (junior high) or 50-yard (senior high) intervals. To find the number of "stations," each with a flag, use the following table:

Number of Pupils	Teams and Members		Number of Flags
20	4	of 5	4
30	5	of 6	5
42	6	of 7	6
56	7	of 8	7
72	8	of 9	8
90	9	of 10	9 etc.

There are as many stations as teams, and there is one more member per team than the number of stations.

As shown in the illustration, the stations are placed evenly round the track, with one team leader, baton in hand, by his own flag at his starting station. Thus each team has a different starting station. The leader ensures that there is one member of his team at each of the other stations, and that the extra member is with him at his starting station. At the starting signal, each leader sprints around the track to his second member, who receives the baton in the correct manner and

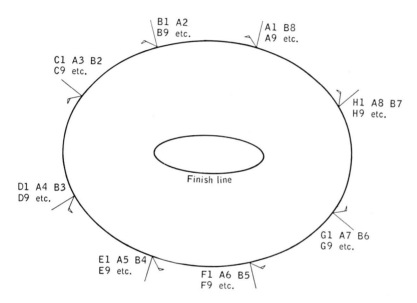

B1 A2 B9 etc.

A1 B8 A9 etc.

C1 A3 B2 C9 etc.

H1 A8 B7 H9 etc.

Finish line

D1 A4 B3 D9 etc.

G1 A7 B6 G9 etc.

E1 A5 B4 E9 etc.

F1 A6 B5 F9 etc.

FIG. 11.3. Progressive circular relay.

takes it on to the third member, etc. When the baton has gone right around, the extra member takes it on from the starting station to the leader who is now one flag further on. With each circuit of the baton, each runner moves on one station, until each leader reaches his own flag again, whereupon he pulls it out of the ground and runs inwards, planting the flag on the small inner circle. First leader in is the winner.

4. *Jumping.* Running broad-jump and high-jump skills can be measured in the usual way for track and field athletics. Standing broad jump can also be tested in outdoor jumping pits. It is useful to have

a fixed board along the side of the pit with 3-inch intervals marked. Indoors, floor markings, either permanent, or of tape or chalk, can be used. These, if kept outside the main court markings, have the advantage of motivating children to practice and can be used in squad work. Another handy method is to prepare roller blinds with painted markings 6 inches apart, and lesser gradations at inch intervals. Subjects jump on or beside the canvas, depending on its suitability and strength. The canvas should be attached to or laid out on the floor when required, and rolled up for storage afterwards.

Standing high jump is usually measured by the vertical jump and reach test, originally popularised by Dr. Dudley Sargent in the last century. A very good method of scoring this is to use a roller blind attached to the wall, so that it travels up and down and can be stopped in the usual fashion by the ratchet notches. If the distance the blind travels between notches is about $1\frac{1}{2}$ inches, then three scales staggered $\frac{1}{2}$ inch apart will cover the distance between notches, and the blind can accordingly be adjusted so that it will be within $\frac{1}{2}$ inch of any student's upward reach. If a partner system is used, the partner adjusts the blind for the jumper, who uses the scale with the baseline nearest his upward reach. The jumper has three trials, and his partner—standing on a stool—observes the point reached by his finger tips each time. The best jump is scored. There are of course, many other varieties of apparatus for this test.

This method of scoring is very quick, and requires no measuring with rulers, no use of chalk, or rubbing out. A group of eight, in pairs, can be tested in a few minutes, much more rapidly than with the usual blackboard and chalk method.

SUBJECTIVE EVALUATION, RATING, AND JUDGING

In such activities as gymnastics, dance, boxing, wrestling, and diving, the assessment and scoring of performances must take into account largely the *quality* of the movement, and this cannot as yet, if ever, be rated purely objectively.

In the past such assessments were sometimes highly unreliable and invalid, but statistical knowledge and techniques have been applied to a large extent, reducing, if not minimising, the weaknesses prevalent in the scoring systems. The rulebooks or regulations governing most of the above sports contain directions for scoring performances, and should be consulted. There are a number of general principles which apply to all these sports which should be considered here.

Let us take the hypothetical example of a school's annual gymnastics competition. If the competition is strictly on Olympic gymnastics lines, then the Olympic gymnastics rules and procedure should be adhered to. But if, as is often the case, it is an individual competition in physical education, and consisting only partly of gymnastic activities, then general principles of rating and judging should be applied.

The fundamental considerations of what the competition is for should first be studied. An outside judge should talk over with the teacher of the school such matters as why the competition is being held, what the pupils have been taught and the standard reached, exactly what activities are to be included, what instructions have been given to the pupils, what costume is required, and what basis the competition is to be marked on. These should be discussed fully, for it is unfortunate if a judge penalises competitors because of a difference in interpretation between him and the teacher.

These principles should then be applied:

1. If possible there should be more than one judge, and three is often a good arrangement. They should be outsiders, so as to reduce the possibility of favouritism or bias.

2. The judges should be experienced in the type of work and in its rating, and thoroughly briefed in the considerations outlined above.

3. Plenty of notice should have been given to both judges and pupils, and the pupils should have had adequate opportunity to prepare and practice, and to know the conditions, costume, and other requirements.

4. The place for the competition should be familiar and suitable, with correct equipment similar to that used in practice. Lighting, run-up space, and spectator accommodation should be adequate. Steps should be taken to ensure that spectators will be quiet and orderly, so that there are no distractions.

5. There should be a sufficient number of representative items, so that the competition is as valid as possible in being a test of ability in the particular field of physical education involved.

6. The contestants should be limbered up, to minimise danger of accident, and to ease tension and nervousness. It is often a good idea

for them to practice several activities "in stream" (that is, one behind the other in fairly quick succession). This will warm the group up, and enable the judges to obtain a general idea of the standard and spread of performance.

7. The competitors should display numbers and not names. There should not be too many in the finals of the competition, since the judges will have an exacting task even with less than a dozen contestants. In any case, too many contestants will cause the competition to be drawn out too long.

8. The contestants should not perform in the same order each time; the order should rotate.

9. When the competition consists of only a few activities, it might be desirable to have two or three attempts at each, to minimise the luck factor, or nervousness on the part of the contestants. R. E. Roper in England in the 1920s observed that in vaulting and tumbling few could produce their best at the first attempt, while most had produced it by the fifth, with the third as mean. However, the usual number of activities, say at least ten, should have this effect anyway. There is also the problem of "weighting" the events. The showier events, which make the spectators gasp, can count too much. It seems possible that a "degree of difficulty" factor, as used in judging diving, may be necessary.

THE METHOD OF SCORING

1. It is usually wise to have some consistent and agreed-on system of scoring, for example, taking into account the approach and take-off, the movement, and the landing and recovery in a gymnastic vault. In some more complex vaults, or in sequences, points might be allotted for each part of the movement.

2. The scale should be as simple and small as is suitable. Most activities can be rated satisfactorily out of ten, or sometimes even only five, points.

3. With sequences of movements, and with inexperienced judges, it may be advisable to divide the judging scale into parts, analysing the movement and allotting appropriate points, and adding them up afterwards—though Gestalt impressions are important.

4. It is advisable to encourage the judges to spread the marks as

much as possible, because a tendency to use a small range of marks often causes difficulty in sorting out the minor-place getters. With practice, judges can discriminate between low-average and high-average performances and score accordingly.

5. Unless the judge has a good idea of the standard, it is often useful to award the first contestants a nearer-to-average mark by one point. These can be adjusted after seeing several other performers. If the judge awards a good vault 8 out of 10 points, and it then turns out that nearly all the succeeding vaults are even better, a ceiling effect will result—or else there will be insufficient room at the top end of the scale. An initial award of 7 points could be made, and adjusted to 8 if the succeeding vaults are no better. Similarly with very poor vaults, initial marks one point nearer to average, possibly adjusted later, may ease crowding at the lower end of the scale. The more experienced the judge is, the harder it is in general to get him to give full marks.

6. If the wrong vault or movement is executed, the judges should award marks according to prior arrangement with teacher and pupils. Usually it is due either to misunderstanding, when the contestant may be given another chance, or the result of at least attempting the right movement, when credit should be given for the parts executed correctly. In top-class competition, no marks are usually given for incorrect vaults.

7. Usually no allowance is made for variations in age and size of contestants, although in small informal competitions, encouragement should be given to the young and those whose physique is less than suitable.

SCORE CARDS

Score cards are extremely important in providing the required evaluation data in the most appropriate form and in the quickest way. They can be grouped into two types: those which are individual, and self-scoring or scored by partner or leader; and those which are for the whole group or class, usually scored by an assistant or the teacher.

It is advisable to have score cards printed for the main evaluation work before the schoolyear begins. Manila or cardboard is best, since score cards are often subject to hard wear. Of course some evaluation procedures, such as measuring growth patterns of individuals, will require special forms.

An all-purpose scoring card can be printed, and used both by individuals and by groups. The form shown in Fig. 11.4, printed on both sides, is suitable.

RECORDING RESULTS

Results of tests and measurement programs should be recorded permanently in a suitable filing system, with adequate indexing. You

Name or Event	1	2	3	4	5	6	Total

Grade _____ Date _____ Event or Name _____

FIG. 11.4.   Simple general purpose score card.

never know when you or another person may wish to use them for research or for other purposes.

A popular system employs a double filing cabinet, one containing individual dossiers for each student, and the other containing summarised material, by classes and in chronological order. In addition, the most important data on each student should be summarised on his cumulative-record card along with general information, and relevant material for the physical educator should be copied and recorded in a small card-index file. The latter should be kept for quick and handy reference on his desk.

The individual dossier for each student usually consists of a cardboard or manila folder, containing all individual material, much of which must be transcribed from test results recorded in the class files. Informal notes and jottings by the teacher, as well as data and notes from the principal, teachers, and parents, and medical officers and counsellors will be filed inside the folder. The folder itself could be used as a summary record form, as a growth chart (see Chapter 12), or as an individual achievement chart. In schools with their own health service, there should be continual liaison over these matters.

The class files will contain class lists and score cards, with grouped and summarised data. Very often, this material will be summarised or classified according to age, physical fitness, and other indices. Norms and other useful data will be housed here.

SELF-RATING AS A TEACHING TOOL

Suppose a child does a stunt—tumbles or vaults—our tendency as a teacher is to comment qualitatively and encouragingly on it; however, once a teacher and class have established mutual understanding, the learning effect can be increased if (1) the teacher from time to time awards points on a ten-point scale, slightly upgrading the weaker brethren, but making it very clear that a full mark is very difficult indeed to get. At first the teacher indicates to the better children why and in what way they fall short of perfection; then it is wise to change after a while to another method: (2) asking the child to rate himself in what he has just done, and to indicate what he thinks his errors were. This is all verbal, but it is evaluation as much as any statistical treatment. One's aim is to bring the youngsters to the stage where they perceive through their proprioceptors and other feedback mechanisms what their errors are. Self-evaluation is an important educational goal and can be lost if all evaluation is external.

CARD FILING SYSTEMS

The summary-card index file of all pupils in alphabetical order, perhaps by grade, will contain such data as age, body type, significant medical information and special atypical characteristics, motor-ability and physical-ability indices, intelligence quotient, and significant data on both physical achievement and sports talent.

It may be a good idea to have a separate cabinet for draft results, score cards, and the like, which may provide useful research material, even though most of the data are summarised in the main filing system. Do not destroy raw scores and draft results unless all the data have been entered in the main files.[6]

Continually keep records and files up to date. Revise T scales and norms, and keep cumulative-record cards, growth charts, etc., entered up to date—and if the work is too much for one person, enlist the aid of colleagues, senior students, other teachers, clerks, or parents. (One of the authors worked closely for three years with a math. teacher who processed all records.)

PERIODIC CHECK-UPS

Periodically—especially at the beginning of the school year, and a month before the end of the course, but preferably every month—*scan* all measurements and test results. Consider which evaluation procedures are proving useful, and which have not. There may be grounds for continuing some of the evaluation work, in the hope that time and opportunity will be found to utilise it, or for discontinuing other work which is not proving worth while. Some tests may need repeating, to check progress and achievement; others, to calculate their reliability. The following are some reasons which might justify testing and evaluation work.

1. To indicate results of a course—what are the achievements in general?
2. To show pupil achievement—how have individuals done?
3. To evaluate the success of a teaching method—is our teaching successful?
4. To provide evidence of a need for equipment or facilities—which can be presented to the principal.
5. To provide data for a case to put forward to school authorities, pointing out benefits of the physical education program.
6. To provide information for parents, enlightening them about the value of the physical-education program.

[6] One of the authors kept individual height-weight graphs for a number of years in a school. His successor, not understanding their value for establishing norms, etc.—destroyed them.

7. To serve as a part of research projects.
8. To compare two experiments, methods, or samples, using experimental and control-group techniques.
9. To provide data for school reports, awards, badges, and the like.
10. To provide data for team selection.
11. To assist in classifying students into ability, and other selected, groups.
12. To motivate pupils and provide incentives and challenges.
13. To provide data for achievement charts and publicity material for notice boards.
14. To trace and assess the growth pattern, posture, nutritional and physical condition of pupils.
15. To provide additional data on medical condition of pupils.
16. To assess physical abilities of pupils.

STANDARDIZING TESTS AND USE OF NORMS

Many tests used by teachers will already be standardised, with norms established. Other tests will need to be modified, or have norms constructed for the particular situation. Others will be adapted merely for informal uses to help improve the education process. Few teachers will have the time, facilities, or personnel available to construct, standardise, and publish tests, as well as to draw up norms for them. Nevertheless, the main procedure in the process of drawing up norms is given below.

When standardising tests, the intention usually is for a test to be adequate for some years, and to be suitable for others to use. The test should therefore be of the highest possible standard, meeting rigorous statistical requirements. Some advanced statistical procedures require rather complex techniques beyond the scope of this book. At the end of this chapter, the reader is referred to several texts where the techniques of advanced statistical method are explained.

Some of the main steps in standardising a test are as follows:

1. Items should be analysed by item analysis, and modified accordingly so that only suitable items are included.
2. The validity of the test should be determined by correlation with one or more validity criteria.

3. The reliability of the test should be calculated if possible by retest, or by the odd-even "split-halves" method.

4. Each subtest of the complete battery should be correlated with each other; if any two subtests intercorrelate highly, i.e., measure the same thing twice (unless desirable), the least suitable subtest should be discarded. This procedure is carried out to ensure that each subtest to a large extent measures some important component of the total variable or ability to be measured, and conversely, that every important component of the ability is measured by one of the subtests.

5. Next, multiple correlation coefficients with the validity criterion should be obtained, so that it can be determined which subtests in the complete battery will make the best combination, both in terms of the coefficient, and in respect of ease of administration. The complete test battery can then be selected.

6. Weight raw scores so that, when combined, each subtest is represented in even proportions. This can be done by three methods:
   a. Simply by multiplying lower average subtest scores by an appropriate number to bring them into line with highest average subtest scores.
   b. By computing T scores for each subtest and adding them.
   c. By computing regression equations.

ESTABLISHING NORMS

The battery should now be tried out on an appropriate sample. A T scale, or separate T scales for each subtest, should be constructed. (S scales or Z scales could alternatively be drawn up for certain purposes.) The T scale is the most versatile and convenient of the standard scales. It is also readily understood by students, and is widely accepted throughout the English-speaking world. These norms may have to be revised from time to time, as standards of performance change. Norms can also easily be compiled for your own situation, using tests which have been standardised elsewhere. With judicious use, the values of norms are tremendous.

USES OF NORMS

1. Norms provide a measure of level of achievement in a field—a

yardstick of ability for pupils of the same type in other schools, the state, the whole nation, or even in other nations. Transcultural comparisons are interesting, as well as valuable, to children.

2. Such data enable *comparisons* of achievement or status to be made between individuals, classes, and schools, or states and nations, using norms of standardised tests which can be applied universally.

3. Comparisons can sometimes also be made between teaching methods, or learning efficiency in the educational process, and different techniques and styles in many activities in the program.

4. Such data can show the rates of growth, learning, and achievement of both boys and girls as they grow older, and can aid in determining at which age to teach or emphasise certain skills and activities to the majority.

5. They can be the basis for the standards or minimum requirements planned or expected in any course, e.g., in an achievement chart. As a result, pupils will appreciate what levels of achievement they should aim for and accomplish, and teachers can assess clearly and quickly the progress being made towards the objectives of the course.

6. In the form of standards, they can provide a graded series of goals to motivate pupils to strive to improve their own achievement— "beat their own record"—and reach successively more difficult and advanced goals.

7. They can provide the basis for class, school, and state competition.

8. They can assist with diagnosis of weaknesses and strengths of individuals and classes or teams, so that appropriate action and practice can be taken.

9. They can indicate improvement, progress, and learning of skills during a course, particularly when achievement or status at the begining and again at the end are compared. Relative benefit or effects of several courses or topics can be compared by using norms with experimental and control groups.

10. Exceptional talents of individuals may be revealed if tests with norms are applied, and special treatment or coaching may be accordingly more effective and less wasteful educationally.

11. In physical activities and conditioning programs, norms and standards lend themselves to self-instruction and self-teaching, in schools, in clubs, and at home.

12. School, county, state, national, and Olympic team selection can be assisted by norms in various sports and events.

13. Norms can be developed both as a result of, and as a stimulus to, research into all aspects of education.

Nonconformity to Norms

However, like most things, norms used to excess involve dangers and weaknesses. Each of us is different from our fellows, and today we are educating as much for those qualities which are different in our pupils, as those things which are the same. We should not try to make all individuals conform to a norm, when growth pattern, physique, and temperament all are destined to make many very different from the norm. One can remember the shock received as a high-school pupil in the 1930s when a teacher, just returned from the United States with a Master's Degree in physical education, began to measure heights and weights, and informed one of the authors that he was 19 pounds underweight. Further, his parents were informed, and became quite alarmed. He has since found that he was destined to be quite tall and ectomesomorphic, and that the height-weight tables the learned doctor-teacher had adopted for all pupils were average weights for height, regardless of range of age and physique.

Norms can be of great value to both teachers and pupil, nonetheless. They can indicate the achievement and standards of nation-wide samples of students, similar to those he is teaching. They can show him differences and likenesses, and whether his students have reached nation-wide standards. If they have not, and if the teacher is satisfied that such shortcomings or deficiencies require correction, he can modify his program accordingly. Deficiencies of a whole class, be they deficiencies in physique, posture, or ability, should be investigated.

Individual deviations from norms require careful interpretation. The teacher must be sure that "abnormalities" of individual pupils are in fact real, and not reasonable and harmless variations, lying well within the distribution range of the group.

Norms Are Useful for Screening and Standards

With individuals, norms have a very useful function as a screening device. Individuals failing to reach a certain norm can be referred for closer study and further examination. There is a danger that an individual, finding he is well below a norm, may suffer through misunderstanding its significance, and the possible upset may do more harm than good of therapy.

On the other hand, the setting of individual norms and standards in the form of achievement charts, and the encouragement of individuals to "beat their own records" and thus improve achievement and skill, can motivate pupils and be of great value to the educational program, so long as *undue emphasis* is not put on the aim of being class champion. It is important with children's sets of values to realize that a football or track hero is no more important than a good citizen, a scholar, or an artist. We all know that the motivating quality of trying to beat our own score in golf can be very great—and many of us make tremendous efforts to do so! We exploit this form of motivation only too seldom in schools, where class and school competition and champions thrive at the expense of self-competition and over-all standards.

RECOMMENDED READING

Baron, D., and H. W. Bernard, *Evaluation Techniques for Classroom Teachers,* New York, McGraw-Hill, 1953.

Glassow, R. B., and M. R. Broer, *Measuring Achievement in Physical Education,* Philadelphia, Saunders, 1938.

Hunsicker, P. A., and H. J. Montoye, *Applied Tests and Measurements in Physical Education,* New York, Prentice-Hall, 1954.

Jordan, A. M., *Measurement in Education,* New York, McGraw-Hill, 1953.

Neilson, N. P., and F. W. Cozens, *Achievement Scales in Physical Education for Boys and Girls in Elementary and Junior High Schools,* New York, Barnes, 1934.

Research Methods Applied to Health, Physical Education and Recreation, Washington, AAHPER, 1949.

Scott, G., and E. French, *Evaluation in Physical Education,* St. Louis, Mosby, 1950.

part iii

APPLICATION TO THE INDIVIDUAL

chapter 12

THE CHANGING INDIVIDUAL

What! my young lady and mistress! By'r lady, your ladyship is
nearer heaven than when I saw you last, by the altitude of a
chopine. Pray God, your voice, like a piece of uncurrent gold, be
not cracked within the ring.

Hamlet, Act II, Scene 2

In the Beginning

WITHIN perhaps six hours of the successful spermatozoon burrowing
its way into the nucleus of the human ovum, growth starts. Of course,
in their turn, the ovum and spermatozoon have also grown. With
certain kinds of bats the spermatozoon may be put near the ovum in
the fall, but nothing happens till the spring. In one kind of worm,
"Seminal fluid from one copulation is sufficient for several months of
viable cocoon production."[1] Children have been conceived by stored
semen after six months of freeze-drying; in fact, the apparently mi-
raculous could happen—a man could beget a child months after he
was dead. Those who say there is nothing new under the sun should
ponder the full implications of such facts. At Columbia University a
doctor has been able to fertilise under the microscope a ripe ovum
obtained during a gynaecological operation and to observe *in vitro*
(that is, independently of a living environment) the whole intimate
process of the fusion of the gametes and the first stages of cell division.
The test-tube baby of Aldous Huxley's *Brave New World* has not been

[1] B. L. Roots, "The Earthworm," *New Biology*, XXI, 110. Harmondsworth,
Middlesex, Penguin Books, 1960.

281

produced yet, but young rabbits have been born from a female rabbit into whom the artificially (i.e., *in vitro*) fertilised ovum of another rabbit has been experimentally introduced.

Whether we like it or not, such experiments of the mid-twentieth century have enlarged our understanding of the beginnings of human growth—the first-cell division of a new being.

Life and Nonlife

We knew long before this that growth of certain kinds could proceed independently of a living environment. There is the often-described experiment in which a piece of chicken's heart has increased in size, while provided with a nutrient medium for over thirty-five years.[2] Though whether this piece of still growing chicken's heart is living or dead is a difficult philosophic question. When one considers that the human male beard, and the nails of both sexes, continue to grow for a while after clinical death, the mystery is seen not to be confined only to the experimental situation.

Growth, a Major Field of Study

As a biological phenomenon, growth is a lifetime study for many kinds of scientist. How does it concern the physical educationist, and with what aspects should he be concerned? First, the schoolteaching physical educationist is dealing with individuals in whom growth is a *major* phenomenon. Second, certain aspects of this complex of growth concern health. Third, certain aspects concern skill.

Thus, those working with human beings in their infancy, juvenile period, or early and late adolescence are, by the nature of the human material, confronted with growth in many of its forms.

Growth Is Partly Inevitable

Growth in this period, as at all times, is concerned with *inevitable* change. This is the first important factor: we are dealing with something not in our power to alter. Just as the prophet of Isaiah told us that no one could increase his stature by taking thought, so, for instance, no correspondence course in increasing height can significantly

[2] Alexis Carrel, *Man, the Unknown,* rev. ed., New York, Harper, 1939.

alter our destined height. Such a course may increase our effective height by altering our posture. It may advise us to wear thick soles and heels, or as in one course, send us two blocks of wood on which to stand, but in this particular dimension our destiny is well-nigh settled at conception. There can be a diurnal shrinkage in height and nocturnal recovery due to changes in the thicknesses of the intervertebral discs. This has been observed by several observers, including Dr. Charles Begg and Depuky in Norway. Other observers, including W. H. Sheldon, have doubted this.[3] Begg measured sitting height immediately on rising in the morning and again in the early evening. Maximum differences occurred in adolescent subjects; one 14½ year old boy showing a difference of 1¼ inches. Begg and others attribute the change to a drop in the muscle tone of the normal antigravity postural muscles—though it may also involve the thickness of the intervertebral discs and their degree of turgor.[4] There is some evidence that certain illnesses may inhibit longitudinal growth. On the other hand, it has been suggested in a very careful analysis by Ebbs that in fact certain diseases seem on the average to increase height somewhat. And of course, malfunctioning of the pituitary may produce a form of giantism, and other endocrine or vitamin deficiencies produce retarded growth. So too, nutrition may affect growth in certain ways, although little in height. Recent studies in Britain, the United States, Canada, Sweden, and New Zealand indicate that the average child is taller earlier than he was a quarter of a century ago; that is, he reaches full stature at an earlier age. The evidence is not so clear that the means of adult stature have increased so significantly. It is, of course, easier to procure information about adolescents' height than about that of adults, because random samples of adults are hard to obtain. Military samples are not random ones, being selected on various grounds, which may or may not include factors affecting height.

MUCH GROWTH IS HEREDITARY

But despite all factors which we know may affect height, for the vast majority one can presume total growth in stature is inevitable,

[3] W. H. Sheldon *et al.*, *Varieties of Delinquent Youth*, New York, Harper, 1949.

[4] Charles Begg, *Degeneration of the Intervertebral Discs*, Doctoral thesis, University of Otago, 1946.

and to a large extent, genetically predetermined. Mothers' anxieties about the linear growth of young children are often reactions to a matter of fate.

There are some factors in individuals which can be changed, and we are reserving those for the next chapter. This chapter is more concerned with awareness of, and the possibilities of purposeful evaluation of, inevitable changes. It will be necessary, therefore, to limit our treatment only to those topics which give understanding or can be usefully applied.

WHAT IS AGE?

Let us consider age first. In its common usage "age" means only the time interval since birth. In that sense it is a simple and unalterable concept—and that is the way we most often use the term. But among educationists and human biologists this is not sufficient. We may hear the terms *mental age, dental age, skeletal* or *osseous age*, or *carpal age* —though not as yet, motor age (except as shown in Gesell's work with the movements of young children). There are two factors which various "ages" can be compared with; the first is the inevitable chronological age (time since birth), and the other is the norm for similar organisms in similar environments. While everyone is normal as to chronological age—though parents are sometimes vague about the year of birth—many will vary from the group or population norm in some particular type of age. A may have lived 10 years, but have the normal teeth of a 12-year-old in that society. B may have lived 10 years, but have a reading age of a 6-year-old in that society. This tag-phrase "in that society" is essential because all norms are calculated in terms of a given society or population. Normal reading ages in Finland are presumably higher than that for the world would be, because Finland is highly literate; and the world norm is lower, because there are still many large populations where literacy is low. (These difficulties of the meaning of normality have been dealt with in Chapter 9.) There is therefore a grave danger, especially in a large country, in thinking that one's country's norm is a world norm. Possibly no other form of loose thinking does more harm than this one, save perhaps, thinking that the norms of others are wrong because they differ from our own. The name for this particular prejudice in thinking is ethnocentricity. Just, as the well-balanced man has control of his egocentric tendencies, so the educated man of today tries to be free from ethnocentricity.

Types of Age

As scientists isolate factors in human beings which vary in time pattern in their development, so more and more special types of age will emerge. Some of these ages are only of interest for classification, or taxonomy, as it is called, others amount to useful information which can be acted upon. Knowing the mental age of a child can guide a teacher as to what to expect, or explain to a parent that Willie's lack of progress is not necessarily due to bad behaviour, laziness, or poor teaching. There is a slight danger of a fatalism of outlook in this and, of course, the ultimate value of such knowledge depends on the degree of its validity (and as is shown often in this book, final validity is hard to come by). In England the much-debated 11-plus examinations which determine irrevocably the sort of high school attended, exemplify the danger of an arbitrary norm of age. Many children, for instance, have in error been classed as of low mental age in performance tests or class achievement, when in fact the real block was in another field, for instance, slight deafness, or deafness for certain frequencies, or partial-sightedness. This serves to show how evaluatory practices should be interrelated. A school physician may find a child is partially deaf (in itself a tricky diagnostic procedure without an efficient audiometer, for which the ordinary "whisper" or watch tests are only crude substitutes), and this information may be put on a card, but unless it gets through to Miss Jones, the new teacher of the fourth grade, it is so much sterile data.

The Pursuit of Certainty

We have, of course, a tendency constantly to search for and earnestly hope for final validity. We put our faith on the label. The uncritical worship of the IQ is in some ways parallel with the fantastic rush for antihistamines when they first became available. We long for certainty. But recent work on intelligence-testing has introduced a concept which many of us felt was lacking before—intelligence A and intelligence B. Intelligence A is the real potential intelligence, and B is that which we manage to measure.

ORGANISMIC AGE

So with ages—some "ages" are more meaningful than others; we can always go back to the final chronological age, however. The various sub-ages we evaluate show us how infinite in variety is man, and we must examine some of these sub-ages—but remember the danger of ignoring the whole. Attempts have been made to produce a combination of all sub-ages and to give a child an all-embracing age called an *organismic age*. This idea, first mooted by Olson and Hughes[5] in 1942 is attractive and ingenious, but also, in some ways, ingenuous, because there are four considerable weaknesses. First, it is well-nigh impossible to isolate with certainty *all* the variables from which to calculate the organismic age. Second, the loading[6] to be given to one factor or another in making such calculations presents an almost insoluble problem. Our third reservation about this concept is the administrative one— that this is an extremely round-about and overdetailed way, quite out of the question for most schoolworkers, for finding out a comprehensive picture of a child. Fourth, the essence of understanding lies in being aware of the *different* factors and the isolation of a simple number as the organismic age, which gives no indication as to how the figure was arrived at. This sort of information is not quite like telling us that adding a banana, an apple, a pawpaw, a pineapple, and a peach will make a fruit salad, but is it much better than that—and is there not a certain parallel? It seems possible that the total picture of a child will be best presented by a mixture of words and figures, the equivalent of a scientifically devised thumbnail sketch. For instance:

A COMPLEX PICTURE OF GROWTH

Elvis is a lank, gangling youth of 13. Already he is 6 feet 4 inches, but only weighs so far 120 pounds. He gives into gravity at the top with a long high kyphosis. His feet, like those of most children who will be taller, are enormous (size 13½), but as yet lack spring, and he drags them. Pressure at school is

[5] Willard C. Olson and Byron O. Hughes, "The Concept of Organismic Age," *Journal of Educational Research* (March, 1942), 525–526.

[6] *Loading* or *weighting* is a term used when one or more factors making up a total score are considered to influence the total score unfairly. These factors can be *weighted* by multiplication or division so as to bring them into proportion.

towards making him a basketballer. At home they want him to be a musician, like his father—born in Vienna—and several generations of his family. He works after hours and does not get to bed till 9:30 and yet has to keep in with the family tradition and rise at 6. He has grown 3 inches in the last 3 months and only put on 1 pound. In classes he often falls asleep at his desk. His verbal IQ is 95, his spatial awareness is 110, his strength is low, his only musical interest is a mild one in the amelodic, writhing cacophony of his famous namesake. Some things are certain—he needs rest, tolerance, and individual help.

PROFILES CAN HELP

It is a truism that adding up the parts does not make the whole in a human being, but in such cases as organismic age, have we even all the parts? Of course not—and of course this must be a question of "weighting." Combining information of separate factors, even when carefully relating each score to a norm, is not unlike trying to estimate a patient's health by adding the difference from the norm of his blood pressure, temperature, haemoglobin level, and blood sugar level. Such information kept separate and used in a total picture gives us more real information than when combined. Displayed as a *profile* it may allow us to see how an individual compares with age norms in a number of factors, and this gives us more angles on a person's age nature. But while *profiles* are better than totted up organismic information, they are always only part-information, just as in the more common use a "profile" of a wanted criminal would be inadequate without full-face and other essential information.

The argument so far is that *age* as such and *subages* add interest, but are no final guide to our actions. This is not to say that *changes through time,* or *rate of change,* are not important; we shall come to those later. Even if we could produce a motor age equivalent to mental age, or breaking it down further, a throwing age equivalent to a reading age or a swimming age or a petting age equivalent to a physical or social maturity age, would we be much further on?

Homo sapiens is the most varied of species in size, life-length,[7] mental capacity, and rate and degree of development. Always in democratic

---

[7] In spite of popular myths about elephants, man lives longer than any other known mammal.

societies he will be found in heterogeneous groups—heterogeneous in size, in eye colour, in skin colour and texture, in genetic background, in racial origin, and in a myriad of observable details and potential capabilities (although there may be homogeneous pockets of similar people within a country). Group him one way and you ungroup him another. Group him in intelligence in your school and, as an individual,[8] he will not be grouped in size. Studies of whole populations in the statistical sense may show that certain characteristics go together.[9]

But whereas such tendencies may be true of large populations, the small sample we teach—the seventh-grade class in Cedar Rapids, Medicine Hat, Liphook, or Oshkosh—will be heterogeneous. And in physical education particularly, we may have to teach children grouped according to some other basis than motor efficiency, physical fitness, strength, endurance, innate motor ability, or any other factor which we might prefer. Most likely, in physical-education classes, we shall deal with a group selected as to a mixture of chronological age, academic achievement, and social promotion—perhaps with some intelligence streaming[10]—and in some cases with a definite socioeconomic background.

What Units Shall We Use?

What are we then to do with this apparent chaos of multiple variables? Is there rhyme or reason in the inevitable changing of individuals of which we can make use as teachers? To the scientist, the anthropometrist, there is much of interest in studying these changes. His studies may ultimately add to the total study of man—normal man —the man in the street, the boy at the desk, the girl in the factory.[11]

[8] Whatever group tendencies relating to intelligence and size may be.

[9] For instance, see Thurstone's monumental longitudinal study (i.e., continuous over a period of years with the same individuals) of California children, or see some of the classical longitudinal studies made by the late Harold Jones and others at the Institute of Human Development at the University of California, Berkeley.

[10] *Streaming* is dividing a grade into several different classes, on the basis of intelligence or of academic achievement, so as to produce homogeneous teaching groups.

[11] See the publication of H. V. Meredith, for instance, or those of Tanner in England. J. M. Tanner's *Growth at Adolescence* (Oxford, Blackwell, 1955) should be compulsory reading for all secondary teachers.

But we, as teachers, while respecting this painstaking labour to evaluate man in general, are fundamentally concerned with evaluating Bill Hochstetter or Mary Lou Jones. We are short of time, probably have no laboratory, and in any case, we shall probably only know, and be able to influence, Bill and Mary Lou directly for a few years at the most.

Yet there is much we can do if we assume the premise that we are teaching children and not basketball or softball, individuals not groups.

We shall now examine those factors in the inevitably changing individual which matter most to a teacher of physical education. It may be necessary to refer to scientific work establishing our reasons for recommending procedures, but this book is not so much a scientific treatise as a guide to the beginner in practical, purposeful evaluation.

CHANGES IN HEIGHT AND WEIGHT

The most obvious forms of growth, as it happens, are the most easily measurable, and also lend themselves fairly easily to purposeful interpretation.

Height

There is no real problem in measuring height, only certain safeguards to be observed and one mechanical difficulty to be overcome. The fancy name for a height-measuring device is a stadiometer, but mother's tape-measure, provided it is new, will do just as well. The simplest means employs a scale marked on a flat wall or a long enough ruler screwed to the wall, and some device which, when held against the measure will project at right angles. The range needed on the scale will be suggested by experience. In an elementary school, a range from 2 feet 6 inches to 6 feet will cover all but the most unusual of cases. In a high school 4 feet to 6 feet 6 inches will cover most cases, although statistics in height suggest that Californians should extend their top height scale (just as in Canada, British Columbian children tend to be taller earlier than eastern Canadians). However, if the scale is to be used on university or high-school basketball teams, obviously scales have got to include up to 7 feet 6 inches.

It will be noted that the units suggested are feet and inches, though of course, in the general world of scientific measurement the metric system is used. It seems sensible on the other hand, to use a system of measurement in which the units are well known to the general population. If one is going to talk about height to parents, children, or most doctors in North America or the British Commonwealth, their most familiar scale of values will be the foot-inch one. However, if transcultural comparisons are to be made, conversion tables may be necessary when doing research work. These can be tabulated or simpler ones to use with a straight-line graph.

HEIGHT MACHINES—STADIOMETERS

What are the mechanical difficulties? The main one is to make sure that the arm or horizontal surface against which the height is taken maintains a 90° angle with the upright—and some quite expensive machines are weak in this respect. Sliding members which move on the scale itself are apt to work loose at the critical angle. For this reason either a block held firm against the scale, or a telescopic tube or bar sliding within another with a completely fixed right angle at the top, is more reliable than most members sliding on the scale itself. The next mechanical problem is estimation of the point of contact. If we were all bald, the tangent between the horizontal surface and the skin over the cranium would be clear, but undoubtedly the varied nature of hair thickness and springiness increases the chance of error between individual and individual. It is interesting that hair counts in weight, but is in a sense discounted in height. One cannot see the contact, one can only feel it; and that in itself may actually disturb the individual's posture somewhat. One of the authors, annoyed by this problem, tried the device of incorporating a bell-push flush with the horizontal arm; this lit a light bulb when contact of a certain pressure was made (see Fig. 12.1). Such a device is really unnecessary where other factors are considered, as will be seen later.

There is also the question of whether the person being measured should stand *free* in space or with his back against a vertical surface.

It is suggested that having the back against a surface enables one to stretch to one's full height more easily.[12]

SIGNIFICANT ACCURACY

But all these questions are affected by the main principles in such measurement: (1) What is to be the significant degree of accuracy? (2) Are changes in individuals more important or less important than relationship to a norm?

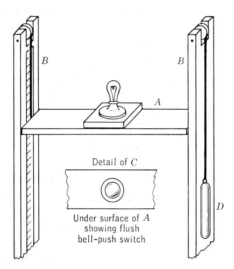

FIG. 12.1. Simplified drawing of consistent-registering stadiometer. *A*, sliding bar; *B*, uprights with pulley mechanism at top, each upright has a scale; *C*, battery housing and lamp; *D*, counterweights.

Although works have been published, including one on the Wetzel grid[13] (which we shall deal with later), which show height measured to a millimetre, such a degree of accuracy is not possible or meaningful where anything so plastic and unreliable, statistically speaking, as hu-

---

[12] Sheldon, *op. cit.*
[13] Canadian Department of Health and Welfare Booklet on the Wetzel Grid.

man height is being measured. A good deal of height-recording has been done to tenths and eighths of an inch, but even this degree of accuracy is of doubtful significance. Of course, in theory the errors of consistency will be quantitatively smaller in measuring a small child than a tall man, but no sliding scale of error would make sense. For practical and useful purposes in schools, it is the authors' opinions that the nearest ¼ inch or ½ cm is the most meaningful degree to which accuracy need be taken.

Although norms for groups may be expressed in fine degrees of accuracy, the question of significance comes in, as has been pointed out before.

SIGNIFICANT CHANGES

In any case, for purposeful interpretation, as we shall show, changes in an individual are as important as, and probably more important than, changes in relation to a norm. As Sutcliffe and Canham quote, "The Nuffield Trust Report implies that *changes* in height and weight are more informative than *actual* height and weight."[14]

How shall the results be expressed? The commonest pattern in North America is in feet and inches, though some workers have used inches and fractions of an inch—sometimes rather inconsistently using decimals of an inch. Height by the way, should be taken barefooted or in socks or stockings. It may seem odd to mention this elementary factor, but experience indicates that this has to be pointed out to children and adults.[15]

To summarise, the diurnal variation and the wavering success in the battle against gravity, together with postural changes, make height a variable quantity which oscillates for a given individual about his own norm, and it is meaningless to state height to a degree of accuracy more than ¼ inch.

WEIGHT

This is a dimension more important in some senses than height, though when studied in isolation or in relation to some other variables, it yields little meaning.

[14] A Sutcliffe and J. W. Canham, *The Heights and Weights of Boys and Girls*, London, Murray, 1950.
[15] Women, of course, have a "social height," as well as an actual one, depending on the fashion in heels.

WEIGHING MACHINES

The only important things about weighing machines are that they shall be valid and reliable. Validity can be either ensured by checks made by the manufacturers or by regular checking against constant, known loads. Machines depending on a spring mechanism lose accuracy more rapidly than ones totally dependent on lever systems. In all machines where delicate knife-edge fulcra are part of the mechanism, these should be inspected regularly, at least every six months. Some expensive spring-balance machines are valid and easily checked. Others, such as the common, compact bathroom scales, are apt to be very unreliable. The advantage of the spring-balance scale is that it is quicker to read, and generally easier to read. Where time is the essence of the contract, as is often the case in schools, there is much to be said for anything which hurries up a laborious process. The main point is that validity must be checked. The steel-yard sliding-weight machines are of two main types. Some have two sliding weights, one taking care of tens of pounds and the other of single pounds. In others, more clumsy to operate, loose weights are hung on a hook to the approximate weight, and the final adjustment is made with a sliding weight. Such machines, while tending to be accurate, are not recommended where speed is essential. The scale used will normally be the pound-ounce one and the same things are true of weight as are of height concerning the metric system. All weighing machines depend upon a certain number of knife-edge fulcra and should be treated with respect.

STONES AND POUNDS

A trap for English-speaking people is that, although in North America human weights are expressed in pounds and ounces, or fractions of a pound, in much of the rest of the English-speaking world, the old unit, the stone (14 pounds) is used still for weighing humans, though, strangely enough, not livestock. If, in reading literature referring to "stones," it is remembered that:

$$
\begin{array}{rcl}
15 \text{ stone} & = & 210 \text{ lb} \\
10 \text{ stone} & = & 140 \text{ lb} \\
5 \text{ stone} & = & 70 \text{ lb} \\
2 \text{ stone} & = & 28 \text{ lb} \\
1 \text{ stone} & = & 14 \text{ lb}
\end{array}
$$

weights can quickly be compared by simple addition processes. While discussing weights, it is worth mentioning that the North American ton is 2000 pounds (although in some contexts "long" tons and "short" tons are used), while the British ton is 2240 pounds. No wonder Continental people and scientists cannot understand avoirdupois systems and their inconsistencies!

DAILY FLUCTUATIONS

Like height, weight has a diurnal variation related to food patterns, bowel habits, loss of water by skin and transpiration, respiration, urination, etc. Therefore weights should be taken at the same time of day. To offset error due to different amounts of clothing, weight should be taken nude, or with a consistent minimum of clothing. It is desirable for these and other reasons that there is some degree of privacy when weighing is carried out. Those thin and those fat, or scarred, or having acne, may be embarrassed at their condition, which is all the more apparent in a state of undress.

A TEACHABLE MOMENT

It should be mentioned here too, that weighing a child is one certain occasion when one is treating him as an individual, and for this reason there is much to be said for the teacher himself doing the weighing. It may provide "a teachable moment" to use Jay B. Nash's excellent phrase[16]—a moment when advice about posture, or diet, a word of encouragement, or a friendly personal enquiry, produces a sincere response. It may be that such a moment of advice on a one-to-one basis may be more effective than any amount of class teaching in health education. The bigger the school, the greater the number of children dealt with by one teacher in the course of a week, the more important it is to preserve these moments of interpersonal intimacy. If weighing and measuring becomes like a conveyor-belt system, or putting sheep through the sheep-dip, it loses much of its potential educational value. The moment when you, the teacher, are interested in X, Y, or Z as a person may be of great importance to that child. This is very much the message of this book, that children are more important than norms,

---

[16] See Jay B. Nash, *Physical Education: Interpretations and Objectives,* New York, Barnes, 1948; and his earlier book, *Teachable Moments,* New York, Barnes, 1942.

that human relationships are more important than statistical analyses in the educational situation, and that the working physical educationist needs *clinical* understanding.[17]

Now what shall be the significant units in weight? Probably the quarter- or half-pound is sufficient. The variables operating even in quite a small child run into pounds. A general statement would be that in the elementary school and junior high school, a quarter-pound difference (depending on somatotype, *q.v.*) may be significant, in the high school half-pounds may be, *ceteris paribus,* as the economists say. But when it is remembered that in one micturition a child may void ¾ pound of urine, that a game of basketball in high humidity and temperature may cause a perspiration loss of 2 pounds or more, it can be seen that quarter-pound units are probably stretching the limit of significant accuracy. Of course, the mother of the newborn baby watches the ounces of its daily weight, but by the time we *teach* children, the variations, even when weighing is done at the same time of day, are considerable. There are also random factors, such as changes in hair style, which may vary weight considerably. At the Olympic Games in 1948, supporters of a boxer tried to reduce his weight to required limits by cutting his hair.

To summarise, weight should be taken at the same time of day, in the same light clothing or nude (on a machine tested for accuracy and consistency), read to the nearest half-pound, or, with smaller children, quarter-pound. There should be some privacy, and the occasion should be regarded as one with educational potentials.

HEIGHT-WEIGHT RECORD

WHY KEEP RECORDS?

What is to be done with the height and weight once obtained? This is an extremely important question and there are several possible an-

[17] But the working teacher needs science behind him just as the general practitioner in medicine (or the nurse) does, but his first duties are human.

swers. There are certain preliminary questions which should be asked:

1. What is the aim in taking the height and weight?
2. For whose benefit is it taken?
3. Who will be told the results?
4. How much useful information can we validly obtain by just measuring three factors—height, weight, and age?

To the first question we must have a clear answer in our minds. If we are practising physical educationists in a school, the aim must surely be *to provide important information about an individual child —information primarily concerned with change in that child.*

If, however, we are scientists more concerned with group tendencies, our aim will be different—but this book is primarily for the practising teacher in the workaday situation, rather than the anthropometrist.

To the second question, our answer must be a composite one. It is: *for the benefit of the child concerned, and his parents and teachers.* Our answer is not: to add to the pool of scientific knowledge. Nor in the composite answer first given can we exclude parents or teachers (in the plural), as the argument will show later.

Weights Are Interesting

The answer to the third question is implied in that to the second. A child tends very naturally to be interested in his own growth. Parents, too, have the same close interest. You, the physical educationist, should be interested, and while one cannot expect most other teachers to be interested in children's growth, except casually, there are always individuals whose growth patterns tell something about the child's performance in general subjects. A fourth person should be added here as an additional recipient of information in some cases, and that is the physician most concerned with the child in question. Counsellors, too, may find such information important.

How Shall We Interpret Our Data?

The fourth question is a very important one. We can treat the basic figures yielded—height, weight, age—in many ways. We can relate

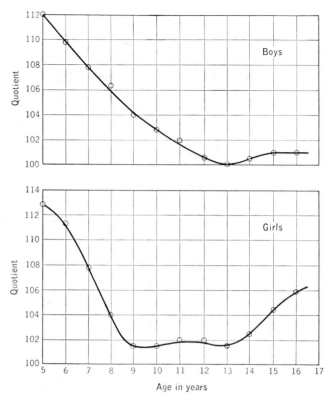

FIG. 12.2. Sutcliffe and Canham's index of chubbiness, $_2\sqrt{\text{Wt. }(lbs.)}$ / Ht. $(in.)^3$. (From A. Sutcliffe and J. W. Canham, *The Heights and Weights of Boys and Girls*, London, Murray, 1950)

two of them to yield a special type of extra information. For instance, W. H. Sheldon has devised, in relation to somatotyping (described later), a reciprocal ponderal index, virtually an index of lankiness, expressed by the formula,

$$\frac{\text{Ht.-in.}}{\sqrt[3]{\text{Wt.-lbs.}}}$$

Sutcliffe and Canham have described an index of chubbiness as

$$\sqrt[2]{\dfrac{\text{Wt.-lbs.}}{\text{Ht.-in.}^3}}$$

which is also an index in a sense of relative density. McCloy recommended a simpler formula 1/3 wt./ht., devised by Kelly. S. E. Finlay has a system of combining these factors to give an estimate of the relative proportions of muscle, bone, and fat in the body.[18] Height and weight can also be combined to give an approximate figure for surface area, and from this can be calculated the basal metabolism.

QUALITY OF GROWTH

The figures can also be combined to yield information on *quality of growth*. R. E. Roper was a pioneer in this, in 1916, in his book, *Physical Education in Relation to School Life*, following it up in the report, "Nervous Instability in the School Child" (1937), and in his book, *Movement and Thought* (Blackie, 1937).

More recent and better known in North America has been the work by Dr. Norman C. Wetzel, a pediatrician whose ingenious double graph system yields information about quality of growth, in relation to norms of such quality.[19]

There would seem, however, to be some upper limit to the reasonable interpretations derivable from merely three measurable factors, and this must not be forgotten. Two dimensions of size and one of time can obviously only yield a limited amount of information about anything so complex as a human being. True, many factors, such as nutrition, illness, endocrine imbalance, and mental health, may affect the growth pattern, but let us realise that we are dealing with a severely limited number of the total variables. We must also remember that variations in growth itself may not be of pathological origin, but may in their turn, affect performance and behaviour. We must consider each case in relation to the total information available and not just as one factor in relation to norms. Of course, parents and children themselves want to know if things are normal; however, neither the average parent, nor the average child, has the faintest conception of

[18] Student Health Service, University of Leeds.
[19] We have certain reservations about his work and so have several leading anthropometrists and pediatricians in the U.S.A., Canada, and Great Britain.

what normality means, and systems of growth-recording which have built-in norms may be very misleading to children, parents, and, indeed, teachers.[20]

EASE OF INTERPRETATION IMPORTANT

It is important when keeping height-weight records that they shall be easily entered and quickly and meaningfully interpreted *in relation to the individual concerned.* That is, the nature of the changes taking place must be immediately clear. Now, we realise that keeping a columnar tabulation of height or weight, as in most records, does tell you how each dimension is shifting. The simple addition or subtraction sum necessary is well within our powers—*when we are dealing with one variable at a time.* Some card systems have additional columns for entering the quantity of change, e.g., plus 1 inch, no change, minus 3 pounds, or whatever it may be. But even an experienced weigher and measurer finds it difficult to look at the changes in height and weight *in relation to each other* by mentally calculating the differences in two columns. A graphic system in addition to the tabulated columns enables one to see at a glance the nature of the change in both dimensions in relation to each other, and to add the third factor of age if necessary.

HEIGHT-AGE AND WEIGHT-AGE GRAPHS

It has been common to graph height against age, and weight against age, but the relating of these two factors tells us little about the individual; even if the two graphs are side by side, it is not easy to see the significant relationship between the two at any given moment in time (see Fig. 12.3).

HEIGHT-WEIGHT GRAPHS

If however, we graph height against weight, with weight on the vertical axis and height on the horizontal one, we can represent any

---

[20] We have no comments to make on the prognostic validity of fortune-telling cards issued by public weighing machines. We like the story of the weighing machine that speaks your weight in a rich deep voice. When the corpulent madam of 250 pounds stepped on it, the impersonal voice called out, "One at a time, please."

individual at a given point in time by one point on the graph. Thus weight $= P$, height $= Q$, and the point PQ indicates both. We can also add the factor of age by writing it alongside the mark made, thus giving *three* factors at once (Fig. 12.4A).

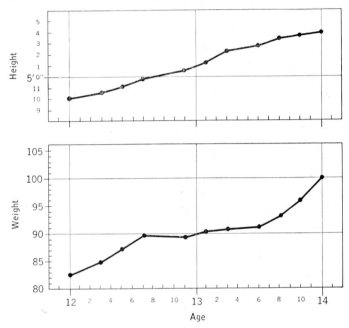

Fig. 12.3.   Height and weight graphs by age for one individual.

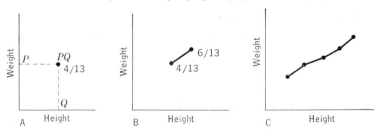

Fig. 12.4.   Height-weight-age graph.

If a second pair of measurements is made two months later, this can be put on the graph as another point, with the new age (in years and months) alongside it (Fig. 12.4B). Thus with several readings, a line of presumed change linking up the points can be made (Fig. 12.4C). There are numerous methods of graphing to be found in the literature of anthropometry, and child health and development. Our concern here is to give an example of a simple method which can be meaningful to teacher, parent, and child—a method which will not cause concern because a child's growth has crossed a line demarcating normality of some kind from nonnormality, and yet will give a teacher some indication of a marked departure from previous growth habits. The teacher, taking into consideration other known factors about the child, can then decide if this change of growth pattern requires action of some sort.

WHAT HAPPENS IN THE INTERVAL?

Before examining what meaning such a line has, we must consider the word *presumed* in an earlier sentence. It is a presumption that if a boy weighs x pounds now and x plus 3 pounds in 3 months' time, that at a point halfway between he weighed approximately x plus 1½ pounds. This is a very dangerous presumption, as can be shown by anyone who troubles to take weighings at short intervals.

In 1936, one of the authors took weighings at monthly intervals of 275 boys. Analysis of the results showed a somewhat surprising pattern. He found that approximately:

20% gained weight in each half-term.
30% gained weight only in the first half-term.
25% gained weight in the first half-term, then lost some.
15% gained weight in the first half-term, but lost more than the gain in the second half.
10% lost in both halves of the term.

So if the boys had been weighed only at the beginning and end of the term, 75 percent would have been recorded as gaining weight, presumably throughout the term, whereas, in fact 70 percent of the boys gained no weight in the second half of the term and 40 percent lost some in that half-term.

INVESTIGATION OF SHORT-TERM CHANGES NEEDED

Further experience with weekly weighings of late-adolescent men and women students at the University of Otago yields similar rather surprising changes in weight over short intervals. This is a field in which we do not know yet the final answer, but just these two samples of information must make us cautious about our presumption. Over the long period presumably these changes in the weight curve are smoothed out, but J. Allan has shown this cyclic pattern in two types of school in Britain. He showed that the weight loss occurred mostly in the last month of term.[21] These and other investigations raise the interesting speculation as to what would be the optimum length of a school term? Term lengths are traditional and not based on any sci-

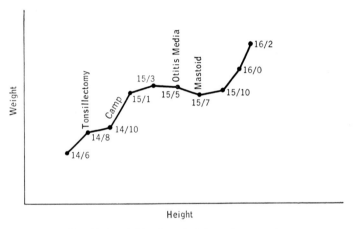

Fig. 12.5.   Addenda to height-weight graph.

entific or pedagogical study. We may not in fact be getting the best work response from children because we have never studied this and other basic issues.

Additions to the Height-Weight Graph

Reverting to our weight-height graph, let us see what we can tell from it and, also, possibly what we can add to it, of clinical interest. Roper has suggested that any extra stress or strain should be noted on the graph. Examination pressure, economic pressure, punishment, illness, bereavement, or other emotional stress, may or may not affect

[21] J. Allan, "Growth of Children in Day Schools," *Lancet,* June 3, 1939, p. 1300.

growth patterns, but are easily entered as addenda on this graph (see Fig. 12.5).

BODY-TYPE A FACTOR

Before attempts to assess changes on this graph, the factor of somato-type or body build, must be taken into consideration.[22] Dr. Wetzel, on his first graph, which is one of weight-height on semi-logarithmic paper, rates physique on a quality scale. But the authors have some reservations about this relating of physique and quality, especially in the adolescent. We consider that crude somatotyping (*q.v.*) gives information of a sort that is useful, but expresses no qualitative opinion. According to Dr. Wetzel, good growth for a certain physique will tend to proceed along specific channels, but we see no clear reason for supposing that in all cases one physique in children is basically healthier than another. It seems probable that at one age, one physique may be better, at another age, another may be better. So, too, quality is related to occupation, interests, and even to culture. For instance, the Hottentots delight in steatopygy. There are, for instance, some people of unusually thin physique who are remarkably healthy. In the older age groups, actuarial information for such careful sifters of data as the Metropolitan Life Insurance Company indicates that, in general, leanness is indeed a virtue in regard to longevity, or, more accurately, avoidance of some of the killing diseases. We shall return to health in relation to body build later, and content ourselves with saying that we doubt the wisdom of qualitative comments on physique *at any one moment* in a child. Just as the assessment of nutritional status is a difficult business by ordinary clinical observation, so we are hesitant at categorising physique in regard to health, purely by the data yielded by only three factors. Even if the norms of disease incidence correlate with certain physiques, there is no quick way of assessing a given individual's relation to the normal variation *for that physique* in health terms.

[22] Whether one is familiar or not with detailed somatotyping techniques is irrelevant. So, too, the validity of a particular technique is here of little importance. What is important is the common sense judgment, which says, "This boy obviously cannot afford to lose weight," or "This boy is overweight and a little weight loss probably would not matter."

DIRECTION OF GROWTH INFORMATIVE

Our view is that taking into account the general obesity or leanness of a child's physique, and allowing for the error due to unmeasured short-term changes, some significance can be attached to the direction of a line linking two points on the graph of weight against height.

Instead of the usual mathematical terminology used in a graph of 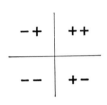 we look at the direction of growth (as indicated by the line joining two points) in terms of a conventional *compass direction*. It can reasonably be surmised that the graph will go in a *general* easterly direction rather than westerly, and in a northerly rather than southerly one. The general direction of growth of most individuals before adulthood will be northeasterly, probably varying between NNE and ENE.

WESTERLY GROWTH RARE

Any growth in a westerly direction means a drop in height (and such things are possible, due to posture changes, collapse of foot arches, and some forms of fatigue[23]), which will of course be relatively rare. Movement easterly will mean increase in height, which may be gradual and regular, or intermittent and irregular. Movement northwards means increase in weight, and southwards, loss in weight. So much is obvious, and similar trends can be shown on weight-age and height-age graphs.

SOME IRREGULARITY EXPECTED

But let us examine the significance of the combined changes. While the general movement is within the northeasterly quadrant, it may be said that the individual is getting larger in both height and weight, with perhaps one factor predominating, or both proceeding in proportion. There are often observed shooting-up periods and broadening-out periods, and these correspond to the known nature of bone growth, rarely in both dimensions simultaneously.

[23] Also changes of a degenerative kind.

IMPORTANT CHANGES

Let us now look at some more significant situations. Suppose the graph goes due north, we can then say the person is putting on weight, but not growing in height. Is this desirable in relation to the body build? If he be obese already, this may be worth watching. Do the eye and palpation tell us that this extra weight is due to a broadening of skeletal development—of thickness of wrists, knees, and shoulder girdle—or to adipose tissue appearing generally locally, or to muscle hypertrophy? This clinical observation of the individual, whom we see as a regular pupil about the place, can guide us as to whether this northwards growth is presumably reasonable or a matter for concern. In most cases it will be reasonable, but in others it may be the occasion for referral to medical opinion. Let it be said quite clearly that a physical educationist cannot diagnose; he can only make observations and measurements that may be useful to physicians. This and the following instances also bring out sharply how the addition of trained subjective judgement adds to the value of objectively gained information.

OBSERVE EASTERLY GROWTH CAREFULLY

Next let us suppose the graph moves due east. What can we say about this? This means height is increasing, but weight is standing still. This means a *relative* loss in weight, since it is a fair assumption that, except in weight-losing obese persons, an increase in height would imply some increase in weight. Putting it simply, when you grow taller, you do not do so by taking it from the sides and piling it on the top. You grow taller by an increase in length in all the long bones, with little or no decrease in their transverse growth. Some long bones, such as the femur, tibia, and fibula, have a marked affect on weight, others which grow at the same time, such as lower arm and hand bones, do not. Thus, in general, growth in bone length should be accompanied by increase in weight. The exceptions to this general rule would be the obese child who happened to coincide in a *fat-losing* and *bone-lengthening* period. Thus, due easterly growth should be looked at in relation to the total picture and perhaps be regarded with caution. If this occurs in a lean person, it should be the occasion for referral to a physician, especially when such a tendency occurs in two successive readings. Easterly growth is more likely to be significant than growth due north.

Growth South of East Sometimes Indicates Ill Health

What about growth south of east? This, in fact, means increase of height with an *actual* as well as *relative* weight loss. Again, what does the general picture suggest? Is this an obese pupil losing fat? It is worth remembering that bone is denser than muscle, muscle than fat. Muscle wastage is serious and generally occurs in specific illness or enforced rest and muscle disuse. Bone wastage is very rare and generally serious.[24]

On the whole, southeasterly growth, except in the extremely obese, is a matter for immediate referral to medical authority.

Recommended Intervals

So far this chapter has not taken into account one important factor. At what intervals should such measurements be taken? It is hard to arrive at a satisfactory scientific answer to this until sufficient experiment has been done on short-term changes. The answer must be a practical one for most of us. How often can we fit in such measuring processes? To do them merely at the beginning and end of the schoolyear gives us but crude information of gross change. To do them weekly is administratively impossible. Our suggestion is that six-weekly or two-monthly intervals, designed to fit in with the school pattern, would be a compromise likely to yield significant information.[25] We have used monthly weighings ourselves in a school, but it seems the aforementioned intervals would yield nearly as much information.

Relate Measurements to Other Data

It is important, of course, that such a weighing-and-measuring programme be geared to the existing physical-education and health setup. It is important too, that the records should be made (or at least seen) by someone who regularly sees the whole child as a moving, living

[24] Of course, only diagnosable by a physician or radiologist.

[25] On the chart shown, the recommended intervals fit in with the New Zealand school year, which is from February 1st to December 10th, approximately.

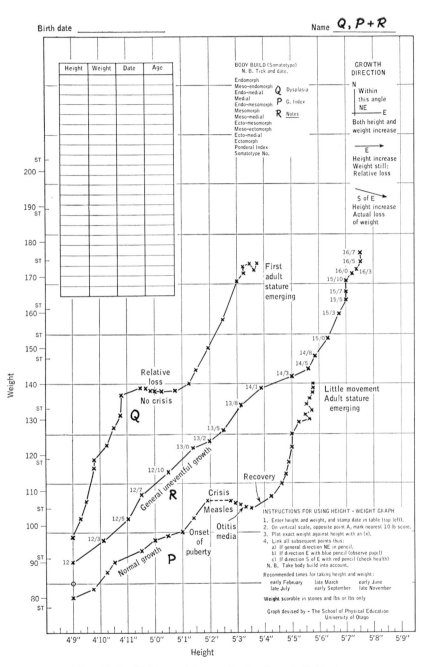

Height	Weight	Date	Age

BODY BUILD (Somatotype)
N. B. Tick and date.

Endomorph
Meso-endomorph
Endo-medial   *Q*   Dysplasia
Medial
Endo-mesomorph   *P*   G. Index
Mesomorph
Meso-medial   *R*   Notes
Ecto-mesomorph
Meso-ectomorph
Ecto-medial
Ectomorph
Ponderal Index
Somatotype No.

GROWTH
DIRECTION

N
| Within
| this angle
NE
+——— E

Both height and
weight increase

——→ E
Height increase
Weight still;
Relative loss

S of E ——→
Height increase
Actual loss
of weight

First adult stature emerging

Relative loss
No crisis

Little movement
Adult stature emerging

Q

General uneventful growth

R

Recovery

Crisis
Measles
Otitis media

Onset of puberty

Normal growth

P

INSTRUCTIONS FOR USING HEIGHT - WEIGHT GRAPH

1. Enter height and weight, and stamp date in table (top left).
2. On vertical scale, opposite point A, mark nearest 10 lb score.
3. Plot exact weight against height with an (x).
4. Link all subsequent points thus:
   a) If general direction NE in pencil.
   b) If direction E with blue pencil (observe pupil)
   c) If direction S of E with red pencil (check health)
N. B. Take body build into account.

Recommended times for taking height and weight:
early February   late March   early June
late July   early September   late November

Weight scorable in stones and lbs or lbs only

Graph devised by - The School of Physical Education
University of Otago

Weight

Height

Fig. 12.6. Height-weight graphs for three individuals.

being. The day-to-day contacts, with observations, of John, Willy, or Mary Lou, are an important concomitant of measurement. Measurements taken by a mechanised system, by an individual who knows nothing else of the child, can be difficult to interpret. It is important to see what accompanies these growth changes. For instance, are there observable changes in the child's motor and social behaviour? Is the progress in academic subjects consistent with expectations, intelligence, etc.? Are any additional strains being added when growth itself is a strain? Are growth changes coinciding with strains known to occur in the home, in the classroom situation, etc.? The height-weight graph, added to by information from individual teachers and counsellors, can be a significant record of the changing and developing child.

SEEING THE WHOLE CHILD

Let us reiterate that in this chapter we are not concerned with research in growth, which is a major field best left to the anthropometrists. What we are concerned with is the obtaining of information about children's growth, the way we store that information, and the ways in which we might use it to fill out the total picture of any one child. Those who have done growth research may find it hard to accept this limited type of growth study; however, the key idea for us is that how a given child progresses in relation to its former status is more important than its relationship to a norm, and this may produce important relevant information affecting the welfare of that individual child.

We have not in this chapter attempted to deal with other inevitable changes, such as the onset of puberty and the development of secondary sexual characteristics. These changes are relevant educationally and will be observed and noted when this appears to be important. Many children pass through puberty with no particular disturbance to their equilibrium, but there are always others to whom it is a major upset. These disturbances may include changes in motor efficiency. Excellent work has been done in America on the somatic development of the child.[26] Much of it is irrelevant for a physical educationist, but knowledge of it enriches his background and may increase his wisdom.

[26] See Recommended Readings.

What we hope is that teachers will try and see children "whole" and will hence pool their information. Particularly, the high-school child needs to be seen as a mass of interacting variables, and as some-

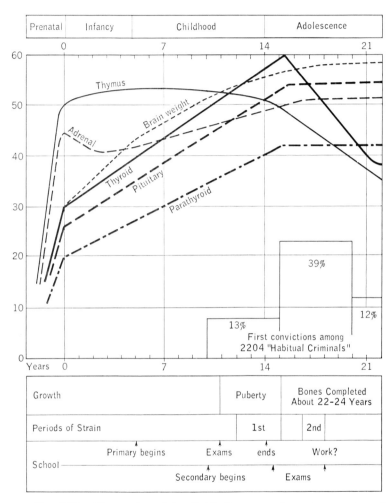

FIG. 12.7. Chart adapted by R. E. Roper to show the complex of variables which change during puberty and adolescence. (From R. E. Roper, *Movement and Thought*, Glasgow, Blackie, 1937)

one who may appear different to different observers. We reproduce here two charts from R. E. Roper's *Movement and Thought*. Roper was one of the first to see the educational importance of growth, and how quite simple records could be shown to indicate strain in a child.

TWO WORD PICTURES OF CHILDREN

We end by giving two word pictures of growing children which we hope will illustrate how we feel the physical educationist could assess

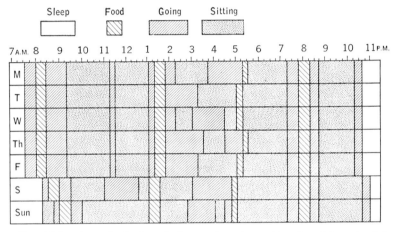

FIG. 12.8.   A method of analyzing strain: time-table of a girl aged 16½, one week before matriculation. Energy is expended 93 hours, or 55.3 percent of the time; time spent in recovery is 75 hours, or 44.3 percent. (From R. E. Roper, *Movement and Thought*, Glasgow, Blackie, 1937)

children, as it were clinically, using subjective judgement combined with some objective information.[27]

CASE HISTORY, N. H.: FAILURE

N. H., when first encountered, was a fair-haired, chubby faced youngster of 15½, who was in my fourth-form (tenth-grade) English class. In class, he showed no interest in English and considerable interest in trying to disturb the general atmosphere. This was actually an intellectually bright class, in a

[27] These are taken from experience.

school of good tone. His written work in English, however, was surprisingly good and the first essay he served up on some controversial subject was mature and well expressed. Thinking I had misjudged the boy's classwork I wrote kind remarks on the essay and expressed the hope that he would maintain this level of work and would also try to profit from his classroom sessions. He continued to be a nuisance in class but maintained the level of written work for five or six weeks, until the boy in the sixth form (twelfth grade) who was doing his written work for him refused to help him any further.

In the meantime, the boy was met in physical-education classes. Here I weighed and measured him, examined his posture and feet, and in further practical classes attempted to teach him various types of skilled movement. In practical classes, being a freely moving particle, he was even more a nuisance than in the English class. If he could interfere with any neighbouring boy by kicking him unseen, or pinching him, he would do so. His own performance level was extremely low. He had no resilience in his feet, nor any sort of muscular drive, although he was solidly built. Seen as a pupil in English and to the ordinary physical-education teacher, he was one of life's little problems—difficult in behaviour and apparently low in potential achievement.

However, when weighing and measuring him, etc., he was found to be more than usually pot-bellied and extremely flat-footed, so on those counts alone he came to see me individually twice a week for special attention. In these sessions it was comparatively easy to establish a friendly relationship with him. There was no need to show off to other boys, and he clearly perceived that I was trying to help. In fact, in these individual sessions I found him pleasant company and that he made some effort to help himself. One Friday I asked him how the rest of his school life was going, and he replied not at all triumphantly that it was getting him down. He had accumulated during the week punishment to the tune of 49 pages of essay-writing (a popular punishment at the school was setting 7-page essays—no comment). On questioning, it was evident that no single teacher was finding him helpful in the classroom, and when later I mentioned his name in the staff common room there were universal imprecations and plenty of abuse. I then questioned his housemaster about him (it was a boarding school). His only reply was "H. is a filthy boy." On further questioning as to what this meant, he replied that he was a bed-wetter and thereby a nuisance. I happened to know the head prefect and captain of the boy's house and had a talk with him. He knew the boy's home because he lived in the same town; the home was one full of stress and strain. On one occasion the boy had seen his father attempt to knife his mother. The school medical officer was also consulted, and his record showed not only that he was an enuretic, but something which confirmed a general impression I had had of immaturity, that he had undescended testicles and endocrine dysfunction.

So when a picture is put together, the child whose various facets are disappointing to his teachers is shown to be someone in need of medical help, affection, and possibly psychiatry. Unfortunately, by the time all this information had been accumulated, and some of it was given reluctantly, this boy had left the school, and no co-operative programme of remedial treatment could be set up.

CASE HISTORY, P. R.: A MEASURE OF SUCCESS

P. R. was an extremely intelligent boy of 16, rather ectomorphic in build, with a certain amount of abdominal fat on him and very asthenic. He was near the top of his class in the fifth form (second grade). On paper, although his handwriting was of a tense, spider-crawl variety, the matter produced was good, particularly in science. He had a huge head, almost hydrocephalic, but was apparently organically quite sound. He had an appalling stutter—the sort that has difficulty in initiating a word; it was apt to be explosive when he did succeed, so his oral contributions in class were few, and embarrassing to everyone. In the gymnasium and on the sports field his coordination was extraordinarily poor, and he was tense and anxious about any effort which involved climbing 6 inches off the ground or jumping over any object at all. Nor could he hang by his hands at all. When his posture was checked he was found to have fairly marked, winged scapulae, which made him look even older than he did already, even when fully dressed, because his shoulder blades could be seen clearly protruding and pushing out of his jacket. His feet were also lifeless and weak. He was so far below the next less-able boy in class that one could not teach him in an ordinary practical class without continually being conscious of what he must be suffering. However, when dealt with individually he was much more willing to try and do things. He was in no way antisocial, except insofar as his difficulty in speech was inhibiting, though he was low in extrovert qualities. He was respected by his peers for his scientific ability, but regarded as very peculiar, physically and socially.

Two things transpired during individual sessions with him. First, he saw quite clearly that he was being helped. At that stage I used to include massaging the plantar muscles of the foot and the foot generally to improve circulation as part of the re-educational procedure. There is not much rationale for this on physiological grounds, but in this instance, through presumably physiological means, there was a release of tension. When his feet were being massaged, the boy could talk relatively freely; sometimes for several sentences on end without a hitch. Good rapport was thus established. After a while I questioned him openly and frankly about the difficulties he had when asked to leave the ground in a jump, or when climbing on to anything. He could not understand them, and then, to my surprise, described what difficulty he had had in learning to ride a bicycle. I had not imagined that it would have been possible for him to ride a bicycle, but it certainly was an indication of hope for the development of other motor skills, many of which were below the level of coordination, daring, and balance required in cycling. On further questioning it was quite clear that for years, even going back into normal childhood play, he had avoided climbing and jumping. Now there may, I admit, have been some psychic trauma involved here. No doubt it could have been dealt with by psychotherapy, but it seemed to me that if he had learned to ride a bicycle, provided the approach to other skills was gradual and in a pleasant atmosphere, he could manage to overcome some of his motor difficulties.

We started by putting a matchbox on the ground and learning to jump over it—the sort of thing which a child of two might accomplish. From this we progressed to a book, trying jumping on one leg and jumping on two legs; then on and off a 6-inch stool; then from this to another stool a foot high; and before very long on to a third stool 18 inches high. He then jumped down from these by stages and learned to jump down from 6 inches, 1 foot, and 1 foot 6 inches. He also learned to jump up on to these heights. Jumping up to a stool 1 foot 6 inches high is well within the limits of normal ability. There were failures at various stages, but by going back each time and making sure no stage was missed, these deeply ingrained difficulties were overcome. After three months of two sessions a week he rejoined the ordinary physical-education classes. I had let him use these individual periods as a substitute, during the re-education period. As it happened, the class he was in was taken over, as he rejoined it, by my new assistant. I said nothing to my assistant about the boy, but a month later asked how he was getting on. He had to think for a moment who the boy was and said, "Quite well. He is not much good—but why do you ask?" R. had now come so much within the range of normality that he was no longer a special problem. I suggest that the gain to him at this relatively low level of skill was out of all proportion in its importance to his psychosocial confidence and for his physical tone.

chapter 13

THE CHANGEABLE INDIVIDUAL

Myself I then perus'd, and limb by limb survey'd!
MILTON, *Paradise Lost*

I am fat and scant of breath . . .
Hamlet

How much in fact one person can change, whether growing or full-grown, is still a matter for both speculation and investigation.

HOMEOSTASIS

The metabolic processes of katabolism and anabolism proceed; the osteoblasts and osteoclasts balance each other, with a slight permanent victory to the osteoblasts; the sodium-potassium balance is delicately kept, only to be disturbed strongly by surgical intervention, trauma, or certain illnesses. The pH of body fluids wavers about a certain level. The blood sugar level stays constant, and even with the diabetic, the teeter-totter between hyperglycaemia and hypoglycaemia can be safely controlled. We are a mass of servomechanisms maintaining homeostasis.

Most of these mechanisms are of little concern to the physical educationist except as part of the background picture of human biology which is essential to his deeper understanding of *homo sapiens* in action. The physical educationist whose knowledge of the human body is only a mechanical one of bones, joints, and muscles is dangerously

ignorant. The reduction of man to the status of an animated marion-
ette is oversimplification to the point of falsehood.

MAN'S SHAPES

Take, for instance, the shape of man—not so much as the artist sees
it, which indeed we must respect—but let us ponder the shape of man
actually moving. What impressions do we form? That tall slender
negro straddles the high-jump bar in a continuous smooth movement:
a stealthy run-up, a smoothly explosive drive, a manipulation of long
slim legs as if they are well oiled in every joint, a floating down—relatively speaking—into the yielding pit. From start to finish a consistent
flow of rhythmical movement. That stout middle-aged couple doing the
rhumba: is their picture the same? Or do their feet, hips, and general
ponderousness produce what is really only something rather foolish-
looking and out of place, like a baby elephant trying to catch butterflies. Or regard that gymnast on the rings in an inverted crucifix
position: arms like hams; veins distended; a mass of corrugated muscularity in arm, shoulder, and torso; and with relatively light legs neatly
held with hyperextended ankles as a mere decoration and balancing
lever in the movement. Or see again that 8-year-old child standing
tense—knees and elbows slightly bent, his antagonist muscles locked,
inhibiting normal reciprocal innervation—wondering if he dare jump
down from the 18-inch high form (bench).

THE SHAPE IN MOTION

Man moving presents an even greater variety of pictures than man
standing still on the weighing machine. For when man moves many
things are revealed, which weight, height, and age do not disclose—
that man has his weight mostly in his powerful legs, with a slight torso
and medium thin arms; that a boy's weight is concentrated centrally,
being a huge mass of fat, flesh, and guts centered somewhere between
his navel and his lumbar-dorsal junction that his extremities are small,
his arms hamming down to a fine wrist, and that he has peg-top legs.
This large man of 220 pounds, with a huge frame draped in layers of
accumulated fat, is showing his son a picture of himself at 17, coming
over the last hurdle in the 440 high hurdles—a hurdle which always
looked like a high jump, but now would seem like an unclimbable wall.

Even these five word pictures show how infinite in variety is man, or for that matter, woman. The weight of one man may be mostly in his strong legs, in another it is central to his torso, in another his weight now is very different, in quantity as well as quality, from what it was in college days.

Skeletal Shape Hereditary

What sort of pattern can be perceived and evaluated in this picture of diversity? Firstly, we can say we are born with and inherit certain aspects of physique. The basic structure of physique is bone shape, and bone shape and proportion seem to be largely hereditary. Thus a child's head shape may be extraordinarily like that of one of its parents. So, too, in proportional terms, allowing on the whole for the complex patterns in heredity, tall parents tend to have tall children—that is, the control of bone-length is apt to be handed on through the genes as part of the genetic instructions. So, too, such bone factors as shape of chest, a slim ankle, or a wide pelvic brim seem to be a product of the action of the genes—whether we like it or not. And there is little beyond elementary nutritional precautions that we can do about caring for our bones in youth. Vitamin deficiencies in youth may affect the deposit of calcium in bones, and thus the more flexible component of bone, the collagen, bends in the weight-bearing regions. But this is an increasingly rare condition. The rate of growth of bones is to some extent controlled by the somatotrophic hormone (STH) of the anterior pituitary, and sometimes hormone deficiencies or surpluses interfere with normal genetic patterns and produce giantism, dwarfism, or, occasionally, an unusual type of bone deposition or formation, such as acromegaly or achondroplasia.

Bone Shape Destined; Aging Modifiable

By and large, however, the basic framework of our physique comes from our parents, and there is little we can do about size, shape, or proportion. We may be able to do something about the rate of changes due to aging—for instance, the general tendency for bones to become more brittle with age, as the balance between collagen and inorganic materials alters. Although the changes themselves are inevitable in the intact being—just as the youthful changes from flexible bones to rigid ones at maturity are inevitable—it may be possible to slow down the process of calcification and delay the loss of elasticity in bone (and for that matter in other tissues which depend on elasticity for full functioning). Jokl and others have produced some evidence of this delaying of aging change.[1] Man, the most long-lived of mammals (despite the myths about elephants), may one day solve the problem of controlling the speed of aging changes. There seems to be no clear reason why he ages at the rate he does.

MUSCULATURE

The major part of the morphogenotype (a technical term meaning the physique we inherit) is skeletal, but musculature also comes into it. Our muscular destiny, however, would not appear to be so fixed as our osseous one. We know quite clearly that we can diminish, maintain, or increase muscle strength by deliberate intention. This can be shown by the isolated preparation in the physiology laboratory, or on the whole human being. It is surprising how little may be needed to change muscle. Rest a muscle by local splinting and deliberate nonuse and it begins to atrophy within a few days. Give it, according to Müller, as little as 5 seconds exercise at three-quarters load per day and it does not atrophy. Give it 20 seconds hard exercise regularly and it hypertrophies—i.e., grows bigger and stronger.[2] It is difficult to think of any of our system-functions that we can more easily modify naturally than the capacity of muscle to do work. There is small wonder that what Fishbein has called the "Big Muscle Business" is a flourishing one.[3] Anyone in normal health can increase strength locally or generally, provided he is willing to do sufficient hard work. It is as simple as that. Most of the correspondence courses in muscle-building (with or without gadgets) ask the pupil to do up to two hours of exercise regularly each day. Such effort yields results; the pupil is happy and the purveyor of ideas feels successful—in one case felt so successful that he stood for the Presidency of the United States.[4] It is not the place of this book to say that physical educationists have looked a gift horse in the mouth as far as muscle-building is concerned. Maybe they have

[1] E. Jokl, *Alter und Leistung*, Berlin, Springer Verlag, 1954.
[2] There has, however, been difficulty in repeating his experiments.
[3] Morris Fishbein, *The Medical Follies*, New York, Boni & Liveright, 1925.
[4] See Mary Macfadden, *Dumbbells and Carrot Strips*, New York, Holt, 1953.

just some sense of guilt at being associated with a commercial racket or anything so simple as strength. It is rare to meet a boy who would not like to increase his strength. Our hospitals house many people whose strength of one or another muscle region has let them down. And of course, the whole corset industry is a monument to women's abdominal muscle laziness.

Are the Bare-Torso Kings Attractive?

But there are some important qualifications to add. Muscles in general have to be attached to bones—pull on bones—and muscle size will not, as far as we know, alter bone size significantly.[5] Nothing will turn short levers into long ones, or vice versa. There is also the sociocultural phenomenon not to be forgotten that, while strength may be useful (or for that matter useless), there is scant evidence that the human female in western civilisation regards strength as the male's most important attribute. In spite of the universal advertising of the idea that the mighty muscled torso attracts the girls, there is some evidence (*vide* Sheldon and Kinsey) that, in fact, the female of today prefers her males gentle and gracious, rather than tough and rugged.[6] There is also clinical evidence from psychiatrists that the bare-torso kings are pandering to what is fundamentally a pubertal homosexual interest or a narcissistic one, neither of which would be found in a well-adjusted adult male.

Strength and Muscle Girth

Another rather surprising factor must be mentioned here. The physiologist tells us that muscle strength is directly proportional to cross section. While this may be true of such purebred and standardised animals as the laboratory frog, mouse, or cat, we cannot be sure that this is true of the more highly differentiated human species. Empirical observation suggests that sheer girth of muscle is not the only factor. Some quite lightly muscled people seem to be able to generate surprisingly high strength, and some large-muscled people, surprisingly low

[5] Though there may be some local bone-thickening at the muscle-attachments and occasionally bony out-growths into the muscle tendon or insertion.

[6] A study by Peter E. Smith, at the University of Otago, New Zealand, specifically on attitudes to various degrees of muscularity in male physique, bears this out.

strength. Strength-testing is referred to in another chapter; however, this factor is mentioned here, because it may be connected with the morphogenotype. What enables a muscle to contract fully is only partially understood. The biochemistry of the nerve-muscle relationship is more fully understood as a result of the work of Eccles *et al.,* but whether all individuals have the same degree quantitatively of nerve-muscle relationship, or whether this apparent difference to produce strong muscle action is more centrally located in the total nervous system—or possibly in the differential speed of the nerve impulse—is not yet fully understood. For the moment we must include variations in muscle power per unit cross section as being possibly, and only possibly, of genetic origin.

Two Kinds of Strength

Mention must be made in this context of recent work which indicates that the firing off of motor units in a voluntary muscle can come from two sources—one primitive, crude, inaccurate, and at times very strong, coming from centres in the lower brain by an extrapyramidal route—and the more familiar (in the sense of more mentioned) cortico-pyramidal route of innervation used in learned skills and tests. In literary terms, the more of the beast in us that we can summon up, the higher our scores will be in a strength test,[7] or contrariwise, the more we can eliminate fear and the unwanted extrapryamidal tensions it may produce in, say, balance-walking, the smoother, easier, and more accurate movements[8] we shall get. Thus these two motor systems can reinforce or hinder each other.

Fat—Dead Weight

The third major tissue in weight is, of course—fat. Fat is dead weight in that it plays no part in movement, beyond increasing inertia at rest or momentum in movement, or providing buoyancy in water. It is a less dense tissue than muscle or bone (it floats in water; bone and muscle sink), and therefore it takes up more room per unit weight in the total physique than bone and muscle, reducing the body's specific

---

[7] See the study by A. Steinhaus and M. Ikai, "Some Factors in the Expression of Human Strength," *Journal of Applied Physiology,* January, 1961.

[8] Thus exemplifying Maja Carlquist's concept of the best movement being the one with the "minimum necessary tension."

gravity. It is also the tissue which seems to vary in quantity and location most markedly, from individual to individual, and from time to time. It is the tissue, too, which seems to cause most trouble in the minds of its owners, and there is some medical horse sense in this. But is it of genetic origin or a result of a pattern of living? The layman probably thinks that he has fairly definite control of the fat situation, and the emphasis in the mid-twentieth century on slimming, whether for aesthetic fashion or health reasons, has increased man's confidence that he is master of his fate in this respect. It is however, not quite so simple as this.

There would appear to be three clear factors. First, the morphogenotype may be such that fat tends to be laid down in very definite local patterns; that there is a very strong tendency for fat to stay put in certain places, except under conditions of extreme starvation; and that the capacity to store, rather than to burn up, fat-producing foods may be inborn in the form of what is sometimes called an economic metabolism. Second, there are in some people developmental phases which seem to be either genetically determined or due to a shift in endocrine balance, and in which there is temporary excess fat locally or generally. The puppy fat found in some late teen-age girls, which makes them at 17 seem chubby and buxom, but which for no apparent dietetic reason sloughs at about 21 or 22 to reveal a sylphlike build, being an example. Third, there is, of course, the fat which comes quite clearly and measurably from eating excess fat-producing foods, particularly carbohydrates. There are of course, a group of physiques which, whatever the diet, seem to store no fat and are in turn the despair of over-anxious mothers, and later the delight of insurance companies. For, although longevity in the Western world is mostly a matter of choosing one's parents wisely and avoiding motor cars, there is little doubt that after middle age the lean are better risks for prolonged life.[9]

Any or all of these fat factors,[10] the hereditary, the developmental, or the environmental, may operate singly or in combination.

[9] Although figures about weight-change and life expectancy, which have long been regarded as final truths, have lately been questioned. See the works of Brozek, and those of Ancel Keys, and the latest Metropolitan Life scales.

[10] The whole problem of fat-intake in relation to atherosclerosis is still far from clear. Recent reports on autopsies of fat-starved Dachau concentration camp cadavers showed frequent atherosclerotic fatty deposits. See report in the *New Scientist*, X, no. 236 (May, 1961), 462.

Morphogenotype and Morphophenotype

In the first case fat does not generally mask the morphogenotype. It may be, indeed, an essential part of it, but in temporary developmental fat, or dietetically acquired fat which is sometimes hard to shift, to the untutored eye at least, the morphogenotype does appear to be masked. W. H. Sheldon's term *morphogenotype* describes the tendency of physique which we inherit. His term *morphophenotype* describes what has in fact happened to that physique at any given movement in time. This distinction between genotype and phenotype is used in many biologial contexts.

Before exploring the general field of somatotyping and the work of leaders in this field, let us examine briefly the means available for evaluating these three main body tissues, omitting, of course, as entities, the respiratory, vascular, digestive, endocrine, reproductive, and nervous systems, which complete our total make-up, and are as important—and probably more so—that we can, in fact, assay.

X-rays and Calipers

In the living, bone size and shape can be assessed by two main ways, X-rays and physical anthropometry, which latter uses calipers and measuring devices. X-rays enable us to examine shape, size, and density of bones wherever they are located—deep within soft tissue or superficially—producing a high correlation between bone dimensions on the X-ray plate and in actuality (measured on the cadaver or during operations). But it is a method of assessment reserved for the radiologist only, and a method that requires highly specialised training for interpretation. Furthermore, it is a method of evaluation which is now used as sparingly as possible under very strict control, because of the dangers of accumulated radiation, particularly in the regions where the gonads are situated. Thus, while this is a highly valid form of evaluation, it is of very limited usefulness.

Lombroso

Physical anthropometry, either of the living or the skeleton, has been of considerable interest to students of racial characteristics, anatomists, and anthropologists. It has revealed some of the patterns of evolutionary processes in comparative anatomy. Sometimes it has contributed to the mainstream of scientific knowledge; at other times it has strayed down attractive but unprofitable byways. The skull has always been a particular hunting ground for the physical anthropologist, having the advantage in the living that its bony landmarks are easily found and, also, in the case of the cranium we have the only region almost completely closed by bone. While the story of man's evolution and posture has been built up from skull and skeleton study,[11] there are errors of judgement, such as that made of the infamous Piltdown skull and in the extraordinary work of Lombroso. It is important to mention Lombroso, if only to distinguish his fundamental philosophical approach from that of Sheldon. Lombroso, a professor of psychiatry (when that field was barely developed) and of forensic medicine, a criminologist and an anthropologist, developed a strongly deterministic theory in the middle of the nineteenth century that there were criminal types assessable from their skulls and facial characteristics. This idea is, of course, frequently suggested in literature, whether classical, modern, or only journalistic, but never had there been such an elaborately worked out statistical (in one sense) treatment of the idea. His major work, *L'Uomo Delinquente* (1893) is a curiosity worth examining, if only to see to what lengths human ingenuity, credulity, and an *idée fixe* may lead a learned and scholarly man. His work has, of course, been entirely discredited, and scientific investigation has shown that criminality is predominantly of environmental origin.[12] However, the mania for labelling, so common in man, still allows us to talk of a criminal type, and we assume all too easily that a teddy-boy haircut is automatically an indication of antisocial tendencies. What vagaries of fashion there are is shown by another haircut, the Teuton or the crew-cut, which in turn has been the symbol of the convict, before becoming the fashion of the college boy—and indeed, some of his professors.

Lombroso and his followers came out with such ideas as these.

[11] The classical articles by Sir Arthur Keith are in the *British Medical Journal*, I, February, 1923, 451.

[12] Though such books as S. and E. Glueck, *Physique and Delinquency* (New York, Harper, 1956), and R. W. Parnell, *Behavior and Physique* (Baltimore, Williams & Wilkins, 1958), may shake our faith in an entirely environmental view.

Small and large heads occur with extraordinary frequency, middle-sized heads being comparatively deficient. Thieves have small, and murderers large heads. The shape of the head is remarkable for abnormality or irregularity. Defective conditions often occur in the cerebral region. The eyes are feline and cold. The lower part of the face has a heavy appearance, the weight of the lower jaw being much above average and the forehead is receding. The ears are large, prominent and outstanding. Wrinkles are strongly marked and occur frequently in the young (see Figs. 13.1A and 13.1B).

PHRENOLOGY

Mention, too, at this point must be made of phrenology, or telling character by means of reading bumps, i.e., palpating the surface morphology of the skull. This is a phoney science, based on a complete misconception of cerebral structure, function, and influence on the external shape of the skull. That phrenologists do occasionally make sound judgement after palpation of the skull can be explained by a highly intuitive and experienced mind operating through its eyes, ears, and touch, and building up a picture—an informed guess—about the person being examined. If such a concept as extrasensory perception operates, this too, may play a part in the accuracy of the picture. But also the subjective interpretation of the remarks made by the phrenologist to the subject will tend to include wishful thinking, for there seems to be, in many of us, a deep-seated desire to believe in magic.

ASSESSING THE COMPONENTS

Reverting to the anthropometrist's assessment of bone size, caliper gauges satisfactorily measure intervals between prominent bony points in the living, provided that there is not much overlying tissue. Thus, wrist dimensions are relatively easy to measure, while shoulder width (bi-acromial) in the obese may be difficult to assess. When there is overlying tissue the question arises of what pressure to exert with the caliper jaws, in order to feel the bone, and this may form an unreliable factor, the degree of meaningful accuracy being reduced. However, much anthropometry has been done by this means. A modern method of anthropometry which obviates this problem is in assessing dimensions by measurements made on photographs taken by a standard procedure. If the scale of the photograph is known and the image

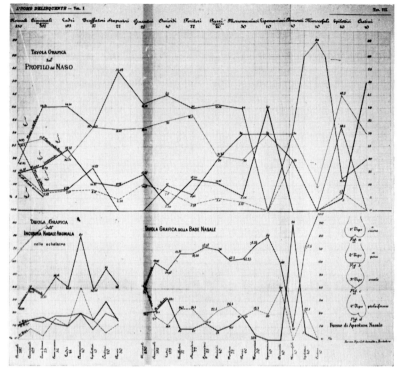

Fig. 13.1A. A graph from Lombroso's *L'Uomo Delinquente* concerned with details of the nose in relation to different types of criminals.

is sharp, very accurate and reliable measurements can be made, avoiding the problem of compressing tissue—but, of course, these are not bone measurements. Thus, apart from radiology, the measurement of bone, the most constant tissue, is largely impossible in any sort of detail. Bone length is, of course, more easily measurable in some bones, e.g., the femur and ulna, than transverse measurements of a bone across the skeleton, or part of it. But even such an important factor in bone length as the length of the neck of the femur or its angle to the shaft—a very variable factor—is out of the measuring range of calipers; so too is the torque in long bones, which may be quite marked.

It is possible to approximate from certain measurements the propor-

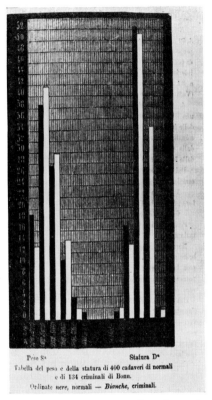

Peso S.   Statura D.

Tabella del peso e della statura di 400 cadaveri di normali
e di 134 criminali di Bonn.

Ordinate *nere*, normali — *Bianche*, criminali.

Fig. 13.1B. One of Lombroso's graphs comparing heights and weights of criminal and normal people (white used for criminal, black for normal).

tion of tissues in the body, and indeed this has been suggested, by S. E. Finlay, as possibly the most wise way of somatotyping. "What is needed is a system for the quantitative description of physique which will make sense, anatomically, physiologically, and biochemically. Recent physiological and biochemical studies have opened the door to this. By these means the body's composition can be analysed and the body broken down into its fat, lean and fluid fractions with a fair degree of accuracy. . . . These methods can be applied to volunteers in the laboratory, but are quite impractical for everyday use. . . . Thus a physique can be written according to its fat, muscle and bone index indicating the relative proportion of these components entering into the physique."[13]

He completes the picture by adding the reciprocal ponderal index of Sheldon. While agreeing with Dr. Finlay that such a complete tissue picture would be interesting, and in spite of his criticism expressed of Sheldonian somatotyping, we feel that there is a certain value in a method of *descriptive* somatotyping which enables one to visualise or recognize a physique.

Descriptive Somatotyping Has Its Uses

Whether the method be that of Kretschmer, Sheldon, the revised Sheldonian methods of Lindgard and Parnell, or Sheldon's own revisions of his original method, there is some virtue in a method which enables description, rather than quantification of components with no morphology, to be made. The danger is in attributing importance to it that is not warranted. As R. M. Elliott has said, "The human mind is insatiably eager to detect positive connections and phenomena within or even beyond the range of its observation. On the other hand, the sobering and disillusioning activity of counting negative instances, by which we detect the failure of a law to apply universally, or what is the same thing, the falsity of the law, is reluctantly indulged in by laymen and even by accredited scientists."[14]

Muscle Measurement

Muscle measurement is only possible with certain muscles, some, such as the psoas and iliacus, being completely inaccessible in the intact body. The circumferential measurement of the tape measure is still the best measure for the layman, whether it be junior gauging his biceps, or teen-age sister taking her "vital statistics" (which, of course, are not entirely muscular). How tight the tape shall be pulled is, of course, relevant as is, also whether the muscle shall be flaccid or contracted.

---

[13] S. E. Finlay, Student Health Service, Leeds University, personal communication.

[14] R. M. Elliott, in the Introduction to D. G. Paterson, *Physique and Intellect*, New York, Appleton, 1930.

With the layman, wishful thinking will no doubt operate; with the investigator, more care must be taken to develop a constant technique and to use a reasonably constant tape. Karpovich *et al.* have suggested means of obtaining constant tension.[15] W. H. Sheldon and associates have shown that diametric measurements made on standard photographs correlate significantly highly with circumferential measurements made on the living, provided three views are taken. Whatever method is used, the measurement includes bone, whatever fat may be present, blood vessels, nerves, etc., and there is in fact no practicable way of measuring the dimensions of an individual muscle in the living person. We have to presume, say, that the changes in upper-arm dimensions are due to increased strength of the biceps, brachialis, and/or triceps, and to include the bone growth in the figure. We can, in fact, talk more accurately of limb measurement than muscle measurement. It should be mentioned that limb measurement of soft tissues as well as bone can be made by radiological means,[16] but no detailed reference to specific muscles can be made. W. T. Dempster of the University of Michigan has done much important work on this complex problem.

FAT MEASUREMENT

What can be done about fat measurement? The commonest way is the circumferential one, but this again is only an approximation—in certain places more valid than in others. The equatorial waist measurement is probably a good index of fatness, as in this particular region fat increases the measurement, while muscle increases tend to diminish it. As a means of roughly checking the effects of a reducing diet, circumferential measurement of say, waist, chest, thigh, and upper arm, combined with weight, may be clinically meaningful. There are now, however, more accurate ways of assessing local subcutaneous fat by the measurement of the thickness of the fold of skin and fat that can be drawn up on almost any part of the body. Callipers which measure to a tenth of a millimetre consistently, and which exert a constant pressure at different widths of opening, have been devised, though we have seen some much cruder instruments used for this purpose. Experiment has provided evidence that skinfold measurements in certain standard regions can be added together to give a valid fat index. This

[15] *Research Quarterly*, XX, no. 3, 33 [1952].
[16] See the *Research Quarterly* for May, October, and December, 1956.

can be combined with other measurements, such as weight, body surface area, etc., to make possible the study of changes through quite short time intervals. Training in using the callipers is required, but with carefully prescribed and practiced procedure, an acceptable degree of reliability between different observers, and from time to time in one observer, can be established.[17] The English Harpenden skinfold calliper is the most efficient calliper we have seen. It must be remembered that, just as with muscle measurement, there can be no direct actual fat measurement in the living—only measurement of samples of tissue in which fat is likely to be the most significantly variable factor.

FAT LOCATION

As was mentioned earlier, the actual morphological location of fat in a given individual would seem to be a largely hereditary matter. There would also seem to be a tendency towards a hereditary age-fat deposition pattern. As W. H. Sheldon has indicated, one can observe certain physiques and predict successfully, *ceteris paribus*, that X will have a battle to keep down excessive fat, and that Y will have little trouble.[18] So too, the trained observer of physiques can predict that in certain male physiques abdominal fat will accrue above the navel generally, or in a limited number of physiques, as Sheldon puts it, as a "subumbilical watermelon."

One of the still unknown factors, at present under investigation in several places, is how much deliberate control of *localisation* of fat is possible, through specifically local exercise, combined with general dietetic control.[19]

EXERCISE AND FAT

It has been popular since the early 1940s to publish elaborate tables to show what a vast amount of exercise is required to burn up metabolically one pound of accumulated fat—and this rather dramatic oversimplification of a complex issue has led to a facile down-valuing of

[17] Though it seems easier to obtain readings on some people than on others. Surgeons suggest that some people's fat is in fact much firmer than others'.

[18] Their reciprocal ponderal index will alter on a pattern. See W. H. Sheldon *et al., Atlas of Men,* New York, Harper, 1954.

[19] Experiments at the University of Wisconsin and the Oregon State University are in process on this difficult question.

exercise. Such tables did our profession a considerable disservice. Like all oversimplifications and overemphases on one variable in a multi-factor situation, this picture is now considered quite inadequate and, in its way, misleading, because it suggests that the best way to weight reduction has nothing to do with exercise. In weight control, diet is certainly important. However, the rational answer, gradually emerging, shows that exercise increases metabolic rate, and this, in turn, affects what happens to the food intake. While "what you put on you must have put in" remains a truism, exercise, and probably other factors of a psychosomatic kind, decide how much of that you put in, you put on—or indeed, whether you take it off in a sensible way. The increase of muscle tone or firmness is also of importance to well-being. In the oversimplified logical extremes, starvation causes weight reduction (not only by fat absorption, which is only the first of several processes), and gross overeating of fats and carbohydrates may, in most physiques (though not in some), cause fat accumulation. The subtleties around the middle between these two extremes are not just a matter of dietetic control. There is no space here to more than mention that water retention (that is, retention of water in tissue) is also an important factor in obesity.

HEREDITY AND ENVIRONMENT

Just as in the twentieth century investigation by psychologists has caused us to place the major emphasis on environment in character formation and mental health, with a corresponding ignoring of heredity and immutable genetic tendencies, so in the far simpler problem of fat control, there often has been neglect of inborn constitutional make-up. The swing back to regarding heredity as a factor has begun in several fields—for instance, in optometry, where myopia, astigmatism, and other abnormalities are now thought to be largely constitutional and not the product of, or even aggravated by, what health-educational syllabuses would call *poor reading habits, inadequate illumination*, etc.

HUMAN CONSTITUTION

This brings us to the fundamental study of the human constitution and, particularly, that part of the soma we call physique, body build, or somatotype. Perhaps we should have said that whether that part where body ends and mind begins is a continuum or whether there are two observably separate entitites remains for many an unsolved problem, into the solution of which one's most deeply held beliefs are apt to intrude. Few now doubt that mind affects body, and body affects mind. Few now doubt that mind operates, in part at least, through the nervous system. But what we mean by *mind* and what we mean by *body* remains as it has for centuries, a field for philosophical speculation, fraught with logical and linguistic difficulties and prejudices. For the physical educationist, it may be better to look at the problem in the way suggested by R. E. Roper, in 1937, as *movement* and *thought*—two functions, rather than as a structure and a function, in the common body-and-mind usage.[20] Plato's body-mind totality has also an appeal to those in our field.

It is not proposed to retrace here the history of attempts to classify human physique systematically. Such repetition and, indeed, plagiarism, would be both redundant and impertinent. Rather, it may be said that this problem has long interested thinkers, and in particular medical men, but only in the last forty years has there been much acceptable yield from the efforts spent on the problem. Nor is the problem finally settled. There are still opponents of the idea on various grounds. It is astonishing how often attempts to give a condensed picture of Sheldon's somatotyping completely misrepresent his basic ideas—and mischievously so.

Some Objections to Classification

One objection is that although there may be blood groups, and many evaluable subgroupings, with skins there appear to be as many skin-types as there are people, and so with physiques; we are dealing with a series of continuous variables,[21] and any attempt at taxonomy is to introduce artificial divisions. There are at least three answers to this; one, the result of clinical experiment, and the others more obvious. Experiment by Woodruff, Medawar, and others, have shown that, although skin grafts normally will only take and stay put if they are auto-grafts, i.e., from some other part of the same individual,[22] it

[20] R. E. Roper, *Movement and Thought*, London, Blackie, 1938.
[21] Private communication from the late Sir Arthur Keith.
[22] Or from an identical twin—the only homograft that will do.

is possible to produce auto-grafts from mothers to progeny (in mice and rats—the experiment with humans is already under way) if the progeny have been injected extremely early in life with an extract from the mother's tissue cells. That is, a tissue of hereditary origin, but not transmitted by the normal genetic mechanism, can be shown to produce specific acceptance reactions in progeny, so that they will accept homo-grafts successfully from the mother.

Another answer is that a rainbow is a continuum in colour produced by differing wave lengths of light, but even without the accurate measurements of the spectrometer it is useful to describe parts of the continuum by the common visible colour terms of red, orange, yellow, green, blue, indigo, and violet.

The third answer is, of course, that untrained observers have for centuries described physique types in literature and medicine, and that anyone trained in somatotyping becomes adept and reasonably reliable in picking them out. As has been pointed out elsewhere in this book, the down-rating of subjective judgement that has come with the development of objective measurement has been ill-balanced, and produced an almost fatalistic abrogation of human judgement. Meanwhile, the dog shows go on, Miss Universe is chosen, the critics appraise the books, the connoisseurs buy the pictures, and the gourmet enjoys his *vol-au-vent* or crepe suzette, knowing perfectly well that their judgements are mostly sound.

ANOTHER OBJECTION—FATALISM

The other main group of opponents of somatotyping are those who think it leads to a fatalistic neo-Lombrosian outlook—in simple terms, "I am like this, therefore I *cannot* do such and such." Quite apart from the tendency to use the negative idea, rather than "I am like this, therefore I *can* do such and such," this is an inadequate view of the outcomes of somatotyping. All human biologists know that there are no hard-and-fast predictions to be made about the majority of human capabilities. In fact, educational and psychological investigation between them are much concerned with the realisation of human potentials—often masked by inhibiting factors of environmental origin. But it is observable and accurate to say that some people are naturally better at some things than others. This has always been the case and always will be; neither political systems nor educational enlightenment is likely to alter it. Some will be born idiots,[23] and some will be born geniuses, and those of us in between will struggle with our limitations. We shall have to learn to accept some of them, and to accept them in others, as well as their virtues and talents. The cerebral palsied, as Dr. Earl Carlson and others have said, have to accept their limitations. For purely physical reasons apart from inborn talent, some cannot be ballet dancers and are unlikely to be painters. So too, the 15-year-old boy, of short parents and heavy, slow-moving build, has to accept the likelihood that he will never be an ace basketballer. The girl with the rotund figure and stout legs, with barely discernible ankles, will have to accept not being a great ballerina. Acceptance does not mean giving up trying; it means trying something else more suitable. While we may not have absolute measures of, say, intelligence (and it is a dangerous extrapolation from the truth to say we have), we have enough to guide us—enough to tell X that his mathematical reasoning powers are insufficient to encourage him to be a nuclear physicist. Many people are in misfit occupations and have unreasonable ambitions. Better guidance could have helped them to live worth-while lives. Learning to accept failure or inadequacy is as important as learning to strive to the utmost with our ambitions, and most people have some potential.

Accepting Physical Limitations

Many of the activities in physical education are of transient interest. The glories of athletic success are evanescent. There is nothing more boring than an ex-athlete revelling in his past achievements. During the few years during which athletic success is of major importance to the ordinary man or woman, we must surely try to help people reach their potential, use their talents, and accept their limitations philosophically. Social or parental pressure may create ambitions in a child that will lead to a series of disappointments, building up a child's sense of inadequacy. There is nothing that whittles away human ego-strength more insidiously than continual failure. Somatotyping, sensibly used, can diminish the failure rate of pupils and increase the rate of success.

It is not the purpose of this book to teach somatotyping. This is far

[23] This is not to ignore such chemically remediable conditions as phenylketonuria.

better done by the authors of books specifically connected with this field. We make only a few points in this respect.

TRAINING AND PRACTICE ESSENTIAL

Experience suggests that it takes months of solid work, testing one's own reliability, etc., before one even becomes a novice somatotyper. It is also necessary to decide whether one uses Sheldon's own method (a revision of which is, we understand, in preparation, as is his long expected book on women's somatotypes), or whether one uses neo-Sheldonian methods, using his terms, but adding either other factors or slightly different meanings. For instance, there are available the methods of:

Bengt Lingard in *Variation in Human Body Build,* Copenhagen, Ejnar Munksgaard, 1953.
R. W. Parnell in *Behaviour and Physique,* Arnold, 1958.
Sheldon S. Glueck in *Physique and Delinquency,* New York, Harper, 1956.

For those who want to build up the whole critical picture surrounding Sheldonism, reference can be made to:

A mimeographed address by Dr. S. E. Finlay, Student Health Service, University of Leeds.
A review by Dr. Howard V. Meredith, of the State University of Iowa in *Child Development,* II, no. 4 (December, 1940).
H. J. Eysenck, *The Structure of Human Personality,* London, Methuen, 1953, pp. 165 ff.
Various articles by J. M. Tanner, C. H. McCloy, F. D. Sills, Ancel Keys, and others.

There have been several attempts (to use the words of S. E. Finlay) to demolish "the house that Sheldon built." But it is our impression that few of the attempts to demolish his "house" show that the authors have followed up all of Sheldon's own writings since his first basic book, *The Varieties of Human Physique* (published by Harper in 1940). For instance, Sheldon's later work on the morphophenotype, as opposed to the morphogenotype, has answered some of the earlier criticisms.

We are not impressed in general with argument by prestige—a frequent technique of the advertisers—but we ask readers to note that the

Institute of Human Development at Berkeley, under the much respected leadership of Dr. Harold Jones, has used Sheldonian methods for many years, and Dr. Sheldon has frequently cooperated in their investigations.

Physique and Temperament

Sheldon's views on the relationship of physique and temperament are even more controversial than his anthropometric ones. We would suggest readers study Parnell's *Behaviour and Physique,* and Glueck's *Physique and Delinquency,* as well as Sheldon's *Varieties of Temperament,* before coming to any conclusion.

The author of this chapter imagines—and admits he may be wrong—that Sheldonian typology, whether it be of physique or temperament, has enabled him to understand the personalities of his fellow men better. He is not alone in this, and others have said that, even after years of studying environment-dominated psychology, Sheldon's concepts provide another criterion for looking at the total complex of personality. It may do no more than make us more tolerant—which would be no loss.

POSTURE—A VARIABLE

There are well over a thousand publications in English on this variable in the human being. Systems of physical education have been built up and others rejected on and around posture as a goal in physical education.

Posture Is Generally a Reaction

For the purpose of this brief section, posture is defined as "the physical manifestation of the reaction of a human being to his internal or external environment." To jump for joy and to double up with pain are both postures. To walk proudly down the aisle with a bride on your arm, or to slink away in disgrace, or to cringe in cowardice are postures.

The simple lateral view of standing posture is a relatively artificial position used occasionally in certain professions, and only very infrequently by most people. To use it as a *sample* of an individual's many postures may be misleading. On the other hand, the capacity to stand in a certain way, acceptable in terms of whatever the fashionable criteria of posture may be, can tell us at least whether a person can stand well in that position or not.

THE ASSESSMENT OF POSTURE

We have listened to those who think that posture is everything, and those who think it is nothing, to those who think it is unalterable, and to those who are sure it is alterable. We have seen ingenious gadgets for the so-called objective recording of posture, and we have seen people who use none, yet appear very knowledgeable.

This is not a book on corrective, remedial, adapted, or individual physical education—though the author of this chapter has specialised in this field and has set up and run a Clinic for Individual Physical Education, well patronised by the referrals of local doctors.

The statements given next are much condensed, and are made after twenty years of practical work in this field, continuous reading and discussion, and some experimental work.

1. We consider that while objective devices may be of considerable help *motivationally,* they do not yield any more useful and meaningful information than the well-trained eye and a skillful pair of hands. The eyes have the advantage that they are binocular and perceive in depth, and can act like a dozen cameras, changing viewpoint. For instance, if an arm masks the lumbar spine in a left lateral view, the eyes can move slightly to the right and see the lumbar spine (or more accurately, the external back in that region). The hands can learn to test tenseness and can distinguish between hard and soft tissues. The camera, sil-houettograph, or conformateur, etc., cannot do these things.[24] They can be a guide to the eye.

2. Most objective recording devices record only the posture at that specific moment in time. A cine-film might improve on this. A close personal inspection, and general observation at other times, give much more information about one individual's variations in posture. For instance, some with a standing lordosis reverse the lumbar curve on sitting; others maintain a rigid concavity.

3. Norms of posture generally set up are not *norms* statistically

[24] We know of at least twenty such devices, but it would be repetitious and irrelevant to describe them here.

speaking at all but represent *ideals* based on cultural and aesthetic values (see Fig. 13.2). Sometimes, and sometimes only, these values include factors connected with physical health.

4. The psychogenic factor in posture is a major influential variable.

5. Postural alteration by re-educational procedures is possible in

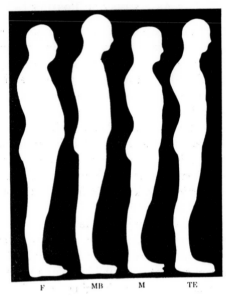

F   MB   M   TE

FIG. 13.2.   Orthograms of posture. Final mean tracings of the four body builds are shown as cutouts. F = fat, MB = muscular-balanced or "average man" type, M = muscular type, and TE = thin, elongated type. (From Charles Weir Goff, *Journal of Bone and Joint Surgery*, January, 1952)

some cases. The methods used are multiple, but an understanding of the general neurophysiological control of posture—an extremely diffi-cult subject—will give a rationale for methods of re-education.[25]

[25] "A mastery of the principles of neurology will rescue many a good theory from an area of unexplained empiricism into the realm of explainable process. It will also promptly debunk and eliminate opinionated methods, some of which have become deeply entrenched because perhaps of the weight of tradition, or possibly, as does occur—here and there even in the celestial realms of educa-

6. Modern studies in that seeming no man's land between psychology and physiology throw light on posture.

7. Exercises to strengthen extensor muscle groups and increase range of movement in joints, or stretch tight muscles (pectorals, for instance), will not generally alter posture, but may help to provide a situation in which the individual concerned can alter it.

8. Nearly all attempts at classifying posture oversimplify and over-accentuate the musculoskeletal shape factor in posture, and ignore psychic factors and those concerned with muscle tension.

In spite of what must seem a large number of sceptical reservations about the examining of and taxonomy of posture, and its re-education, we feel confident in saying that something is known about posture, and we can do some things that are generally beneficial to the individual concerned.

A NEW WAY OF ASSESSING POSTURE OR ATTITUDE

The author and his colleagues have devised an entirely new way of describing posture which is still being tested out. It emerged as a side-product in an attempt to carry out research on the relations, if any, between posture and somatotype.

Sherrington, the great English physiologist, who unravelled some of the tangle of influences which control posture, physiologically speaking, spoke of posture as an "attitude." We like this word much better, because it implies something *dynamic,* not *static,* and also implies *relationship.* One has an attitude *to* something or *because* of something.

Two articles in *Impulse* (an annual modern dance publication) by a psychiatrist, one called "Posture, a Gesture towards Life," and the other, "Your Actions Speak So Loudly," inspired in our minds one of the factors in our new system.[26]

It consists basically in the assumption made from clinical observation that there are at least three interrelated components in the visual manifestation of any posture.

1. The first is the familiar one—the shape in space, or the *musculoskeletal* or *curvilinear* factor.

---

tion—from sheer inertia" (S. U. Lawton in D. L. Zirbes, ed., *Symposium on Posture,* New Brighton, N.Y., Phi Delta Pi Fraternity, 1938).

[26] Douglas Gordon Campbell in *Impulse,* 1951, 1954; Impulse Publications, 160 Palo Alto Avenue, San Francisco 14, Calif. See also Erwin Straus, "The Upright Posture," in *Psychiatric Quarterly,* XXVI (Oct., 1952), 529.

2. The second concerns muscle tension, and is one which we call the *myotonic* component.

3. The third is a psychogenic one which involves reaction to environment. This we call the *psychodynamic* component of posture.

The problem, of course, is to isolate and rate these in any acceptable and consistent manner.

We can report that we have devised a means of rating the first component—the curvilinear—which correlates between 0.7 and 0.8 when different people rate the same photographs independently. This rating includes the ventral abdominal outline, plus the back outline, in the lateral view, as well as the shoulder position, the head position, and the hang of the arm.

The assessing of the second, or myotonic, component is still being studied, and some success has come in an experiment which shows that humans can learn to rank muscle tensions in correct order of tenseness, through palpation by the fingers. We have devised a rigidity-flaccidity rating scale.

The third component, about which we feel most confident clinically, is still under investigation in terms of assessment. We have postulated a 7-point scale, from apparent high dominance-aggression to apparent apologetic-submission. The word *apparent* is stressed, because we are most definitely *not* saying the visual manifestation shown in posture tallies with the *actual* personal mental attitude to a situation. We know, for instance, that people can put on an act. William Sargant, in *Battle for the Mind,* cites a cogent example of how an attitude of dignity and contempt enabled a British colonel to frustrate his German inquisitors, and also helped him to stand solitary confinement and three years in the notorious Dachau concentration camp.[27] It was Margaret H'Doubler, at Wisconsin, the doyenne of modern dance major courses, who said long ago in her own words, that when you put yourself in a certain attitude, you are apt to sense the emotions associated with that attitude. This enables an actor, of course, to add emotional strength to his performance. There is also a reasonable neurophysiological ex-

[27] William Sargant, *Battle for the Mind,* London, Pan, p. 207.

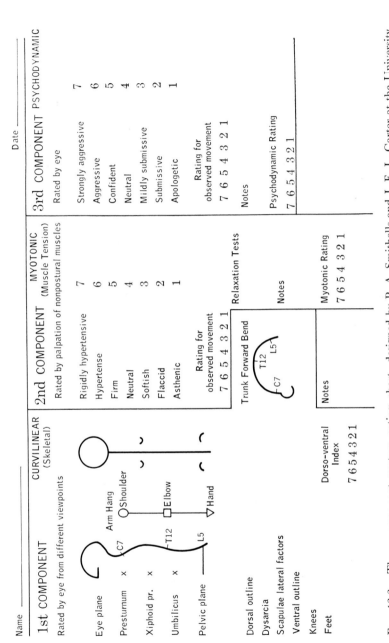

Fig. 13.3. Three-component posture rating chart, designed by P. A. Smithells and J. E. L. Carter at the University of Otago.

planation as to why this happens, which appeared long after Dr. H'Doubler made this empirical observation.

Posture Still Important—But Not for Amateurs

To conclude, the evaluation of posture is a specialist field in which much interesting work remains to be done. None should attempt to enter this field without a very thorough preparation in the basic sciences appropriate to the problem, a strong personal interest in individuals, and the sensibility and sensitivity of a good clinician.

OTHER MODIFIABLE VARIABLES

We have only attempted to deal with two modifiable variables in the changeable individual. Of course, there are many others—skill, strength, speed, power, endurance—which have been worked on by C. H. McCloy, T. K. Cureton, E. Jokl, C. Diem, P. Høgberg, E. Asmussen, E. Howhu-Christensen, A. Schiotz, Harrison Clarke, F. Hellebrandt, H. J. Montoye, T. H. Pear, F. C. Bartlett, L. Morehouse, P. V. Karpovich, A. Steinhaus, G. L. Ranik, H. de L. Mellerowicz, E. A. Müller, M. Hettinger and P. Hunsicker, G. L. Rarick, and scores of others, too numerous to mention here.

HABITUAL MUSCLE TENSION

We would have liked to devote time and space to what we consider a fundamental objective of physical-education teaching—the reduction of habitual superfluous muscle tension in action and rest. This is certainly an important modifiable factor in the changeable individual, and much of the pioneer work has been done in the United States. The leaders in this field, e.g., Jacobsen, Rathbone, and Sweigaard, have often differed sharply, just as those working in relaxation-for-childbirth training differ markedly, reflecting e.g., the Russian, French, British, and American methods. However, the difference is over method and technique, and possible explanations as to why a method works. We suspect that there are several valid ways of teaching relaxation, and that the present neurophysiological picture of body-mind relationships shows that there are often more ways than one of altering habits.[28] This is too technical a field to more than mention here, but its practical relevance to physical education is considered important.

We have the ability and the opportunity to alter some of the structural and functional manifestations of growing children—and some only. Sometimes these alterations are of major, long-term importance. It is for us to evaluate in our minds and policies which are the most important changes to consider and deal with, in terms of children's immediate and long-term welfare. We have mentioned some we feel to be central—physique, attitude, and muscle tension. Elsewhere we have stressed the importance of strength and skill. These seemed to be important enough tasks, laid upon us, which it will take all our professional lives to master.

RECOMMENDED READING

Bogen, H., and O. Lippman, "Gang und Character," *Zeitschrift für Angewändte Psychologie,* Beiheft, LVIII, Leipzig, Verlag Barth, 1931.

Brophy, John, *Body and Soul,* Toronto, Oxford University Press, 1948.

Darwin, Charles R., *The Expression of Emotion in Man and Animals,* New York, Appleton, 1910.

Dunbar, H. Flanders, *Emotions and Bodily Changes,* 3rd ed., New York, Columbia University Press, 1946.

Feldenkrais, M. *Body and Mature Behavior,* New York, International Universities Press, 1950.

Jokl, Ernst, "Physique and Character," *Proceedings of the Congress of the 2nd World Lingiad,* Stockholm, 1949.

Rathbone, Josephine L., *Corrective Physical Education,* 5th ed., Philadelphia, Saunders, 1954.

Sherrington, C. S., *The Integrative Action of the Nervous System,* rev. ed., New Haven, Yale University Press, 1948.

Straus, Erwin, "The Upright Posture," *Psychiatric Quarterly,* XXVI (Oct., 1952), 529.

Todd, Mabel E., *The Thinking Body,* New York, Harper, 1937.

[28] P. A. Smithells, "The Rationale of Relaxation Teaching," a paper (so far unprinted) given to a conference of obstetricians, physiologists, and physiotherapists, at the Post Graduate School of Obstetrics and Gynaecology, Auckland, January, 1958; See also Wilfred Barlow, "Anxiety and Muscle Tension Pain," *British Journal of Clinical Practice,* XIII, no. 5; also his, "Psychosomatic Problems in Postural Re-education," *Lancet* (September 24, 1955), 659.

chapter 14

THE INDIVIDUAL AS A PERSON

I am what I am . . .
POPEYE

Inherent Ability

All aspects of education can have an influence on the development of the personality. Some are more likely to than others. Some subjects "take" with children because of inherent talent. We suspect, for instance, this is true of mathematical ability beyond the elementary phases of computation. What percentage of the population has such inherent ability, and how much its development depends on good teaching we are not so sure about. The rate of production of scientists and technologists in Soviet Russia, forty years ago a largely illiterate country, has shaken Western educationists and politicians, and has led to some healthy reexamination of both teaching and learning methods.

All Need a Sense of Achievement

Whatever the truth about special talents, it is fairly certain that a sense of achievement, a sense of having mastered some skill, or overcome some difficulty, is of importance to the personality. Success is generally elating, failure depressing. The well-balanced personality is not necessarily highly successful in all he does, but it seems that some measure of success is necessary if he is to believe in himself. In adult life there are probably fewer chances of success—significant success which makes you believe in yourself—than in childhood. Many people have jobs which are humdrum, at which they reach the peak level of achievement quite soon, and from then on coast on a plateau. This applies particularly to impersonal jobs in industry and those of a clerical kind. Those with jobs which bring them into personal relations or demand high skill have greater opportunity for success—or failure.

In the school years there are many forms of experience, many occurrences in which there is success or failure. These are also formative years in which environment of an artificial kind (home environment being of a more *natural* kind) impinges in many ways on the waxing raw material of heredity. Let us assume that the home or home-substitute plays the major part in personality development; let us realise, too, that in education we can, and willy-nilly do, modify the home influences.

ALL CHILDREN MATTER

Let us also assume as part of our credo that *all* children are worthy of educational attention, whatever their social status or basic abilities. Can we assume that, to the growing mind in our sort of society, success or failure in physical skills and attributes is at least as important—and probably more important—to belief in oneself at school age (elementary or high school), than success or failure in classroom subjects? It is more important to be a football hero, to one's contemporaries, *at that time,* than to win a math prize, or write good poetry. To put it another way, children tend to rate play success higher than work success—in our sort of society, at present. Perhaps this is not only true of children. Are there talent scouts from universities scanning our junior high schools for math scholars or high-class linguists?[1] Presumably the sport-accompanying panoply of cheer leaders, drum majorettes, bands, and organised fans has the teachers' blessing.

How does all this affect the individual as a person? How does this total situation help Hank or Marlene to believe in himself or herself, as a person who succeeds. We can be fairly sure that for the moment anyway—and as alumni memories are long, for some years after—the men on the squad, the girls in the team, or those who wave pompoms

[1] It might also be said that in the U.S.A. an exchange of values between sport and academic work is desirable, i.e., sport for all and special attention to the academically most capable.

feel the more important for the experience, feel they are persons in their own rights. No doubt too, with the prevailing values, the most weak and clumsy little lad who cheers, gets some kick from being in the crowd and being able to say "I was there when Palooka High scored the touchdown in the last five seconds against Lincoln."

But What About the Unselected?

But we do not know the negative effects of a system which continually applies the laws of natural selection to its *athletic* situation, while having a different philosophy about its *schoolroom* education. To offset the effects of a big-time sport in schools, colleges, and universities, we have other programs, intramural ones, restricted ones, adapted ones, and so on. Such remarkable developments as wheelchair basketball and square dance, archery for the blind, and so on, emphasise this provision of incentive-to-improve for the handicapped. In fact, our charity and kindness to the markedly underprivileged or handicapped is well developed. But between the football hero and the halt and the maimed lies the great bulk of our school population, the abilities of whom represent the major bump in the distribution curve. The question must be asked, how many of these children feel more significant *as a person* as a result of our physical education? The intramural programme may give them their turn at shuffleboard, their bit of square dancing, their little bounce on the trampoline, but how much sense of lasting as opposed to transient success do they gain from these? The good player has the goal of a team and honour ahead of him; the haemoplegic has the excitement of taking part in something seemingly denied to him because of his limitations—but what of the vast majority of youngsters between these two extremes, each of whom has a right to be an individual, a right to pride?

Motivating the Majority

The commonest device used for the mob is competition—a pale shadow of the competition at higher level, with limited possibilities of any sort of success that counts. The child can perhaps choose what he wants to do, but what criteria has he by which to choose? It is at this point, and probably with this large group, that evaluation has an important part to play.

A prerequisite to its effectiveness is that the teacher has a sincere and dominant belief that each child matters equally as *a person*. This is a difficult view for teachers who themselves have come from far above the norm, and who may have achieved their main self-confidence through athletic success as performers and coaches.

THE RIGHT TO BE A PERSON

If the teacher holds this view of the inherent right of the child to be a person, then, and only then, can he use evaluating techniques towards that goal. If to him, however, evaluation is essentially and fundamentally a means of selecting the *best,* he must first re-examine his philosophy of physical education.

Particular techniques for particular activities are mentioned later but as this book is at pains to emphasize, technique without philosophy can be meaningless.

BASIC NEEDS IN SELF-ESTEEM

What are a child's basic needs for self-esteem as far as matters that come within our preview are concerned? A tentative list might be:

BOYS

1. To regard oneself as being of acceptable physical appearance.
2. To have reasonable strength.
3. To be not clumsy.
4. To be not fearful or cowardly.
5. To have succeeded in the mastery of some worth-while skill.
6. To have mastery of physical skills associated with mixed company.
   (Note: In (3) and (4) a negative way of putting the idea is used because positive words, expressing the exact meaning wanted, do not come to mind; skillful, agile, dextrous, brave, or tough are too far on the positive side.)

GIRLS

1. To regard oneself as being of acceptable physical appearance.
2. To move with grace, poise, and rhythm.
3. To be not clumsy or ungainly.
4. To have had some success in some appropriate and appreciated physical skills.
5. To have mastery of physical skills associated with mixed company.

6. To have mastery of techniques associated with future demands on the physique, e.g., retention of figure in adulthood, regaining of figure after childbearing, etc.

These lists suggest *objectives* or needs which might be *felt* without having been verbalised or implanted by teacher suggestion. That is, it is assumed that most children could see sense in such objectives.

Additional Objectives

To these might be added objectives and needs less likely to arise spontaneously in a child's mind—beyond the reach of most children's insight and foresight. Of course, not all children will be able to achieve each of these needs, but most of them can partially achieve them.

Extra objectives which a teacher might add, with explanation and justification, might be:

1. The capacity and knowledge of how to relax excess muscle tension.
2. The capacity and knowledge of how to train for extra strain.
3. The capacity to compensate for occupational effects of, say, sedentary work.
4. The capacity to keep one's feet in good health.

Each of these objectives, arising in the child's mind or the teacher's, is capable of stage-by-stage evaluation if the teacher has a clinical approach to children—that is, sees the child as a whole in relation to its basic attributes, drives, and needs, and not as a pawn in the game of promoting the teacher's objectives—as successful coach, tumbling teacher, dance creator, or whatnot.

With each objective it is possible:

1. To assess the present situation.
2. To assess basic difficulties.
3. To plan a series of progressive goals.
4. To chart progress regularly towards these goals.
5. To evaluate progress periodically and check the suitability of the goals.
6. To make a final assessment on leaving school.

Physical and Health Education Inseparable

Some may argue that some of these matters stray into the field of health and personal development, but the writers can see no sharp margins between physical education and these fields, and can in fact see no virtue in a physical-education philosophy that does not have clear health goals. To exemplify the kind of approach we advocate, let us take two hypothetical children.

Cy Rankin is in the tenth grade. Aged 14½, he has grown fast lately, and his height-weight graph shows a tendency to an easterly direction (see Chapter 12). He is in a gangling phase of rapid pubescence. A greasy skin has proved a good bed for incipient acne. His posture slumps, and he raises his head in a peering way. His teeth obviously need attention. So far, he has no athletic success. Not nimble enough for basketball, or rugged enough for football, he has been offered shuffleboard and badminton, but has had no satisfaction from either. The first seems to him trivial, and his eyesight is not good enough for the latter. Although he is beginning to like girls at a distance, he is shy and has neither psychosexual confidence nor social skill. He has above average intelligence.

There are of course, millions of Cy Rankins or their equivalents in our schools. Let us go through the processes recommended:

1. *Assessing the Present.* The height-weight record yields growth direction; the pubertal development is seen by general observation; the posture pattern appears on our posture record. The motor-skills record shows the lack of significant achievement. The medical record may or may not have spotted the eyesight defect. General observation reveals his incipient heterosexual interest.

2. *Assessing Basic Difficulties.* The record has a note of approximate somatotype—low grip strength, low motor-fitness score. The eyesight is tested briefly on charts and, if found deficient, referred to the school health or medical service for further diagnosis and remedial action. The counsellor can supply any background psychological details, including intelligence, which has some bearing on the capacity to see and interpret his needs.

3. *Progressive Goals.* A talk on care of the skin, a demonstration of how to modify posture, and a conditioning practice of the desired posture is introduced into the child's normal living. A set of exercises which will improve arm, back, and leg strength is prescribed; these can be done at home or during the free-play period at school. Volleyball—a good game for tall people, with an easily visible ball, and not

too rapid and continuous movement—is prescribed as a possible athletic goal. Introductory square dancing is brought in for co-recreational experience, together with stress on cleanliness of clothes, and good grooming to offset skin troubles—about which reassurance is given. In volleyball, strength exercises, postural check, and square dance, *specific* goals are introduced and shown on an achievement chart (mimeographed), which the boy can self-score.

4. *Periodic Charting of Progress.*   Once a month the boy is seen for a few moments with his achievement chart and general self-evaluation. This is an opportunity for encouragement, instruction, and, in particular, seeing the boy as a changing, whole personality. However busy the teacher, he is never too busy to see some children—in fact nearly all children, individually. He must plan his teaching so that this is possible.

This emphasises the all-important necessity of developing highly motivational, self-propelling activities which can go on purposefully with the rest of the class, while individuals are seen. That is, good class organisation is a must. And indeed, *evaluation* techniques may be the secret of establishing self-propelling methods. For instance, *Team Dodge-ball* is a game that lends itself to perpetual upgrading in measurable success.

Suppose a class of forty-eight boys is in six teams of eight. One team is identifiable by pinnies, bands, no shirts, or something. They attempt to knock out all the remaining five teams (using one or two volleyballs) in as few seconds as possible. No one may run with the ball, and dodgers can defend themselves by making a clean catch of a ball thrown at them, placing it immediately on the ground. Each child, by the way, on being hit, retires temporarily to a pen for hit dodgers. The time for team *A* is recorded. Then *B* has a go. A good team of eight with a class of forty-eight can clear the floor in one minute if they learn to pass and mark rather than throw wildly. A continuing record of team progress is kept.

This game is mentioned in parenthesis to exemplify the sort of device the writers have in mind. It is self-evaluatory and progressive, and the teacher can be free to carry out individual evaluation of another sort.

5. *Periodic Evaluation.*   Once a quarter the whole picture must be looked at in a more protracted way, and discussion must be held with the boy about future objectives and the suitability of the present ones,

6. *Final Assessments.* It is important that, before a boy leaves school, he should discuss his past progress, his present status, and his future needs with his physical-education teacher. Too many children leave school having no clue as to their total physical-education experience, its meaning, and what their future needs are likely to be. To some it is a case of "thank goodness that's over." But if this is ever so, it is a criticism of the lack of philosophy, perspicuity, and evaluatory sense of the physical-education teacher.

A SECOND CASE

Without developing it in similar detail, the case of a hypothetical girl might be:

Diane Jankowska is a 15-year-old, and fat to the point of embarrassment. She dresses inappropriately, sucks "lollies" incessantly, and is always around the local soda fountain. Her mother wants her to learn ballet; she wants to be an ace basketball player. However, both goals are way beyond her potential. She has a sense of failure because of her shape, appearance, and failure to attain goals. Boys do not like her, more for superficial reasons than fundamental ones. She stands and walks splayfooted, drives to school in a car from a home half a mile away, and is thoroughly spoilt. She is a potentially good swimmer. Her growth curve veers towards the vertical, northerly direction.

As an exercise, the reader is invited to evaluate, diagnose, and suggest remedial action and future evaluatory procedure.

Persons, Not Specimens

So far, the individual is thought of as a person, and the hope is expressed that a sense of evaluation, and an understanding of the philosophy of evaluation, does not lead a teacher to think of a child as a specimen whose potentialities and achievement are only of interest in their relationship to a norm. The true scientist is perhaps totally impersonal in manner and aim, but we are first of all practicers of the art and craft of physical education. Science is our handmaiden, not our overlord. What we attempt to show is that scientific method can make humanity, kindliness, and personal interest more meaningful, without losing one iota of compassion. But the individual inevitably is part of a group and can only temporarily be considered as a unit, so it is necessary now for us to look at individuals and groups.

chapter 15

THE INDIVIDUAL AND
THE GROUP

You must not, when you have gained a victory, use any triumph-
ing or insulting expression, nor show too much pleasure: but endeavour to console your adversary, and make him less dissatisfied
with himself.

BENJAMIN FRANKLIN, *The Morals of Chess*

ISOLATION VIRTUALLY IMPOSSIBLE

IT IS debatable whether an individual can exist in isolation. With
the rare exception of the hermit or the isolated, stranded aviator or
sailor, all of us are related to groups all of the time. Even the hermit
was once a member of a group. Thus, in a sense, the last chapter deals
with only a partially true concept. Cy got his genes from parents, his
jeans maybe were Levis, and even his highly personal acne must have
originated in bacilli present in a group.

STATUS IN THE GROUP

This chapter stresses the place in a group held by an individual, his
past, present, and future status in the physical-education situation. We
must bear in mind that status within a physical-education group is
only partly modifiable, and is in any case the outcome of many forces
operating outside physical education. We cannot trace such assumptions
back to their source, but emphasise once more that physical education
is an eclectic field, which has to accept the substantiated findings of

psychologists and social scientists. For example, there is now so much evidence of the long-term effects of infant relationships with mothers or mother substitutes,[1] that we cannot ignore its causal impact on later social behaviour. So too, the tendency to different patterns of development in the only child, as compared to say the third of four siblings, may be a factor beyond our control, but which we may take into account in evaluating group behaviour and status in physical-education situations. Sociologically, too, we must realise the pressure of the culture pattern—the gradually but unevenly changing traditions of a given society and their heavy pressure on group mores. Probably no country is more involved in such changing group values than the United States. The welding into a unity of an originally polyglot collection of people emigrated from differing national groups, emigrating for such different reasons as those of the Pilgrim Fathers, the forty-niner miners, the refugees from Hitlerism, or the original negroes, is one of the most rapid, and in many ways, astoundingly successful social upheavals and re-sortings in the history of mankind.

PRESSURES TO ADAPT ARE HIGH

The pressure to adapt, to form a new unity out of disparate sub-groups, has been urgent and powerful, and, it may be suggested, has provided such a necessary drive to conformity to group ideals that the momentum of the drive has taken it, at times, beyond the point of immediate usefulness. This has been suggested by several prominent American authors. This, combined with values set by democracy, has led to a general philosophy that the well-balanced personality is socially acceptable, lives easily in the group situation, and is found to be identified in viewpoint with the group—putting perhaps a valuation on extrovert sociability somewhat higher than in other countries. If these general factors are true for the majority of situations—and it is American sociologists such as Riesman and philosophers such as Barzun who have stressed these points, then our evaluation of group status in physical education will tend to place emphasis on social adjustment, regarding the child who is "in" with the group, and a "regular fellow," as the ideal. Pressure will be all the more active in a profession which attracts well-socialised extroverts, and which is con-

[1] E. J. M. Bowlby, *Child Care and the Growth of Love,* Baltimore, Penguin, 1953.

cerned with the pageantry of sport, involving millions emotionally in titanic struggles of the grid, the diamond, and the court.

Therefore, prima facie, it may be thought to be the task of physical education to develop and encourage group loyalty, even group worship (i.e., worship of the group).

Are There Dangers?

Undoubtedly, we in physical education handle many socialising activities in sport—social, folk, and square dance, and recreation and outdoor education. We provide much group fun, group comradeship, chances for an individual to obtain group and peer status. We see a lonely child develop friendships; we see an isolated individual become at times a happy participant in group pleasure. No scientific evaluatory technique is needed to demonstrate these positive things.

But are there hidden dangers? In satisfying the vast majority are we, perhaps, hurting or inhibiting a minority who may have an important contribution to society to make, and yet fundamentally find no satisfaction in group pleasures and group enthusiasms. Even though our national culture pressures and our professional tendencies may highly value group acceptance and group fun, are there not individuals who should have the right, provided they are not antisocial, to be asocial, to prefer solitary or relatively solitary interests—to reject as their form of personal pleasure being in a mob training for the team? An extreme example might be creative persons, who could provide some of the lasting glories of a cultural heritage, as opposed to the evanescent and lesser glories of, for instance, athletic success. History will no doubt remember Jesse Owens and Babe Ruth; yet presumably the archaeologists of the twenty-fifth century, if any, will be more interested in digging up the remains of one of the efforts of Frank Lloyd Wright, the compositions of Aaron Copeland, the poems of Ginsberg, or Sandburg, even the wit and comment of Mencken, than the records of games at Ebbetts Field or in the Rose Bowl.

Individualism Also Allowable?

Of course, some creative people are also athletic—Paul Robeson was once an All-American footballer, whatever his group status may be now. Still some creative people are highly individualistic, and some are anti-athletic and uncomfortable in a hearty group situation, finding the crowd "lonely"—to adapt an immortal phrase from Riesman. This urging of respect for the asocial individual does not imply that all such individuals are better that way—asociality may be a form of incipient neurosis. However, provided an individual has developed a positive, constructive interest, have we the right to press him to accept group values? Is not the inalienable right to equality also one to freedom, of a certain sort? That rugged explorer, Captain Scott, dying near the South Pole, wrote in his last diary entry a message for his wife concerning his son's future. It included this passage, "Make the boy interested in natural history if you can; it is better than games; they encourage it in some schools. I know you will keep him in the open air." How proud he would have been to know that his son, Peter, would become one of the world's best painters of wildfowl in their natural habitat.

INDIVIDUAL AND GROUP IN THE PLAY SITUATION

One of the situations where the individual and group have to come to terms is behaviour in the game situation.

As has been pointed out by Huizinga, in his remarkable *Homo Ludens,*[2] one of the essential characteristics of all games, whether the informal ones of kiddies in the sandlot or big-time sport, is that they have a framework of rules. The rules may be simple and traditional, handed on verbally and spontaneously with occasional modification, or they may be formally set up and revised by an official body from time to time. This is true of all games. Three things differ from time to time and place to place.

In some places there is conservatism about rules. Chess, for instance, a complex game, has not modified its rules substantially for centuries. On the other hand, the rules in basketball change frequently, so frequently that a rule has had to be made not to change the rules more than every so often. The rules of cricket have stayed substantially the same for a century; obsolete rules about catching the ball in your hat being four runs for the other side have disappeared (top hats were once the fashion in cricket), and new ones come in occasionally. In rugby football, one of the parents of American football, the number of

---

[2] London, Routledge, 1949.

rules has increased considerably in the last half-century. This brings us to the second point.

Game Rules Differ

In different places the same game may have different rules. In the United States the keyhole under the basket is retained, in international basketball, the sides of the keyhole diverge towards the backline.

Sometimes differences about rules lead to two forms of a game developing, for instance, two international games—with no love lost between them—rugby and rugby league. The story is even more complex, since Canadians play a game they call rugby, which is, except for a few rules, the same as American football, but which has no connection at all with rugby as known in Britain, South Africa, France, Australia, or New Zealand.

Game Rules Are Not Laws

It can already be seen that sports rules are more like local traffic rules than the laws of the physical sciences. But there is still another important difference to consider, and that is how strictly the rules are interpreted, and, even more significant to us as educationists, what forms of behaviour are tolerated towards the rules and in those situations where the rules do not operate. Custom varies from place to place and sport to sport, and from individual to individual. Usually, the Davis Cup player, or any other respectable tennis player, does not challenge the umpire's ruling on whether a ball was in or out. He may not be able to control his chagrin at losing a point and may perform antics or scowl. But in baseball, on a doubtful point, players, coaches, and public all give their interpretation of the situation in no uncertain terms, and so do, no doubt, television viewers. In a crowd, even the man who happened not to be looking when the incident occurred, because he was buying a popsicle, will still shout a confident opinion.

Fair Play and Sportsmanship

Many people who support the idea of major games playing in schools and universities do so on the grounds that they develop character, and a trait somewhat evasive of definition, called sportsmanship.

The argument leading up to this topic, which is essentially an individual-group one, has, it is to be hoped, indicated that the rule situation in games is a very variable one in general. Yet one more variable might be the different capabilities of umpires and referees. We must be careful in regarding sportsmanship as being a constant. At its best it may mean certain characteristics which are good, e.g.:

1. Winning with modesty.
2. Losing with gracefulness.
3. Giving an opponent the benefit of the doubt.
4. Not contesting the umpire's decisions.
5. Never showing a selfish and personal reaction.
6. Playing the game in the spirit rather than the letter of the rules.
7. Never taking advantage of a mishap to an opponent.

DOES THIS REALLY HAPPEN?

These could be called desirable characteristics, and few would challenge the epithet. But, in fact, do they in any way represent the actual situation in most sport? Certainly there was a time and place when such characteristics were found in a considerable number of players in certain games. The players wanted it that way, and the spectators did too. The crowd disliked unsporting play and individuals felt a duty to the group to show their sportsmanship. In those days and places, such values in sport may have been one of the factors in the complex of influences in building character.[3]

SOCIOLOGICAL INVESTIGATION NEEDED

Evaluation in this field is difficult, and it is important before attempting it to clear the ground by historical and philosophical speculation. The whole history and contemporary development of games and sport is a wide-open field for sociological study, but mostly it can only be

[3] A topsy-turvy argument sometimes comes out which says, "These high ideals of sportsmanship derive from the concept of chivalry, from the graces and customs of the highly privileged, men of leisure, the nobility of another age. That day is past; democracy has ousted privileged classes, such traditions are outworn and out of place in a modern classless society." The argument is glib, but ignores the fundamental question of whether there are *good* values, compatible with our ethical ideals in, say, religion. It is difficult, and self-restraint is needed to play chivalrously. But it is also difficult to turn the other cheek, or for the Confucian to live up to the similar idea expressed in the phrase, "If a man spit on thy face, let it dry before thou answerest."

done by those with a thorough training in the social sciences and psychology. David Riesman, in *Individualism Reconsidered,* indicates in a fascinating section on the development of American football how such a topic can be tackled, at least in the historical situation. Brian Sutton-Smith at Bowling Green University, P. V. Gump, and others have studied the detail of, and behaviour in, children's spontaneous games. The late Frederic Cozens and Florence Stumpf, in their stimulating survey *Sport in American Life,*[4] have showed the complexity of the problem and the increasing penetration of sport into different aspects of life. Ernst Jokl, Matti Karvonen, and their colleagues have made a brief world study with interesting statistics and interpretations in *Sports and the Cultural Pattern of the World.*[5] The international symposium *Sport and Society*[6] is another source book of ideas and information. So too, the publication by the Birmingham University staff, *Britain in the World of Sport, Sport and the Community,* report of the Wolfenden Committee (London, The Central Council of Physical Recreation, 1960), and the UNESCO publication, *The Place of Sport in Education* (1956) are also essential reading for anyone interested in ideas of sportsmanship or the significance of sport.

ONLY ASSUMPTIONS SO FAR

The key to this problem lies perhaps in sentences in "Reflections on Fair Play," a chapter by Berno Wischman, a leading German coach, in *Sport and Society:* "In spite of the important place which sport holds in the lives of many millions of people, its ethical values, and its influence as a civilising agent have received very little serious study. Indeed philosophers and intellectuals have consistently disdained to give sport their attention."[7]

[4] Chicago University Press, 1953.

[5] Institute of Occupational Health, Helsinki, 1956.

[6] Alex Natan, ed., *Sport and Society; a Symposium,* New York, British Book Services, 1958; see also, F. J. J. Buytendijk, *Mensch und Tier,* Hamburg, Rowholt, 1958.

[7] One might add, except the great Harvard mathematician-philosopher, Alfred North Whitehead, who, in *The Aims of Education* (London, Williams & Norgate, 1932; reprinted many times), writes: "I lay it down as an educational axiom that in teaching you will come to grief as soon as you forget that your pupils have bodies. This is exactly the mistake of the post-renaissance Platonic curriculum. But nature can be kept at bay by no pitchfork; so in

Dean Seward Staley, of the University of Illinois, has long felt this lack. It is to be prayed that in the latter half of this century this topic will become one of major interest.

UNANSWERED QUESTIONS

We have no answers of any validity to fundamental questions such as:

1. Does playing games increase respect for rules in life generally?
2. Is the violence in some sports an outlet for aggression, or does it build up more aggression?
3. Does a dominating interest in sport in late adolescence have a tendency to delay emotional maturity?
4. Does an audience watching violent combative sport—e.g., boxing—go home more aggressive or less aggressive?
5. Is playing in the spirit of a game more desirable than playing according to the letter of the rules?

True we can make a few comparisons, through attitude tests, and tot up the figure, but here, right in our laps, one of the main fields of interest of many physical educationists is in a state where our powers of evaluation are limited. They are all the more limited if we consider evaluation is primarily a matter of measurement, and that the only truths are expressed in numbers.

Here is a central problem for us. In the long run statistical technique may help us in parts of the evaluation, but in the sorting out of the problem, in the formulation of ideas, in the working out of methods of investigation, our verbal and philosophical analytical power will be far more important.

LET US FORMULATE THE RIGHT QUESTIONS

This brief chapter provides no answers; it merely tries to pose some of the questions and to say this is an important issue, in which evaluation can help. Not only may there be a serious conflict of ideas and ideals between educationists and sports promoters—and a struggle for power—but also, even with relatively similar culture groups, there can be marked differences of opinion. New Zealand is sometimes con-

English education, being expelled from the classroom, she returned with a cap and bells in the form of an all-conquering athleticism."

sidered the most British of the Dominions. In some things it may be, but in this issue of sportsmanship—the pressure on the individual by the group—there is evidence both objectively collected by attitude tests, and even more clearly shown in writings, of a markedly differing set of values. To illustrate these we quote two passages which show, possibly more sharply than any test, how strong the differences are.

"I was both saddened and angered upon reading a few days ago a statement by a visiting rugby commentator in which he is reported to have said, 'Why all this nonsense of playing the game for the game's sake?' " the Governor-General, Lord Cobham, told pupils of Marlborough College[8] at assembly this morning.

"I would like to ask this man this question," said His Excellency. "For what conceivable reason other than the pleasure of playing the game can games be justified if games do not breed the gracious acceptance of defeat and increasing generosity of outlook? If they do not foster good fellowship, then, in heaven's name let us all take our exercise by bowling a hoop or walking up a mountainside."

Lord Cobham described the commentator's question as an oddly dense one. He added that one more statement by this man required correction. The commentator had said that in test matches the country's honour is at stake.

"Certainly it is," said His Excellency. "When one plays any game or indeed indulges in almost any form of human activity one's honour is at stake, but it has nothing in this world or the next to do with winning or losing. This is a matter of skill and sometimes luck, but the honour lies in trying one's hardest, in playing the game in the spirit and not in the letter of its laws, in winning with modesty and losing with gracefulness."

Lord Cobham is a well-known English sportsman, county cricketer, etc., and a university graduate.

Rugby football was the best of all our pleasures: it was religion and desire and fulfilment all in one. Most New Zealanders can look back on some game which they played to win and whose issues seemed to them then a good deal more important than a lot that has happened since. This phenomenon is greatly deprecated by a lot of thinkers who feel that an exaggerated attention to games gives the young a wrong sense of values. This may well be true, and if it is true, the majority of New Zealanders have a wrong sense of values for the whole of their lives. But to be frank, and since we live in a hard world, and one that has certainly not in my time got any softer, I found in war-time that there was a considerable virtue in men who had played games like pro-

[8] In Blenheim, New Zealand.

fessionals to win, and not, like public-school boys and amateurs, for exercise. New Zealanders, when they went to war, found it easier to get down to the moral plane of a German soldier, and were even capable of thinking a ruse or two ahead in the game of total war. I don't know that the cunning and professionalism of my fellow countrymen is to be commended on abstract grounds, but these are comfortable qualities to have about in war-time. It was only that they looked on war as a game, and a game to New Zealanders is something that they play to win, against the other side and the referee, if necessary. Personally, I still prefer games that way and find them more interesting.[9]

Let us finish this chapter by asking some important questions about the individual and the group in our general context.

1. Is our philosophy going to be that only those pupils who succeed in becoming stars in team or individual sports should be the heroes of our educational society or indeed our society in general?
2. Are we to consider that the boy who actively dislikes the hearty, gregarious situation, the rough-and-tumble of the body-contact game is any the less worthy as a citizen?
3. Are we going to recognise that the boy or girl who acts, plays the violin, becomes a ballet dancer, writes poetry, collects butterflies, withdraws into the world of higher mathematics, may make an even more important contribution to our culture than the very best games player?
4. Because we ourselves tend to be gregarious and highly socialised people, with many mesomorphic interests and ego-satisfactions, are we going to avoid the temptation to see ourselves as a desirable norm?

A quotation from R. W. Parnell's *Behaviour and Physique* crystallises an idea: "How are teachers of physical education to acquire a comprehensive outlook if their bias in physique and culture deprives them of an 'inborn' understanding of two thirds of their pupils with different somatotypes."[10] What is meat for one child can be poison for another.

Or, to quote one of the authors from a speech given to the Second World Lingiad Congress in 1949: "All possible 'racial', national, ethnic, supposed or real differences apart—are there not personal differences within any social group which should be more considered? Have we not as gymnastics and sports teachers tended to expect our

[9] John Mulgan, *Report on Experience* (published posthumously); Mulgan was a New Zealand novelist who died overseas during World War II.
[10] London, Arnold, 1958, 58.

charges to fit into too few categories? Even within the gymnasium there are natural monkeys (who immediately recognise the gym as a jungle substitute) and those who hate apparatus work (and think of the gym as a torture chamber)."[11]

Finally, a quotation from one of the several wise utterances of Pope Pius XII on sport and physical education: "Sport which does not serve the soul is nothing more than a vain movement of the body's members, an ostentation of passing attractiveness and ephemeral joy."

RECOMMENDED READING

Bartlett, F. C., *The Mind at Work and Play,* London, Allen & Unwin, 1951.

Brew, J. McAlister, *Youth and Youth Groups,* London, Faber & Faber, 1957.

Hare, A. P., ed., *Small Groups,* New York, Knopf, 1955.

Huizinga, J., *Homo Ludens,* London, Routledge, 1949.

Isaacs, Susan, *The Social Development of Young Children,* London, Routledge, 1952.

Layman, E. M., *Mental Health through Physical Education and Recreation,* London, Burgess, 1955.

Pope Pius XII, *Sport,* Sydney, Australian Catholic Truth Society, 1956.

Riesman, David, *Individualism Reconsidered,* Glencoe, Ill., Free Press, 1954.

Riesman, David, *The Lonely Crowd,* New York, Anchor, 1954.

Trotter, W., *Instincts of the Herd in Peace and War,* New York, Macmillan, 1916.

[11] P. A. Smithells, "Physique and Temperament in Relation to Physical Education," Dunedin, New Zealand, 1949.

chapter 16

GROUPS AND GROUP
RELATIONSHIPS

IMPORTANT, BUT LITTLE UNDERSTOOD

FOR several reasons this will be the shortest chapter in this book. The field of intergroup relationships is certainly one in which the physical educationist tends to find himself. It is also the field of evaluation in which as yet we have least understanding, and a branch of the social sciences which so far is in its infancy.

We think however, that this is an extremely important field, and, looking ahead, one in which our profession must interest itself. It is obvious, for instance, that the Olympic Games are no longer a competition between individuals but, as used by journalists, a means for the increase of intergroup tensions, or as supposed evidence for the superiority of a way of life. In the political field, intergroup relations in a shrinking and nuclear-armed world are a matter which may affect our continued existence, personally—and also professionally.[1] It is no exaggeration to say that some people fear, while being politically on the American side, that some of her leaders see international conflicts as a football game, in which someone will suddenly say "Let's go!" into the famous red telephone in Omaha, and then there will be Armageddon. When President Eisenhower, Mr. Macmillan, and Mr. Khrushchev have all said in differing terms that there is no defense against nuclear attack, we know that to imagine one has a special heavy-defense platoon to loose on to the international grid is an act of self-deception.

---

[1] E.g. the attempts already manifest and sometimes successful to cut down time on physical education in schools and universities and to give the released time to math and physics.

If international conflict is like a game, it is like a game of chess played with explosive chessmen, not a physically active game—and there is the possibility of obliteration of all the pieces.

Tension Provocation and Tension Reduction

It seems possible that cultural exchange of art exhibitions, orchestras, dance groups, and writers' conferences may have more influence on assuaging tensions than rugged international competition. It also seems possible that some people regard a university as a great one because of its football and basketball prowess. All these questions need examination by the social scientists. It is dangerous for us to make assumptions that the fields we work in reduce intergroup tension. They may do, at times. To visit an Olympic Village during the pre-Games practices is a heartening experience. It seems that the young and active people can understand each other immediately, in spite of the barriers of language. To see Zatopek lolloping round the practice track talking with an American friend is a reassuring sight. At the best, in some sports, great depth of understanding between representatives of groups can occur. But one remembers too, the description by the colour-tolerant New Zealander, of the immortal Jesse Owens, fresh from his triumphs in the 1936 Olympics, coming into a café for a glass of milk at Berlin and being shunned by some of his teammates, whose upbringing had conditioned them to this attitude.

At the time of writing there have been leading articles in that internationally most respected of English daily papers, the *Guardian* (formerly the *Manchester Guardian*), deploring the decision of the New Zealand Rugby Union to send a New Zealand team which contained no Maoris to South Africa. This action about "only a game" has produced a protest from the heads of all the Christian churches, Roman Catholic, Protestant, and others, in New Zealand. A petition of 155,000 signatures (out of a population of 2,250,000) has gone to the Prime Minister on this subject. The Prime Minister, rightly or wrongly, does not think it is the business of government in a democracy to interfere with sport.

We Must Investigate

No one really understands these problems, because we have not yet attempted to find means to evaluate them satisfactorily. But it is no longer possible to say that sport has nothing to do with intergroup relationships. It is perhaps time to say that some sports seem to provoke more intergroup hostility than others,[2] but whether this is actual—referred through the many spectators to their cultures—or whether this is tension whipped up by an unscrupulous press, is not known.

There are signs that some people see that these topics of intergroup misunderstanding and tension are worth studying; the attention of readers is called to two such investigating bodies, both centred in the United States. The Division of Human Rights, at United Nations Headquarters in New York, studies this field. Also, the recently formed Institute for Conflict Resolution at the University of Michigan, Ann Arbor, is concerned particularly with studying forms of conflict, including intergroup type, objectively and constructively.

In such developments there lies hope. We, as a profession, need to be alert to such things, and to be aware that the effect of our work at the intergroup level is as yet not understood.

---

[2] It seems possible that the sports involving violent bodily contact provoke most intergroup hostility. Perhaps there is identification and projection of unresolved personal aggressions in spectators and press alike in these socially permissible situations. Perhaps, too, such sports attract more aggressive people in their audiences.

part iv

APPLICATION TO VARIOUS ACTIVITIES

chapter 17

THE APPLICATION OF EVALUATION TO GYMNASTICS

WHY USE THE TERM GYMNASTICS?

THE authors feel bound to use this term initially on a world basis, rather than according to American usage. On a world basis, gymnastics includes more or less all of those subdivisions used in the United States, i.e., callisthenics, stunts and tumbling, correctives, heavy apparatus, conditioning work—all of which may appear in one gymnastic lesson. We also feel bound to do some ground-clearing before dealing with evaluation in this controversial field.

Gymnastiki in classical Greece was the physical component of a complete education. In Europe the term is still used frequently in education to indicate the basic central part of physical education to which most time is given. A physical-education teacher in Britain or Scandinavia or Austria, for instance, may still be called a "gym-teacher," even if the teaching of gymnastics, of one sort or another (and, as will be seen, there are many sorts) is only part of his job, and he spends much time on games, track and field, swimming and skiing, and may even take his pupils camping. What is more, although he may centre his timetable round a *gymnastic* core, regarding what in the United States tend to be called conditioning programs as the basis of his work, he is just as likely as his American confrere to be aware of, and skillful in teaching, a wide vocabulary of activities in the fields of *sport, games, dance,* and *outdoor education,* and to realise the educational and recreational implications of what he does.

AMERICA AND THE GYMNASTIC APPROACH

Many American leaders on the men's side, and rather less on the women's, have regarded the views of that brilliant leader, Clark W. Hetherington, as final when, as far back as 1910, he replaced a "drills" program by a play-dominated one. Hetherington had the wisdom to see the limitations of the mass-callisthenics approach in the California schools. Jesse Feiring Williams, another influential leader, consistently opposed the basic claims of formal exercises. This is quite clear in his *Principles of Physical Education,* the many editions of which have come out from 1927 to 1959. These two thinkers have had a widespread influence on the basic philosophy of American physical education.

Opposed to this viewpoint have been isolated leaders and university teachers like William Skarstrom at Wellesley, Harrison Clarke at Oregon, Mabel Lee at Nebraska, Charlie Pond and T. K. Cureton at Illinois, Arthur Steinhaus and Ernst Jokl, and, most of all, the late C. H. McCloy, who became, particularly in the years of his retirement, a world figure. McCloy had a wide personal knowledge of physical education elsewhere than in the United States. A pioneer in tests and measurements, an authority on kinesiology, and, like Carl Diem—mentioned elsewhere—always an example of the practices he preached, McCloy felt that Americans had made a serious mistake in rejecting a gymnastic basis in physical education. Although loaded with honorary degrees for his intellectual and scientific work, he unashamedly espoused the cause of building up muscle tone, either to a level for the maintenance of general health, or to a level for special kinds of athletic performance. What he did not do was to regard this as the only goal. By the time of his death in 1959, his views on this had not persuaded more than a few of his professional colleagues in the States.

SPECIFIC EXERCISE IN EUROPE

In no country of Europe, democratic or totalitarian, monarchical or republican, have the practice and process of building physical fitness through hard and fairly specific exercise held less than a major place in physical education during the last sixty years. The methods used are many, and are always developing in terms of shifting educational values and the emergence of new physiological information. It must be emphasised that the "drills" rejected fifty years ago by Hetherington and others were rejected also in most parts of Europe, slightly later, but rejected and replaced by more effective and educationally acceptable forms of specific exercise. Hetherington's influence meant the almost total elimination of German, Swedish, Danish, and other European methods, and also—more important—the concepts behind them. Later in this chapter some more detailed reference is given to these concepts.

Misconceptions about Gymnastics

Many of the arguments put forward against the European gymnastic approach have become outworn shibboleths, but it is disturbing to hear people talk of such things as "militaristic Swedish callisthenics." The Swedes have been in no war for 150 years, and are thoroughly democratic. True, they are certainly *formal* people, who set a high standard in all things they undertake, but they are also one of the major sporting countries of the world, in yachting, skiing, track and field, soccer football, and, in fact, in a huge range of energetic outdoor sports which men and women, young and old, indulge in to a high level of physiological demand. They, together with the Danes, have led the world in the folk high-school movement, a remarkable form of democratic adult education.

Cultural Differences

There are two main differences in Europe and in the United States. In Europe, taking exercise is largely a personal business. In Britain, for instance, the heroes—Robin Hood, King Arthur, Dick Turpin, and Bonnie Prince Charlie—are, for adults, historical figures to whom they do not see themselves related. In America the pseudo-mythical figures of Daniel Boone, Buffalo Bill, and Davey Crockett seem nearer at hand, and the businessman in his gay hunting costume who steps out of his jeep, rests his gun on a fence, and takes a potshot at a deer may subconsciously see himself as a frontiersman. So too, the massive-shouldered archetype of the football hero may be an image through whom vicarious exercise is had by many. It is all too easy to mistake the idea for the fact. Not that the Europeans do not watch sport—they do, in their millions and with much excitement—but it is in general as a recreational spectacle, and not as a substitute for their own activity, nor as a form of exercise by proxy.

CULTURAL PROBLEMS

We find it hard to believe that the total rejection of the gymnastic approach by most American leaders was based on any form of evaluation which would command respect today. It seems possible that it was fundamentally a cultural rejection of a pattern which has been described by several writers on the development of American culture values. An observable general pattern has been that first-generation immigrants may cling nostalgically to European customs, but the next generation, in a desire to become good Americans, reject things dear to their parents. The son of the Polish immigrant may be slightly ashamed of his father's accent and customs, though not, say, of his father's skill as a scientist. This pattern is found frequently in the British Dominions too, where something may be rejected because it is English, and not because of any fundamental criterion. In some aspects physical education has a tendency to be culture-dominated, sometimes to the exclusion of scientific good sense.

Certainly we expect certain games and sports to have marked cultural biases. Some, however, as mentioned in Chapter 19, do cross cultural barriers—soccer, field hockey and basketball for instance, though curiously soccer has never been highly popular in North America, while in South America it has had a phenomenal growth.

It might be said that on a world basis, except in the United States, and to a lesser extent in Canada, the transcultural, international aspect of physical education is the gymnastic one—remembering that the term is used here strictly in its wider and older sense. One of the aims of this book is to foster and develop the international aspects of physical education so that we may someday achieve the status of other professional studies, such as law, the pure sciences, or anthropology. For this reason we reject as insufficient, when thinking of physical education as a whole, concepts of physical education which are wholly culture-dominated. We are suggesting, therefore, that re-examination of former strongly held viewpoints is a desirable, and possibly profitable, professional undertaking.

It is not intellectually sound to reject something absolutely on the grounds that it is apparently undemocratic or apparently authoritarian without some penetrating investigation. For instance, fine though democracy in the United States may be, it is not difficult to find forms of authoritarianism there, even aggressive authoritarianism. Some such quite undemocratic behaviour may be found within the coaching situation in a college or high school. So too, if practices rejected as undemocratic are common in European democratic countries, the whole situation must be examined in detail, before any valid evaluation can be made.

We are not here recommending the reintroduction of outmoded callisthenics, or even modern exercise systems. We are asking that there shall be an open mind, and some re-evaluation. The Chicago-trained American woman psychologist who in conversation somewhat surprisingly said that at school she had enjoyed callisthenics more than anything else in physical education, followed this up by saying it was the only time she could hide her skill inadequacy. She may unintentionally have said something quite profound—the sort of thing about which we know very little, in our good-humoured extroversion.

THE REJECTION OF DRILLS

Another point to be emphasised, before evaluation can be mentioned in detail in this field, has been stressed in a previous publication.[1] It seems highly probable that in rejecting callisthenics, Americans made several assumptions:

1. That callisthenics were the core of European physical-education schemes (which they were not).
2. That callisthenics were easy to teach, whereas in fact they are extremely difficult to teach properly.
3. That callisthenics were meaningless posturings. There are plenty of men of medical and scientific eminence who think otherwise.
4. That callisthenics could be taught with practically no fundamental training.[2] It is impossible to teach proper callisthenics—since they were devised in the country of their origin—without much detailed training in performance, and also kinesiological background.
5. That since Ling, Nachtegall, Tyrs, and Jahn, things in Europe have not changed. This is just not true. There is constant gradual change.

[1] P. A. Smithells, *The Atlantic Gap,* Dunedin, New Zealand, 1948.
[2] New Zealand, Australia, and Britain made this mistake to some extent too.

CALLISTHENICS ARE NOT THE BASIS OF GYMNASTIC APPROACH

These points are not at all intended to indicate that callisthenics should be the basic form of physical-education teaching. Indeed, one of the authors, when in charge of the physical-education programme for the whole school system in New Zealand twenty years ago, vigorously *excluded* nearly all callisthenics, knowing that the ordinary non-specialist teacher could never have sufficient kinesiological and gymnastic know-how to teach them. The correct performance of modern callisthenics is almost equivalent to ballet in detailed accuracy of position. To attain mastery of detailed position it is inevitably necessary to give precise and definitie instruction. So is it in golf.

Pehr Henrik Ling (not, as *Life* said in 1949, a nineteenth-century Swedish Bernarr McFadden), a modest experimenter, hard thinker, and successful national poet, gave the general impression that apparatus work was *introductory* to free-standing work.[3]

BOSTON, 1889

In the final section of this ground-clearing, reference should be made again to the classical report of the famous 1889 Boston Conference on Physical Training. This is a remarkable document which shows clearly some of the first major conflicts between protagonists of various European national schools of thought. In 1889, Dr. Seaver, of Yale, was saying, "Whatever system we take it must be adapted to the circumstances in a scientific way so that we get results that shall mean something. If we make mistakes, we can again change and modify. That is the peculiar genius of America. We are not afraid to try something new, to launch out into seas unknown to us."

ARE MINDS STILL OPEN?

Is this open-minded liberal spirit still so prevalent? Or, as Whyte, in the *Organization Man,* and others, have suggested, is the United States in a conservative phase?[4] Has physical education got caught up in the insidious process of status-seeking? There is not time or space in this

---

[3] According to the late R. E. Roper, in a personal communication.
[4] William H. Whyte, Jr., *The Organization Man,* New York, Simon & Schuster, 1957.

book to include differentiated descriptions of the various gymnastic approaches used in different parts of the world. The subtle differences between for instance, Jalkanen, Idla, Medau, Carlquist, Bode, Bertram, Mensendieck, and Bjorksten, in modern women's rhythmical gymnastics, to take one section of the gymnastic approach alone, are still unevaluated in detail, though a trained eye generally can detect quickly, from a few movements, which of these is which. So too, the exact relations between movement training (in its several interpretations) in Britain, and some of the functional gymnastics of France[5] and Austria,[6] are not yet satisfactorily sorted out. It is much to the credit of some American women leaders that they have been at pains to observe these developments; but, apart from those who are kinesiologists (still only an empirical science), one wonders what the criteria are by which such systems are judged, or whether American observers, seeing relatively finished demonstrations, realise how much subtle detail there is in the teaching—or the purposes—behind individual movements.

Gymnastic Literature Is Inadequate

The literature in this field is still inadequate, and there is the basic difficulty of describing movements adequately in words (or for that matter by numbers). It may be a fair generalisation to say that over the last thirty years, European leaders have been experimenting so much in their physical practices that they have in general not been inclined to give these the permanence that the written word tends to impart. Meanwhile, many American leaders have been busier with other things than *experimenting* in movement, generally, though mention should be made in passing of an increasing consciousness on the women leaders' part that experiment in actual movement is an essential concomitant to cogitation. This is exemplified, for instance, in the basic movement programme, under Dr. Laura Huelster at the University of Illinois, in which a staff of women with differing backgrounds and experience practically, are attempting to devise a new approach in the service programme. A fine example can be seen at Michigan State in the work of Janet Wessel and her colleagues.

[5] Georges Hébert, *L'Education physique, virile et morale par la methode naturelle*, IV, Paris, Vuibert, 1944–1945.
[6] Gaulhofer, Streicher, and Liselotte Diem, for instance.

EVALUATORY METHODS

Rating Scales

But what evaluatory mechanism and processes have we available in this field? Maybe we can use rating scales as judges do customarily in competitive gymnastics, comparable to the judging of diving; however, such methods assume:

1. That the judges have identical criteria.
2. That they know what they are looking for.

These are considerable assumptions. In competitive Olympic gymnastics of the German kind for men and women, there is, of course, a very long tradition in assessment of such work on the horizontal bar, the parallel bars, the rings, the pommel horse, and the long horse. The Germans have over a century of experience in judging this work, and many other nations have experienced judges too.

Competitive Free-Standing Work

When it comes to a sequence of free-standing exercises, the compulsory sequences will have been constructed with certain criteria in mind (and the appearance of these sequences in Olympic gymnastics bears out the point made about the difficulty of certain types of callisthenics). With these, judgement is more difficult, for these are true *callisthenics*—if the word's original meaning of "beautiful strength" still holds good. At the Melbourne and Rome Olympics, the amazing variety of women's free-standing work made judgement difficult.

Training Subjective Skill—Empathy

But how does a judge get his training and is it objective? Of course it is not, though it may be highly reliable and, as far as we can pin down that elusive quality, valid. A gymnastic judge, of whatever genre of gymnastics, learns to judge through the experience of his own nervous system, and in particular his eyes and his proprioceptors.[7] He develops to a high degree a faculty common to all of us, called *em-*

---

[7] Would that our profession would take the trouble to understand some principles of neurophysiology, from such teachers as Dr. Frances Hellebrandt, of the University of Wisconsin.

pathy—the capacity to feel, in a sense, the movement and associated feelings of others. As a mere spectator we can ache after watching a wrestling match, or in a sense, feel the blows of a boxer. We can leap with the ballet dancer's *entrechat*, and sense the loss of security of the man who slips on the banana skin. Centuries ago Aristotle argued that the emotions of the spectator were purged when watching the downfall of the hero in great tragedy. In this he foreshadowed aspects of psychotherapy. Today we might say, using the findings of physiology, that, as the eyes observes others moving, there are relayed to kindred muscle groups, volleys of efferent impulses by either the corticopyramidal route or by the more primitive hypothalamic extrapyramidal one. These volleys, while not enough to overcome the inertia of the limbs concerned, may produce subliminal contractions in the limbs, which in turn produce vasodilation in the region, though little actual movement; thus, in common parlance, we may actually feel warm while watching others being vigorous.

Analytical Vision

The judge of movement, where no external measuring criteria exist, needs to develop his eye and his sensorium to provide five sorts of information:

1. *The ability to isolate in perception the required phase of a movement*—the *slow-motion eye*. To obtain this, long experience at watching complex and rapid movement is essential.

2. *The ability to perceive skeletal relationships*—the general shape of the position, including such things as full extension of joints, or the degree of flexion in joints, and alignment or symmetry of limbs. This might be known as the anatomical *X-ray eye*. A background of anatomy, physiology, and kinesiology is essential.

3. *The ability to perceive muscle tensions*, necessary and unnecessary, at isolated phases or points in a movement, or in the movements as a whole. This is the *empathy-forming* function of the eye. A background of personal proprioceptive experience is essential.

4. *The ability to perceive flow or rhythm* in a movement which may be a quality desired. This is probably a combination of (3) above and the next quality. For this kinesiological study of qualities of rhythm is essential.

5. *The ability to produce a mental image of how a movement should*

appear in its best form. This comes by at least two nervous mechanisms. The one is memory of other performances, giving a value scale, in which the best performance ever seen in reality, or on photo, film, or television, is resurrected in the mind as an image for comparison. The other mechanism, probably connected neurologically, is the *ideatory* one, by which, *before* making a movement ourselves, we, as it were, picture in advance in our mind's eye the sort of movement we are trying to make. That is we, ahead of our actual movement, perceive inwardly (*see* is an inaccurate term) how we shall appear at either the central phase of a movement—say the top position of a vault or a jump—or we visualise a *sequence of the portions of the movement*—starting position, run-up, flight, landing or follow-through, and finishing position. This pause before actual movement, when we gather ourselves before starting, has been called *Der schöpferische Pause,* the creative pause.

IDEATION

In movements like dives, vaults, dance, and individual callisthenics, where we may perform independently of others, this creative pause is, for some people, very important. It may be unconscious or deliberate. There is a slow-motion sequence of Jesse Owens preparing to do his world-record long jump at Berlin, in 1936, which is an excellent example of this. As he stands half-crouched ready for the run-up, he quite obviously gathers himself, concentrates his alertness, before starting. There is some danger in overideation however, in situations where an opponent in a game makes a rapid movement which demands counter action. In boxing it may be useful, but in baseball or cricket it may lead to anticipating a type of pitch or bowl which is, in fact, not pitched or bowled. How many of us have hit in our ideatory phase, a homer, or a six, which in fact was a strike, or which felled our wicket!

SUBJECTIVE JUDGEMENT TRAINABLE AND UNAVOIDABLE

The fastidious statistician may complain that all this is subjective and therefore not valid. It is subjective, and inevitably all of us depend on subjective judgements in most things we do. The hope is, that we train ourselves to be aware of likely errors and biases in our judgement, that we train ourselves to know what to look for, and to use our miraculously evolved nervous system to the best advantage in developing the perceptive powers which lead to:

1. The slow-motion eye.
2. The X-ray eye.
3. The sensing of muscle tensions through empathy.
4. Rhythm sense.
5. Ideatory sensitivity.

THE MAIN COMPONENTS IN GYMNASTIC MOVEMENTS

Whatever the system be, whatever the ingredients, there are certain basic movement patterns in gymnastics. Rather than classify by country, one tends in Europe to classify by individual leaders. There are, for instance, at least three main trends in Denmark, four in Sweden, three in Finland, and several in Britain and in Germany. However, as our readers will tend to be American, an analysis of individual leaders' techniques, emphases and supporting theories would be academic. We therefore prefer to analyse under headings indicating *types* of movements, in order to give a framework of reference. With each heading we suggest some criteria that might be used in evaluation.

FREE-STANDING MOVEMENTS

These are known generally in the United States as callisthenics. Such work can be graded in difficulty into exercises suitable for a kindergarten, a football squad, or the inmates of a home for senior citizens. The only apparatus used is the floor. They may include:

1. A series of *held* end positions, in which the intermediate movements are unimportant.
2. A linked series of swinging movements in which *flow* is all important.
3. A combination of (1) and (2).
4. Movements aiming at certain qualities (rather as in American modern dance). These movements may be:
   a. *Simple* movements, requiring little strength, and within the normal range of movement of joints.
   b. *Difficult* movements requiring hyperextensions and increased range of movements beyond normal range (e.g., bridging movements, span-bends, or sideways splits).

c. *Difficult* movements requiring great strength (e.g., one-arm push up).

d. *Difficult* movements requiring unusual balance ability (e.g., one-arm hand-stand).

e. *Difficult* movements requiring spring (e.g., backward somersault or leaping to touch the toes with horizontal-abducted straight legs).

f. A combination of any or all of these. (It may be realised already that advanced free-standing work, e.g., Olympic, ground exercises include much that is actually tumbling, or to use the British term, agility work.)

The various exercises may be: (1) separate or linked; (2) prescribed or voluntary. Their purpose may be: (1) the demonstration of an extreme level of skill; (2) developmental, compensatory, or remedial (e.g., stretching of iliopsoas or pectoralis major, or toning up of glutei).

THE EVALUATION OF FREE-STANDING MOVEMENTS

1. The purpose must be known and agreed on with the other judges, if any (in the teaching situation the teacher is often the only judge), and with the performer (in the schoolteaching situation the pupils must be aware of the goal—in most circumstances).

2. The purpose known, basic points of judgement can be put under headings, e.g.:

   a. Rhythm or flow.

   b. Ability to reach end positions.

   c. Achievement of anatomical and kinesiological purpose.

   d. Stillness.

   e. Balance

   f. Flexibility.

   g. Strength.

   h. Spring.

   i. Relaxation of muscles not in use.

   j. Ease.

   k. Bearing.

   l. Correctness of position.

   m. Beauty of performance (a total impression).

3. These basic points can be:

   a. Tabulated under headings with *rating scales,* so that either a total mark or profile may be given.

   b. With the experienced judge, whose training will tend to integrate the analyses of all these points, *a total mark* without breakdown may be given.

c. An *error* method may be used, in which the performer is assumed to have, say, 80 per cent of available points; points are subtracted for errors, and any special virtures are marked up.

INTEGRATED OBSERVATION

Just as the experienced aircraft pilot checks with a glance of the eye some two hundred dials, and spots the one not reading in the normal region, so the experienced teacher of gymnastics can form a Gestalt impression of a movement and pinpoint errors without specific analysis of all factors. In the learning phase, just as the pilot is drilled to go down a list of actions on take-off or landing, so the new teacher needs to analyse in detail a particular piece of practical teaching.

There is no mathematically objective way of eliminating prejudice in evaluating free-standing movements. There are obvious traps, such as letting beauty of the performer be confused with beauty of the performance, or letting one's own particular foibles dominate, but the basic problem is knowing thoroughly what is being attempted.

FREE-STANDING EXERCISES WITH SMALL APPARATUS

The purpose in these may be:

In this form of gymnastics, an external object is used to add *interest, range, quality,* and *strength* to the movement. Common objects are hoops (small or large), small or large rubber balls (inflated or medicine), light Indian clubs (not now used for the complex patterns of the old club swinging), sling-balls, skipping ropes (jump ropes), flags, or the heavy German iron ball with a handle. Some patented gadgets are also used.

The criteria for evaluation are much the same, though an extra detail may be *the capacity of the performer to keep an even and consistent relationship mechanically with the object used.*

EXERCISES USING PARTNERS

1. Extension of joints.
2. Strength development.
3. Balance.

4. Synchronisation.
5. Functional muscle demand through combative activities.
6. Mechanical assistance in increasing a factor, e.g., the support in upward jump in threes, or in a combined arabesque-like balnace.
7. Mastery of complex patterns.

Fig. 17.1.   Gymnastics with small apparatus—ball work. (*Evening Star,* Dunedin, New Zealand.)

Fig. 17.2.   Gymnastics with small apparatus—hoop work. (*Evening Star,* Dunedin, New Zealand.)

These exercises may involve using small apparatus—sticks, balls, quoits, hoops. These may add to the skill, strength or beauty of the movements. Some of these activities come under the classification of that vague term *stunts.*

Gymnastics with Heavy Portable Apparatus

The most obvious example of this is in weight-training and weight-lifting,[8] which is a form of gymnastics which has had a dramatic increase of interest during the last twenty years. Some prejudices have been overcome, thanks, in part, to American research. But there are also group activities with the timber baulk, and with other heavy objects, which have been introduced in the last twenty-five years. There is not space here to describe evaluation in detail in weight-training (it is well written up elsewhere). The obvious objectives are:

1. Strength.
2. Power.
3. Rapidity of strong movements.
4. Increasing the range of movement.
5. Lifting techniques.
6. Synchronisation in groups.

Gymnastics with Fixed and Portable Apparatus

This tends in Western countries to be of two main types, singly—in contrast—or as a mixture. The common terms, on a world basis, are given, but historically these terms are not very accurate.

German Apparatus (fixed)

Rings
Parallel bars—even and uneven
Horizontal bar
Trapeze
Balance beam—approximately 4″ wide and 4′0″ from the ground

Swedish Apparatus (fixed)

Wall bars (stall bars, rib-stalls)
Beams (booms)—2½″ wide, and adjustable from 6″ to 10′0″
Climbing ropes and inclined ropes
Windowframes

[8] Weight-training enthusiasts may dislike being classed as a form of gymnast, but in our use of the word, they use a specialized form of developmental gymnastics.

Fig. 17.3.   Gymnastics using the Swedish beam. (*Evening Star,* Dunedin, New Zealand.)

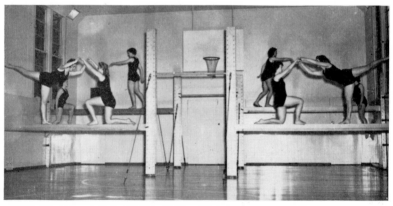

Fig. 17.4.   Gymnastics using the Swedish beam. (*Evening Star,* Dunedin, New Zealand.)

Miscellaneous Portable (used to some extent in both German and Swedish)

Vaulting buck
Vaulting box
Vaulting stool (New Zealand)

High plinth (vaulting table)
Tumbling mats
Landing mats
Trampoline
Trampette, springboard, beatboards, etc.
Pommel horse, long horse
Beam saddle (Swedish), bench saddle (British)
Swedish bench or form (with hooks)
Balance bar (wide or narrow)
Modern combinations of elements of these, especially in British countries

The skilled evaluation of the use of these cannot be given in a general book of this kind, but it may be appropriate to point out several ways in which gymnastic systems differ, in method and purpose, since there is singularly little differentiation seen in America.

ENDS AND MEANS

First let us consider *ends and means*. In general, the claim of apparatus gym-teaching in Scandinavia is that it helps to make you strong, flexible, courageous, etc., for no *specific* purpose; i.e., the *end* is not for most to be a gymnast (though some of course, do make gymnastics a sport).

In German-apparatus teaching, the aim for many (especially for men—women are more divided in their aims) is to be a gymnast, and in Germany itself, as in the Turnervereine in America, the emphasis on gymnastic competition is remarkable, going far beyond physical prowess. This difference between the approaches of two gymnastic systems is fundamental.[9] In one, gym makes you strong, etc. In the other, you make yourself strong in order to do the most demanding gymnastic feats, such as the "crucifix" on the rings.[10] At one time, the feeling between the two schools of thought ran high (both indeed were caught up in patriotism), but lately it is not rare to find Sweden enjoying German equipment as a sport, and Germans frequently use Swedish equipment in their educational work. The Norwegians and Finns, in

---

[9] And indeed the physiques of those who perform at top level in each tend to differ. See A. D. Munrow, *Pure and Applied Gymnastics*, New York, St. Martin's, 1955; and P. C. McIntosh, ed., *Landmarks in the History of Physical Education,* London, Routledge, 1957.

[10] There is also of course a mystique in the German Turnverein of considerable importance to its members.

contrast to the Swedes and Danes, have compromised between the two schools of thought for many years—as have several other Eupropean countries.

The second point is *lesson structure*.

LESSON STRUCTURE

In America, the custom is to separate callisthenics, stunts, and tumbling, and heavy apparatus. In Europe the combined lesson is often used, thus:

1. *Limbering up* with (a) callisthenics (rhythmical and linked), (b) a vigorous minor game, (c) free play on the equipment, or (d) a vigorous known dance. (The purpose of this section, in general, is physiological, circulation promotion,[11] and psychological preparedness.)

2. *A stretch and strengthen section* (compensatory, developmental, conditioning). In this section pair-work, stick-work, medicine balls, Swedish benches, beams, ropes, wall bars, etc., are used to make high *local* demands on strength, and are used also for promoting flexibility. There are also activities demanding balance. The movement may be entirely *formal,* with emphasis on exact end position, or relatively *functional.* The apparatus allows more exact localisation of effort by fixing one region while others move.

Sections (1) and (2) take up one-third to one-half of the session and are, as it were, devoted to preparing the body and mind generally. Section (2) undoubtedly has the strongest and most specific effects on the body. It may well be physiologically much the most valuable.

3. *The recreative section of the lesson.* This section tends to be a more recreational one, in which the challenge is to courage, spring and mastery of form, and perfection in movement (except in the functional schools of thought, where form is secondary to function). Tumbling mats, horses (buck, pommel horse, long horse, box), swinging ropes, swinging rings, etc., are all used.

The Pattern of the Whole Lesson

The general lesson moves from purposes which initially are physiological and anatomical to a latter section in which the main emphasis is

---

[11] The authors are aware that there is controversy about the need for warming up.

on skill and the mastery of difficult and exciting tasks. Sometimes this latter part includes ball skills, dance, minor games and relays, or such practices as track and field techniques, resuscitation, lifting, etc.

The evaluation of the first part is essentially the application of very specialized know-how, in terms of anatomy, physiology, kinesiology, and a long-established vocabulary of some thousands of graded activities. A well-trained gym teacher shows a large vocabulary[12] of activities of both developmental and recreational kinds, on each piece of equipment, and has a mastery of whatever type of free-standing exercise he may use, if any. He is able to apply in the lesson, too, the teaching of relaxation; in the second half of the lesson, general games' skills may be used. The lesson may end with a ball game, a dance, a relay race, or a game on the equipment, such as "shipwreck." After this there may be a *finishing* or *quietening* activity.

EVALUATING THE LESSON

In the evaluation of the lesson as a whole different criteria are needed at different stages, although there are some criteria which apply at all stages. Some of these are:

General Criteria

Is the atmosphere one of willing effort?
Is the purpose of the activities clear to the participants?
Is there a feeling of good-humoured freedom?
Is time wasted by "dead spots" when nothing is happening?
Is time wasted by poor organisation, such as queuing for activities, poor lesson design?
Is the teacher aware of every pupil and particularly the less able ones?
In appropriate parts of the lesson is responsibility delegated to pupil leaders?
Does the lesson stress self-discipline rather than imposed discipline?
Is the teacher quick to observe difficulties?
Does the teacher modify his lesson appropriately where planning is inadequate?
In group (squad) work is the lesson self-propelling?
Has the teacher absolute control when necessary?

It will be seen that the modern European lesson is far from being

[12] It is no exaggeration to say that a well-trained gymnastic teacher knows twenty-five purposeful ways of jumping from a height.

one of authoritarian domination, and uses democratic techniques in appropriate parts. What it does stress is purposefulness and effort, in the belief that there is little time in which to do all the desirable things, and that an atmosphere of hard work and individual effort is not undesirable as a contributory process in either the physiological or the character-forming processes of education as a whole.

In the three main sections of the lesson these particular criteria are also valid.

For the First Section—Limbering Up

1. Does the lesson get off the mark quickly without time-wasting formality?
2. Is the introductory activity chosen:
   a. Pleasurable?
   b. Already well known to the children?
   c. Reasonably informal, giving pupils freedom in space and time?
   d. Of sufficient general cardiorespiratory demand?
3. Is it well-linked, so that there is good "flow"?
4. Does it occupy all pupils?
5. Does the section end with a definite tidying up of the class into some appropriate formation—free-spacing or fixed-floor pattern—ready for immediate work on the next section?

For the Second Section—Stretching and Strengthening

1. Is there a reasonable mixture of rhythmic and static movement?
2. Is there realisation of stretch or muscle contraction?
3. Are end positions reached and held?
4. Is equipment ready and used in a planned, efficient manner?
5. Is the dosage in each particular movement sufficient to gain the desired physiological effect?
6. Is the stretch reflex avoided in extension exercises?
7. Are some of the exercises done in the pupils' own time and to the pupils' upper limit?
8. Does the teacher give clear and concise class corrections?
9. Does the teacher move among the pupils and give individual encouragement?
10. Are there at least some *functional* movements?

It is in this section that the knowledge of kinesiology, corrective work, and applied anatomy and physiology is paramount. This is more the case when this section is concerned with formal movements designed to give a specific isolated effect. For instance, to the well-trained

European gymnastic teacher there are some ten variations of what to the American is merely "chinning." Each of these ten variations is also gradable as to difficulty, so that it can be performed by a very weak child or by an extremely strong man, each at his own level, each according to his need. When it comes to graded abdominal exercises, there are some hundreds of these, varying from those suitable for use immediately after childbirth to those suitable for a boxer. So too, specific relaxation teaching and testing can be included in this section.

FOR THE THIRD SECTION—SKILL-BUILDING AND RECREATIVE WORK

This section, being devoted to recreation and skill-building, has so many criteria, each specific to the activity in mind, that it would be impossible to outline them all.

GENERAL QUESTIONS

1. Is the equipment well arranged so as to:
   a. Bring rapidity of turns?
   b. Provide return activities where appropriate?
   c. Be adjusted to a level which will produce real effort? (For instance, in astride-vaulting (leap-frog), the top of the buck or other object should be at least the height of the chest *above* the take-off point, be it floor or spring board, beat-board or trampette. It is impossible to do a good vault over too low or too high an obstacle.)
2. Are ability groups used in a class of heterogeneous size and ability?
3. Is a vault or tumbling activity clearly conceived as having definite parts, all of which go to make a finished whole?
   a. Standing position at start.
   b. Run up.
   c. Take-off.
   d. Flight.
   e. Landing.
   f. Finishing standing position or straight through run-off, in stream-vaulting, or roll into some other movement.
4. Are spotters (catchers) clear about the technique required?
5. Does the teacher notice general faults and give class corrections?
6. Does the teacher analyse individual faults?
7. Does the teacher encourage children to such proprioceptive self-awareness that in the end they analyse their own faults?
8. Does the teacher understandingly encourage the clumsy, the timid, and the tense?

9. Does the teacher finish off the lesson neatly and tidily, leaving the class calm and ready to go back to the classroom?

It would take a whole textbook to analyse these evaluatory criteria further. It takes all of three years to give a teacher a knowledge of these basic criteria, along with all the other skills necessary for a physical educationist. It takes years of apprenticeship to put these into practice well. Teaching gymnastics requires intense observation and intellectual concentration. Long ago, gymnastic teaching ceased being merely a do-this, do-that, automaton drill.

Posture Is Only Incidental

So far, no mention has been made of posture and coordination. These two were specific goals in early gymnastic teaching. We have dealt with posture elsewhere, and have shown it to be so complex, that we would make no claim for the special teaching of it in gymnastics. However, it may be a time of opportunity for drawing attention to it—but to some children the gymn can be a torture chamber, while to others it is a return to the jungle. How a child specifically reacts to a gymnasium, a gym class, or a gym teacher, probably determines his posture more than the teaching of it—on that occasion.

Coordination

So too, coordination is a complex function, neurologically speaking. As yet, it is undecided whether this is a general ability or a highly specific one, and we prefer at this stage to make no claims, beyond saying that many gymnastic activities demand a high degree of co-ordination, even in quite simple movements. It seems unlikely that performing complex coordination movements produces any *general* effect, but that it probably enhances the learning of other coordination exercises.

Functional Gymnastic Systems

In Europe there have been some gymnastic leaders who have rejected the idea of gymnastic exercise with an exactly prescribed form. For instance, using a vaulting horse, they will have their pupils regard this as an obstacle to be negotiated—as quickly as possible, or as quietly as possible—but with no prescribed form. This is somewhat the approach used with climbing apparatus in elementary-school playgrounds in some parts of America; the equipment is there as a challenge—to

Fig. 17.5. Functional gymnastics—new outdoor climbing apparatus in a New Zealand high school. (Education Department, New Zealand.)

Fig. 17.6. Functional gymnastics—challenging apparatus in a New Zealand elementary school. (Education Department, New Zealand.)

defy gravity, to use courage, to brachiate (bear the body weight on the arms)—and any anatomic-kinesiological benefit is incidental. The French, Austrians, and to some extent the Hungarians, have developed whole syllabuses on this nonformal basis, and indeed the approach goes back to some early German ideas. Others, such as the late Count Thun Hohenstein, have devised special functional approaches. This eccentric nobleman devised an impressive gymnastic training based on the movements of animals—but unfortunately left little written record of his experiments. For a time there was hostility between the formal and functional schools in Europe, but latterly some compromise and reciprocation of ideas has been noticed. In Sweden, for example, much of Maja Carlquist's junior work is taken functionally.[13] A child is encouraged to take a running leap at the wall bars and cling on, but at other parts of the lesson exactness of performance is required.

POSSIBLE USE OF COMBINED FUNCTIONAL FORMAL WORK IN AMERICA

It is the authors' view that this functional work, with strong cardiorespiratory demand and, at times, exactness of form, may commend itself to American men—if only they will learn how to teach it. It is distressing for a visitor to walk through well-equipped American gymnasia, and to hear from leaders that they no longer use expensive and useful equipment, usable in a variety of ways for developmental work, both functional and formal. It would seem as if they had accepted unquestioningly, at second hand, some of the strong views of the influential leaders of forty years ago, without re-examining their assertions—in spite of the fact that some of these same modern leaders have training in evaluation, and could be expected to have had the open mind that should come with scientific training.

MOVEMENT TRAINING AND BASIC MOVEMENT

A development in the last quarter century, originating from many sources (Hébert in France, von Laban in England, and others), has been the idea of a *basic training* in movement which will prepare people for all manner of activities and, according to some thinkers, will enable them to apply their training to new motor learning situations.

[13] See F. Maja Carlquist, *Rhythmical Gymnastics,* Toronto, Ryerson, 1955 (English ed., London, Methuen, 1953); also the books of Liselotte Diem.

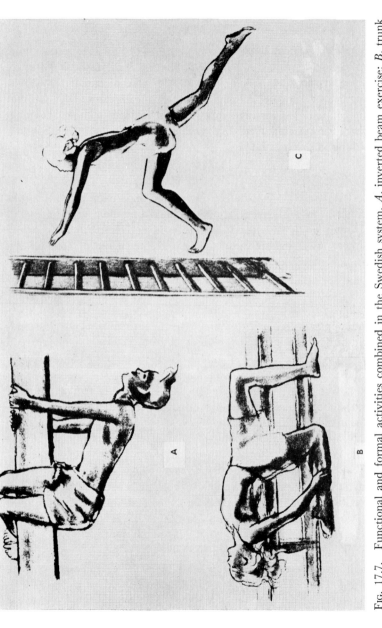

Fig. 17.7. Functional and formal activities combined in the Swedish system. *A*, inverted beam exercise; *B*, trunk exercise on a bench; *C*, leap to the wall bars. (Drawings by G. Lagerstedt, from Maja Carlquist, *Rhythmical Gymnastics*, London, Methuen, 1955)

HEBERT

Georges Hébert, in France, outlines his work in a huge six-volume, finely illustrated series, *L'Education Physique par la Methode Naturelle* —a thought-provoking book. He (and to a large extent Gaulhofer, Streicher, and Liselotte Diem) advocate a training on the basis of natural human movements: crawling, standing, walking, running, climbing, lifting, throwing. The vocabulary he gives in his books is astonishing in variety and size.

VON LABAN

The late Rudolf von Laban, who was the main stimulus in this field in Britain, had a different approach, analysing type and quality of movement methodically, and in terms which overlap to some extent with those used in American modern dance. Laban's followers in Britain have developed this to an astonishing degree in both elementary and high schools, using in general, adapted Swedish and newly devised equipment in a completely new way. A few well-stated claims for its educational and aesthetic soundness have been made,[14] though the extremist supporters seemed to make extravagant claims at first (a tendency in our profession), going almost so far as to say all games should be taught by this method, rather than by the methods accumulated by trial and success over many years.

To us this question remains open, and as yet we are not aware of any satisfactory special forms of evaluation applied to this work. Indeed, the task is difficult, and it seems virtually impossible at times to evaluate method independently of the infectious enthusiasm of the teacher. We feel that Britain, after a half-century of being a copier of European gymnastic movements, has now become a leader. We feel that after initial hostility, particularly from male leaders, this work has now come to stay. It has also established itself as a separate entity from dance yet remains on good terms with it.

ORIENTAL GYMNASTIC SYSTEMS

We in the West know too little of these. Some farseeing leaders, Josephine Rathbone Karpovich for instance, have gone to the East to

---

[14] And evolving many new types of approach. See Ruth Morrison, *Educational Gymnastics,* London, Spiers & Gledsdale, 1957; also *Educational Gymnastics for Secondary School,* published by the author, 1960.

D'une main, le bras bas et allongé; l'autre bras servant de balancier.

A deux mains, l'objet maintenu avec les bras bas et allongés (1), ou élevé à l'épaulement (2).

Hissage d'un objet le long d'une paroi verticale.

Le lever sur place.

La difficulté de tenue de l'aplomb du corps provient de l'étroitesse ou de la nature de la base d'appui des pieds en meme temps que du poids de l'objet et de l'incommodité de sa forme.

D'une main, le bras bas et allongé.

A deux mains à hauteur de ceinture.

A l'épaule.

Sur la nuque et l'épaule (coltinage).

Le portage sur base étroite mais horizontale.

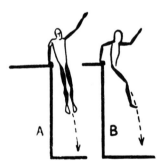
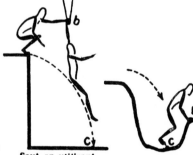

Saut en conservant l'appui d'un bras le plus longtemps possible pour diminuer le choc à la chute (saut de côté en A et de face en B).

Saut en utilisant l'aide d'un bras par suspension à une barre (b) pour réduire la vitesse de chute ou allonger le saut.

Chute avec appui retardant des bras (en B) avant le poser des pieds (en C).

Entrainement au saut en profondeur vertigineux.

FIG. 17.8. Functional gymnastics—French natural method of Hébert. (From G. Hébert, *L'Education Physique, Virile et Morale par la Méthode Naturelle,* Paris, Librairie Vuibert, vol. III)

study such well known and long respectable fields as Hatha Yoga, but it would seem that there are many long established practices in the East—whether as specific developmental systems, or as training for dance, or eastern combative sports—which might well be of interest to Western man.[15] Not only might the actual practices be useful, but nothing but good would come from Western man acknowledging that his Eastern brother can teach him something. There is also a psychosomatic side to Yoga which may have much to teach us. We know for instance, of a busy Indian cardiologist who does an hour's Yoga each morning, and finds particularly that it gives him peace of mind all day.

SUMMARY

So, let us summarise this all too brief survey of practices under the general heading of gymnastics. We can say that whatever the system, whether its purpose be developmental, recreational, aesthetic, or sporting, the ultimate evaluation depends on the teacher. In particular, certain special forms of discrimination—all products of the teacher's own nervous system—which he has developed through that tremendous receptor organ, the eye, and through his own proprioceptive sensibility. Just as a good musician can play great works without the music before him (entirely by subjective skill!), and he or a critic knows whether he is playing correctly and well, so a competent gymnastic teacher develops his judgements.[16]

In this chapter the author has attempted to aim the ideas towards North American readers, particularly those in the United States. Canada seems much more aware of European developments, and several leaders have been at pains to use European ideas, as well as American.

Were this chapter written for Europeans, the stress would be on the dogmatism which the enthusiastic leaders of each particular gymnastic system seem to develop. The supporters and particularly the inventors of one particular gymnastic school are apt to think they have found

---

[15] Mahlkamb and Lethim from India for instance.

[16] It may be argued that the analogy of a musician negates our stated concept of scientific justification. In fact, however, some of the artistry of playing can be reduced to mathematical terms of time patterns and sound frequencies.

FIG. 17.9. Two contrasting pictures: *above,* old-fashioned gym class, North America (Ewing Galloway); *below,* modern gymnastics, 1959, New Zealand.

the *ne plus ultra,* and to underestimate the contribution of other leaders. Some are also apt to overclaim for their systems.

An Antipodean Viewpoint

To us at a distance, not caught up in interschool-thought quarrels, it seems a pity that, concomitant with so much good work, and skilled and purposeful exercise, there should be such professional intolerance. Until we can shake ourselves free of these culture and personality-dominated prejudices, we will never be truly a profession. It seems that the somatotonic or somatorotic[17] personality, while successful in the field of action, may be very insecure in the field of contemplation, exposition, and professional cooperation. This is to be seen on both sides of the Atlantic—and indeed in the Antipodes too. The main difference to those of us who know both sides of the Atlantic, is that we expect the European physical educationist to be a first-class practical teacher, with a wide and detailed practical vocabulary. Whereas, on the other hand, we find the American leaders broader in theoretical background, but often not directly concerned with practical teaching, save in specific sports.

RECOMMENDED READING

Bode, Rudolf, *Expression-Gymnastics,* 5th ed., Lund, Sweden, Sydsvenska Gymnastik-Institutet, 1948.

Lindhard, J., *Theory of Gymnastics,* London, Methuen, 1934.

Knudsen, K. A., *Textbook of Gymnastics,* London, Zv. Churchill, 1947–1948.

Ministry of Education, Great Britain, *Physical Education in the Primary School,* London, Her Majesty's Stationery Office, 1953, Part I, "Moving and Growing," Part II, "Planning the Programme."

Morrison, Ruth, *Educational Gymnastics,* London and Liverpool, Spiers & Gledsdale, 1957.

Morrison, Ruth, *Educational Gymnastics for Secondary Schools,* Liverpool, College of Physical Education, published by the author, 1960.

Munrow, A. D., *Pure and Applied Gymnastics,* New York, St. Martin, 1955.

---

[17] See W. H. Sheldon, *The Varieties of Temperament,* New York, Harper, 1942; or R. W. Parnell, *Behavior and Physique,* Baltimore, Williams & Wilkins, 1958.

Randall, M., *Modern Ideas on Physical Education,* rev. ed., London, Bell, 1960.

Staley, S. C., *Conditioning Gymnastics,* New York, Barnes, 1927.

Thulin, J. G., *Gymnastic Hand-book,* Lund, Sweden, Sydsvenska Gymnastik-Institutet, 1947.

Wessel, Janet A., *Movement Fundamentals,* New York, Prentice-Hall, 1955.

chapter 18

EVALUATING DEVELOPMENTAL WORK

But you who are wise, must know that different nations have
different conceptions of things: and you will therefore not take it
amiss, if our ideas of this kind of education happen not to be the
same with yours . . . several of our young people were formerly
brought up at the college of the northern provinces: they were instructed in all your sciences: but when they came back to us they
were bad runners; ignorant of every means of living in the woods;
unable to bear either cold or hunger; . . . were therefore fit
neither for hunters, warriors, or counsellors: they were totally good
for nothing . . .

> Spoken answer to an offer by Williamsburg College
> in 1744 to give six Indians a college education;
> quoted by Benjamin Franklin in an essay, "Re-
> marks Concerning the Savages of North America"

THE medical experimenter can try out ideas on animals. He can
keep cages full of carefully bred, almost identical organisms, having
deliberately controlled their heredity. He can also exert remarkable
control on their environment, perhaps altering only one variable at a
time. He may remove an endocrine gland, transplant a tendon, de-
cerebrate a cat, feed one particular food, replace a kidney, or provide
a diet deficient in one factor. He can, in fact, at times design experi-

ments where cause and effect can be established with a high level of certainty. He can repeat his experiments—or others can repeat them—and he can use sampling techniques, and by these means he can well satisfy the strict criteria of evaluation. But he cannot ask a guinea pig, "How does that feel?" nor can the guinea pig give him any verbal help from its own insight, hindsight, or foresight. Different scientists can work on inanimate substances, on animate but inarticulate plants or animals, or in that world where life and nonlife seem indistinguishable, in the world of viruses.

EXPERIMENT WITH THE INANIMATE AND NONVOCAL

In fact, much of the methodology and apparent certainty of science has been built up by careful experiment on things which have no expressible view on the experiment. Some of the biological sciences have switched their main emphasis from taxonomy to behaviour, as is shown by the work of Hooton, Yerkes, Kohler, and Zuckerman on apes; of Richdale on penguins; or of Tinbergen on sticklebacks; and by the charming books of Konrad Lorenz, for instance. Much of this socio-behavioural study, ethology, has to be interpreted in terms of basic needs—the need to eat, to defend oneself or a zone, and to reproduce—and there is the constant possibility of the error of anthropomorphism coming in. That is because when an organism reacts in a situation parallel to a human one, we are in danger of assuming that it is aware of the situation in a way similar to that in which a human being would be aware. The zoo keeper who, on being asked the sex of a hippopotamus by an old lady, replied, "That is a question, lady, which should only be of interest to another hippopotamus," was expressing such a viewpoint.

LESSONS FROM ANIMALS

We can probably make some valid deductions from animal behaviour, by comparing behaviours before and after some given factor has operated. For instance, thyrodectomised rats on an iodine-free diet change remarkably when the thyroxin or iodine is given. It is also possible to produce reversible changes which seem to restore a situation, after controlled disturbance, to very much what it was before.

EXPERIMENTS ON MEN

It is proper to ask how much we can experiment with human beings and if there are any essential differences. We do, of course, experiment with human beings when they are ill. We try the effect of some medicament, injection, diet, or environmental change. A large part of medical and surgical treatment is based on successful experiments made upon persons who are clearly seen as ill or damaged. There are also, sometimes, volunteers who act as "guinea pigs." The well-known Harvard "Common Cold" Experimental Station on Salisbury Plain, in England, is an example. The British conscientious objector who submitted to starvation diets during World War II, in order to test a nutritional theory, or the psychologists at McGill University who exposed themselves to simple repetitive tasks to the exclusion of all other interests, until they were quite disoriented, are examples drawn from many such cases of voluntary submission to human experiment by the healthy. There were also, from 1933 to 1944, more sinister experiments in Nazi Germany made by medical men on prisoners in concentration camps. There was deliberate mating of young people of desirable Nordic stock, on a human stud-farm basis. There was also the huge fanatical attempt by Hitler, through genocide, to alter the "racial" nature of the German people. And, of course, the United States of America represents the greatest experiment in human history, involving a new cultural pattern out of people who only recently came from well-established old ones. By and large, we tolerate experiment where treatment for illness is not well established, if the experiment is successful. And we frown on experiments made on the well made against their will.

HUMAN RIGHTS

The human being, we consider, has an unwritten inalienable right in these matters. There are some questions still not clearly answered. The question of *wittingly* raising the level of radiation is one. An experiment on a remote Pacific Island may be concerned with the defence strategy of one group of people, but the side results of the experiment unwittingly may ultimately affect the lives of people not concerned with the experiment. So too, we use the word *ill* somewhat loosely. It is a truism that one can be diseased without knowing it. Some diseases show their presence by painful or embarrassing symptoms, which cause action to be taken. Others develop to well past the danger point before the ill person has any awareness of them. Mass radiology uncovers some such cases, and experiments, such as those at the Peckham Health Centre, have revealed that even those who may feel and act fit may in fact be seriously ill at a presymptom, or, as it is called, prodromal phase.[1]

And then of course, there is again the main difference between experiment on conscious man and on animals or plants. The person experimented upon can communicate his views as to what he thinks is happening, either in response to question or by introspection, as in Aldous Huxley's celebrated experiments with mescalin, described in *The Doors of Perception,* or in some of the brain operations described by Dr. Wilder Penfield, O.M., and others. What is more, provided there is a common language in the situation, these communications can have many shades of meaning. The language of gesture and facial expression alone allow us to communicate more than animals. The missionary doctor palpating for a fulminating appendix in a Papuan native, can use his eyes on the patient's face to confirm the estimations of his finger tips—but do not let us be so ethnocentric as to think the same gesture universally means the same thing. For instance, shaking the head means no in many places, but in Turkey the negative is expressed by sharply lifting the head. Thus we can summarise by saying that experiment on the apparently well human being should only be made with his consent, but that it has some advantage over experiment on nonvocal subjects or noncommunicating ones.

VALUABLE TYPES OF EXPERIMENT

Bringing the focus down to physical education and programmes aiming at *development*—that is, development by intentional behaviour, as opposed to development that goes on just by the passage of time (the normal "programme" of growth,[2]) what can we hope to do and what can we evaluate? We can never divorce the experiment from the

[1] G. S. Williamson and I. H. Pearse, *Biologists in Search of Material,* London, Faber, 1938.
[2] Supplied with the genetic "instructions."

time factors, but we can make reasonable assumptions by comparison of one situation, in which we deliberately interfere, with another similar one, where we do not, after the interference has operated for a significant time.

Let Us Limit the Target

Now what can we test in this field? We cannot easily test "the spiritual and moral qualities which contribute the fullest measure of living in a democratic society[3]—even if they are an aspect of fitness. Let us set our sights a little lower and on a more definite target, and let us not give up or rationalise into a cloud of verbal evasion, because we are dealing with a situation of many variables and probably few ultimate truths. One narrow concept of development concerns physical fitness, and its possible improvement. Let us admit that an increase in the more physical aspects of fitness may not make us morally, spiritually, or democratically superior. Let us admit too, that physical fitness is a multiple concept. Let us admit *strength* is only part of physical fitness.

Two Kinds of Strength

There are two aspects of, or kinds of, strength that may be useful to our physical well-being. One is the sheer force exertable by voluntary muscle at a given instant,[4] the other is the capacity, through our cardiorespiratory machinery and motor neurones, to keep up a certain level of output of strength.[5] Both of these types of strength may be important in the daily life of the ordinary citizen and, of course, matter more to some than to others. Each of us needs sufficient voluntary strength to overcome gravity without a continual conscious effort and to do our domestic chores or other jobs without muscle fatigue. Even in a push-button world there is an argument for some reserve of strength,

---

[3] *Fitness of Youth,* statement by 100 Delegates to AAHPER Conference, Washington, September 1956.

[4] Even this has low reliability and depends on motivation. The explanation of this lies in the dual mechanism, neurologically, by which muscles are stimulated to contract—a crude, primitive mechanism for general movement and a cortical one for learned and accurate movements.

[5] Sometimes called *endurance.*

for the unexpected effort—the suitcase that has to be lifted out of the auto, the car that has to be dodged—the rapid strong action that may be needed by anyone only very occasionally, as it were, the reserve tank to be used when there is danger or the push-button circuit fails.

IS EXERTING STRENGTH A PLEASURE?

It can be argued too from experience that exerting strength itself can be a pleasure to the majority of people. This is a pleasure vicariously obtained through the cowboy chase on the screen, the power of a car (which of course, bears little relation to functional efficiency—within the law), and perhaps indirectly confidence in an intercontinental ballistic missile with a nuclear fission warhead. Some need more satisfaction through executing strength directly than do others. It seems probable and reasonable that the highly mesomorphic find basic satisfaction in outlet through violent strength. The Gluecks' clear finding that, in Boston youngsters at least, there is more mesomorphy among delinquent boys than in a matched sample of nondelinquents, is not entirely surprising.[6] This does not mean that weight-lifting is a cure for delinquency, but it may mean that the sort of person who might become delinquent may enjoy and find satisfaction in violent exercise. It may mean that violent exercise of a socially acceptable sort might provide an outlet for forms which might otherwise be used antisocially. It would seem possible that the ratio in a given person of motor tissue to dead weight had some bearing on this problem. In fact the described jumpiness of the ectomorphic, and the sloth of the endomorphic, may be in part the product of something so simple as such power-weight ratios. It is also conceivable (and here former athletes whose morphogenotype are well draped in adiposity may resent this) that habits of activity enjoyed in youth and established in the motor-neurone network, remain frustrated in the well-ballasted tackle, become sedentary. Sir Alan Rook at Cambridge University,[7] has recently established that athletes have a normal life span, living neither longer, nor less long than nonathletes, and this might appear to lend force to the cynicism

[6] Sheldon Glueck and Eleanor Glueck, *Physique and Delinquency*, New York, Harper, 1956. This has been criticised on the grounds of methodology by some people.

[7] Also Montoye and colleagues at Michigan State.

attributed at different times to President Hutchins of the University of Chicago, to Mark Twain, and to others: "The only exercise I take is acting as a pall-bearer at the funerals of my more athletic friends."

Hidden Classifications

However, what is not apparent is a possible hidden classification in such findings as Rook's. It is to be wondered how many of the athletes followed up in his major survey altered substantially in tissue balance.[8] When it is remembered that the major male sports at Cambridge are rugby football and rowing, both requiring a high proportion of meso-morphy, and both predominantly sports of youth and low carry-over value, it is conceivable that, if the findings of the Metropolitan Life Insurance Company about acquired adiposity and life expectation are true, then some of these highly mesomorphic athletes might have lived longer had they kept their calories down and their exercise up. Of course, another factor operates too in that longevity seems to be in part a functional affair of a genetic pattern. But just as with delinquents, who should have chosen their parents more wisely, this is not just a simple hereditary factor, but also an environmental one.

The Retention of Strength

Thus, returning to strength, there are seen to be several grounds for its development. There are also arguments for its retention. Possibly because the hands and arms are man's most expressive and versatile motor organs (outside speech), we are apt to think of strength (with abhorrence for some) as bulging biceps, tying knots in pokers, or rip-ping the Manhattan telephone director into sixteen pieces with the bare hands. In fact, arm strength is of relatively little importance, once we are adults. Possibly because we admire hand-skill in so many fields—the artist's, musician's, surgeon's, or craftsman's—we may have a natural revulsion to the brawny arms and shoulders associated with our ancestors and a cruder sort of life (although books with titles like *How to Build Mighty Arms* have a ready sale). Man's supremacy has come through his manual skill, not strength, and there is something atavistic in the worship of gross strength in the upper limb—this amazing skill-organ.

[8] How much the morphophenotype changes on a laid-down pattern is also puzzling.

WHAT REGIONAL STRENGTH MATTERS MOST?

But it is not in arm strength that we lapse as we age, so much as back strength, abdominal wall strength, and foot and leg strength. The toll of tired backs, disc injuries, back pain, the corset industry and the "fat man" business, and the success of commercial physical culture in general, bear witness to failure in these vulnerable regions. They are, it could seem from modern medical experience, valid enough reasons why we should each of us *know* how to maintain voluntary muscle strength in these regions which let us down through weakness. The same is probably true for cardiovascular strength, though here the means of evaluation and of maintenance of an adequate level are more debatable. As has been shown by many recent publications, including Hunsicker's classical collation in the *Research Quarterly,* for March, 1957, there is plenty of material available in the measurement of voluntary muscle strength. There is also much work on means of gaining or maintaining strength, gradation of exercise dosage, general and local exercise, static and dynamic movement, exercise using external weight, exercise using the body weight, and so on. It is not the place of this book merely to repeat in abbreviated form what has been done elsewhere. We would, in this matter, only call to the attention of readers that, thanks to the work of Müller in Germany, it seems probable that relatively little exercise will maintain muscle strength, and that the dosage of work needed to cause hypertrophy is also much lower than might be expected—though one of the authors suspects from clinical experience that individuals differ markedly in this respect.[9] The work of Morgan and Adamson at Leeds University on *Circuit Training* has also made an important and educationally attractive contribution to strength-gaining as part of a school's physical-education problem.[10]

RELATIVE EFFICACY OF STRENGTH-TRAINING METHODS

There are three aspects of strength development and its evaluation which do demand attention and, it would seem to us, have been somewhat neglected in many places. We put them as questions.

[9] Müller's work is controversial; see a stimulating article by G. T. Adamson, "Milo or Müller?" *Journal of Physical Education,* LI, no. 153.

[10] R. E. Morgan and G. T. Adamson, *Circuit Training,* New Rochelle, N.Y., Soccer, 1958. Also A. S. Lewis, of Canterbury University, New Zealand, with his "Target Training," *New Zealand Journal of Physical Education,* no. 18 (July, 1959), 17.

1. Granted that general strength may be increased by general whole-body movements (as in sport, dance, or functional gymnastics of the Central European sort), or by deliberate localised exercise (as in weight-training, Scandinavian gymnastics, physiotherapy, resistance-training, and many other forms of conditioning exercises) [11]—granted these two main alternative approaches, have we any evidence of their relative efficacy in regard to specific basic strength needs, such as abdominal strength, back strength, or foot and leg strength?

2. Different protagonists of different methods ever since the 1889 Boston Conference have sworn their methods are the best, with the full, but unscientific, confidence of having seen them work with groups of people. Opponents of such methods have been equally confident in rejecting claims, sometimes on psychosocial grounds, and sometimes on such attractive but somewhat specious grounds that, in effect, certain exercises are not "natural." [12] Some also will say, for instance, that Americans are so democratic that they do not like and will not do exercises to command. Meanwhile Miss Prudden, whose approach is both formal and functional, has made it clear, as did William Skarstrom in his day, that some Americans do not object to doing exercises to command. [13] These general statements are a prelude to a question. What do we really know about *motivation* in relation to developmental work?

3. The third question is not unconnected with the other two and is concerned with cerebral understanding, know-how, insight. How much do we know about the understanding people may gain about how to help themselves to restore, maintain, and increase voluntary strength?

Differences and Cults

These three questions we consider raise issues which are central to the problem of developmental work in our field in the mid-twentieth century. We have had bickerings, enthusiasms, and cults, and almost holy wars between respected professional leaders, such as that in the *Physical Educator* in 1953. There has been so far we feel more opinion than detached evaluation, and this is perhaps why the Kraus-Weber

[11] See an excellent and comprehensive list of these in C. S. Staley, *Conditioning Exercises.*

[12] For a closely argued statement of "natural" movement, see Frode Andersen, *Journal of Physical Education* XLVII, no. 142 (1955), p. 105.

[13] And no one can deny the enormous growth in the last decade of commercial ventures in the form of physical culture studios.

Tests caught the profession with its intellectual pants down. We feel that these are basic questions, which were perhaps answered with too much confidence before we had the means of evaluation to really assess the problems.

The localised versus general-exercise approach has, of course, at times caused angry splitting of opinion in Europe, but the solutions that have come there have been more in the form of compromise than the divided camps found in the United States. The Scandinavians, particularly the various followers of Pehr Henrik Ling (incidentally an Honorary Fellow of the American Academy of Physical Education), in early days stood strongly for the theory that methodical zone-by-zone exercise of the body was necessary to reach all muscle groups and to exercise them through their full range. Thus for many years the table of exercises for the first two-thirds of the lesson made marked local demands on strength and flexibility. The Central Europeans, and to some extent the British, took the view that *vigorous* general activity would reach these same muscle groups and joints, as an incidental occurrence of a more "natural" kind, rather than the deliberate and overformal procedure of the Swedes.[14]

The word *vigorous* must be emphasised, because all European schools of thought believe in a strong workout in which the participant had to exert his will and make high physiological demands on himself, to the point where there is free perspiration, accelerated cardiorespiratory action, and the feeling of being really vigorous. It is inconceivable to a European physical educationist of either main school of thought that shuffleboard, bait-casting, or desultory square dancing[15] could be regarded as a workout or as the main requirement in physical education, whatever their recreational value.

POSSIBLE TESTS

It seems possible that evaluation techniques could be worked out which would test out the relative effects in performance of strength and flexibility tests of:

1. Highly localised exercise.

[14] In a limited sense they were right in that individual muscles are not represented on the cerebral cortex.

[15] Square dancing is, of course, not a desultory activity, but it can become a soft option and demand no effort of the pupil.

2. General wholebody conditioning exercise.
3. Various game forms of exercise.

All three of these forms of exercise are taken from the potential vocabulary of school or college physical education. The fact that American investigators have been able to alter scores in the Kraus-Weber Tests by very short periods of training requires careful interpretation. While disregarding the tests as total-fitness tests, and regarding them primarily as muscle-strength tests for certain muscle groups (ignoring for the moment the most contentious toe-touching tests), the fact that people can be quickly trained to pass them does not invalidate them as such tests. Müller's work has shown that strength can be increased rapidly when deliberate attempts are made, and it is a commonplace of teaching experience that people can improve their maximum score on all-out tests such as sit-ups, squat-thrusts, chins with very little training, if they make the effort. The evaluation required consists of an overhaul and evaluatory inspection of activities common in physical education to see which of them in fact do cause alteration in strength of local muscle groups and which do not. The answer is surely to improve on the Kraus-Weber Tests, ignoring such double talk as the suggestion that there is any meaning in a distinction between "medical" and "physical education" tests in this context (though there obviously is in other contexts). The validation of muscle-group strength tests can be measured directly by the methods of Harrison Clarke, McCloy, and others, and also in some cases checked by electromyography, though quantification still presents a difficult problem here.[16]

It needs little knowledge of kinesiology to see that vigorous volleyball or basketball involves greater range of movement, and more muscle groups, than does archery, shuffleboard, or golf. Cinematographic studies of volleyball, using an analysing projector showing one or two frames per second,[17] or a still picture, would enable quantitative verification of what direct experience suggests, e.g., that there is a very full

[16] Though the factor of motivation will always remain an uncontrollable variable. It is no answer to say that a constant stimulus will solve this. It may help, but some people will not promote maximum effort. Nor, for instance, can we be sure that pulling against an *unyielding* load (as in cable tensiometer tests) will stimulate the greatest effort in all people. The subjective realisation of success can be a spur to greater effort.

[17] We strongly recommend the relatively cheap SPECTO analysing projector, made in Britain.

range of movements in ankles, knees, hips, shoulders, and wrists, and that there is a continuous active demand on dorsal extensors. We have, in fact, the means to evaluate local effects in general activities.

SHOULD MUSCLES BE USED?

We can assume that clinical evidence suggests that maintenance of abdominal-wall strength and dorsal-extensor strength is desirable, but we can take the matter further and examine the principle so often advocated by Scandinavians that it is desirable and possible to keep all the main voluntary muscle groups at a certain level of efficiency. We need not suppose that this idea is a purely occidental and Scandivanian idea. The Hindu or Javanese dancer and the practicer of Hatha Yoga go even further than the Scandinavians in control, strength, and range of movement. Anyone who has seen Uday Shankar or Ram Gopal dance realises that they have remarkable control of many little muscles of the neck (rectus-capitus posticus, intraspinatus, intertransversalis, etc.) and of the eyes and face, which we Western folk have never developed. The Germans have a proverb, "Rast ich so rost ich" (literally, "If I rest, I rust!"), and in a general sense this is true physiologically of voluntary muscle. What we cannot say yet is what are the reasonable limits in our society in such a process. We can say the corset industry indicates our concern with a certain figure shape, in which we are content to use synthetic muscles. We can say many people's backs let them down and might not have done so had they been stronger and used more wisely.[18] We can say that people's foot posture—that is the neural control of the antigravity muscles in leg and hip, and leg and foot—fails them, to their own discomfiture, but there are other regions, not yet shown so clearly, as being important and which merit study.

LIMITATIONS TO THE RECREATIONAL APPROACH

Those with a predominantly recreational approach to physical education will not see this area of evaluation as important, but on a world basis they are in a minority. This field where kinesiology and evaluation

[18] See the work of Sills, *et al.*, on relative back and abdominal strength in relation to back pain; e.g., F. D. Sills, "Sports, Medicine, and Exercise Therapy for the Back," *Proceedings of the Central District Association of AAHPER*, Sioux Falls, South Dakota, 1953.

meet is of particular interest in Germany and France, Scandinavia, the Latin countries, whether in Europe or South America, and increasingly in the East. It is the field where we come nearest to our most powerful potential allies—in the world of medicine.

In America medical men once dominated physical education, perhaps excessively. Physical educationists threw off this yoke gradually and embraced education and psychology, but in doing so at times they may have shown some of the fury of the convert. The new espousal was a fortunate one historically, for it coincided with the period of the evolution of sound methods of evaluation. This development of understanding in evaluation gave physical educationists a new respectability: they began to talk the language of the educational scientist. Earlier they had been the doers, the active men, in something of the same relationship to medicine as the nursing profession still is.

A BETTER LIAISON WITH MEDICINE NEEDED

Now, with academic standing, surely they are ready to work with medical men again, in the field of research and practical health education. Now these fields of intellectual understanding overlap, and possibly in this very field of evaluation, physical educationists may know more about scientific procedure than most medical men. Many medical men would not know a standard deviation from a chi-square. A rapprochement is surely due, and it is in the fields of evaluation, kinesiology, and psychology that it is most likely that it can occur.[19] Since medicine dominated physical education, medicine itself has become more scientific and more broken up into separate disciplines. It still has superior social status to us and always will have, but there are now more fields where we can work together. It is perhaps a tribute to the Europeans that the veteran Swedish leader, J. G. Thulin, received an Honorary M.D. on his eightieth birthday, and that the most honoured of European physical educationists is Carl Diem, M.D., Honoris Causa. Many of the other leading European-born physical educationists are fully trained physicians.

[19] A recent visit to the United States by one of the authors confirms this view. In the period between medical domination by M.D.'s and the modern emergence of leaders brought up to the doctoral level in physical education, there was a period of inspired leadership by those who came sideways into the profession from psychology, physiology, anthropology, and education.

WHAT MOTIVATES WHOM?

The second question, of *motivation* in relation to exercise, is a more difficult one for evaluation. With what certainty do we know that a sample group of persons in a given culture will or will not respond to a certain set of stimuli? This is quite a sociological problem. It has often been said that Americans do not like being given orders. The same is frequently said of New Zealanders. Although Americans are of much more mixed stock, the pioneer founders of each country left their mother countries dissatisfied with conditions there. Conditions at the time concerned included a highly stratified society with much giving of orders by those above to those below, and much formality at the upper-class levels.[20] Even more recently each country has known an influx of refugees from authority in Europe. This is not to say that authority cannot run amok in the United States. The incidents of the early 1950s have not died from memory entirely, nor can it be said that Americans are not interested in the monarchy, judging by the published attention to the doings of the British royal family. But it is true to say that there is in the make-up of the former colonial settlers a feeling of pride at having shaken off unreasonable authority. That they have allowed other forms of more subtle authority to appear and influence them is not to deny the main principle. There is no denying either that formality and a dominance-submission situation were often main factors once, in say, Scandinavian physical education, or in another more strongly patriotic way in the Turnvereine of Jahn in Germany, or the Sokols of Tyrs in Czechoslovakia. But maybe Americans have to rethink the question of teacher-pupil relationships and not be afraid of making demands. The appraisal and overhaul of high-school teaching at present in process—e.g., the Conant Report—is not overdue.[21]

[20] It is ironical to find that societies which attempt to be classless fall into a pattern of class levels relatively soon after the original class-yoke is thrown off; see Vance Packard, *The Status Seekers,* New York, McKay, 1959.

[21] In Dr. James B. Conant's *21 Recommendations for Improving Public Secondary Education,* the only reference to physical education is in a sense a negative one: "B. The Elective Program. The other requirement for graduation should be successful completion of at least seven more courses, not including physical education. *All students should be urged to include art, music in their elective programs*" (page 48). There is no cause for complacency on our part. Dr. Conant has made some later comments on physical education which show awareness of the need for reform—if not the direction of the reform.

EXPERIMENT NEEDED

This question of *motivation* must remain unanswered for the present. It is to be hoped that there will be carefully thought-out experiments made, using specific techniques on carefully sampled groups. One essential factor is that, if European conditioning methods are to be part of the experiment, the teaching groups must be efficient *by European standards,* and yet acceptable as people to those on whom experimental teaching is tried. As David Riesman has shown, in *Individualism Reconsidered,* American football developed from English rugby in the 1860s because American players could not understand or properly interpret the rules of rugby as printed (this sort of failure to interpret from the printed word could spoil an experiment in comparative developmental work completely). One of the writers has seen, in person, so-called callisthenics at adult and child levels in America which were such a pale imitation of the type of work originally conceived and practiced that the session would have been boring to anyone. Many older American gymnasiums are well equipped for developmental work, but few of the teachers would know how to use the apparatus as it was originally intended (see Chapter 17). Wall bars (stall bars, rib-stalls) have to the trained European, hundreds of uses both formal and functional, which can be exciting and demanding to anyone, but without basic training and vocabulary, their use can be a bore.

SO FAR, LITTLE VALID EVIDENCE

The answers given so far in American publications on questions of the effect of conditioning exercises have been dialectically skillful. There have been some pontifications with emotional overtones, on the subject of the undesirability of "strength" as a main physical-education objective—but little evidence of any consequence.

Developmental work has, of course, different functions in different situations, and part of the way to suggesting appropriate evaluation is to discuss those functions at different age levels and in different situations.

THE INFANT AND YOUNG CHILD

The healthy child is intermittently restless. It explores its physical environment; it accepts the challenge of the pull of gravity. It accepts the challenge of its own built-in stretch reflexes. Let a baby grasp your finger, and then move the finger up—the baby will hang on. This is not an act of the baby's will. It is unlikely that it makes any choice in this matter at all. Its myotatic reflexes give its muscles the chance to develop. Swaddle it tight, and the stretching and grasping movements are not possible. Gorer, the social anthropologist, has suggested that such frustrations of movement in the young may reappear later in forms of adult aggressiveness, petulance, and temperament. As the child becomes more mobile—from creeping, to clambering, to walking and running, throwing and jumping—its own physiological make-up, neuromuscularly (and, of course, in terms of somatotype), prompts it onto the path to development. No elaborate quantitative evaluation is necessary. An examination of the environment in terms of opportunity for challenging self-chosen exercise is sufficient. We must ask, "Has this child a chance to indulge its motor drives so that there is possibility of achievement?" We do not expect persistent or adult-organised developmental activity. Like Wordsworth's child in "Ode on Intimations of Immortality in Early Childhood":

> See, at his feet, some little plan or chart,
> Some fragment from his dream of human life,
> . . . .
> But it will not be long
> Ere this be thrown aside,
> And with new joy and pride
> The little Actor cons another part . . .

It is not the place of this book to chart the development of motor abilities. This has been done very thoroughly by Gesell, McGraw, Harold Jones, Anna Espenschade, and many others. The main statement to be made is that exploration of the environment involves muscle exercise, and this means a gradual slight hypertrophy and increase in strength. The recent work done in Germany by Müller, Hettinger, and others, at the Max Planck Institute for Applied Physiology,[22] which indicates how little load is required to produce an increase in strength with young adult males, has made us think twice about earlier concepts

---

[22] It is interesting to consider that at first quite a few leaders in the United States trained in physiology and evaluation took Müller's work at face value, since it came from such a reputable source. However, many have failed to get similar results.

of "overload." We cannot with certainty say yet what is the desirable load for young children; we can only say that frustration of drives to move around or removal of all challenges to the exertion of strength is both unnatural and maybe prevents what would be normal strength development for any given child. All children need a certain minimum of strength for locomotor purposes—to withstand the impact of a world of bumps, to save themselves from a fall, to lift and carry things —but the situation does not lend itself to quantification. Perhaps our main task is to evaluate the environment in terms of opportunity by a series of questions.

Does this child's environment:

1. Allow it to move freely?
2. Allow it to climb and hang by its hands?
3. Allow it to lift and carry objects at least a half of its body weight?
4. To run so far that it can get up to its maximum speed?
5. To throw things as hard as it can?
6. Present challenges to it which can only be dealt with by effort?

At this point someone will be asking about danger. An environment, entirely hazard-free, would inhibit movement, but obviously certain hazards must be removed. These things are amply considered in safety-education syllabuses. A possibility greater than the hazards so often stressed is that urban living, with the diminution of the opportunity for adventurous life of the Huck Finn type, will prevent normal development. Rising building costs mean smaller apartments, and all the more need for movement space. How many urban children in the mid-twentieth century ever have a chance to climb a tree? And then, of course, there is the other challenge produced by so-called progress. The opportunity for exercise by proxy, for vicarious play, has increased enormously. It is not so much that watching the television or the drive-in movie keeps you inactive, but, because it so often involves watching movement, we identify ourselves with the images on the screen so much that we think in fact we have had the exercise. While we watch, empathy is at work, and very probably very low-level action currents operate in our muscles giving us a slight sensation in our own bodies of having made the movements we have been watching. We are not only deprived of the exercise, but deluded to some extent into thinking we have had it.

As far as the young child is concerned, we adults have the chance of providing the exercise-stimulating environment, the challenges to strength, and also have the possibility of actually seeing that a child does use these, by at times denying him second-hand pleasures.[23] It is we adults who by our ingenuity have produced this lazier way of life. It is not child-invented, but because it is often superficially very attractive to a child, he may prefer it to what otherwise he would naturally do.

THE YOUNGSTER (7 TO 11)

In this phase we begin to move into a more evaluable area. The self-chosen activities have a wider range, and include more activities where we can measure what is happening; also we can offer more specific challenges. This phase of development is regarded as a very stable one from the health angle, both mental and physical. It tends to be an uncomplicated stage. The child at this phase, granted normal health, is becoming independent in some of his choices, chooses an environment outside the home limits part of the time, and is highly mobile. He is also considered as being very receptive, and soaks up experience like a sponge. Some natural sex differences of interest appear, and some are, of course, imposed; but there will be many children who are not clearly differentiated in the sex difference of interest. Particularly, there will be girls who enjoy the rough and tumble of boys' activities. Overanxious mothers who think this will mean that their daughter will grow up unfeminine are merely sowing the seeds of hostility in their children, if they try to imprint adult patterns too early. The fantasy about physical-education teachers and sportswomen being unfeminine is, to outside observers, quite extraordinary. In New Zealand, for instance, where girls are extremely energetic in all kinds of sport compared to the American girl, they are much in demand as wives.

A TIDE TO BE TAKEN

The most important thing about this phase, as far as exercise and strength are concerned, is that it is one which is important from the view of timing. Although many sail through the puberty period with no visible disturbance of equilibrium, to others it will be a period of stress and strain. This calm period before puberty is an excellent one for

[23] The wisecrack, "In America parents obey their children," is not entirely irrelevant.

developing habits and conditioning them so firmly that they persist through the disturbed period. During the disturbed period we are often reluctant to learn to develop new habits; in fact, we may be quite resistant to teaching at all. In fact the prepubertal period is of formative importance, particularly for exercise, skill, and strength interests. In growth and development there are tides which must be taken at the flood, thus the fourth to eighth grades become crucial in our field. The child who has enjoyed physical challenge during this period, has mastered skill, and knows how to develop strength if he or she wishes, has an investment which may carry the child through a period when the disinclination to be active occurs, and when all manner of distractions impinge. The junior high-school child can be one of the most responsive to an energetic physical-education programme.

To evaluate strength exercise needs in this period we can ask another set of questions. Do the child's three main environments—school, home, and self-chosen—

1. Provide plenty of challenge involving effort and exertion?
2. Provide not only opportunities for energetic whole-body skill but knowledge of how to prepare by training for such physical demand?
3. Give the child an understanding of its own growth and development and clear indication that it needs exercise both general and local?
4. Give a child a knowledge of its own body in such a way that the child can help itself, e.g., in gaining strength if it wishes?
5. Give the child an awareness that it is moving into a phase of life where its natural drive for activity will be thwarted and replaced by seemingly attractive but less active interests?
6. Give the child some scales of achievement in strength and skill by which it can evaluate its own progress (not so much in relation to a norm as to its own previous level)?

Of course there are many practices in society and in school life which may tend to put the emphasis elsewhere than on these central physical needs. The competitive organisation of sport—if this means that the few represent the many, and the few get most of the care while the many watch and cheer—may act in an opposite direction, but there is nothing incompatible with anything suggested and the development of maximum levels of achievement and interest in sport. There is only the serious implication for us which we are not always prepared to face that, in physical education, all children are equally important, whereas in sport, natural selection operates. This is perhaps too young an age to understand that localised strength, e.g., back strength, abdominal-wall strength, foot strength (the three voluntary muscle regions in which most adults fail) is actually of importance to health, and that exercise is now recognised to be important in relation to cardiac trouble and obesity; however, at this stage understanding is not the main point. The pleasure of hard exercise, the know-how of building and maintaining strength and endurance and the sense of achievement from skill are the important things; the whys and wherefores can come later.

THE PUBERTAL AND EARLY ADOLESCENT CHILD

Some children may be unaffected by puberty in terms of any gross change in their physical make-up or emotional stability, but most children (with no major abnormality) begin to shift their emphases in interest as they move through the teens. Inevitably as they move towards adulthood their relationships with their parents alter; inevitably their new maturer body is a different persona in which to live. Some will continue with their prepubertal interests barely unaltered, but they themselves have changed. Others will shift interests towards vocational goals, homemaking goals, academic interests, or merely the desire to get power through the amassing of money. Even if an individual barely alters physically and in interests, the fact that those around him alter inevitably makes its impact on him. So we have a time of flux, a time of distraction, and of shifting relationships and values.

CAUTION ABOUT NORMALITY NEEDED

This is not the place to describe the psychosomatic picture of puberty,[24] or the psychosocial complexity of later adolescence, but mention of their very nature, their tendency to flux and change must be made, for the whole problem of evaluation is tied up with the nature of the material evaluated. In brief, we must be very cautious about what we call "normal" in this period. We must regard evaluations as only true for a moment in time, with little predictive value, perhaps throwing little light on what has gone before, and being only of slight diagnostic

---

[24] Excellently done in F. K. Shuttleworth's studies in the *Child Development Series*, Berkeley, Ill., Society for Research in Child Development, Inc., and the Institute of Human Development, 1951.

or prognostic value. We are dealing with a multivariable situation in which many variables are shifting at different speeds and in different directions, and with marked difference in emphasis in different individuals.[25] The error we make too often is to assume that it will continue in the same direction. This is a period when some earlier promise is not followed by expected progress, and where with others, new talent suddenly emerges. But although it may be a period of instability and change, what does go on through this period is what was there before.

This is a key question for us. What we call memory goes on. The child does not forget what twelve times twelve is; he does not forget how to tie his necktie (if he learnt before) or how to thread a needle, or eat without smearing his face what is on the spoon or fork. Although his inclination to do these things may alter, he still has the means, preserved—we can presume fairly safely, in the light of modern neurophysiology—in the neurone circuits or patterns of his brain and total nerve network. That is, he can do what he did before, but maybe not so well because, though the main motor pattern be there, the relative limb lengths and weights may have altered, and the movement is not so smooth. This may cause embarrassment which creates further tensions, and which in turn further destroy the smooth, simplified nerve-muscle patterns of a well-learnt movement. Thus, we have the phenomenon of clumsiness, the manifestations of which are physical, but which is certainly a psychosomatic thing.[26]

THE PAST DETERMINES THE FUTURE

Thus, *what went before* is of importance, and hence the crucial nature of the period dealt with in the last section. The mere fact that a boy could do something once is an indication to him that he might do it again, even if there are temporary difficulties due to a changed mechanical situation. But if a person in this period is at all clumsy, or embarrassed for some quite irrelevant reason, say, an acne-marked face, or because he is in love, he may tend to be more reluctant to learn new things in which his very incompetence will concentrate unwelcome attention upon him. The road to self-awareness (as Roper

[25] See Fig. 12.7, p. 309.
[26] Clumsiness has not been studied sufficiently. An excellent starting point is T. H. Pear's "What Is Clumsiness?" *British Journal of Educational Sociology*.

has suggested) leads past the hill-difficulty of self-consciousness. This reluctance to learn new things may mean a swing away from that whole area of interest, and much may be lost. This is not to say that we should not teach new skills to young teen-agers, but rather to say that our capacity to do so and the willingness of teen-agers to learn them may increase if there has been a good foundation laid before. It may be necessary to go back to that foundation rather than presume we can go straight on.

Would it be wrong to say that we lose more pupils than we catch in the ninth and tenth grades? The number of pupils whose whole-hearted interest we lose in the eleventh and twelfth grades is a reflection not only of our own teaching methods and their content but on what went before. This sounds like a trite platitude, but it may be truer of the world of physical skill, and of interest in healthy living, than of more purely intellectual or vocational school content—for physiological reasons.

As one grows older surely the general importance of physical activities diminishes as a proportion of the total interests we have, and the proportion of other interests increases. This is not always realised by coaches and physical educationists, because they are sometimes people with whom major interest in physical activities has persisted as a dominant factor, whereas with the majority of people the interest diminishes—or changes from an active to a spectator role. This is to say, do not expect more than a fraction of your pupils to be like you. Do not expect smooth, even development, but realise that what has happened before to your pupils has a profound effect on the influence you are likely to have on them, for quite simple physiological reasons.

QUESTIONS TO ASK

Therefore, in evaluating exercise and strength needs, rather difficult questions have to be asked from those for the previous section. Some are:

1. Has this child already been given fundamental skills and knowledge about its body—training, gaining, and preserving strength—etc.?
2. Is the impact of puberty-adolescence having a major, medium, or minor impact on this child? (Information from growth charts, observation, reports from previous teachers, relevance to somatotype, etc.)
3. Is physical activity likely to be a major, medium, or minor part of this

child's interests? (Information elicited by questioning, knowledge of dominant interests, somatotype, etc.)

4. What are the minimal healthful living skills I can give this child as an investment? Does he know how to help himself?

5. What is the best way to motivate this child toward physical activity in terms of his present status, interest, and probable future life pattern?

Such questions are of course fairly searching and demand that the teacher use time and ingenuity in devising means of getting valid answers. Some can be obtained by pencil-and-paper methods, provided it is made quite clear that honest answers are required and will not be used against pupils. This means a degree of detachment on the part of the teacher in which he must accept attack on, and rejection of, some of his pet interests. It also involves the teacher in making clear to children before evaluation that there is wide choice of good activities, that it is wise not to be too ambitious, that some ambitions lead nowhere, that we have to accept our limitations, etc.

Attitudes Towards Girls' Athletics[27]

There will be more social pressure to become sports heroes operating on boys than on girls in the present American culture. However, it is well to realise that there are many other civilised cultures—and an increasing number of them—where the athletic woman is much respected and without any loss of femininity. Cultural attitudes may change in such matters, but whatever the cultural pattern in these areas, more individuals will have ambition than will have aptitude or opportunity. It is conceivable that in placing great emphasis on a particular type of sports hero, rather than a variety of them, society creates more frustration among the many who aspire but cannot achieve and must therefore play their part in a passive, supporting role. What to an outside observer seems as like pantomime-pageantry around, say, football in America,[28] may be a product of failing to understand the differences in ability between people and to cater for them.

Active and Passive Participation

Of how many people can it be said that their interest in, for instance, football, is one of active participation, and in fact, a truly self-chosen

[27] See E. J. Jokl "The Athletic Status of Women" in the *British Journal of Physical Medicine,* Nov., 1957.

[28] Not that the soccer world does not occasionally indulge in ballyhoo too.

one rather than one in which they have been caught up in a strong tide of social pressure. The guidance towards healthful living and sound recreation of teen-agers is as tricky as vocational guidance; it requires the aid of evaluatory procedures rather than hearty enthusiasm, and, above all, a realistic picture of individuals, in which their other interests and aptitudes are taken into account. This is an overwhelming argument for not tangling physical education up in the sport program. These should work in harmony together and, inevitably, have to share facilities and work out allotments of time, but their aims, objectives, and means are essentially different. This is not to decry in the least the evaluatory capacity of sports coaches, who often, without much in the way of objective assessment, make very sound judgements and prognoses and, of course, do immeasurable good to individuals (mostly a minority) who come into their care, and who have the special natural aptitudes which flourish in the hands of a good coach. But let us beware of any general slogan such as "You too can be a football hero!"—which is very misleading.

Shades of the Corset Maker Appear

In this period begin to emerge adult weaknesses requiring as much special attention as adult needs. Faults of body mechanics tend to increase. A lax abdominal wall gets worse. Weak feet get more tired, and protest. There is often general fatigue in the rapidly growing, leading to very reasonable sprawling and slummocking. There is also, in some, ambition about the figure or about strength; some girls will be concerned with having a trim flat tummy, boys, with a strong torso and legs. Others will find that they need strength and knack for lifting and carrying. And as we have emphasised, without doubt we all need a certain reserve of strength, over and above our likely daily demands, for the emergency when we may suddenly have to take an extra load, and this may happen to anyone, even in the most civilised, push-button civilisation. The reserve tank of strength is an idea that must be approached through mental understanding, and through discussion and argument, for some will be resistant to conviction. The arguments for the firm abdominal wall are all around us among the adults, and so, too, are the arguments for the strong back, because backaches of various kinds are among the most common of complaints, and certainly some of them could be prevented by better strength and muscular habits. There is no problem in persuading the boy or girl with athletic ambitions that strength-training is in his interest, and hence there is little need to use mental understanding of the desired goal as motivation; with others it may be necessary. It is not enough to give localised exercise in callisthenics, and say, "that is good for your back, etc." This is an insult to the intelligence, and in sharp contrast to teaching methods used with other subjects where the aim is at full mental grasp of an idea. One could have hoped that as a result of physical-education training existing in the universities this would have led to a more intellectual approach in physical-education teaching, and less of the "Jump to it" teaching or the "You too can be like me" approach.

Adult Degenerations Are Often Local

It will be seen that as age increases we recommend an increased attention to specific physical needs. While the recreational content of physical education broadens out continually from the infant to the late teen ages, the pattern with specific needs narrows down. This is because, in general, the adult whose general exercise dosage drops shows the results of this in certain specific regions of the body and this localised degeneration of function proceeds through life.

General Adult Needs

Before studying in detail the regions of specific need, it is of course apparent that besides specific needs adults young or old sometimes have need to go into training for a specific purpose. They are going on a skiing or hunting trip; they are suddenly going to make a high extra demand on themselves in a cardiorespiratory sense and also in sheer muscle load. While they need not train like a mile runner, it is as well to make some preparation for the extra load to come. It is worth remarking here that because of our mechanical ingenuity, skiing (and to some extent golf with its auto-buggies) [29] has lost the built-in training it used to have. Before the days of chair-lifts etc., the only way to gain

---

[29] And suction cup sticks for picking up the ball. It only remains for someone to invent a good golf-club swinging machine and a rangefinder, and our part in the game is entirely passive. We could even control it by radar from the 19th hole.

altitude in order to have a good run down was to walk up hill on skis. To increase friction sealskins were put under the skis. It is hard for a modern skier to imagine the hard work of trudging up hill on oblique or zigzag tracks with the extra weight of skis on one's feet and the softness and slipperiness of the snow to overcome. One sometimes walked for three hours to get a twenty-minute run downwards. But the walking was training and strengthened many muscle groups, as well as the cardiorespiratory function. Modern skiing techniques are concerned primarily with balance, and little strength is needed for downhill or slalom running—*except* when the emergency comes, and suddenly great strength is required, and strain being thrown violently on joints whose surrounding muscles may be ill-trained to take it.

REGIONAL NEEDS

But training for extra load apart, what are the regions of the body which in so many adults show signs of wear and tear quite early in life?

The abdominal wall is perhaps the commonest. It is not used much in ordinary sedentary city living, and because of our faulty eating habits it is a region which suffers by distension from within and deposition of fat on both sides. It is in most body builds the first region where "condition" is put on. With women it has the added strain of stretching during pregnancy, and, of course, it is a region for which artificial supports are big business. The protuberant belly is the main crude index of obesity. Insurance companies (such as the Metropolitan Life) have long since made obesity a reason for raising premiums. The insurance firms are thus doing a nice piece of evaluation on this topic. The control of the abdominal wall presents only two problems: knowhow and the will to control the situation. Many people have neither. Diet alone will not control abdominal tone. Nor will general exercise help, except in some builds, and it fails remedially once the tone is lost. There are some hundreds of graded movements for exercising and gaining control of the *different* muscles making up the abdominal wall.[30] Also it is rarely realised that doing abdominal exercises alone will not necessarily maintain the abdominal wall in the optimal posi-

---

[30] I.e., for using different combinations of the same muscles.

tion. This, like all other postural problems, is a matter of neural control and the "grooving" of new habits.

Thus to evaluate a programme on this single topic alone, the following questions can be asked:

1. Do these pupils understand the parts played by carbohydrate and fats in obesity?
2. Do they realise that the intake of these foods should vary with the total activity output?
3. Do they realise that different body builds behave differently in relation to the eating of fat-producing foods? Does each individual have a clear concept of his own build in regard to the problem?
4. Do they know a graded series of exercises, from the very simplest to really hard ones, which will tone up the transversalis muscle, the external and internal obliques, and the upper and lower segments of the rectus?
5. Do they understand pelvic-tilt control in relation to the abdominal wall?
6. Do they realise how much controlled breathing, especially exhalation, during the performance of abdominal exercises increases their efficiency?
7. Do they understand the basic mechanism and means for changing postural habits, and its application to this problem?
8. Do they realise the possible outcomes of a slack abdominal wall, e.g., aggravated varicose veins, loss of general vitality, failure to help uterine displacement, loss of pride in appearance, possible changes in bowel habits, expense in purchase of larger clothes, corsets, etc.?
9. Do they realise that only a multiple attack on this problem will solve it—that diet alone will not succeed, that exercise alone will not succeed?
10. Do they realise the remarkable change in feeling of well-being that can come from mastery of such a problem.
11. Do they realise that there is hope of real success for almost any case?

If readers of this book will ask themselves how many of these questions they could answer with certainty when they were in the twelfth grade, they would have a nice evaluation of the teaching of conditioning work in their school. There is no need to use numerical methods of evaluation in this field, except as a means of creating incentive, e.g., loads, number of repetitions of exercises, girths, weight changes, etc. But the basic evaluation of the school program is what *knowledge* it has given the pupils; this could be tested both practically and by means of paper tests.

The Back

A second region which shows wear and tear in adults is the back. Long before disc troubles were a popular diagnosis, people had lumbago, sciatica, low back pain, "fibrositis," and, at the other end of the spine, stiff necks, crooked necks, and vague neck aches. Unfortunately this is nowhere near so easy a problem to deal with as that of the abdominal wall. The intervertebral discs are one of the first of human tissues to show aging changes, and the original investigations in this field, by Schmorl in Germany, included a very large sample which showed degenerative changes in a surprising number of adolescents.[31] How much of this degeneration is inevitable (possibly of hereditary origin), how much is due to misuse of the spine, and how much is due to sudden trauma is not yet clearly known. But the physiological evaluation by electromyography (Floyd and Silver) indicates that the human back is very vulnerable in certain positions of extreme flexion, in which the normal protective function of the muscles is cut out.[32] It is also known that muscular weakness may play a part. It is known too, from industrial experience, that this region is particularly prone to damage in lifting, heaving, and twisting operations. It is in fact a region where the preservation of strength, and particularly knowledge of sensible use, is important. There is little doubt, too, that sedentary life makes no demand on back strength. That it plays some part in posture is true, but the part is a minor one compared to the factor of balance and self-awareness.

Thus evaluation of a conditioning program in relation to backs would stress knowledge of sound use and means of preserving strength. The neck region, the most potentially flexible part of the spine, has not been dealt with here. It is a very technical problem rather neglected in occidental physical education, the chief defect developing being loss of mobility. As yet we have not the certain knowledge to hand on to children.[33]

[31] A. S. Beadle, *The Intervertebral Discs,* Medical Research Council pamphlet no. 161, London, H. M. Stationery Office, 1931.

[32] W. F. Floyd and R. H. S. Silver, "Patterns of Muscle Activity in Posture and Movement," *Science News XXII,* Baltimore, Penguin. See also *Journal of Anatomy,* LXXXIV (1950), 132; and *Lancet,* I (1951), 133.

[33] Smithells and Gresham have shown that neck posture may be related to malocclusion of teeth; see *Year Book of Dental Science,* 1954.

THE FEET AND LEGS

The last region, like the first, is an easy one to deal with in many cases; it is that of the feet and legs. These too in an automatised society suffer neglect through disuse and misuse, but there are many remediable causes of common forms of foot trouble. How much do our twelfth graders know about their feet, and what that can we do to help them *now*—and more particularly *in the future?* A set of questions such as the following could be used as part of the evaluation of this part of the conditioning program. The other part would include practical tests and demonstrations of good and bad foot habits. What do these children know about:

1. Choice of footwear and the effect of footwear on feet.
2. The best way to stand, sit, and walk so as to reduce strain on the feet.
3. How to keep feet plastic and mobile.
4. Means of strengthening intrinsic or extrinsic muscles of the foot.
5. Means of strengthening the musculature of the whole leg column (as needed for skating and skiing).
6. The hip-knee-ankle-foot relationship.
7. Occupational footstrain and means of alleviating it.

What is to be said of objective methods of foot-recording? The only well known device is footprinting. This can be of help in observing changes in a given individual, but we cannot accept the idea of norms or even quality ranks in footprints. Those who have worked for years on foot posture re-education know that in general it is the trained eye which can pick out the feet which need help, just as they know that athletes can have flat prints, and high arches can mean rigidity and poor function. The ultimate test of a foot is whether it works well in standing, walking, running, and jumping.

Roper in *Some Aspects of Children's Physique*[34] measured ankle flexibility in relation to foot functioning. Morton has devised his staticometer for measuring how the weight-bearing function of a foot is shared. Many others have attempted to pin down in some formalised way the minor foot defects with which a physical educationist could be expected to deal. It is not the place of this book to go deeply into corrective work. We believe our profession has a considerable responsibility for children's foot health, but we also believe that the relevant evaluatory techniques have to be learnt with the re-educa-

[34] London, Her Majesty's Stationery Office.

tional ones, and these are outside our immediate scope.

Finally, some reference should be made to experiments in the effect of conditioning work on educationally subnormal children. J. N. Oliver, at the University of Birmingham (England), has carried out some of the classical experimental work in this field with remarkable and, to many, surprising results.[35]

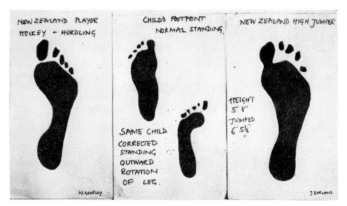

FIG. 18.1. Footprints may be half-flat, yet come from excellent feet. Also, they are modifiable in one individual.

TARGET TRAINING

We feel that a New Zealand development, *target training,* has been so successful motivationally that we should describe it more fully than in a footnote. Derived, of course, from the "circuit training" of Morgan and Adamson, it was developed by A. S. Lewis in the Student Recreation Programme at Canterbury University, Christchurch. It sets a time—the *target* in which a certain number of tasks have to be performed. Once this *target* is reached there is a higher one. Lewis and others have found it exceedingly popular and physically demanding.

[35] *British Journal of Educational Psychology,* XXVIII, pt. 2 (June, 1958), 155–165. "The effect of physical conditioning exercises and activities on the mental condition of educationally sub-normal boys." "The Slow Learning Child," IV (July, 1957), 27–35; "Motivation of Educationally Subnormal Boys through Physical Activities," *Medical Officer,* XCVII, no. 2 (January, 1957), 19–22; "The effect of systematic physical conditioning on the growth of educationally subnormal boys."

Score Sheet

Target Training Exercises	Number of Times		
	Beginner	Standard	Super
1. Running-lengths of gymnasium	30	40	40
2. Climb rope to touch beam	1	2	3
3. Squat with 50 lb. bar-bell	2 sets of 10	2 sets of 15	2 sets of 18
4. Alternate punch upward with 7 lb. dumbells	60 60	80 80	100 100
5. Double skips	15	20	30
6. Backward arch from lying face down	12	15	20
7. Press bar-bell 50 lbs.	2 sets of 7	2 sets of 10	2 sets of 12
8. Splits jump. Jump from squat, one foot forward.	20	30	40
9. Heave to chin bar from arms stretch	8	10	12
10. Standing broad jump (height plus standard)	5 x ht. + 15 in.	6 x ht. + 15 in.	8 x ht. + 18 in.
11. Press-up to arms straight from lying	15	20	25
12. Sit up from lying on back	20	24	30
13. Step up on double bench	25 each leg	40 each leg	50 each leg
14. Bar-bell curls 50 lbs.	8	10	15
15. Jump from side to side over medicine ball	20	30	40
16. Duck walking	width	length	length
17. Squat jumps (burpees)	15	20	25
18. Shoot baskets	10	15	20
Target times	25 min.	26 min.	28 min.

Enter completion times on score sheet below

Dates							
Beginner Standard Super							

There are eighteen exercises of a general nature to perform in Target Training. These have been chosen because of their suitability as standard exercises and their variety which places loads on all parts of the body in turn. These are not the only suitable exercises and the list may be changed from time to time.

The exercises can be done in any order except that similar ones should not be done following each other, e.g. rope climb and chinning the bar, medicine ball jump and split jumping. The order in which the exercises appear could be used though this may be possible if others are using the apparatus required. No warm-up is necessary but the run should be done first.

Three grades of work-doses are given. Beginners or unfit persons should start at the Beginners or Light Grade and when the Target Time for the complete set of exercises has been bettered three times they should move on to Standard or Middle Grade. This grade will satisfy the majority of students who should seek to improve their times at each repetition. Those requiring a better state of fitness for a special purpose may progress to the Super or Heavy Grade when the Standard Target time has been bettered *three* times. It is estimated that Target times set should be within the ability of every student who seeks to improve his or her fitness. . . .

Challenging amounts of work have been set out on the work list. The amounts must all be completed even if it means several attempts; e.g., a total of 10 chin-ups even if this cannot be achieved in one attempt. Those doing the training should use a watch with a second hand or ask for a stop watch so that their training periods can be accurately timed to the second from start to finish.[36]

SUMMARY

In this chapter we have deliberately overlapped with the chapter on evaluation applied to gymnastics, hoping that one may reinforce the other, and believing in general that conditioning is the weakest field in American practice. This is not to say that some of the research is very good; it obviously is painstaking and thorough, but how often does it result in action? Neither of us is a physiologist, and so we cannot evaluate the contributions in postgraduate research in applied physiology, which we know goes on in many places in America.

[36] Quoted from instructions used by Mr. Lewis in the Student Recreation Programme. Modified forms of this are used with and enjoyed by women students and high school girls.

In general, though, we agree with the pithy statement of Morehouse, "The United States is now a nation virtually without physiological ideals." We see in our own younger country, relatively recently a frontier one, signs of American influence. These come mainly through the mass-media of communication and through commerce.

The influence of the United States, intentional and unintentional, on both highly civilized countries[37] and on newly fledged ones is immense. Rather than only attempt to thwart here at home those parts of American influence about which we have doubts, we feel it is better for all to attack it at its source. Europe in general, we consider, will look after itself, but we eye with suspicion the Coke bottle in the jungle and the jukebox in the bazaar. We feel that some of your leaders in America, over the years, have misled you on this question of conditioning exercise and have sent you chasing vague democratic and social miasmas. A valiant few have fought steadily for narrower but more certain aims. It is our hope that their judgement will prevail, for your own sake, and for the sake of those whom you influence.

It is obvious too that we have not re-traced the whole field of strength-testing which has a vast literature of its own in standard textbooks and periodicals—but there still remain some unsolved problems about its evaluation.

[37] New Zealand has both a higher productivity per capita and a higher *general* standard of living than the U.S.A.

chapter 19

THE APPLICATION OF EVALUATION TO GAMES AND SPORTS

THE PROBLEM IN GENERAL

THERE are in most games some built-in evaluatory devices, whether the games be the informal ones of small children, the host of minor ones taught by teachers and recreation leaders, or in what might be called national and international sports.

These devices may be a *situation* which finally decides an issue, such as when the king is takeable in chess, when a child is found in hide-and-go-seek, or when a batsman is caught on the fly. On the other hand, there may be built-in numerical evaluation such as the score in golf, billiards, darts, or the distance for a long jump, the target values in archery, or the time for the downhill run or slalom in skiing. From the structure and pattern of the game rules, by giving certain situations certain values, individual or group prowess is indicated. With team games, in which many contribute in different ways to a common end, there may be no built-in evaluation of individuals. All kinds of football, for instance, give a final result which gives no indication of which members of a team in fact contributed most to the total situation. In soccer—by far the most popular football game in the world—the official goal score 5-3 tells nothing of individuals. The initiated will know that the goal keepers are extremely unlikely to have scored goals, the full-backs too; there is a possibility that a halfback did, and a probability that the forwards scored the goals, but no indication which of the five did so. But in any case the raw match result tells nothing of missed opportunities, how luck operated, who made the openings which enabled the scoring to happen, which defence player made a misjudgement, etc.

431

Common Forms of Evaluation

In general, the detailed evaluation of one single team-game result is customarily done by a lengthy verbal report, describing the sequence of incidents. These, allowing for inaccuracies of observation, can often give a clear and valid picture of a game, and an individual's contribution to the group situation.

The Sportswriters' Craft

The craft of the sportswriter and commentator on radio or TV must be respected as forms of evaluation. Indeed they are sometimes the interests of very gifted writers.[1] It is interesting to note, however, that the supplementing of this verbal evaluation varies markedly in different countries. In Britain, the "home" of soccer once (it is now a second-class power in this game) and of rugby, the post-mortems and the through-the-season evaluation of these two football games tends to remain dominantly verbal. The goals scored and the tries made are noted, but only these specific actions are evaluated numerically.[2] In the United States, what might be called the numerical evaluation of the components of a game, and particularly an individual player's contribution to these components, is a highly developed craft in coaching, journalism, and commentating. The charting and reckoning of yardage gained, forward passes attempted and completed, and so on, is all carefully tabulated. What is more, whereas in most parts of the world, the details of the game fade with the passage of time—even the next day there is some loss of definition of detail—in American football, the whole game is often filmed in slow motion, and postmortem study of the game often reveals to a coach detail which was missed or obscured on the actual occasion. To British people, used to soccer and rugby, this filming business has seemed a fantastic expense, because during a game of soccer, which lasts 1½ hours, the ball

---

[1] Neville Cardus, the cricket commentator for the *Guardian,* one of the most widely respected English newspapers, is also at times their music critic. Paul Gallico, an American, whose book, *The Snow Goose,* became a classic, was formerly a sportswriter in the U.S.; see his book, *Farewell to Sport,* New York, Knopf, 1938. John Arlott, the best known BBC commentator on cricket, is also responsible for poetry programmes.

[2] In rugby, the weight of the players, and the scrums (scrimmages) and line-outs won, are recorded.

is in play for some 48 minutes in the game, with one 5-minute interval, no time-outs, and no substitutions. In rugby the ball is in play for approximately 32 minutes. To film this amount of play would be prohibitive in cost, even to a professional team. But in American football, the ball is only in play for just under 10 minutes during a full match, and a great deal of time between plays is available for evaluation. There are also official built in evaluatory devices in the 10-yard lines, and intermittent surveys by the men with the chains.

TRANSATLANTIC COMPARISONS

Two general comments might be made. In America evaluation in major sport has been thoroughly developed by a combination of highly trained judgement in coaches and objective recording of all measurable incidents, whereas in Europe this type of evaluation in the goal games (soccer, rugby, hockey, net ball, basketball, lacrosse), has tended to remain predominantly verbal. The other comment may have no significance, bearing in mind that correlation does not necessarily mean causation, but in general the *increased* attention given to evaluatory detail has coincided with a *decrease* of actual play. This is, of course, less true of basketball than football.

COACHES EVALUATE SKILLFULLY

What contribution has the kind of evaluation recommended in this book to make to sports and games? We feel fairly confident in saying that in most sports, both these inbuilt rule mechanisms and the emergence of skilled coaches have provided these sports, when played at a *high* level, with sufficient evaluatory devices and techniques for their present problems. We can admire the judgement and critical acumen of a good coach, who may know nothing whatever of statistics. It seems doubtful if statistical evaluation of the major games themselves so far made, or to come, will ever make any significant contribution to the improvement of major sports playing. The validity of performance prediction of highly skilled individuals, chosen from two standard deviations above the norm, and playing in a complex situation with a number of other individuals and many variables, seems likely to be very small in team games. Perhaps our services are needed elsewhere, and perhaps we can be a little humbler and appreciate more the largely subjective skill, but often accurate judgement, of the great coach.

Track and Field

In track and field we may be able to help more, but extrapolating from data already established is not an accurate form of prediction. The curve of time improvement for the mile race was a fairly regular one, and then suddenly altered its course by a quite unpredicted jump in the immortal mile race in Dublin, in August, 1958, which produced an astonishing new time. In New Zealand we have seen a high jumper (height 5 feet 8 inches), whose ceiling over two or three years seemed to be 6 feet 1½ inches, suddenly raise it to 6 feet 5½ inches at an international meeting. In short dashes and the broad jump we may say that a plateau is reached, but in nearly all other events, the future is unpredictable in terms of degree of improvement. We suspect that the contributions of science to athletics is in general a *post hoc* one rather than a predictive one. In track and field, a happy hunting ground for the scientists—with the possible exception of Richard Ganslen and the pole vault—science justifies a method kinesiologically after it has been discovered accidentally, or by inspiration.[3] It is as well to point out though that accidental discovery of new truth, or serendipity as it is sometimes called, occurs in many branches of science —the discovery of how penicillin operated, by Fleming, was indeed an accident, in which a prepared mind suddenly saw significance in a contaminated culture plate. Newton's famous falling apple is in this category. So too, the hunch has often helped the scientist at some unexpected movement, when deliberate reasoning and calculation have got him no further. It appears that the accumulated experience of the outer world, stored in neurone circuits in the cortex and elsewhere, can suddenly organise itself without volition, in a way that brings the birth of a new idea or a new explanation.

There are several ways in which evaluatory procedures can be useful in relation to sport. The three main ones are: (1) classification of sport; (2) study of change in sport; (3) guidance of individuals in choice of sport.

---

[3] An exception might be the development of the Held javelin.

THE CLASSIFICATION OF GAMES

We wish to call the attention of readers to an isolated article by Roger Caillois on the "Classification of Games," published in *Diogenes* (available in university libraries) in November, 1956.[4] This is no statistical study, but an attempt to give a badly needed classification system for games and sports, and one which we think is important.

Briefly Caillois suggests, in this extremely scholarly article, that there are three main groups of games:

1. *Agon* (or struggle)—A contest with artificially created *equality* of chance against an adversary, human or not human.
2. *Alea* (dice)—Games played against destiny or chance; based on *inequality* external to the player.
3. *Mimicry*—Games of pretence or illusion.

Examples of *agon* games would be the typical team or target ones, in which each combatant or side is faced with the same rules, restrictions, goals, etc. In some sports, e.g., boxing and wrestling, weight ranges are used to equalise opponents. In golf a handicap system is used. In archery or target rifle-shooting, all fire at the same target from the same distance, and have the same number of shots. Even in children's spontaneous play, rules which make the opportunity equal for both sides are nearly always introduced. Besides the written or understood rules of how the game is played, there are also interpretations of rules which involve the concept of *fairness*. Briefly, in agon-type games there is an assumption of *fairness*. Whether all players enjoy best the closely fought game decided in the last minute or the last round is not certain. There was a time when this doubt about the outcome was of major importance—in terms of pleasure. The situation in the last innings where one run is needed, the bases are loaded, and there are two strikes on the last batter, and three balls on the pitcher, can raise a crowd to a frenzy, just as can a close finish in a mile race, in which tension is built up over several minutes. One of the authors had always presumed that this last-minute uncertainty (found particularly in basketball) was one of the most stimulating experiences in sport and more important than the ultimate result. One day, addressing

---

[4] I am indebted to the late Mr. A. R. D. Fairburn, poet, for calling my attention to this article.

a student audience which contained university footballers who had completely thrashed another team by a huge margin, he remarked that this must have been a poor game, but to his surprise, the players themselves were emphatic that this was the sort of victory they really enjoyed. Maybe values in this field are changing.

The most obvious *alea*-type games are those of chance—roulette, dice, or lottery games; however, some measure of the alea inequality comes into those team games in which noncontrollable factors operate. In cricket, for instance, the state of the ground and the way it is expected to change are very important. A rainstorm or a drying surface can completely alter the predicted performance of players. In football games or tennis, the sun's position may be important, and the spin of a coin is used to decide who shall have the advantage. So some games combine alea and agon.

Games of *mimicry* are commonest with younger children—in cowboys and Indians, acting games, charades, etc.—though in a sense the peculiar garb of the drum major in a football band might come in this category, and the human mascots certainly do. If the wider concept *play* is used, of course, the antics of the Shriners, or various other male groups in conventions, show the basic pleasure in mimicry.

Roger Caillois goes further in his classification by suggesting that there are three main factors operating which may occur singly or multiply, in the different types of sport. These he calls:

1. *Paedia* (a child)—Spontaneous exuberance, childlike play or form.
2. *Ludus* (a game)—The deliberate creation of difficulty in a game.
3. *Ilinx* (a whirlpool)—The challenge of gravity and equilibrium and centrifugal force.

Paedia, for instance, does not appear in chess, nor rarely in serious football. It may appear at the Harlem Globetrotter's level in basketball, and there have been well-known cricketers and soccer players who delighted spectators with their sense of fun and unrestrained exuberance. Perhaps we are tending to lose paedia in the increasing seriousness of sport.

Ludus is known to any golfer who lands in the sand trap. Here is artificially created difficulty in an agon game. So, too, the delicately balanced high-jump bar, the offside rule, the time limit, the mechanically propelled moving target, or blindfolding in blind man's buff, are artificial difficulties introduced. In the latter case we have mimicry, with ludus.

Ilinx is to be seen in any children's playground, circus, or gymnasium, or in skiing or skating: the defiance of gravity in balance, swinging, spinning, or allowing oneself to use it under control in the dive, slalom, or fly-away from the horizontal bar.

There is no quality value inherent in these terms, nor a quantity value, but they do give us a new means of looking at different sports and taxonomically comparing their contents. One may use a chart for comparison as shown in Fig. 19.1. Each characteristic can be noted —or even rated on an A-E, or other, scale—and some general conclusions drawn.

Name of game:

	Paedia	Ludus	Ilinx
Agon			
Alea			
Mimicry			

Summary:

FIG. 19.1.   Chart for comparing the contents of sports.

A nice point about Caillois' introduction of mimicry is that it joins once more the *play* we see in the theatre with other forms of *play*.

It is also interesting to see which forms of game, sport, or play tend to be restricted in their elements and characteristics, and which involve many factors.

The authors regard adventurous camping very highly as a form of physical education in which many different objectives are reached at the same time. When analysed in Caillois's terms it is shown to contain all his components. Camping itself is mimicry in that one pretends to live as a pioneer, it is full of paedia in its simple childish pleasures, and there is ilinx in plenty in the challenge of gravity in exploring, canoeing, bridge-making, tree-climbing, and pioneering. The rules in competitions, etc., are such that it is equal for all in terms of difficulty; thus it is agon in one sense; yet it is full of artificial difficulties and provides ludus; still the chance operation of wind, rain, snow, and heat may have a profound effect, and are the alea components.

Altogether we can be grateful to Roger Caillois for enabling us to take a new and more detached look at things which are familiar to us, and this is indeed a form of evaluation.

CHANGE AND SPREAD IN SPORT

The spread of sport through the world and changes in its nature are major phenomena of the twentieth century. At present the study of these changes is in its infancy, although some detailed studies have been made by Dr. Carl Diem, probably the greatest living scholar in the field of physical education.   .

The best methods to be used for studying change in sport are probably those of the social sciences. We refer again to Riesman's chapter in *Individualism Reconsidered*, on the early development of American football. Luckily for the investigator of modern major sport, there is a mine of written resources in the nineteenth and twentieth centuries which can be tapped. Source material before that is difficult to find. One might say that there have been fine compendium studies of the history of sport and physical education, such as Mitchell, Van Dalen and Bennett's work, but only recently has there appeared work in which certain detailed fields are studied with all the care and methodology of the historian. For instance, such works as Carl Diem's, *Körpererziehung bei Goethe, Byron als Sportler,* and his monumental three-volume *Olympische Flamme,* are solid and detailed historical works. So too, *Physical Education in England since 1800,*[5] by Peter McIntosh, and the more recent volume he edited, *Landmarks in the History of Physical Education,*[6] show an attention to documented detail and care in interpretation, often missing from more compendious works.

THE SPORTS ETHNOGRAMS

Recently one of the authors has devised—as an evaluatory tool for quickly depicting the evolution and changes in sport—a device called the sport ethnogram. The sport ethnogram is a graphic device for briefly describing the cultural diffusion of a given sport or form of play. It

[5] London, Bell, 1952.
[6] London, Routledge, 1957.

also enables rapid comparisons to be made between the development of one sport and another.

We know three things for certain: (1) some sports are found in almost identical forms in many different places; (2) some sports are highly localised or limited in their spread; (3) some sports differentiate into many subforms.

The following terms are used:

1. *Origins and kindred games*—primitive forms of the game before it is in any way formalised, and similar game forms (place and kind).
2. *Formalisation*—the point at which definite rules are produced on some local unit basis (place, date and person or body).
3. *Diffusion pattern*—where the formalised game is found geographically (places, dates).
4. *Subdiffusions*—local diffusion within a country, geographically or socially.
5. *Vectors*—the main means whereby it has spread from the parent-source.
6. *Sub-vectors*—additional means of diffusion or subdiffusion.
7. *Derivatives*—derived game forms, whether formalised or not (name, place, date, subdiffusion of these).
8. *Status*—(a. level to which played, internationally or intranationally, e.g., Olympic, limited international, national, zone, highly localised;
   (b. sex of players (male or female, or mixed);
   (c. individual or team (group) contest.
9. *Prognosis*—expected future development, e.g., continued diffusion, diffusion ended, regression, etc.
10. *Sociocultural notes*—significant comments on class, economic, or political aspects.
11. *Source material*—bibliography, etc.

The visual diagram moves through time from left to right. It gives a condensed general picture of the development and present status and location of the sport. Nearly all the facts are available, if not in general histories, within the countries themselves. It is proposed as a long-term project to collect relevant information and build up a service of charts and tabulations of all major sports. The example shown of a sport ethnogram makes it clear that one can take a family of related games and show as it were the family tree.

A SAMPLE INVESTIGATION

One could also take one game and go much deeper into the detail of its development. For instance, although lacrosse is a team goal

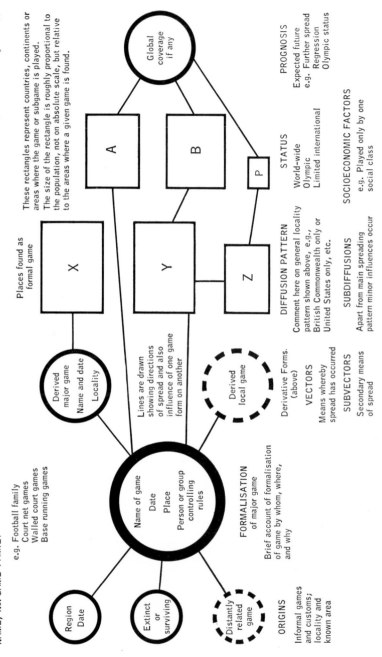

Fig. 19.2. Ethnogram.

game, it is not similar to other well-known games in origin. Its evolution was from an informal game played between American Indian villages, using a long flexible stick, the end of which was bent round and bound to the main shaft, with two small leather thongs at right angles to each other (making the cross—hence *la crosse*). The evolution from this to the mayhem of box lacrosse, or the graceful type of lacrosse played on a women's national championship level in England, or between Oxford and Cambridge men, or between men in the suburbs and villages in Yorkshire and Lancashire, makes a fascinating study. At some stage, though French settlers provided the name, British influence may have suggested the formal goal, similar to that in soccer, field and ice hockey, and handball (the international game), but for some very odd reason the names of positions on the field in lacrosse are in part taken from fielding positions in cricket (a nongoal game). Point, coverpoint, and third man (three main defensive positions in lacrosse) are as well-known to the cricket fan as shortstop, left field, and right outfield are to a baseball fan. But quite apart from using the ethnogram for a world history of a sport, it can be used as a tool in evaluating local development and history. For instance, using lacrosse again, in the 1880s it was a major men's game in New Zealand, matches being played between New Zealand provinces (as they then were called), and also against Australian states (New Zealand and Australia are entirely separate countries, with 1250 miles of rough ocean between them). Now lacrosse is rarely played in New Zealand—in two private girls' high schools only. No one knows why this change has happened. The historical picture of the sociocultural factors influencing this one particular small problem—the rise and fall of a particular sport in one country—is an evaluatory study, and one in which a condensed picture could be given in an adapted sport ethnogram.

Such a task would require much examination of press reports, correspondence columns, high-school annual reports, club minute books (if they still exist), and general documentary collation, interpretation, and evaluation.

One other virtue of the sport ethnogram is that it may let individuals see the place of a sport that interests them on a world basis, and thus diminish their ethnocentricity and the arrogance that sometimes goes with it. In parenthesis one wonders what future historians might make of the term *World Series,* when the only reference to this pretentious title will be found in one country only.

Historical Writing Extremely Difficult

Thus so far we have stressed the more nonstatistical evaluation of sports and games. Before leaving this topic, it may be said that such historical writing is very difficult, and involves long and patient search for and perusal of original documents or photostats. It is research more suited to a doctoral than master's degree thesis. Too many theses of a semihistorical kind use superficial evidence, obtained by writing to prominent individuals and asking their views. We receive, in this isolated and distant university, what can only be called naïve enquiries from those doing theses in the United States, asking for brief summaries of some sport or activity in this country. Often the subject in question is one that has never been fully investigated in a scholarly way here—nor in many other places. The theses written from our replies must be souped up collations of impressions, and not a very valuable exercise in evaluation or the development of the critical faculty. Such work brings no credit to a profession badly in need of it. There is little doubt that we are low on the totem pole scholastically in most universities—and one of the causes is substandard postgraduate work, in some places. Plans in the making for accreditation for bachelor's degree courses in the United States are a good sign. Let us hope they are extended to the postgraduate level.

THE GUIDANCE OF INDIVIDUALS IN SPORTS

This chapter must make some reference to the possible use of evaluatory methods in the guidance of individuals in the choice of a sport. This may be of considerable psychological benefit to them in that its use may in some cases prevent frustrated ambitions of children and parents. This does not mean that the wise evaluation tells every boy under 6 feet 6 inches to keep out of basketball, but it does mean that we can enable people to see their own talents and limitations with some detachment. This may be useful in recreational guidance and, even more useful, it may be evidence to use on overambitious parents wanting to "make a man" of their son, or realise through him some of their own frustrated ambitions.

While it is obvious that in some sports a breakdown of component skills is easy to make, and it is possible to devise valid and reliable tests of these component skills, it must be realised that there are some important variables hard to evaluate—and also both known and unknown pressures operating which to ignore would be folly.

ATTITUDE-TESTING

Just as in the 1920s and 1930s, industrial and vocational psychologists were optimistic about aptitude-testing, by using, for instance, a set of small assembling tasks, as a test of mechanical ability, so we may have been optimistic in the validity of prediction of our basic skill-testing. More and more the industrial testing expert likes to see the subject in the full workshop situation, and perhaps we have to include in our test routines exposure to the actual game situation, in addition to basic skill-testing. This is probably more important in the situation where a subject scores high on the basic skills than where the score is low.

For instance, a child who can neither catch nor throw (say a softball or basketball) is unlikely to show high catching or throwing ability in the game situation; on the other hand, one who scores high in these skills in the test situation may in the actual game situation find himself distracted by the anxiety of that situation, the defence tactics of opponents, or the attempts to put him off by crowd and opposing players. Basically, the nearer the test situation can be to the game-playing situation, the more valid the testing is likely to be.

GROOVING SKILLS

The point must be made, however, that in general the more a person's basic skills are grooved by frequent repetition over a period, the less likely are these skills to desert him when faced with a total game or stress situation. The air pilot has a drill for the relatively dangerous tasks of take-off and landing, and these drills are brought to automatic level; hence, in the most disturbing situations he still carries out the routine without error.

Prediction

From this can be seen another basic idea. The predictive validity in skill tests is likely to be higher when the skill tested has been thoroughly learnt and practised frequently over a long-enough period to groove the skill. Thus, for instance, ball-skill tests of various types administered to in-coming ninth-grade children, with a view to guiding them into various sports, may be very misleading. It may produce a down-rating in scores for some who might with a deal of practice be good players, but who may be either slow learners or have had relatively little practice in the skills tested. More practice will, of course, increase the reliability too. What we need, and what as yet does not seem to be well established in our profession, are tests which indicate learning speed, an aspect of motor educability which is important for us to know in planning children's work. It would be useful to say to Hank, whose score on a basket-shooting test is low, "You can improve your shooting by shooting fifty baskets every morning," but while such advice is in general sound, it is clear: (1) that some children will need to practice more or less than fifty shots per session; (2) some children will need to practice twice every day, and some every other day—or on some other pattern.

Dosage of Practice

In fact we do not, in general, have clear and well-established evidence even of an empirical kind as to the best pattern of dosage in practicing basic skills. Obviously well-established coaches have routines and patterns of practice which they have developed with experience, and in which they believe, and just as important, in which they get their players to believe—but by and large we have no clear information.

Throughout education we have shown perhaps too great a tendency to cling to traditional learning units unquestioningly. Basic questions such as, "What is the optimum length for a school term?"; "What is the optimum length or pattern for a school day?"; or in more detail, "Although, say, 40-minute sessions may be the best length for study on a single subject in the morning, is it also the best length towards the end of the school day—or towards the end of the school term?" Or again, "Is a 5-day timetable or a 10-day timetable better?" Most of these basic questions we answer either by convention or convenience of organisation.

An Interesting Experiment

An article by J. M. Harmon and A. G. Miller is very stimulating to thought on this topic and illustrates from a simple experiment how far we may be from the best pattern of practice for basic skills.[7] In this classic experiment a new skill was taught to four matched groups of novices in four different time patterns. Each group had nine practice sessions only. The *first* group worked three days per week for three weeks. The *second* group worked on an *additive* basis (borrowed from a well-known growth pattern in the biological sciences). This group had practices on the 1st, 2nd, 3rd, 5th, 8th, 13th, 21st, 34th, and 55th days. Inspection of this progression will show that each new day number is the sum of the previous two. The *third* group practiced daily with no week-end break. The *fourth* group practiced once per week.

Conclusions were, briefly, that the second pattern was significantly superior to the others, and a follow-up study by G. F. Longley showed similar superiority with another kind of additive time schedule, with a slightly shorter total period (forty-three as opposed to fifty-five days), and slightly less improvement.

A Challenge to Our Basic Assumptions

Of the many interesting studies on time factors in learning in our literature and that of educational and industrial psychology, we mention this one because it challenges some fundamental assumptions we may make.

A further experiment should also be mentioned which shows that the time pattern for one skill in one game may be markedly different from that best for another game. Olive Young, in her "Rate of Learning in Relation to Spacing of Practice Periods in Archery and Badminton," found that there was some significant difference in the best arrangement of learning sessions in these skills.[8]

There is a vast fund of suggested practices for basic sport skills in our literature, and also many experiments on learning patterns. As yet

---

[7] "Time Patterns in Motor Learning," *Research Quarterly*, XXI, no. 3.
[8] *Research Quarterly*, XXV, no. 2, 231.

we have no final and certain answers, and our general counsel is to experiment either empirically or scientifically—not that these two terms are mutually exclusive.

A Basic Difficulty

The basic difficulty in evaluating this sort of problem can best be understood by those who trouble to learn their neurophysiology and associated psychology and endocrinology. Oversimple kinesiology, in which muscles are made to appear to have volition, and to act as if entirely under the control of the will, is misleading. The delicate and ingenious feedback mechanisms by which information is transmitted to higher centres from muscles has only recently been thoroughly investigated. The realisation that efferent impulses along the main alpha motor fibres which fire off muscles can be stimulated *either* by the *corticopyramidal* route used predominantly in the learning or learnt process, *or* by the lower brain–extrapyramidal route in situations of emotional tension, is itself a logical explanation as to why in strength, skill, or performance-testing general results may show low reliability or low validity, or both. Each one of us is as it were propelled by two inner neuromuscular drives—a primitive, crude one, making general, rather inaccurate movements—dominant in anger or fear, or situations of self-preservation—and what might be called the more civilised and educated motor self, capable of beautiful precision and harmony in movement.

How much of each of these two motor selves is operating in a given motor situation we can barely guess, but it can on the one hand keep us humble about the meaning of test results, and on the other make us take the maximum care to remove fear of the testing-situation; and to realise that we ourselves can produce tensions in our pupils which will spoil their performance. So too, we can motivate pupils by encouragement, but what we may consider to be sound encouragement in one pupil may have the opposite effect in another.

Finally, it may be said that there are still unknowns in the sports situation, such as tactical sense and the capacity for what might be called face-to-face active-opponent sports, both to estimate the opponent's moves and also to influence them, not only by our skill, but by our suggestive powers—maybe of a subhypnotic kind. We still have a lot to learn.

chapter 20

EVALUATION AND AQUATICS

THE aquatics teacher has much to gain from the use of purposeful evaluation techniques, because quantitative measurements of distance, weight, and speed provide good yardsticks of success. Work by Cureton in the United States,[1] Highmore in England,[2] and Carter in New Zealand[3] has shown clearly that buoyancy (from specific-gravity tests) and ankle drag or weight in water (from flotation tests) greatly influence *what* aquatic skills he will be good at, and *how* he will carry out those skills.

For example, to excel in synchronised swimming or lifesaving towing, a swimmer needs to have a low specific gravity, and little or no ankle drag. His or her body type will need to be relatively high in endomorphy, or fat-muscle ratio, because fat floats and has a lower specific gravity than muscle.

Several studies have investigated the relationship of physique and of buoyancy to different aquatic activities. Carter found that while over 35 percent of women tend to float horizontally in fresh water, less than 5 percent of men achieve this—either swinging to the vertical, or sinking completely. Again, women "sinkers" were found to be very rare, yet 30 percent of the men sank in fresh water. Over 90 percent of the men swing to the vertical; that is, they cannot maintain a horizontal floating position.

[1] T. K. Cureton, *Physical Fitness of Champion Athletes,* Urbana, University of Illinois Press, 1951.
[2] G. Highmore, "Problem of the Male Non-Floater," *Journal of Physical Education Association* (England), November, 1957, p. 92.
[3] J. E. L. Carter, "Buoyancy and Flotation," *New Zealand Journal of Physical Education,* nos. 6, 8 (July, 1955; April, 1956).

These findings on buoyancy and flotation also influence the style which the swimmer must use, as well as the stroke he may have to choose. For example, in the breast stroke, the glide after the leg drive will vary greatly. The flat floater can develop a long glide, and thus be suited to distance swimming. The vertical floater and the "sinker" cannot afford to glide far, because the former will start to swing to the vertical, and the latter will start to sink as forward momentum is lost. For these reasons every swimming teacher should test the buoyancy and angle of flotation of each of his pupils.

TESTS

The aquatics teacher can administer several purposeful tests at various stages of the aquatics course, from beginning swimming to competitive swimming.

1. The tests developed by Cureton and adapted by Carter are the vertical buoyancy test, and the horizontal floating test. The *vertical buoyancy test* is designed to assess the average specific gravity of the swimmer's body, by measuring the time in seconds for it to rise to the surface in 7 feet of fresh water. If the swimmer does not rise, the test is reversed, and time taken to sink seven feet is measured. Tables are provided for converting times to specific gravity.

The *horizontal floating test* is designed to measure the approximate angle at which the swimmer's body will float in fresh water when in a prone, extended position. The starting position is one of horizontal floating in at least 7 feet of water. In both tests, the swimmer takes a maximum breath. The final position of the swimmer's body, when it ceases to swing, can be graded thus:

1. Floats flat, legs within 6 inches of the surface.
2. Floats at an angle of less than 45°, but with legs more than 6 inches below the surface.
3. Floats at an angle greater than 45°, but less than vertical.
4. Floats vertical or nearly so.
5. Sinks completely.

2. *Water safety tests* should be given initially to see how safe each beginner is in deep and shallow water. Those who are classified as "unsafe" should be confined by a rope or boom to the shallow end for

tuition. Water-safety tests include such skills as ability to glide and regain the feet in shallow water; to swim on the front and on the back for at least 20 yards, including turning over, stopping, and turning round, and treading water; to scull on the back with arms only, and to move along on the back using the legs only; and to dive and recover an object in water up to the swimmer's neck.

3. *Basic skill tests* should also be carried out early to enable the teacher to assess the standard of swimming of his pupils, diagnose major weaknesses, plan his teaching programme, classify pupils into ability groups, and to choose leaders and assistants. Basic skill tests include such items as swimming a length (two widths may be easier to organise) using each stroke, e.g., crawl, breast stroke, back crawl, and towing kick on the back. Where appropriate (as in the breast stroke), leg action alone and arm action alone can be tested and the number of strokes per width scored. Simple diving and lifesaving skills should be included.

4. *Achievement charts* are used to show the pupils the framework of the course and the progressive goals to aim for. These have high motivating qualities, challenging each pupil to attain fresh goals and master new skills.

Another form of chart is the grading chart, according to which pupils are graded on, say, a five-point scale according to swimming ability and achievement. Each pupil is to endeavour to improve his grading by two points during the course: e.g., a pupil, initially on grade 1, must try to reach grade 3 during the course. Charts such as these require a careful organisation; a system of pupil assistants is needed to help beginners, and the best swimmers may possibly assist in marking achievement and grading the weaker pupils.

5. *Progress tests* are given periodically to note improvement, check weaknesses, and modify later tuition and practice. Results from these can be used for marking achievement on the chart. At the end of the aquatics course, the pupils may be retested in the basic skill test, thus recording their improvement.

6. *Special tests and examinations.* In lifesaving, synchronised swimming, diving, water polo, etc., are usually conducted by the national parent body or association controlling that particular aquatic sport. Pupils showing special aptitude and interest should be encouraged to practice the skills and reach a high enough standard to be able to

enter these examinations, e.g., those of the Royal Life Saving Society.

7. *Rating of style and watermanship.* The teacher, in an effort to get his pupils swimming with good style and enjoyment, may devise rating scales. These can assess excellence of style in the various strokes, and might include emphasis on arm style or leg style separately, as well as on simple stunts and the techniques of synchronised swimming. In this way, recognition of effort and achievement can be given to those who may be keen swimmers, yet who are not good enough or interested enough to take part in competitive swimming.

8. *Competition.* One form of evaluation in aquatics is the holding of class competitions, and the selecting of teams for school and inter-school tournaments. These contests can motivate youngsters a great deal. The section on rating and judging in Chapter 11 should be consulted, as well as the regulations in the handbook of the parent association for each aquatic sport. The local representative of this parent body should be consulted, and may be of assistance.

chapter 21

DANCE AND RHYTHMICAL
ACTIVITIES

If you beat the drums hard enough even the philosophers will
dance.

ALDOUS HUXLEY

Why dost thou not go to church in a galliard, and come home in
a coranto? My very walk should be a jig: I would not so much as
make water but in a sink-a-pace.

Twelfth Night

EVALUATION CONTINUOUS

BECAUSE of the association in the United States between dance and
rhythmics, we have grouped these together, though readers will observe
that there is considerable reference to rhythmic activities in the chapter on evaluation applied to gymnastics.

Whether it be a highly formalised form of dance, such as ballet or
some kinds of folk dance, or whether it be a freely interpreted form
of dance, with no fixed steps, positions, or patterns, evaluation goes on
all the time. The critical eye of the dance teacher who knows what he
wants is indeed an incisive evaluatory instrument. Systems of dance—
folk, social, ethnic, or interpretative—have tended to throw up their
own internal criteria. From the *poussette* to the *cabriolet;* from the
percussive stamp to the whip-action of *anacrusis;* from the corté-turn
to the sword-dance *lock;* or even to the *mudras* of Indian dance

451

we find reference points in most dance forms. These refer to specific movements—qualities or quantities of movement. There is no point in discussing them here.

Since we two male authors consider that dance should form a substantial part of any physical educationist's training, and a part of the school's physical-education programme for both sexes—at both elementary and high-school levels, we feel that we can at least suggest some problems in evaluation which we have met in this field.

The Attitude of Men

The first is the obvious one of *attitude,* with men. Although the world over and throughout history, dance has been a predominantly male activity, in this era, in certain of the newer countries such as America and New Zealand, and also in some of the Anglo-Saxon countries, there is a pervading feeling that dance is really a "sissy," female activity. It is our impression that this is not only a mistaken attitude, but in fact shows moral cowardice on the part of the men who hold the attitude—though there is some slight truth in the statement that to some forms of dance, and to some only, and only in some places, there have been attracted males of narcissistic, or homosexual tendencies. The latter, particularly in newer countries, are particularly frowned on, and maybe an aura entirely due to this has affected male attitudes to dance. As Ted Shawn, that excellent pioneer in men's dance, has pointed out in his *Dance We Must,* it is only recently that males have played a subordinate part, even in ballet.

In some countries, Denmark and Russia, for instance, it is the policy of ballet directors to eliminate homosexuals from ballet companies, not so much because they are not good dancers—some are excellent— but because it gives ballet a bad name and keeps heterosexual male dancers away, and girl dancers prefer dancing with heterosexual partners. This is not an attempt to decry homosexuals, who have a difficult enough life as it is (and it is wise to study Dr. Kinsey's first report before dismissing homosexual behaviour as very rare).[1] But we do feel that this whole question of attitude to dance by males needs airing and investigating more thoroughly—perhaps by psychologists and

[1] A. C. Kinsey, *et al., Sexual Behaviour in the Human Male,* Saunders, 1948.

sociologists, who may be better equipped than physical educationists to make such investigations.

AN EXPERIMENT IN NEW ZEALAND

In the meantime we can only report on nine years of compulsory modern, folk, and ballroom dance for men in the physical education school where we work. After initial difficulties, hesitation, and opposition, it is now established that men take part in dance generally with-

FIG. 21.1. Physical education majors in a dance of their own composition, undertaken voluntarily. Of the five men in the picture, two captained their high schools in rugby football, one represented New Zealand in basketball, another has sprinted for the New Zealand combined universities team. (*Evening Star,* Dunedin, N.Z.)

out question (except perhaps by some in terms of too much of the available time being given to it). The majority get something from it, as sampled opinion, given anonymously, shows. The men consider that they get:

1. An extremely good workout, especially in modern dance.
2. That it improves markedly their kinaesthetic awareness, with a carry-over into other fields.
3. That it produces better "differential" relaxation (i.e., relaxation of muscles not actually involved in an action) in them.

Some would go further and say that the aesthetic pleasure and the concomitant knowledge of music gained are both pleasurable and valuable. As some of the men more favourably inclined have represented New Zealand in rugged sports, we suspect from close personal knowledge of students, that this is no sign of lack of masculinity, but rather the overcoming of a cultural prejudice.

Subjective Evaluation Mostly Inevitable

We feel that most dance situations are self-evaluatory, and that the evaluating of actual dance is best done by skilled, subjective methods. There are, however, two fields where we feel as objective as possible evaluatory methods might well be devised and applied. These fields are (1) predictive tests which analyse basic dance and rhythmic ability, if there be such a thing. These might enable teachers to classify their pupils and plan their teaching more wisely; (2) tests which show whether an actual improvement in basic dance ability has occurred as a result of teaching and practice, or whether it has not.

We suggest that the former field of predictive tests needs much further study. One study done here gave interesting results about the latter question.[2]

A standard stimulus in the form of percussion and piano, and other music on a tape, was used initially on two parallel classes in a girls' school where no dance was taught. Standard instructions were given about rhythmical movements, time patterns, etc., which the pupils had to interpret from the taped accompaniment. Four experienced judges, not concerned with the teaching, acted as assessors. For approximately twenty-five weeks, one class was taught dance only in its weekly physical-education session, while the parallel class acted as a control group and had an ordinary physical-education lesson of gymnastics and games skills. At the end of the experimental period, the same four judges rated the children in each class as they underwent the identical test as at the beginning. There was a significant improvement in the ratings given to the experimental class that had a weekly dance lesson, whereas the control group had improved only slightly.

[2] J. C. McC. Smith and J. C. Greaney, *An Analysis of Rhythmical Ability in Third Form Girls,* unpublished thesis, Otago University, 1957.

More Experiment Needed

More experiments of this sort are, we feel, needed, and it is hoped similar experiments may be done with men, when the opportunity presents itself.

The testing of rhythmic work, except in the case of rhythmical gymnastics with a prescribed form, presents much the same problems as the evaluation of dance. We have little doubt that though objective performance and predictive tests will be a valuable adjunct, the main testing device, and the most efficient, is trained human judgement, in spite of the errors that may creep in through personal relationships and idiosyncrasies of taste.

Readers are referred to various studies in this relatively untilled field, quoted in the *Research Quarterly*. We would emphasise too the basic difficulty of describing movement in words and the importance of dance writers sharpening their semantic sense. It may be necessary as Eleanor Metheney and Lois Ellfeldt have suggested in the *Research Quarterly* of November, 1958, to invent new terms rather than use old ones of indefinite or ambiguous meaning.

chapter 22

EVALUATION AND OUTDOOR EDUCATION

ALTHOUGH camping happens to be a field in which the authors are widely experienced, and although they have built up a campcraft certificate taken at university level, and have themselves been some of the chief examiners, this chapter will be a limited one. We feel that techniques in outdoor education of all kinds tend to have a strong cultural bias.

Although one of us has visited some twenty American and Canadian camps in summer and winter, we feel hesitant about attempting to outline any comprehensive evaluation policy. We feel that such paternal figures as Julian Smith, and those who work with the American Camping Association, the Boy Scouts, the Girl Scouts, the Campfire Girls, the Conservation Officers, and many others, provide forms of evaluation as part of their daily work.

CAMPING, AN EXTRAORDINARILY VALUABLE MEDIUM

We will, however, display our prejudices and any doubts we may have. First, let us make a sweeping statement. Through camping—of a kind we shall describe in some detail—we feel that more of the aims of physical education can be reached *at one time* than through any other medium of which we know. This begs the question about aims, but we accept a general, broad grouping into physiological, psychological, social and spiritual, and even intellectual, aims—put forward by many thinkers. Lest it be thought that we are backwoodsmen, devoid of knowledge of ball games, track and field, gymnastics, aquatics, and dance, we would like it to be known we have played between us some thirty-five different ball sports, to say nothing of taking part in and teaching the other fields mentioned.

To justify our assertions, let us look closer at camping—or rather, the kind of camping we mean.

ONE IDEAL KIND OF CAMP

We consider that the ideal camp is that for about eight to thirty-two people. It is tented with small sleeping tents, with a large tent for community use in wet weather, and good store, tool, and utensil tents. We do not fundamentally object to a hut for wet-weather programmes, but only fear that it may be retreated to too often, and thus remove some of the hardship and hardening effect of camping. With younger children, one is essential.

The camp should be located near relatively safe water, preferably on a bend in a river, small bay, or point on a lake. Potable water nearby, and plenty of timber for burning and construction are essentials. A playing field is not. We feel that to bring city games to camps is only justified when the campers never get those games elsewhere—or unless the camp is used for training games-and-playground leaders, such as in the excellent Youth Leadership Camps run by Mr. Gordon Wright, Supervisor of Physical Education for Ontario, at Lake Cuchiching, near Toronto.

The temptation, we feel, is to put the clock back and go into the wilderness, and then set about bringing the town to the wilderness and putting the clock forward again by chromium-plating the camp and filling it up with modern laboursaving devices, and urban activities.

The first objective for the camp is to make it reasonably weather-tight, so that normal living, including cooking outdoors, can go on whatever the weather. Of course, it must be reasonably hygienic, too —but we suspect that this can become a fetish and can go far beyond anything to do with health.

The second objective, included with the first, is to keep everyone busy helping the camp in two main ways. The *first* is by allotted tasks —giving individuals actual responsibilities, and breaking the camp into subgroups of not more than eight. Lord Baden-Powell, the founder of

Scouting (not an American invention, as was told to us when visiting America), long before the study of social dynamics, pointed out that a group of ten boys is fundamentally different from a group of up to eight, and that something tends to be lost in the larger group.

But besides *allotted* tasks, we think a camp should have general *unallotted* tasks, which all campers should feel they must do. For instance, the collection of firewood, the clearing and tidying up of surrounding ground, the removal of hazards, the beautification and improvement of the campsite, should be, we feel, a general responsibility. We often say ourselves that this *unallotted* work is a main test of whether an individual has realised a fundamental of camping—that the welfare of the community depends on each individual's voluntary effort, or, to put it in the form of an old English slogan, "Work of each for weal [welfare] of all."

The third objective is a *challenging programme*. This should require skill—many new skills in fact—observation, endurance, and enterprise. It should involve physical, cultural, and intellectual activities, both in and outside the camp.

Outcamping

We are particularly keen on outcamping—purposeful expeditions for small groups which, in turn, set up small camps or overnight bivouacs, at a level a degree more primitive than the main camp. Quite apart from the fun, adventure, and new skills learned, these separations into small groups both ease the strain from living in a bigger group, and also raise the level of tolerance and interpersonal communication in the subgroup. At the appropriate ages, say below 10 and above 16, we feel that such outcamps may well be of mixed groups. We have in the course of twelve years sent out some sixty-five groups of mixed men and women university students, without faculty, to set up outcamps, and we are quite sure that the situation has not been abused. As one camper said, "You do not feel like indulging in individual and selfish pleasures when you are in a busy outcamp."

Recreation in camps, as we have already hinted, should be different from that in urban life. Preferably, we feel, it should be appropriate to the camping situation, and on the whole, use relatively primitive materials—although it is obviously more sensible to bring bows and arrows with you rather than spend days whittling them. We favour such things as archery, horseshoes, small-bore rifle-shooting, *pateca* (a Brazilian form of volleyball with a homemade outsize shuttlecock—the making of which is an excellent camp craft), and of course, canoeing and swimming. We would emphasise hiking to increasing distances, so as to build up stamina, and thorough training in map and compass work, whether in sport form as orienteering, or in practical use for map-making, trail-blazing, and surveying. So too we feel camp crafts—using the axe, the saw, the knife, and the entrenching tool—are in a sense recreational. So too, knotting, splicing, lashing, and whipping, with various size of twine and rope, are valuable. The use of these in pioneering, bridge-building, etc., is a practical challenge.

Skill Competition

For instance, we have devised a form of competition which is self-evaluatory and highly challenging. Men, youths, or girls are divided into groups of three. Each group is given a spade, a bush-saw, a tomahawk, and a length of ¾-inch rope. The project set is to erect a 6-foot-long horizontal bar 8 feet from the ground, with another below it at 5 feet. Once erected, each trio member must in turn circle up on the lower bar, turn round, sit on the lower bar and circle up on the top bar. Finally, all three must hold the balance support (balance hang) position on the bar at once.

To start with, each trio is given a two-minute huddle to plan their course of action. The word to go is given, and from then on it is a race against time. The first team to finish with the right height of bars and with all three perched aloft wins. Our record from start to finish is 17½ minutes—and this included cutting all timber some way away from the site of competition.

Of course such a competition assumes skill, both in campcraft and gymnastics, but since, in New Zealand, even our top footballers and cricketers, who may be physical educationists, have to know all these things, we have no problem.

Gadgets

Two comments on the practical side we must make in regard to gadgets. Gadgeteering and boon-doggling can become an end in themselves instead of a means to an end. While admiring, say, the crafts so ably written up and explained by Bernard S. Mason in his books, we have observed with educational doubt books advocating the making of useless gadgets, neither aesthetic nor functional.

Intellectual Studies

Regarding intellectual studies at camp, we feel these should grow out of the natural surroundings, and answer in fact the asked or unasked question, prompted by the impact of the environment. The general opportunity for nature study, of flora, fauna, rocks, stars, climate, conservation, and route-finding and surveying, provides almost limitless opportunities for teaching and discussion at any level.[1] In fact, one of the outcomes, it is to be hoped, is heightened curiosity about the environment, and the man who knows trees has far more to offer than the baseball coach, in a camp.

Camping is Self-evaluatory

Basically we feel that a camp is self-evaluatory, that any trained camp leader evaluates through his senses and his wisdom all the time. Check lists, interest profiles, sociometric charts, etc., may be of some interest to those who have to survey many camps, but we think that they are superfluous for camp leaders generally, and maybe the right sort of person for surveying camps in general does not need a check list, but an open and experienced mind.

Camping is an ancient craft handed on from person to person. It is, we feel, far better caught than taught. Too much self-conscious analysis may destroy its very essence.

Varieties of Camp

Before justifying our assertion made at the beginning of this chapter, passing reference must be made to forms of outdoor education, of which we are aware, but feel not inclined to treat in this book. The large permanent camp, whether private or charitable, which children attend for eight weeks, has, we feel, to be very different, *sui generis,* from what we regard as educational camping in its finest form. Tented

---

[1] Our observation is that, at camp, discussion tends to be freer, and even the most inhibited normally take part.

and primitive camping is tiring for campers and leaders alike, and perhaps ten to twelve days is the wise upper limit of duration. The common American summer camp, we realise, has to be run in quite different ways, with counsellors, sports' leaders, and enough creature comfort, medical attention, and safety to enable children to stand and enjoy a long session away from home. Having met camp directors *in situ*, having discussed such matters with leading figures in the American camping world, and having visited the impressive Indiana headquarters of the American Camping Association, we are sure that such camping has thrown up its own evaluatory services—and leaders are aware of pitfalls and uneducational developments.

SOCIAL RESEARCH NEEDED

We do suggest, however, that there is a field for psychosocial, and perhaps socioeconomic, investigations here, particularly as to family social dynamics, e.g., the effect of separation from parents on both parents and on children in the most outdoor part of the year. We realise, having spent a July in New York, the desirability of getting children into other than an urban environment, but we still feel that not all the implications of the present pattern have been evaluated.

So too, with day camps, winter camps—such as the delightful elementary school one we visited in Michigan—and other ingenious camping forms, we do not feel competent to deal.

PHYSIOLOGICAL GAINS

Lastly, let us justify our observation that through no other medium are so many aims of physical education realised as through certain kinds of camping.

Physiologically, camping makes demands of adaptation. We are exposed to greater temperature change, the impact of heat, cold and humidity, and our own homeostatic mechanisms have to operate at a natural level. Our skin, that enormous sense organ, is subject to all manner of new stimuli, hardening through friction and pressure, exposure to weather, smoke, slivers, scrapes, etc. Our voluntary muscles do more lifting, carrying, swinging of tools, pulling, and pushing, over many more hours daily, than in ordinary life. There are also many cardiorespiratory demands.[2] Sleeping, relatively in the open air, is a rewarding physiological experience. In camp the level of sheer physical fatigue is raised. While in ordinary life, the psychological limits of fatigue are generally reached long before the physiological limits[3] (not that the two are entirely separate), in camp we go on and on out of enthusiasm, and develop more physiological fatigue and enjoy the balm of rewarding sleep which it produces.

Psychological Gains

Psychologically, camping is a continual challenge to our mastery of ourselves and our environment, and our capacity to get on with and tolerate other people. Our city ways and our normal persona[4] are dropped, in fact and in analogy. To have to get up in the rain with half a dozen other people at 6 A.M. and cook breakfast on a reluctant, smoky fire for a hungry mob, means that the normal facade we present, with lipstick, lacquered hair, aftershave lotion, and impeccable manner, disappears, and we see each other face to face. It is harder to hide our weaknesses, and easier to see our virtues—easier in fact for most of us to be our true selves. There is also the continual challenge to skill, the challenge to learn to do something today which we could not do yesterday, and the sense of achievement which comes with this, so important to our self-esteem. In contrast to the play situation, where we may be continually rejected, in camp everyone can progress, and no one becomes a star, nor are there any fans—"spectatoritis" is not present. There is no World Series in camping, nor exercise by proxy.

Social Gains

Socially, camping is the great mixing medium. It is almost platitudinous to say that at camp people learn to understand one another better, that interpersonal tolerance and sincerity increase. In a camp with work for all, we each depend on each other. Gone are the

---

[2] Alan Barry, in Australia, and F. C. Coates, in New Zealand, have done some pilot studies on the physical effects of camping. More work of this kind would be valuable, though, as Barry suggests, the long-term effects are hard to assess.

[3] See S. H. Bartley and C. Chute, *Fatigue and Impairment in Man,* New York, McGraw-Hill, 1947.

[4] From the Greek actors' masks through which the sound of their voices came (*per sona,* in Latin). Jung frequently used this term.

impersonal tap (faucet) and switch, the elevator, the eerie self-manoeu-vering pickup arm, remote control, supersonic TV switch, and the automatic coffee dispenser with the hygienic, disposable paper cup. Someone has to wash the dishes, hew the wood, draw the water, see the fire is safe, trench round the tents, or we are all uncomfortable. We suggest that people get to know each other better doing shared tasks, working side by side, than they do in school life in town. So too, intersexually, more real understanding and companionship develops than in studying a list of analysed techniques on how to behave on your first date. Not that our urbanised civilisation, and urban control of the mass media of communication, does not necessitate this sort of treatment of human relations, but camping produces actual situations far more akin to the real problems of, say, marriage than does any desiccated classroom treatment.

For the sociologically minded it is rewarding to construct sociograms and social-distance scales for a group before taking them camping, and then do them again at the end of camp. We have found that even with delinquent children the sociogram pattern alters markedly, and the level of antisocial tension drops. Camping provides so many opportuni-ties for constructive use of destructive tendencies. Using a spade, shovel, or pick; axeing and sawing; swinging a mallet, a mall, or a sledgehammer; blazing a trail through new country—all involve de-structive acts which give a socially acceptable and useful outlet for the aggression there is in all of us, and particularly in many disturbed children.

But it is not only the chance to have a bash at something—to strike with might and main; there is the discipline of felling the tree in the direction required, or respecting the axe edge, which if chipped will no longer give us either the satisfaction of cleaving, or the reward of the achieved task. Out of destruction can come forth purpose and sense of achievement.

Spiritual Gains

Spiritually, camping brings us close to nature and God's handiwork. It enables us to see ourselves more in perspective, in time and space. Our life is seen as but a span, compared to the age of rocks and rivers, mountains and trees. Our status is seen in perspective, halfway between the microcosm of the small patch of grass or forest floor, and the macrocosm of the skies. We can, by lying face-downwards, see the extraordinarily varied forms of life, vegetable and animal, that inhabit one square foot of the earth's surface. At the same time at night we can lie on our backs and see the infinite universe. Seeing ourselves on a scale of size and time values in all the infinite variety and beauty of nature, we can become more humble than among the pride-forming paraphernalia of the city, where all around are man's own creation and the thousand golden calves which we bow down before.

In the midst of nature we can, like the Psalmist, lift up our eyes to the hills and help will come from there. We can, with Wordsworth, Keats, Whitman, Shakespeare, Thoreau, Milton, and others, sense the essential truth of nature, and see how truth and beauty are, as Keats implied, essentially the same.

> "Beauty is truth, truth beauty,"—that is all
> Ye know on earth, and all ye need to know.

So too, we find our personal relations improve and, as another poet has said,

> One touch of nature makes the whole world kin.

and we understand better some of the eternal values,

> One impulse from a vernal wood
> May teach you more of man,
> Of moral evil and of good,
> Than all the sages can.

With Blake who doubted, but hoped that Jerusalem could be built even among "these dark Satanic Mills," we can hope too,

> To see the world in a grain of sand,
> And heaven in a wild flower;
> Hold infinity in the palm of your hand,
> And eternity in an hour.

It is a far cry from poetry to statistics, it may be thought—from the sensory to the intellectual—but man is a unity, and, as this book tries to show, science has no monopoly of evaluation. We make no apology for trying to look at things in our field as a meaningful whole.

RECOMMENDED READING

Barry, Alan, and P. Rigg, *Y.M.C.A. Pioneer Course at Camp Yarramundi,* Sydney, Y.M.C.A., 1958.

Coates, F. C., and G. F. Briggs, *Disciplined Adventure Camp,* Sydney, Y.M.C.A., 1960.

Cox, Jack, *Camp and Trek,* London, Lutterworth, 1956.

DesGrey, Arthur H., *Camping,* New York, Ronald, 1950.

Gatty, Harold, *Nature Is Your Guide,* New York, Dutton, 1958.

Hammott, Catherine T., *Camping,* New York, Pocket Books, 1955.

Hazlewood, Rex, *Camping for Boys and Girls,* London, English Universities Press, 1950.

Jaeger, Ellsworth, *Woodsmoke,* New York, Macmillan, 1954.

Mason, Bernard S., *Woodcraft,* New York, Barnes, 1939.

Mason, Bernard S., *Woodsmanship,* New York, Barnes, 1945 and 1954.

Ministry of Education, Great Britain, *Organized Camping,* 2nd ed., London, Her Majesty's Stationery Office, 1951, Pamphlet No. 11.

Perry, Ronald H., *Canoe Trip Camping,* Don Mills, Ont., Dent, 1953.

Swanson, William E., *Camping for All It's Worth,* New York, Macmillan, 1952.

V-Five Association of America, *How to Survive on Land and Sea,* 2nd ed., Annapolis, Md., U.S. Naval Institute, 1956.

Warren-Wren, S. C., *Camping with a Purpose,* Kingswood, Surrey, Andrew George Eliot (Right Way Books), 1952.

INDEXES

INDEX OF NAMES

INDEX OF SUBJECTS